An Economic History
of Nigeria 1860–1960

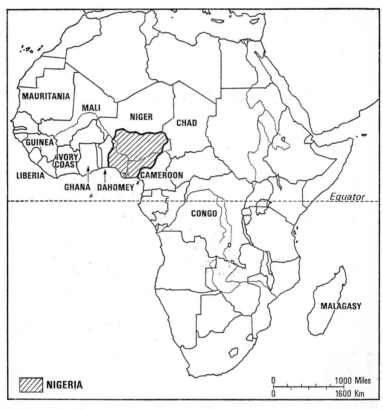

MAURITANIA

MALI

NIGER

CHAD

GUINEA

IVORY
COAST

LIBERIA

GHANA DAHOMEY

CAMEROON

Equator

CONGO

MALAGASY

0   1000 Miles
0   1600 Km

NIGERIA

I Geographical location

An Economic History
of Nigeria 1860–1960

R. Olufemi Ekundare

AFRICANA PUBLISHING CO. New York
A Division of Holmes & Meier Publishers, Inc.

Published in the United States of America 1973
by Africana Publishing Company, a Division of
Holmes & Meier Publishers, Inc.
101 Fifth Avenue
New York, N.Y. 10003
© 1973 R. O. Ekundare
Printed in Great Britain

Library of Congress catalog card no.: 72–94209
ISBN: 0 8149–0135–X

To my wife, Stella Adeola

Contents

Tables

Figures

Foreword

It is no exaggeration to claim that this book opens a new chapter in the historiography of Africa. There have been distinguished monographs on specialized aspects of African economic development, notably trade and more recent economic policy. Some very impressionistic assessments have been made about the course of economic change in Africa more generally. But, between the very specialized research, the excessively general and the large literature on present-day problems of economic growth in African countries, there has been virtually nothing. This is the first systematic study of the general economic development of Nigeria, including its long pre-colonial story, and, with this, it stands as the first academic economic history of any black African country. Scholars and students from many lands will therefore give it a warm welcome.

For a historian primarily concerned with understanding processes of economic change in Europe, the area of study to which this book is a contribution provokes much salutary thought. Where one field has been tilled and tilled again, long past the point of diminishing returns except where new tilth is created by fresh ideas and new evidence (when reploughing is vital), the other offers virgin land for cultivation with the prospect of rich yields. For the historian in Europe, written evidence, particularly legal evidence, stretches back into the mists of pre-Carolingian times; and post-classical archaeology offers its own wide *œuvre* of data. For the economic history of African countries before the colonial period archaeology produces little, where most indigenous artefacts were of mud, and an oral tradition has left little tangible evidence for evaluation by the historian's traditional techniques. Only now are Western social historians beginning to explore the new world – here a very ancient world – of 'oral history'. Paradoxically, even when evidence becomes more abundant, with the arrival of colonial administrators, that data has encouraged traditions of study which mask some of the most important attributes of the economy. Alien intruders, concerned more with political stability and a small export sector of cash-crops, collected information which ignored much of what is now misleadingly called the 'traditional economy'.

In economic history no less than political and constitutional change, colonial countries have been too often seen from the deck of a British vessel, standing offshore, by squinting down a British municipal drainpipe; studied lop-sidedly primarily from the point of view of the colonists, the metropolitan economy and those economic functions and business institutions linking the colonial territory to the home country. The obverse of this tradition, in its own way equally uncritical, has been a blanket condemnation of the economic oppression resulting from this imperial connexion – the financial drain, the blockages to general economic growth and industrialization, the distorted pattern of development.

This book's attempt to study the economic impact of imperialism in more objective terms (Mr Ekundare is a trained economist) is a welcome step forward out of the ruck of uncritical assertions buttressed by selected, piecemeal evidence. It is always inadequate to speak of 'underdevelopment' and 'economic imperialism' as universal entities which can be discussed meaningfully in the abstract, without consideration of the differences which occur in specific contexts. Beyond the most superficial level of analysis, these assumptions darken counsel. Both underdevelopment and the economic consequences of imperialism vary dramatically according to context: the differences can be as important as the similarities, perhaps more important. The debate about economic imperialism now needs to be reassessed in terms of specific national examples (and contrasts), examined in depth and quantified where possible. This is, for Nigeria, a first step towards that goal and an important basis for comparative analysis.

The full flood of data, from which reliable national income estimates, output, growth rates and investment flows can be quantified with some assurance, has come only with the development plans adopted since independence. For this section of the book Mr Ekundare is, therefore, able to tread on firm ground. Here, and for the later colonial period, the responsibility of the academic economic historian is crucial – if indirect – to the guidance of policy, even if his first professional responsibility is to get at the truth for its own sake. Policy objectives are determined in the light of a diagnosis made about the significance of current events and past trends, often in the absence of detailed, objective investigation. The myths of the past – creatures of the present which endow them with significance – thus beckon to the future. The transcendent duty of the historian and the economist, no less creatures of the present but with professional toolkits of scientific procedures, is to get the record straight; to draw conclusions in the light of the totality of relevant facts critically evaluated; not to produce facts selected to agree with the conclusions of a predetermined model. In the subsequent free play of argument and critique such proximations to truth as are attainable by fallible mortals will be realized and, at the same time, the surest intellectual base established for solving present problems and determining future objectives.

Peter Mathias

All Souls College, Oxford
8 September 1972

Preface

In this book I have attempted to present a systematic account of the economic history of modern Nigeria; although the exercise took a few years to complete, it can only serve as an introduction to a vast subject which has remained largely unexplored. The period I have covered, 1860–1960, corresponds roughly with the period of colonial rule.

Economic history is primarily the history of growth; consequently one has to make use of economic statistics in illustrating the trend of economic events, and it is in this respect that the economic historian faces his most difficult task. Before the advent of British administration in Nigeria, a few European explorers visited the country and recorded their personal judgements about the economic and social conditions of the people. Such records, which contain very few reliable statistics, are useful in so far as they help one to imagine conditions which could have existed, and to compare these with the unwritten sources handed down orally through generations. Official colonial reports on Lagos, which began in the second half of the nineteenth century, concentrated on government administration and foreign trade. However, by the 1920s regular government departmental reports were being published. Many of the statistics in these reports differed from those published by the central government. On the whole, one has to adopt the latest of the conflicting statistics. Up to and including 1960, economic statistics on Nigeria were grossly inadequate, and those that were available could have been better presented. Nevertheless, it is possible to piece together the fragments of statistical data and make some reasonable judgements about the history of economic developments in Nigeria.

A subject as young as this will inevitably advance rapidly. New interpretations and emphases will come in very quick succession to replace old notions, once more attempts have been made to learn about man's economic past in Nigeria. I hope by this book to have succeeded in provoking interest in it, and that more scholars will endeavour to develop those aspects which I could only mention briefly, and those that I did not mention at all.

I have made a conscious effort to make the book useful to undergraduates, and to students for the Advanced Level of the General Certificate of Education. It should also provide all Nigerians with the essential links in the economic history of a rapidly developing and changing country. References to other works in this field, mentioned briefly in the text, are given in full in the Bibliography.

I acknowledge with great pleasure the help and co-operation I received from the following institutions: the Public Records Office and the Commonwealth Relations Office Library, both in London; Rhodes House and the Institute of Commonwealth Studies Libraries, both in Oxford; the National Archives, Ibadan; the University of Ibadan Library; and the University of Ife Library.

I am grateful to the publishers of the *Nigerian Journal of Economic and Social Studies* and *African Affairs* for permission to employ material which originally appeared in their publications.

My thanks to Professor S. A. Aluko, Department of Economics, University of Ife, for encouraging me to devote more time to the study and teaching of economic history. My colleagues in the same department have also been very helpful with their advice.

I am greatly indebted to a number of people who at various stages read the manuscript and made useful suggestions. It is a pleasure to be able to acknowledge the help of Dr R. M. Hartwell, Reader in Social and Economic History, Nuffield College, University of Oxford, and Professor Peter Mathias, Chichele Professor of Economic History, University of Oxford, both of whom read the manuscript in its final stage.

I need hardly add that none of the individuals or institutions I have mentioned are responsible for any imperfections or errors which the book may contain.

Richard Olufemi Ekundare

University of Ife
October 1971

Part 1   Introduction

1   An introduction to Nigeria

The Federal Republic of Nigeria, which became a sovereign nation in October 1960, is politically, economically and population-wise, one of the greatest countries in the continent of Africa. Indeed, its importance in Africa gives it automatic recognition as a country with the greatest political and economic potential in the 'Third World'.

The area of the Federation of Nigeria is 356,669 square miles, which is more than three times the size of the United Kingdom, and which can be compared with the size of France and Italy put together. The country lies roughly between 3° and 15°E longtitude and between 4° and 14°N latitude. The longest distance from east to west is over 700 miles, and from north to south, 650 miles. The country is delimited westwards by the Republics of Dahomey and Nigeri, eastwards by the Cameroons Republic, northwards by the Niger and Chad Republics, and to the south by the Gulf of Guinea, which includes the Bights of Benin and Biafra, with a coastline stretching from a point near Ikang in Calabar to beyond Badagry.

The belt of mangrove swamps, which is up to 60 miles in depth in some places in the coastal areas, gives way to highlands as one approaches the northern areas. The coastline is intersected by an intricate network of creeks and rivers, and by the huge Niger Delta which is conspicuously placed midway along the Nigerian coastline. Successive belts of tropical rainforests with scattered hills lie beyond the mangrove swamps, and further north of these is the savannah grassland, which gives way to the semi-desert conditions at the extreme north of the country. Although the northern extremities of the country abut on the desert, the Nigerian frontier with the Republic of Niger lies well within the limits of the rainy season.

The river Niger, which is about 730 miles long (inside Nigeria), and from which the country derives its name, is the third longest river in Africa. It provides, through its tributary, the Benue, the longest uninterrupted waterway into the interior of Africa. The Niger rises in the mountains to the north-east of Sierra Leone and

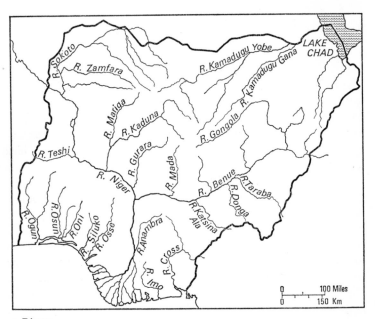

2 Rivers

flows for the first two-thirds of its 2,600 miles outside Nigeria, before entering the country from the west and running in a south-easterly direction until it receives the water of its principal tributary, the Benue – which rises in the Republic of Cameroons – at Lokoja, about 340 miles from the sea, from where it flows due south to the delta to empty itself into the Atlantic Ocean. The other important tributaries of the Niger, all rising within the country, are the Sokoto (390 miles), Kaduna (340 miles) and Anambra (130 miles), while the tributaries of the Benue include Gongola (330 miles), Katsina Ala (215 miles) and Donga (175 miles). There are a number of other important rivers in Nigeria, including the Kamadugu Yobe (290 miles), which flows into Lake Chad in the extreme north-east of the country; the Ogun in the west; the Benin and Escravos in the mid-west; the Sombreiro and Bonny river systems with Port Harcourt as the outlet; and the Cross river system with Opobo and Kwa rivers.

Nigeria is a tropical country. The climatic conditions along the coastal areas in the south are more stable than for the rest of the country. There are two main seasons in the year, the dry and the wet seasons. In the southern half of the country, the rainy season lasts for about six months – from May to October – while the nor-thern half of the country has a shorter period of rain. The dry season, which is of a longer duration in the north, brings with it the dry, north-easterly cold wind – the harmattan. The harmattan is most severe in the north, but its severity and duration reduce towards the coastal area. In the south, the annual rainfall ranges between 60 and 150 inches. The coastal area is hotter and more humid all the year round and has the highest annual rainfall. The range of temperature is not as wide near the sea as it is inland. Lagos, the capital city, on the south-western edge of the country, has a temperature range of between 66° and 92°F (19° and 33°C), for both the rainy and the dry seasons; while Maiduguri, in the north-east of the country, has a range of temperature of between 47° and 110°F (8° and 43°C). For the whole country, the hottest months of the year are March and April, while the wettest are May, June and October.

POPULATION

The total population of Nigeria was 55,670,000 according to the last population census, taken in November 1963. The results of this census created a great national controversy as it was widely believed that they were inflated for political reasons – to influence the allocation of seats in the House of Representatives, the federal parlia-ment.[1] The population census figures for 1952–3, which generated no open controversy,[2] and those of 1963, are contained in table 1.1,

[1] See S. A. Aluko, 'How many Nigerians? An Analysis of Nigeria's Census Problems, 1901–63', pp. 371–92.
[2] Although the population census for 1952–3 was not openly challenged, probably because the British were still very prominently around in the country, in Southern Nigeria it was believed that the census was manipulated by the colonial government in order to guarantee Northern domination in the First Republic.

and shown according to the twelve states arrangement created in May 1967. In 1971 it was estimated that about 64 million people lived in Nigeria, thus making Nigeria the tenth largest populated country in the world.

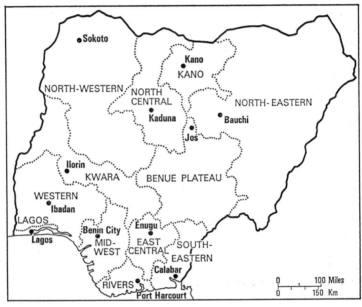

3 Political divisions: the twelve states

From the point of view of population, the Western State, with approximately 9·5 million – about 17 per cent of the total population – heads the list. The North-Eastern State, with about 7·8 million – 14 per cent – and the East Central State with about 7·2 million – 12·9 per cent – occupy the second and third positions. In 1963, the average density of population was 156 per square mile. It varied considerably from state to state, being as high as 1,045 in Lagos, 626 in East Central and 347 in Kano, and dropping as low as 84 in Kwara and 74 in North-Eastern.

It is estimated that the annual population of Nigeria increases at an average of about 2·5 per cent. While the population growth in most areas of the country conforms to the national average, the population of Lagos has been increasing at a slightly higher rate of between 3 and 4 per cent per annum. Beside the normal net increase in the population through the gradual fall in the infant mortality rate and in the death rate generally, Lagos has been the main target for urban migration. Lagos, as the federal capital, offers a great attraction to many Nigerians; the capital cities of the other states

TABLE I.I *Nigeria: area, population and density*

State	Area (square miles)	1952–3 census ('000)	1963 census ('000)	1963 census Density per square mile
North-Eastern	105,300	4,201	7,793	74
North-Western	65,143	3,397	5,734	88
North Central	27,108	2,354	4,098	151
Kano	16,630	3,398	5,775	347
Benue Plateau	38,929	2,295	4,009	103
Kwara	28,672	1,195	2,399	84
East Central	11,548	4,567	7,228	626
South-Eastern	10,951	1,904	3,623	331
Rivers	6,985	747	1,545	221
Western	29,100	4,357	9,488	326
Mid-Western	14,922	1,492	2,536	170
Lagos	1,381	501	1,444	1,045
Nigeria	356,669	30,417	55,672	156

Note: Details may not add to total because of rounding.
Source: *Annual Abstract of Statistics, 1963*, Lagos, Federal Office of Statistics.

are also absorbing a large number of migrants. The major cities and towns grew considerably, nearly doubling, within the decade 1953–63. In 1963, there were 183 towns each with a population of 20,000 and over; and of these 72 were in the Western State, 25 in the North-Eastern State and 19 in the East Central State. Also, there were 24 towns each with 100,000 and over, and of these 12 were in the Western State. The Western State, therefore was the most urbanized in the country.

Nigeria has at least 250 distinct ethnic groups and the principal ones are: Hausa, Yoruba, Ibo, Fulani, Ibibio, Tiv, Kanuri, Ijaw, Edo and Nupes. The 1963 census showed that the Hausas accounted for 20·9 per cent of the total population, while the Yorubas were 20·3 per cent. Each of the two ethnic groups occupies large areas of the country: the Hausas are to be found principally in all the six Northern States, while the Yorubas occupy Lagos and the Western State and some areas in the Kwara State.

TABLE 1.2   *Population of Nigeria by ethnic*
              group, 1963

Ethnic group	Population ('000)	Percentage
Hausa	11,653	20·9
Yoruba	11,321	20·3
Ibo	9,246	16·6
Fulani	4,784	8·6
Kanuri	2,259	4·1
Ibibio	2,007	3·6
Tiv	1,394	2·5
Ijaw	1,089	1·9
Edo	955	1·7
Others	10,850	19·6
Non-Nigerians	102	0·2
Unspecified	10	*
Total	55,670	100·0

* Less than 0·1 per cent.
Source: *Population Census of Nigeria, 1963, vol. III,*
         Lagos, Federal Office of Statistics.

HISTORICAL BACKGROUND

Before the archaeological discoveries of recent years, it was thought that the peoples of Nigeria – and for that matter, the whole of black Africa – had no established history, as it was thought that most parts of West Africa were uninhabited until very recent times. However, the archaeological discoveries of such things as axes, knives, spear and arrow heads have indicated that a palaeolithic civilization existed in West Africa. As in most other parts of the world at that period, the peoples of Nigeria lived in primitive huts and caves, surviving on wild fruits, on the animals killed in the chase and on fish from the rivers. The forest areas of Southern Nigeria, with abundant wild fruits, rivers teeming with fish and the salt of the mangrove swamps and the seawater, were obviously the first areas where a long-established habitation was possible. At that stage there was no organized farming as such, but the early inhabitants soon observed that some of the seeds of the fruits they had consumed and thrown carelessly into the bush germinated and later yielded fruits, thus providing the people with their first practical lesson in farming.

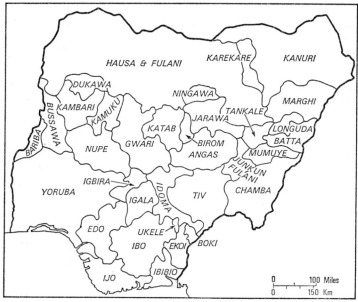

4 Major ethnic groups

It is believed that the neolithic arts were introduced by those tribes which filtered into Nigeria from the Sudan in about 7000 B.C.[1] However, the neolithic, aeneolithic and iron ages are believed to have existed simultaneously at different places in West Africa.[2] Iron ore, which existed in abundance in Nigeria, had been worked for many centuries, for a number of indigenous smelting furnaces in different stages of development have been discovered. It is also believed that the arts of using copper and bronze were introduced into Nigeria from Upper Egypt by the Yorubas, who moved down

[1] P. A. Talbot, *The Peoples of Southern Nigeria*, vol. I, p. 15.
[2] Oliver Davies, *West Africa Before the Europeans*.

from the north-east around 2000 B.C. The Yorubas, who made Ile-Ife their capital, were followed into Nigeria by the Bariba (Borgaua), the Bassava, Nupe, Dakkaherri and the Jukon. Ile-Ife is believed by the early Yorubas to be the origin of man. This belief is probably due to the fact that the Yorubas found at Ile-Ife clear evidence of an advanced culture through stone carvings, iron, silver and bronze sculptures. By about A.D. 900, great civilization had grown among the Nupe and the Yorubas, who were later followed by the Benin culture. From these three advanced ethnic groups came the extraordinary fine bronze and brass works, the art of engraving on brass, pottery, and carvings in wood and ivory. The kingdoms established by them were well organized and controlled by a hierarchy of nobles headed by semi-divine sovereigns. Most of the archaeological discoveries, e.g. Ife and Benin bronzes, depict the figures of the sovereigns, and nearly all the other carvings show life built around the sovereign. In addition, a number of sculptures and carvings depict the gods and goddesses with which the divine sovereigns were strongly associated. Undoubtedly, the early arts of iron, bronze, brass and other carvings and sculpture were controlled by the semi-divine sovereigns. The arts of carving and sculpturing could not have advanced and survived unless they were controlled or 'financed' by a person – the divine sovereign – who could afford to provide subsistence for the artists in their time-consuming and painstaking jobs. By implication, therefore, a kind of division of labour, however backward, existed in these kingdoms. Nearly everybody produced his own food, either by collecting wild fruits in the forest or by growing a limited range of crops. The sovereigns, on the other hand, maintained themselves, their nobles, priests, artists and armies by collecting tribute or 'tax' in kind from their people.

The constant movement of invaders from Egypt and the Sudan into West Africa developed a fairly reliable network of communication through the Sahara desert. Indeed, it laid the foundation for the trans-Saharan trade which developed between North and West Africa: by about A.D. 1000 Kano, in Northern Nigeria, had developed into a strong and prosperous trading centre, and most of the earliest cultivated crops and some domestic animals were introduced into Northern Nigeria from Egypt.

The Hausas are believed to have occupied Northern Nigeria by about A.D. 1000. By the middle of the thirteenth century, the kings of Mali were converted to Moslems, and they in turn began spreading the Moslem religion into the neighbouring areas. This brought the Fulanis to penetrate into the Hausa area by the middle of the fourteenth century. By the start of the fifteenth century, Moslem missionaries were known to have arrived at Kano. Around the same period some of the main cities in Northern Nigeria – Kano, Zaria, Katsina and Sokoto – had grown into great centres of commerce. Fine breeds of horses had been developed, and donkeys, camels, cattle, sheep and goats were to be found in large numbers. The fine leather works and leather trade at Kano had also developed.

The most important and advanced groups of peoples which thus emerged and were prominent at the end of the eighteenth century were the Yorubas and the Bini in the south, and the Hausas, Nupe, Fulanis and Kanuris in the north. These main ethnic groups had each founded a monarchical and civilized form of government completely independent of any European influence. In the nineteenth century the Yoruba kingdoms extended in the west across what are now Dahomey and Togo Republics to Accra; in the north and the east they extended to the banks of the Niger, and in the south-east to Benin.[1] The King of Benin was a Yoruba and it was believed that the King (Obi) of Onitsha was a descendant of the Oba of Benin. By the middle of the nineteenth century, a series of civil wars had broken out among the Yorubas; they lasted for many years, and were finally brought to an end in 1886 by a treaty which the Governor of Lagos concluded among the Yorubas. However, the main result of the war was the disintegration of the Yoruba kingdom and the confirmation of the independence of the various Yoruba groups from the Alafin of Oyo, hitherto the ruler of the entire Yoruba kingdom.

In the nineteenth century, more vigorous efforts were made by the Fulanis to introduce Islam. It was in 1802 that the quarrel between the King of Gobir and the Muslim Fulani leader, Othman dan Fodio, led to the invasion of the Hausa land by the Fulanis. As a result, the Fulani Empire was established over the Hausa land, and fourteen emirates were created under the overall control of the son of

[1] Daryll Forde and P. M. Kaberry (eds), *West African Kingdoms in the Ninteenth Century*.

Othman dan Fodio, the Sultan of Sokoto, who held the title 'Commander of the Faithful'.

The other ethnic groups were not as organized. It has been established, however, that most of the ethnic groups now inhabiting Nigeria came originally from either Egypt or the Sudan or both. The early history of Nigeria – political, social and economic – had a strong tie with North Africa.

POLITICAL CHANGES

The Federal Republic of Nigeria has undergone a number of political changes in the last 120 years. The first direct British political interference in Nigeria came in 1851, with the British military action against Lagos in an effort to force the King of Lagos (Kosoko) to abandon the slave trade. In 1861 Lagos was ceded to Britain and was administered as part of the Gold Coast (Ghana). In 1886 a number of British companies around the Niger amalgamated into the Royal Niger Company, and the charter of the new company gave it power 'to administer, make treaties, levy customs duties and trade in all territories in the basin of the Niger and its affluents', thus bringing the northern territories of the country under the influence of British traders. In the same year, the British government proclaimed the Oil Rivers Protectorate over the Niger Delta and established the Colony of Lagos. It was not until the Niger Coast Protectorate came into existence in 1893 that there was any well-organized government machinery. Even at that stage, the British government had to strive to conclude a number of treaties with the local chiefs in order to have a strong foothold. By 1897, however, the whole of the Yoruba land had been annexed to the Colony of Lagos as its protectorate.

In 1900 the British government took over the administration of the northern territories from the Royal Niger Company and proclaimed the area the Protectorate of Northern Nigeria, with Sir Frederick Lugard as the first High Commissioner. At the same time, the Protectorate of Southern Nigeria was created to replace the Niger Coast Protectorate. In 1906 the Colony and Protectorate of Lagos became part of a new Protectorate of Southern Nigeria. Finally, in 1914, the Northern and Southern Protectorates were amalgamated to become Nigeria.

From 1914 until 1922 there was a Nigerian Council, purely advisory and deliberative, for the protectorate, and a Lagos Legislative Council for the Lagos Colony. The two councils were abolished in 1922, and in their place a larger legislative council was established in 1923 to include, for the first time in the political history of Nigeria, four elected members – three from Lagos and one from Calabar. A separate town council was also set up for Lagos. The first election to the legislative council was held in 1923, on a franchise based on income and property. The council legislated for Southern Nigeria, while the Governor-in-Council was responsible for legislating for Northern Nigeria. In February 1924, the mandated territory of the Cameroons (a German colony before the first world war) was joined and administered with Nigeria. The last of the political changes before the second world war took place in April 1939, when the Northern and Southern Provinces were broken into Northern, Eastern and Western Provinces.

The 1923 constitutional arrangements came to an end in August 1946, when a new constitution was introduced. The Richard's Constitution provided for a central legislature for the whole country, and three regional Houses of Assembly for each of the three provinces. Although the Constitution was to have lasted for nine years, political agitation by the few enlightened Nigerians led to its early review only two years after its introduction. The next constitution, the Macpherson Constitution, which came into effect in June 1951, afforded increased regional autonomy and extended to Nigerians a fuller share in shaping policy and in the direction of executive government action. It was this constitution which introduced representative and responsible government into Nigeria. The desire for greater regional government autonomy, and the need for a more precise definition and clarification of functions as between the central and the regional governments, led to the first major constitutional crisis in March 1953. The crisis led to two constitutional conferences, one in July–August 1953 in London, and the other in January–February 1954 in Lagos. As a result of these conferences, a new constitution which introduced a federal system of government came into force in October 1954. The new Federation thus created consisted of five parts: the Northern, Eastern and Western Regions, the federal territory of Lagos and the quasi-federal territory of Southern Cameroons. Following another constitutional conference in London in May–June 1957, constitutional arrangements were concluded for granting regional self-government to the Eastern and Western Regions in August 1957. The Northern Region also became self-governing in 1959. After more constitutional conferences in 1959 and early in 1960, the British government decided to grant political independence to Nigeria. During the negotiations for independence, Southern Cameroons decided to leave the Federation of Nigeria in 1959. On 1 October 1960 the Federation of Nigeria became an independent and sovereign nation within the British Commonwealth.

In 1962 the Mid-Western Region was created after being carved out of the old Western Region. On 1 October 1963 a republican constitution was introduced into Nigeria by the federal parliament, and it operated until January 1966. Following a series of political crises in 1965, the Prime Minister of the Federation, the Western Region Premier, the Northern Region Premier and the Federal Minister of Finance were assassinated on 15 January 1966 in a *coup d'état* led by some army officers. On the day following the *coup*, the administration of the country was handed over by the remaining members of the federal cabinet to the General Officer Commanding the Nigerian Army, Major-General J. T. U. Aguiyi-Ironsi, who suspended the office of President, the Prime Minister and Parliament, and vested legislative and executive powers in the federal military government comprising a Supreme Military Council and a Federal Executive Council. He also appointed military governors to administer the regions. On 29 July 1966 Major-General Aguiyi-Ironsi was assassinated in a counter *coup* in which the Military Governor of the Western Region, Lt-Colonel Adekunle Fajuyi, also lost his life. After the few days of confusion which followed the counter *coup*, General Yakubu Gowon (then a Lt-Colonel) took over on 1 August 1966 as Supreme Commander of the Armed Forces and Head of State.

The two *coup d'états* in 1966 created a deep rift between the Hausa and Ibo army officers. Following a series of clashes between Hausa and Ibo civilians in Northern and Eastern Regions, some of the Ibo leaders led by Emeka Ojukwu, who was then a Lt-Colonel and the military governor of Eastern Region, felt that the Ibos as a group should constitute themselves into a separate country. However, one of the major political issues in Nigeria, that of the creation of more states in order to protect minority interests, was solved by the creation of twelve states out of the existing four regions, on 27 May 1967. Three days later Ojukwu announced that the territory comprising the former Eastern Region had seceded from the Federation of Nigeria. He gave the name 'Biafra' to this area. As a result of this event the civil war broke out in July 1967.[1] It lasted for about 30 months and ended on 12 January 1970, after Lt-Colonel Effiong, the man to whom Ojukwu handed over power after he fled the country on the night of 10 January 1970, made a radio broadcast announcing the surrender of the rebels. Effiong ordered an orderly disengagement of the rebel troops and led a delegation to Lagos to negotiate a peace settlement. On the night of 13 January 1970, General Gowon welcomed the surrender of the rebels, and thus Nigeria was kept together as a Federation. At the celebration of the tenth anniversary of Nigerian independence on 1 October 1970 General Gowon announced that military rule in Nigeria was to continue until 1976, and that the military government would endeavour to surrender power to a civilian government through an orderly constitutional process.

THE NATIONAL ECONOMY

Agriculture is the mainstay of the Nigerian economy. In 1970 about 70 per cent of Nigeria's labour force were employed in the agricultural sector. Nigeria has a wealth of agricultural resources. The country has a vast area of arable land on which almost all tropical crops can be grown. Agricultural production consists of local crops for domestic consumption and a number of export crops; a number of agricultural products are both consumed locally and exported, for example, palm oil, groundnuts and cotton. When compared with the total area of the country, the area of land under cultivation remains relatively small. In 1968, the average acreage under cultivation per farmer was 1·02 for the three Eastern States, 4·28 for the six Northern States, 2·43 for the Western State, 2·07 for the Mid-Western State and 2·45 for the whole of the country. However, Nigeria is self-sufficient as far as food production is concerned – except in fish and dairy products – and this has also

[1] See Sir Rex Niven, *The War of Nigerian Unity*, and A. H. M. Kirk-Greene, *Crisis and Conflict in Nigeria: A Documentary Source Book 1966–1970.*

been increasing in recent years. The important crops for domestic consumption include guinea corn, groundnuts, yams, maize, beans, cassava, plantain and cocoyam. Locally consumed foodstuffs constitute about 75 per cent of the country's total agricultural production. Livestock production is also a major means of livelihood in the six Northern States.

Agricultural export crops earn an average of between 65 and 75 per cent of Nigeria's foreign exchange, and provide the most important source of revenue for the federal as well as state governments through export produce and sales taxes. They also provide funds for the marketing boards – funds which are used, among other things, for agricultural research, scholarship awards and for the development of the agricultural areas. The most important agricultural export crops are groundnuts, cotton and benniseed, grown mainly in the Northern States; and cocoa, palm oil, palm kernels and rubber from the Western, Mid-Western and the three Eastern States. It must be added that the Northern States supply all the country's cattle, which provide exports of hides and skins.

Nigeria is the world's largest exporter of groundnuts, with about 36 per cent of the world trade. She also ranks as the second largest exporter of cocoa in the world, supplying about 20 per cent of the world trade. Her export of cotton seeds represents about 18 per cent of the world supply, and the country's share in the world trade for vegetable oil is about 11 per cent.

Nigeria is also rich in mineral resources. Some of the country's minerals which are of considerable economic significance include coal, tin ore, columbite, gold, limestone, petroleum oil and natural gas. The potentially economic minerals – those not yet commercially exploited – include lignite, iron ore, china clay, leadzinc, wolfram and tantalite. Other mineral deposits which are known to exist in Nigeria include radioactive minerals, precious stones and metals, including diamonds, silver, phosphates, salt, asbestos, diatomite, ilmentine and xenotine.

Coal is the oldest of the economic minerals of the country. The bulk of Nigeria's coal produced since mining began in 1915 has been consumed internally by the Nigerian Railway Corporation. The only coalfield in the country is at Udi, in the Central-Eastern State. Apart from the alluvial mining of gold from the goldfields in Ilesha division of the Western State, the gold deposits of Nigeria, reported officially to cover a large area, have remained untapped. Nigeria supplies about 5 per cent of the world output of tin ore, and is thus the world's sixth producer of tin. Columbite, which is a by-product of tin, is also produced in large quantities. Nigeria is the world's largest producer of columbite, accounting for about 95 per cent of total world supply. Limestone deposits which exist in many of the states are produced for internal consumption in the production of cement. The production of petroleum oil and natural gas are of recent origin, dating back to 1956. These minerals now exist in the Mid-Western, Rivers and South-Eastern States. The production of petroleum oil was interrupted by the civil war but has now been fully resumed, with the result that Nigeria is the tenth largest producing country in the world.

Generally, the Nigerian economy has expanded rapidly since the end of the second world war. Some efforts have been made to develop and improve the infrastructure of the economy. Through a number of development planning schemes, transport, communications, and a number of social overheads, such as water supplies, education, health and social welfare have been greatly improved. The main ports of Nigeria include Lagos (Apapa), Burutu, Warri, Sapele, Port Harcourt, Bonny, Calabar, Degema and Okrika. The ports at Lagos and Port Harcourt handle the bulk of the Nigerian ocean shipping. The railway systems, which in 1969 covered some 2,178 miles, continued to provide passenger and cargo services between the Northern States on the one hand and the Eastern and Western States on the other. However, the limited and rigid railway systems have been unable to cope with the rapid growth of the economy in recent years, and as a result a network of roads has developed. For example, between 1950 and 1966 the total mileage of roads increased from 28,042 to 55,256, of which the total mileage of tarred roads increased from 1,024 to 9,476. Along with the improved roads, the road transport system was developed, linking all the states of the Federation. The air transport system, with Lagos and Kano as the main airports, has been improved substantially in recent years to cope with the increasing demand for commercial flights. The total cargo carried (inward and outward) on international air routes increased from 373 tons in 1950 to 2,965 tons in 1965.

Over the last two decades, industrial growth has become a crucial factor in the pace and pattern of Nigeria's economic development.

The expansion in industrial production has been made possible partly by a number of incentives given to foreign private investment, including tax reliefs, and partly by increased government capital expenditure on the infrastructure of the economy, the supply of power and land for industrial estates. The bulk of industrial production in Nigeria has concentrated on providing import-substitution goods such as textiles, cement, metal products, beer and soft drinks, soaps and detergents, and building construction materials.

TABLE I.3   *Gross domestic product at 1962 factor cost, 1958–67 (£ million)*

	1958–9	1960–1	1964–5	1966–7
Agriculture, forestry and fishing	672·2	799·9	866·7	869·5
Mining	10·2 (1·5)*	15·8 (5·5)*	47·5 (35·4)*	114·4 (101·0)*
Manufacturing and crafts	45·3	57·0	78·8	93·1
Electricity and water supply	2·8	4·2	8·1	10·7
Building construction	35·3	55·4	65·0	81·3
Distribution	127·9	154·7	194·9	200·9
Transport and communication	40·8	53·4	67·2	62·7
General government	39·8	49·7	52·1	51·6
Education	23·8	29·5	43·0	48·2
Health	4·0	5·3	9·4	9·3
Other services	21·8	25·3	30·7	41·4
Total	1023·9	1250·2	1463·4	1583·1

* The contribution of petroleum oil to mining.
Source: *Digest of Statistics*, vol. 19, no. 4 (1970).

The foreign trade of Nigeria has expanded consistently in the last two decades. The total value of external trade increased from £152·1 million in 1950 to £385·6 million in 1960 and to £571·9 million in 1969. The increase in domestic exports has been more consistent than the increase in merchandise imports. However, the cost of import items has increased considerably. In response to the various development projects which began in 1946, increases in the imports of machinery, transport equipment and industrial materials became noticeable. For example, in 1968 these items put together accounted for about 60 per cent of the total value of imports. The volume and the value of exports have also increased. The world prices for the 'traditional' agricultural export crops of cocoa, cotton, groundnuts and palm products continued to fluctuate; however, these items earned more than 50 per cent of Nigeria's foreign exchange. Between 1955 and 1965 the country experienced annually a consistent adverse balance of trade. The sharp increase in the export of petroleum oil, which has now become the most important single item of export, has been largely responsible for the annual favourable balance of trade since 1966. A phenomenon which has become noticeable in the last decade has been the increase in Nigerian trade with the East European countries.

The overall growth of the Nigerian economy in recent years is shown in table 1.3; and the immediate future prospect can be seen in the light of the new Development Plan 1970–4, which was launched in November 1970.[1] The new plan is expected to involve a total expenditure of about £1,600 million, of which 80 per cent is to be financed within the country. For the remaining 20 per cent, the government planned to raise external loans; however, a contingency plan has been made to resort to internal borrowing if for any reason at all external loans cannot be raised.

The plan estimates a net total expenditure (i.e. excluding federal and state underspending) for the public sector of the sum of £780 million; table 1.4 gives the major allocations.[2] The federal government plans to establish efficient administrative services and an appropriate economic infrastructure throughout the country. It also hopes to promote even development and fair distribution of industries in all parts of the country.

On the basis of investment projections, based partly on past performances and partly on the investment requirements of the economy, it is estimated that the entire private sector should provide over the plan period a gross investment of £815 million, consisting of about £692 million for the incorporated businesses and £123 million for the rest of the economy.

[1] *Second National Development Plan 1970–4*, Lagos, Federal Ministry of Information.
[2] R. O. Ekundare, 'Nigeria's Second National Development Plan As A Weapon of Social Change'.

At this very early stage of the plan period, one cannot prophesy with any degree of certainty the possible achievements of the various development projects as conceived under the plan. 'No matter how brilliantly-conceived and expertly-designed and formulated, the success or failure of a plan depends largely on how it is executed.' One of the major problems facing any development plan is

TABLE I.4 *Second National Development Plan: major items of expenditure*

	£ million	Percentage of total planned expenditure
Transport	242·6	23·7
Education	139·9	13·5
Agriculture, forestry and fishing	132·7	12·9
Defence and security	96·4	9·4
Industry	86·1	8·4
Health	53·8	5·2
Fuel and power	45·3	4·4
Communications	42·6	4·2

the gulf between those who formulate the plan and the political or military authorities that will execute it. However, given the basic strength of the Nigerian economy, and the various policy reforms contemplated in the plan, it is reasonable to expect that the investment targets will be achieved. A good indicator for optimism is the size of the Nigerian market defined in terms of physical area, population and purchasing power. Given the rich and diversified resource endowment of the nation, and a lasting political stability, the economic growth of the country should proceed uninterrupted. Moreover, the selective economic incentives provided by the government should provide the encouragement needed by private investors. It must be realized, however, that the regulation of the economy through the incomes policy, the mobilization of financial resources, the regulation of consumption and expenditure, the problem of distribution and – above all – the successful execution of the plan, can only be realized with prompt and timely government decisions and actions.

2   An outline of pre-1860 foreign contacts and their effects

THE TRANS-SAHARAN TRADE[1]

The first regular foreign contact with Nigeria was with North Africa. By the use of camels, caravan trade routes were developed across the Sahara between West and North Africa, and for a long period these routes were the only ways to and from West Africa and the outside world. There is no evidence of regular contact with any part of southern Africa. This is perhaps understandable because there were no trade incentives in the south. The caravan trade is at least 2,000 years old. Indeed, it has been suggested that the Carthaginians crossed the desert and discovered West Africa many centuries before Christ, and that they established commercial contacts on the coast, exchanging their manufactures for the African products by means of a process of barter called the 'dumb trade'.[2] This had nothing particularly significant about it other than the practical expediency of conducting trade transactions by hand description because of the language barrier.

'Trade bridged the Sahara, one of the world's most formidable barriers to human intercourse.' Between the eighth century and the nineteenth century a number of states and empires sprang up along the caravan trade routes in Western and Central Sudan. The caravan routes known to exist around the seventeenth and eighteenth centuries were grouped into three: the Taghza–Timbuktu route in the west; the Ghadames–Air route to Hausa in the centre; and in the

[1] For a more detailed and interesting account of the trans-Saharan trade, see E. W. Bovill, *The Golden Trade of the Moors*, and A. Adu Boahen, *Britain, the Sahara, and the Western Sudan 1788–1861*.
[2] Allan McPhee, *The Economic Revolution in British West Africa*, p. 28.

east, the Fezzan–Kawar route to Bornu. On each of these routes, which were interconnected, were long waterless stages which heavily laden camel caravans had to pass at great peril. The journey across the Sahara used to take between two to twelve months depending on the distance to be covered, the incidence of animal diseases, reliable cases for water supply and favourable weather conditions, such as the absence of sandstorms. Many of the early

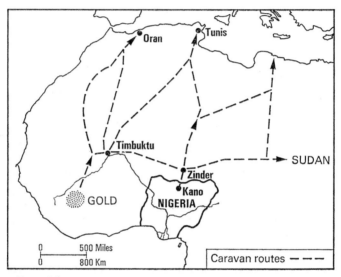

5 Trans-Saharan caravan routes

caravan routes were abandoned through the failure of wells and pasturage which were necessary to sustain the traders and their camels in the course of their journeys. 'Nothing illustrates the dangers and ravages of the trans-Saharan traffic more than the hundreds of skeletons that littered the routes.'[1] Where the wells and pasturage did not fail, repeated warfare among the desert kingdoms led to the decline of trading contacts and activities, particularly along the western route. However, the central and eastern routes which passed through relatively peaceful kingdoms grew in importance.

Along these caravan routes to North Africa were carried such items as gold, dyed cloths, leather goods and slaves, which were

[1] Boahen, *Britain, the Sahara, and the Western Sudan*, p. 120.

exchanged for salt, Arab dresses, cowries and a number of European goods such as Manchester cotton, French silks, glass beads from Venice and Trieste, paper, mirrors, needles and guns. The Arab merchants acted effectively as middlemen in the exchange of the West African products for European manufactures. The caravan routes also promoted a great deal of inter-West African trade. For example, the valuable trade in kolanuts, most of which came from Ghana,[1] was largely controlled by the traders of Kano.

A number of cities played significant roles in the caravan trade. These included Timbuktu, Walata, Jenne, Goa, Katsina, Kano, Bornu, Zaria – all of which are south of the Sudanese States – and Marrakesh, Fez, Algiers, Tripoli and Tunis in North Africa. Timbuktu was a central point of distribution in the early days of the caravan trade. The fact that it lies on the river Niger made it a convenient resting spot for the caravans. During the eighteenth and nineteenth centuries, the persistent confusion of war around Morocco brought a steady decline to the western caravan routes, and increased the traffic on the central and eastern routes thus enhancing the commercial importance of Kano, which developed into a commercial metropolis. The population of Kano, which was estimated by Clapperton in 1824 at between 30,000 and 40,000, included a large foreign element of rich Tripolian Arabs, and Salage merchants from Ghana trading in kolanuts.[2] The opening of the caravan trade routes during the dry season always brought an influx of traders to Kano. It was also the centre of a rich agricultural district which produced adequate foodstuffs for its great population. In addition, Kano owed part of its prosperity to the industry and skill of its craftsmen, especially the weavers, the leather workers and the dyers, the products of whom attracted many traders from many parts of Africa.

[1] Ghana was known as 'the Gold Coast' until she attained political independence on 6 March 1957.
[2] D. Denham and H. Clapperton, *Narrative of Travels and Discoveries in Northern and Central Africa in the Years 1822, 1823 and 1824*; and Henry Barth, *Travels and Discoveries in North and Central Africa*, vol. II.

REGULAR EUROPEAN MARITIME CONTACTS

It was not until the fifteenth century that regular European maritime contact began with West Africa. A number of obstacles had prevented the exploration of the coast of West Africa. There was the problem of building ships capable of undertaking long-distance voyages on the vast ocean, and the other main problem of navigation. However, by the early fifteenth century a better sailing ship (the caravel) using lateen or triangular sails had been developed to take the place of oared vessels; and the compass was also developed to enable seamen to keep to their course for several days while sailing on the high seas and out of sight of land. Another problem was that the Arabs in North Africa and the Middle East had established a strong triangular trade with India, Europe and West Africa. The Europeans wanted a number of Indian goods, including precious stones and spices, but could only get them from the Arabs. European goods which were acquired by the Arabs were also used in exchange for the West African products and slaves, which were again sold to European merchants. The European countries, which had relied on a bewildering number of Arab middlemen for their trade with the East Indies and Africa, realized by the beginning of the fifteenth century that such trade had become more profitable. Naturally, the Europeans wanted direct contact with the countries of the East Indies and with fresh markets in other countries, in order to eliminate the extortion practised by the Arabs. Gradually, a new seaborne trade began to develop along the coastal lands of West Africa, thus providing direct contacts between Europe and West Africa. The slow-plodding camel caravans of the desert areas were gradually out-rivalled over the centuries by Atlantic sailing ships. Although these sailing vessels were very small by modern standards, they were very large when compared in carrying capacity with a camel caravan. The sailing ships also provided a quicker means of contact and commercial exchange than the camel caravans across the desert.

The Portuguese

The Portuguese were the first Europeans to come to West Africa. The first descriptive account of the Portuguese exploration dates from the middle of the fifteenth century, when Alvise Cadamosto, a Venetian in charge of an expedition fitted out by Prince Henry of Portugal, better known as Henry the Navigator, visited the river Gambia.[1] By the time Prince Henry of Portugal died in 1462, the Portuguese had established some trade contacts along the coast of West Africa. However, the most significant effort made by the Portuguese to establish trade in the interior of West Africa was in 1485, when one John d'Aveiro opened up trade with the ancient kingdom of Benin. By about 1580, almost a century later, the Portuguese had successfully increased their trading activities in West Africa, and as a result they established a number of trading posts.

At first, the Portuguese imported from West Africa pepper, ivory and gold. These items of import are reflected in the names given to certain parts of West Africa, such as the Grain Coast, the Ivory Coast and the Gold Coast. The Portuguese started the Atlantic slave trade during the fifteenth century, and this attracted many other European nations to West Africa.

West Africa derived two main economic advantages from the Portuguese trade. First, the Portuguese introduced a number of new crops, including tobacco, rice, cassava, groundnuts, sweet potatoes, red pepper, guava, sugar-cane, oranges and limes. They were in the position to influence world commerce at this period: besides their trading interests in Europe, they established trade contacts with America, India, China, the East Indies and Latin America. It was possible, and indeed probable, that some of the products in the other tropical countries where they had trade contacts were introduced into West Africa in exchange for local products. Secondly, through their trading activities the Portuguese popularized the use of two main currencies, the cowry and the manilla.[2] These were first introduced into West Africa by Arab traders from North Africa, and were soon adopted extensively as the media of exchange in order to ease the inconveniences of the barter system which had prevailed for centuries.

The British

Towards the close of the fifteenth century, the Portuguese protested to King Edward IV about the English traders who were

[1] W. Rodney, *A History of the Upper Guinea Coast, 1545–1800.*
[2] Marion Johnson, 'The Cowrie Currencies of West Africa'.

alleged to be upsetting the Portuguese trading interests in West Africa. An English expedition fitted out in 1481 was prevented from sailing by the influence of King John II of Portugal. Despite the protests of and pressure from the Portuguese, the British continued to explore trading possibilities in West Africa. Captain Wyndham commanded an expedition which reached the Bight of Benin in 1553. In 1588, Queen Elizabeth I granted a charter to the first English–African company, and during her reign many voyages were made by Englishmen to the West Coast of Africa, including the voyage of James Welsh who visited Benin on two occasions. The second and the third British companies to trade in Africa were granted charters in 1618 and 1631 respectively. By the middle of the seventeenth century, more English traders became interested in the West African trade, particularly in the slave trade. One of the few important companies to trade in West Africa was the 'Company of Royal Adventurers of England trading in Africa', which was granted a charter by King Charles II in 1662. The company was given the sole trading rights from the Straits of Gibraltar to the Cape of Good Hope in South Africa. After the company had operated for about ten years, it sold its forts and factories to the Royal African Company.[1] As interests in Africa grew in England, it became clear that the monopoly of the chartered companies could no longer be maintained; consequently the African trade was thrown open to all British subjects in 1698.

For a long period, European contact with West Africa was confined to the coastal areas. The West African chiefs and their peoples here did not take kindly to any infiltration of Europeans into the interior, as this could interfere with their trading interests as middlemen between the people in the interior and the European traders. In addition, the unhealthy conditions for Europeans in West Africa prevented any successful exploration of the interior. But the desire of British merchants to explore trade possibilities in this area led to the founding of the African Association in 1788.[2] The association was prepared to support financially any project for the exploration of Africa. In 1796 it employed the services of Mungo Park to trace the course of the river Niger. Mungo Park made two voyages, but died on the second one in 1806 without actually completing

[1] See K. G. Davies, *The Royal African Company.*
[2] See Robin Hallett (ed.), *Records of the African Association 1788–1831.*

his mission.[1] Later British expeditions followed the encouraging results of Mungo Park's work: other important explorers of the river Niger included Clapperton, Richard Lander, John Lander, Barth, Baikie and McGregor Laird, who founded a trading company with a particular interest in Nigeria. McGregor Laird accompanied the 1832 commercial expedition from England, which arrived in the Niger Delta and ascended the river Niger beyond Lokoja in the first iron steamer to make a sea voyage.[2] Many other unsuccessful attempts were made to open trade in the interior, including the Niger Expedition of 1841, which was supported financially by the British government. The climatic conditions were the major obstacle to British success in West Africa. However, when quinine was eventually discovered as an effective remedy for fever, which had hitherto claimed many lives, both European and African, later explorers began to make progress. In 1854 Baikie led the first successful expedition to make use of quinine.[3] The expedition visited parts of the Benue, carried on trade with the people of the area and returned to the coast after four months, during which not a single member of the expedition died.

The use of sailing ships for sea voyages was one of the factors which limited the Europeans' commercial contacts with West Africa, as it took these vessels many months to complete a single voyage. However, with the development of the steamship in the first quarter of the nineteenth century, ocean traffic between Europe and West Africa increased. The foundation of British shipping, indeed of modern shipping, in Nigeria was laid by McGregor Laird, who founded the African Shipping Company in 1849. Encouraged by the success of Baikie's expedition of 1854, in which he took part, Laird contracted with the British Foreign Office in 1856 to supply a steamer every year for five years, to promote trade in Nigeria.[4]

[1] Joseph Thomson, *Mungo Park and the Niger.*
[2] K. O. Dike, *Trade and Politics in the Niger Delta 1830–1885*, p. 61n.
[3] W. B. Baikie, *Narrative of an Exploring Voyage up the Rivers Kwora and Benue*, London, 1856.
[4] A. F. Mockler-Ferryman, *British Nigeria*, London, Cassell, 1902, p. 56.

THE SLAVE TRADE[1]

Before 1807

The first shipment of African slaves to Portugal took place in 1441. The early slaves sold to wealthy men were well treated, and it was soon regarded as an important moral duty to convert as many Africans as possible to Christianity. However, by 1485 the Portuguese trade with Benin had already been established, and they also possessed a small settlement on the tiny island of São Thomé. This settlement first drew its labour force from Benin through the supply of slaves.[2] It was in this connexion that the Portuguese first realized the value of African slave labour on plantations. By the beginning of the sixteenth century the Spaniards had joined in the trade. The first batch of slaves from West Africa arrived at the Spanish island of Haiti in 1510, and another batch arrived in Cuba in 1521. By a stroke of irony their import into the mainland Spanish colonies was stimulated by the humanitarian zeal of the Spanish missionaries.[3] In 1514, the benevolent Las Casas, first Bishop of Mexico, began to denounce the cruelties inflicted on the Red Indians and to plead that Indian slaves should be replaced by Africans, whom he believed could stand the conditions better. The extensive market for slaves would not have been created had the importation of slaves been limited to Europe. Europeans were used to working on their farms, and the weather in Europe – particularly the winter – was too cold for Africans to be of much use. However, with the opening of the New World – America – there began a great demand for cheap slave labour in the tropical parts of America, where conditions were unfavourable to white labour and that of American Indians. In fact, when the African slaves were brought to America it was discovered that the conditions were unfavourable to them too.

The market for slaves, like any other market, depended on supply

[1] A number of books have been written on the slave trade, including Sir R. Coupland, *The British Anti-Slavery Movement*; Frank Klingberg, *The Anti-Slavery Movement in England*; Christopher Lloyd, *The Navy and the Slave Trade*; Thomas Clarkson, *History of the Abolition of the Slave Trade*, London, Frank Cass, 1968, 2 vols; James Bandinel, *Some Account of the Trade in Slaves from Africa*; and P. D. Curtin, *The Atlantic Slave Trade: A Census*.
[2] Michael Crowder, *The Story of Nigeria*, pp. 68–9.
[3] Coupland, op. cit., p. 18.

and demand. For the Spaniards who later joined and took a vigorous part in the trade, their main interest was the working of the gold and silver mines in South America for which slave labour was needed. They also requested slaves for their American plantations. By about 1576 there were some 40,000 African slaves on the Spanish American territories. But why were Africans so readily available for use as slaves? It is important to realize that the institution of slavery had existed in Africa long before the Atlantic slave trade. Most criminals, for example, thieves, were executed, and those who were fortunate enough to escape punishment by execution ended up being sold into slavery. 'The slave trade was a "blessed means of saving" the victims.'[1] When the Atlantic slave trade began, the supply of slaves came mainly from captives in inter-tribal wars, but at the same time the punishment of criminals became lucrative as they were exchanged for European manu-factures.

It was not till 1663 that a regular English slave trade began with the grant of the monopoly thereof to 'The Company of Royal Adventurers of England trading with Africa'.[2] The other European countries which joined the Spaniards in the slave trade had no direct economic interests on the mainland of America, as their main commercial interests ended in supplying slaves. On the supply side, Africans themselves offered their fellow men to be bartered for guns, gunpowder, gin, rum, beads, iron and copper bars. At first, the slaves exported were either prisoners captured in inter-tribal wars, or persons sentenced to die for crimes committed. However, as the trade became more lucrative deliberate slave raids were carried out among the Africans. The Europeans had to wait on the coast for the African middlemen to supply them with slaves. For two reasons the Europeans never made any serious attempt to travel into the interior to purchase slaves: first, the tropical climate and diseases checked any enthusiasm they might have had about fetching slaves themselves; secondly, the African middlemen who operated through their rulers on the coast resisted any attempt by the Europeans to penetrate into the interior. Having bought his slaves, the dealer marshalled them, men, women and

[1] Bandinel, op. cit., p. 74; Talbot, op. cit., vol. 1, p. 40; Rodney, op. cit., pp. 260–70.
[2] Coupland, op. cit., p. 22.

children, in a caravan for a march to embark on the ship on the coast. They were usually fettered to prevent escape and were often locked in the 'slave-stick' – a long pole with a crutch at the end for fastening round the neck. The slaves were made to carry on their heads the loads of foodstuffs and other baggage necessary for the journey, or the ivory or other African produce which the dealer might have bought. On reaching the coast, the slaves were taken on board the ships for their long and miserable voyage to America. No accurate export figures of slaves are available, but it has been estimated that by the middle of the eighteenth century over 100,000 slaves were shipped yearly to America, and that more than half of these were transported in British ships.[1] In fact, this figure may have been grossly understated, because the Royal African Company alone transported about 91,000 slaves to the English West Indies within a period of thirty-nine years (1673–1711).[2]

As the end of the journey to America approached, the dealers examined their slaves and prepared them for sale. Wounds, caused by storms or ill-treatment on board the ship, were nursed, and as far as possible concealed so that the buyers or their agents could not detect them. But the agents of the slave-dealers often complained that the 'parcels of negroes' landed were 'bad' or 'mean' or 'much abused'. Finally, on board ship or in the public slave market, the slaves were put up for sale by 'scramble' or 'auction'.

The prices for slaves varied from time to time, depending largely on the volume of demand relative to supply. In the seventeenth, eighteenth and nineteenth centuries, the average price paid by an African slave-dealer for a male slave varied between 40,000 and 60,000 cowries, which, according to the average rate of exchange, was equivalent to between £3 and £8.[3] However, the European slave merchant bought each male slave from the African dealer at a price which varied widely between £4 and £25, depending largely on the age and strength of the slave and also on the bargaining position of the dealer. The net sale price of a male slave in

[1] Sir Alan Burns, *History of Nigeria*, p. 103. This figure probably excludes many thousands of slaves who died on the voyage to America and those who were jettisoned.
[2] K. G. Davies, op. cit., p. 361.
[3] Robert Huish, *The Travels of Richard and John Lander*, p. 380; Robin Hallett (ed.), *The Niger Journal of Richard and John Lander*, pp. 94, 193.

the West Indies between 1600 and 1750 varied between £13 and £40.[1] However, the net sale price increased between 1751 and 1850 to between £40 and £60. Generally, the sick and the injured slaves were lumped with the helpless women and children, and sold off cheaply as 'refuse'.

The Atlantic slave trade, therefore, figured prominently in the triangular trade which developed, linking three continents – Europe, Africa and America.[2] The slave trade on its own was too expensive for the shipmaster; consequently it had to be operated along with other items of commerce. On leaving Europe the shipmaster stocked his ship with manufactured goods, which were bartered for slaves and other products, such as ivory, on reaching the West African coast. The slaves were taken to America and sold. The shipmaster then purchased cotton and sugar which he carried to Europe for sale; thus completing the triangular trade.

1807–1861

From the inception of the slave trade, there were groups of people in various European countries who were convinced that it was wrong. Prominent among these groups were the Christians – Quakers, Wesleyans and members of the Church of England. Since the beginning of the eighteenth century, the British share in the slave trade had exceeded those of the other European countries, and it was up to Britain to take the lead in its abolition. One major factor which helped this movement was the gradual industrialization of England. It has been said that the 'abolition of the slave trade was only one manifestation of the major changes from the era of mercantilism to that of industrial revolution and aggressive free trade'.[3] However, many members of the British parliament at that time had derived their wealth directly or indirectly, e.g. through ocean shipping, from the slave trade; consequently they were reluctant to support the move for abolition. It was also thought by some that stopping the slave trade would lessen the number of British ships in use, and that if Britain gave up the trade but France

[1] See Bandinel, op. cit., p. 86; and A. Boahen, *Topics in West African History*, p. 110.

[2] D. Mannix, with M. Cowley, *Black Cargoes*.

[3] J. B. Williams, 'The Development of British Trade with West Africa, 1750–1850', pp. 194–213.

did not, the French would use many more ships to cover the British share of the trade as well as their own, and France might easily become stronger than her on the sea. However, some other members of parliament who favoured the abolition of the trade formed themselves into anti slave trade committees. Granville Sharp, William Wilberforce, Thomas Clarkson, Henry Thornton and Charles Grant were among the people who fought vigorously to end the slave trade. The abolitionists were encouraged by Judge Mansfield's famous judgement in 1772, freeing slaves setting foot in England. Even then, the Bristol and Liverpool merchants who had made fortunes out of the slave trade continued to block every effort to stop it. After a long struggle between the slave merchants and the abolitionists, a law was passed in 1807 which made the trade unlawful to British subjects. It has been suggested that by the time the slave trade was abolished in 1807 the merchants were no longer making fortunes out of slavery and therefore could support abolition.[1] In fact, the economic position of the West Indies had changed by the time of the abolition. First, the British West Indies islands had more slaves than were needed for the economic operation of the plantations. Indeed, some of the surplus slaves were being re-exported to non-British islands in the West Indies. Secondly, the use of slaves on the rich French and Dutch West Indian islands which the British conquered between 1792 and 1802 constituted a direct economic threat to the planters on the old British islands. Thirdly, British West Indian sugar could no longer compete effectively in Europe with the cheaply produced sugar from Brazil and Cuba. In addition, the rapid growth of British industries reduced 'the once formidable slave interest to manageable proportions and enabled the abolitionists to attack it successfully'.[2] The growth of British industries had increased the demand for a number of raw materials such as cotton and palm oil: for example, the textile industry needed more cotton than could be obtained from the West Indies, and the growing use of machines in Britain increased the demand for palm oil and groundnuts. Africa also provided a ready market for British manufactured goods. The abolition of the slave trade, therefore, was necessary in order to encourage the 'legitimate' trade. 'Indeed by 1805 only 2 per cent of British export tonnage was employed in

[1] Eric Williams, *Capitalism and Slavery.*
[2] W. K. Hancock, *A Survey of British Commonwealth Affairs*, vol. II, part 2, p. 158.

the slave trade.'[1] It is also believed that the abolition of the slave trade would have been delayed if the American Revolution had not occurred, because this was thought to have cut off direct British interests in America.[2] One can conclude that both the economic changes in the West Indies and Britain, and the humanitarian and moral considerations, helped to bring the slave trade to an end. Undoubtedly, 'the importance of West Africa to England, as to most European countries, was that it provided the source of valuable commerce, and fitted admirably into the economic philosophy of the day'.[3]

The financial aspect of the slave trade did not end in the expenses of fitting out a slave trade expedition, paying for the slaves, feeding them until they were finally disposed of in the slave market, and the wealth which accrued to both the African and European slave-dealers. Britain had to persuade the Africans and other European countries to abandon the trade.[4] The French were the most difficult to deal with, mainly because of the Anglo-French political and economic rivalry. To persuade Spain and Portugal to outlaw the slave trade was an easier task. It was mainly a matter of money – British taxpayers' money. Portugal, which enjoyed the larger share of the trade, was induced in 1815 by the remission of £450,000, disguised as an 'idemnity' for captured slave-ships, to sign a treaty which confined her trade to the transport of slaves from Africa south of the Equator to her 'possessions' across the Atlantic. By 1815, Britain managed to get all the other European nations employed in the slave trade to give it up. However, it continued despite this agreement, and for the next forty years British sailors, ships and money were used in the attempt to stop the trade completely. When the British parliament abolished slavery throughout the British Empire in 1833, she paid the West Indian planters the compensation of £20 million. The successful battle against the slave trade and slavery was conducted by a number of nations, but Britain was the most active of them all. In fact, the British government was forced to modify both her economic and political policies towards Africa

[1] Boahen, *Topics in West African History*, p. 117.
[2] Coupland, op. cit., p. 62.
[3] E. C. Martin, *The British West African Settlements 1750–1821*, p. 1.
[4] Many nations had forsworn slavery before Britain, but none of them took any practical and positive step to stop the slave trade.

before she could successfully persuade the other European countries
to join her in stopping the slave trade. Indeed, some of the African
rulers were surprised at the sudden change of British policy.[1] The
attempts by the British to substitute legitimate trade for the slave
trade were not entirely successful at the initial stage, as it continued
in many areas including Lagos and Badagry. There continued to
be ready markets for slaves at Brazil and Cuba. For a long time
after the official abolition, a strong competition developed between
the slavers and the legitimate traders in West Africa. However, by
1860 many areas of the West African coast had been cleared of
slave-trading.

Social and economic effects

The Atlantic slave trade produced both social and economic problems which were interrelated. It gradually drained the population
of many parts of Nigeria.[2] A considerable number of able-bodied
men and women were taken away as slaves, leaving behind old
men and young children. Many families were separated for good.
Villages were often destroyed during slave raids, and inter-tribal
wars led to constant bloodshed among the people. Inevitably, there
developed a general feeling of mistrust and hatred among the various
tribes. Indeed, the Yoruba civil war in the second half of the nineteenth century was a by-product of the slave trade.[3]

It also diverted the efforts of many people away from agriculture
and industries. The loss of able-bodied men meant a decline in the
number of farmers and in the volume of agricultural production,
resulting in famine in many areas. The trade gave no urge to exploration and it denied the growth of other legitimate kinds of
commerce. It was not until towards the end of the period of the
slave trade that the demand for palm oil began to increase. In 1818,
1,465 tons of palm oil were exported from West Africa to England.
This was increased to 8,164 tons in 1831, 15,773 tons in 1840 and
to 21,722 tons in 1850.[4] By 1860, 40,216 tons of palm oil and some

---

[1] Crowder, *Story of Nigeria*, p. 128.
[2] *Report of the House of Commons Select Committee on the Slave Trade in
1848.*
[3] J. F. Ade Ajayi and Robert Smith, *Yoruba Warfare in the Nineteenth Century.*
[4] *Accounts and Papers*, P.P., XXXIX, 3 February to 12 August 1842; and
Accounts and Papers, P.P., III, 12 December 1854 to 14 August 1855.

417,000 lb of cotton were exported to England from West Africa.[1]
The palm oil trade would have grown much faster had it not been
that legitimate trade and the slave trade went on concurrently for a
long time in West Africa. The European customers loading palm
oil and other legitimate produce at the mouth of rivers or along the
coast were often interrupted, and obliged to wait, to the loss of
profit and the ruin of the crews' health, while slave-dealers took all
hands on the coast to complete their slave cargoes.[2] Whenever there
was demand for slaves most of the Africans abandoned every other
employment, to either hunt for slaves or be hunted as slaves; and in
consequence, a number of vessels trading on the coast would be
lying idle for want of legitimate trade. For many centuries, the
slave trade provided an effective barrier against the development of
agriculture and industry, and against the entrance of legitimate
commerce.

It has been argued that the slave trade did not drain the population
of West Africa as much as people have feared.[3] It is claimed that the
average annual export of slaves did not exceed the annual natural
growth in population. This gives the impression that the exported
slaves represented a 'surplus' in African population. It has also been
argued that the slave trade in West Africa 'was part of a sustained
process of economic and political development'.[4] Both arguments
raise fundamental economic issues. In the first place, it is implied
that West Africa was overpopulated. However, there is no evidence
to prove that the export of slaves, which inevitably reduced the
number of people who inhabited West Africa, led to an increase in
the *per capita* income of the people. Since the slave trade was
handled mainly by the Obas, Emirs and their chiefs, there is no
doubt that they obtained direct material and monetary gains through
the sale of slaves. However, such material and monetary wealth
was negligible in the context of the entire population, and was
obtained at the expense of considerable loss of economic welfare.
Indeed, the items of exchange for slaves, and the items on which the
revenue from the sale of slaves was spent, included gin, rum and

[1] Talbot, op. cit., p. 62.
[2] T. F. Buxton, *The African Slave Trade and its Remedy*, pp. 230–1.
[3] Curtin, op. cit.
[4] J. D. Fage, 'Slavery and the Slave Trade in the Context of West African
History', pp. 393–404.

other luxury items, which did not contribute to capital formation. The institution of slavery which existed in West Africa before the Atlantic slave trade was insignificant, and the few slaves that existed supplemented family labour on the farms, performing some domestic services. The Atlantic slave trade, therefore, brought a large number of free men into slavery. Inevitably, the slave trade reduced agricultural production, and thus the real income of the people. 'The proposition that slavery was an essential condition of [African] economic development was untenable.'[1] It is also difficult to accept that the slave trade contributed positively to political development, because it brought a series of inter-tribal wars which led to the disintegration of a number of indigenous kingdoms.

[1] Christopher Wrigley, 'Historicism in Africa: Slavery and State Formation', pp. 113–24; Rodney, op. cit., pp. 260–70.

3   Social and economic conditions by 1860

THE INDIGENOUS SOCIAL AND POLITICAL STRUCTURE

The social structures of the various peoples of Nigeria are very diverse, but common to all is the strength of the family tie. A family usually consists of a man, his wife (or wives) and his children, and a large number of collaterals claiming blood or kinship affinity with him.[1] The word 'family', therefore, means more here than is usual in most European countries and in America. It is customary for the poor members of the family to look for help from any rich member, and such help is often regarded as obligatory. The property of the wealthy member of the family is regarded as the common property of all. As a result of such a family burden, it has been very difficult to raise the standard of living of the people above subsistence level. A large proportion of the surplus income of the rich man was usually spent on providing subsistence for his poor relatives. The extended family system, therefore, provided a kind of social security peculiar to Africa. The ultimate aim of the system was to help each member of the family to be able to cater for himself and to ensure that those who were permanently or temporarily helpless, e.g. the old, the sick and the unemployed, were not neglected to suffer.

Until the nineteenth century, when the European nations increased their economic and political activities in Nigeria, the areas now known as Nigeria were completely free from any form of European domination. Many of the natural rulers acquired the right

[1] T. O. Elias, *Groundwork of Nigerian Law*, pp. 287–8.

to govern the people by conquest.[1] A number of small units of 'unlimited monarchy' existed in all parts of Nigeria. The natural ruler dominated every aspect of life in his area. He was the custodian of the land within his domain.[2] He allocated farmlands to each family according to subsistence needs, while the stool-lands (land attached to the chiefdom) and waste land remained unallocated, the non-stool land being directly controlled by him.[3] Any kind of trade approved by the ruler had to be accepted by his people however much they detested it, e.g. the slave trade. On the other hand, if the chief forbade any trade, however lucrative, it had to cease immediately; as happened on several occasions with the palm oil trade whenever the natural rulers wished to press their claims for more customs duties from the European traders.[4]

THE FISCAL SYSTEM

The natural rulers devised various means of raising adequate revenues for running their respective administrations. Revenues were collected in kind, mainly in foodstuffs, and provided for the 'rulers' and their officials. The gradual adoption of a few commodity-currencies, e.g. iron rods, bracelets, manillas and cowries, simplified to some extent the payment of taxes. Even then, the bulk of the population continued to pay in kind by supplying foodstuffs and by performing services, e.g. providing labour on the farm and serving as warriors.

The structure and organization of the indigenous tax systems varied from one part of the country to another. The indigenous fiscal system in the emirates of Northern Nigeria was the most advanced. 'Most of the old established Hausa Kingdoms had embraced the Islamic faith, and under its influence they had by the early sixteenth century developed a well-organized fiscal

[1] Relevant to the early conquests were the Holy War of Usman dan Fodio and the Yoruba civil wars. See Crowder, *Story of Nigeria*, pp. 90–123.
[2] T. O. Elias, *Nigerian Land Law and Custom*, London, Sweet & Maxwell, 1950.
[3] A. K. Ajisafe, *The Laws and Customs of the Yoruba People*, p. 6.
[4] It is known that in 1857 the King of Ijebu (Awujale) stopped the oil trade with the Europeans in his area. He demonstrated his firm intention by executing some natives who had been found carrying oil to markets secretly, in defiance of his orders. Talbot, op. cit., p. 200.

system . . . .'[1] In communities conquered by the Emirs it was not unusual to raid for taxes. Such communities usually paid very heavy taxes which were arbitrarily imposed on no recognized basis, while semi-independent tribes paid just as much as their normal rulers could enforce, and were raided at will.

In Southern Nigeria, a largely rudimentary indigenous tax system existed. A satisfactory feature was that in most of the Yoruba kingdoms tax assessments were based on the ability to pay. But it was equally true that some greedy 'rulers' occasionally boosted their revenues by confiscating goods owned by their subjects. Usually goods were confiscated from various sellers on local market days. Also in Southern Nigeria, in the early days of European contact with Nigeria, European traders were made to pay taxes in the form of customs and shipping dues for the support of the indigenous governments. Some European traders also had their property confiscated, and fines were often extorted from them for various offences ranging from trading with the 'natives' without permission to competing in local trade with the 'natural rulers'.[2]

Generally, the subsistence nature of the Nigerian economy did not allow for any flexibility of resources. However, in some well-organized areas of Northern Nigeria the principal taxes included the Zakka or tithe on corn, the Kurdin Kasa or land tax, the plantation tax on all crops, the Jangali or cattle tax, and the Sokoto Gaisua – a varying sum, probably of religious origin, paid chiefly in horses and slaves by all other emirates to Sokoto and Gando. There was also the Kurdin Sarauta – an accession duty paid by every chief or holder of office on appointment.[3] Lastly, there was the death duty (Gado), which passed the estate of the deceased to the Emir when there was no recognized heir.

AGRICULTURAL PRODUCTION

The economic resources of Nigeria depended largely on agriculture, and the bulk of the population were engaged in farming. In each

---

[1] Lord Hailey, *An African Survey*, p. 453. See also Sir Charles Orr, *The Making of Northern Nigeria*, pp. 153–4.
[2] For a detailed account of the experience of the early European traders, see Dike, op. cit., and G. I. Jones, *The Trading States of the Oil Rivers*.
[3] A similar tax existed among the Yorubas.

chiefdom, the natural ruler was responsible for allocating farmlands to the families which wanted them. Invariably every family needed land, as it was the only means of providing basic foodstuffs and domestic materials. The head of a family took land from the natural ruler and, in his turn, reallocated it to a member of the family. Subject to good behaviour and to the performance of his duties towards the chief, usually on paying regular tribute in kind, the family could retain the land perpetually.

Farming consisted of a series of simple but primitive operations. The system of farming universally adopted was that of shifting culti-vation.[1] This was particularly the case in most forest areas where farming was the main economic activity. First, the land was cleared by cutting down the trees, leaving stumps of young trees of about two to three feet on the ground, so that after the soil was exhausted, i.e. after the land had been cropped for two or three years, the trees could grow up again for a period of from five to fifteen years, during which the land rested and was replenished by the foliage from the trees. The trees which had been cleared on the land and some undergrowth were allowed to dry in the sun. This operation usually took place during the dry season just before the rainy season was about to begin. In the savannah areas, no systematic clearing of the bush was undertaken. Instead, the farmland was set on fire to burn down the already dried shrubs and grass. At that stage the farmland provided firewood, which was usually collected by children and women for domestic use. In the forest areas, after the firewood had been collected, the remaining waste on the farmland was burnt, leaving the ash, which was the only form of manure. Small 'game' were usually trapped and killed for providing meat while the farmland was on fire. The effectiveness of the system in maintaining soil fertility was determined by the length of the fallow period, which depended on the extent to which the crops grown had impoverished the soil. The longer the period of fallow the more fully the land built up its fertility level, if there were no other forces acting against it, such as erosion. The shifting cultivation system suited many areas in Nigeria, particularly areas with low population densities. Apart from the 'bush' farming, cultivation on a much smaller scale, in the form of gardening, was carried on inside the villages and towns where some open spaces separated

[1] This system is still widely adopted in Nigeria.

the compounds (a collection of mud-houses). In fact, something would be planted wherever there was space: all along the town walls, around the compound wall and on any open space in front or at the back of the house. On these small plots or 'gardens' were planted crops such as vegetables, beans, pepper and maize, which were easy to tend by very young children and old people who could not undertake to walk long distances to the 'bush' farms.

Locally manufactured knives, cutlasses and hoes constituted the farm implements. Ploughing was completely unknown. There were two types of hoe – a large heavy type and the small hoe. The heavy hoe was used in making 'earth heaps' or farm ridges for planting root crops, and for constructing the drainage system on the farm. The lighter hoe was used for weeding and other less heavy work. The knives and cutlasses were used for clearing the bush, cutting grain stalks and for digging out root crops, such as yam and cassava.

The principal articles of food grown were guinea corn, maize, millet, beans of several varieties, yams of various species, sweet potatoes, pepper of various kinds, kolanuts and vegetables of all sorts. Cotton was also grown to provide raw material for the indigenous domestic cotton industry. In addition to these, the palms grew wild in the bush, providing the vegetable oil needed by the people, and there were a number of wild plants providing fruits, e.g. paw-paw and mangoes. Agricultural production was largely on the subsistence level in most villages; but in fairly big towns, where some degree of specialization existed, surplus agricultural products were exchanged for local industrial products, e.g. hoes, knives, cutlasses, mats, pottery and leather products (slippers and hand-bags).

It was customary for the entire family to provide labour, especially during the planting and harvesting periods. There was no special class of 'farm labourers' as such, as each family possessed at least a farmland, and provided labour on it. Some slave labour existed to supplement the family labour when necessary: on the farms owned by chiefs, farm labour was provided mainly by slaves.

LOCAL INDUSTRIES AND CRAFTS

Although the bulk of the working population of Nigeria were farmers, some people were engaged in local industries and crafts.

Natural and geographical factors dictated the location of industries in Nigeria. The canoe industry developed along the coastal areas and the river banks. Dug-out canoes were made from logs cut and hollowed out with axes made by the local blacksmith. It required much skill to produce a canoe with sides and bottom of uniform thickness. The final process involved burning the inside of the canoe in order to produce a smooth and shiny surface. Small-scale fishing industries also existed along the coast and the river banks, making use of locally manufactured canoes and fishing-nets produced from local fibres.

In Nigeria, cotton had been grown and manufactured into cloth for many centuries past. Spun, hand-woven in simple cloth and dyed with colours obtained from native plants, it provided most of the clothing of the people. Nearly all the ginning, spinning and weaving equipment was made of wood. There were two types of loom. The one used by men was a narrow upright type worked with pedals, and was commonly adopted all over Northern Nigeria. It produced narrow strips of cloth about five inches wide. The looms were placed in a half-open shed, usually in the inner court-yard of the compound, and each loom was operated by one man. Apart from the shuttle and the wooden posts which were often provided by the weavers themselves, the other tools – the iron rods used as pedals and the iron bar upon which the finished strips of cloth were wound – were manufactured by the blacksmith. The loom used by women weavers was an upright broad loom of between twenty and thirty-six inches wide, installed inside the house. This type was adopted mainly in the south, particularly among the Yoruba women. Cloth dyeing was a special industry of its own, and in all parts of Nigeria vegetable dyes were derived from certain local plants. In most Moslem areas of the north, where women were kept indoors according to religious practice, men were engaged in cloth dyeing, while the job was handled largely by women in the non-Moslem areas of the south.

Long before the nineteenth century, the people of Nigeria had been mining iron, tin, gold, salt and other minerals. Ironworks existed in many areas, including Ijebu-Ode, Ilorin, Bida and Awka. The workshop of the blacksmith was usually divided by a screen which separated the section which contained the furnaces from the one in which he sat. The bellows of the furnaces were either of the split-bag type made of animal skin and used mainly for heavy works, or the small single-bag type used for minor works. The bellows were operated by hand, holding the sticks fixed on the top of each bag. A clay tube passed from the bellows to the shallow furnace in which charcoal was burnt. The charcoal was made out of wood or palm-kernel shell.

The technical process of ironwork was simple. The bulk of crude iron ore was held over the fire in the furnace until it became red hot and pliable. It was then placed on the anvil and gradually hammered into shape. The change from furnace to anvil was repeated several times until the object had been given its final shape. It must be added that the blacksmith also produced his own anvil, hammers, files and other working tools. In fact, there were occasions when the blacksmith undertook the mining of iron ore as well. The local smiths forged spears and arrows, which were used for hunting as well as for inter-tribal wars; tools of husbandry, and household tools were made from locally mined iron. Local smelting of minerals also helped to develop specialized handicrafts. The terracotta figures found in the tinfields round Nok and south-wards to the middle Benue valley, the brass figures and ornaments of Bida and the Ife and Benin bronze heads proved that a long-established sculpture industry existed in Nigeria.[1] There was also a well-established glass-manufacturing industry at Bida. It was believed that the glassworkers brought their traditional art from Egypt, which was claimed to be their original home.[2] The embossed brass and copper work of Bida was famous, and the designs of their goblets, in which brass and copper were beautifully blended, were extremely elegant. Bida also had a prosperous bead-manufacturing industry, which refined the crude or plain beads brought into the country from North Africa by Hausa and Arab traders. Alluvial tin-mining also existed in the plateau district of Northern Nigeria.[3]

Naturally, the fine timbers of the southern districts of Nigeria encouraged the art of the wood-carver. Wood carving was famous in most parts of Southern Nigeria, and in most villages and towns

[1] Basil Davidson, *A History of West Africa, 1000–1800*, p. 200.
[2] S. F. Nadel, *A Black Byzantium*, p. 274.
[3] W. H. Laws, *Nigerian Tin-Mining Expedition*, Canada, 1903: Afr. S. 888 (1), Rhodes House, Oxford.

carved gods and goddesses were displayed in public places, e.g. the chiefs' palaces, and in the shrines.[1]

In Northern Nigeria, there was a long-established leather industry, utilizing the hides of domesticated animals. Sokoto and Kano provided markets for many kinds of leather goods such as saddlery, slippers and handbags. Closely associated with the leather industry was the hide and skin industry, which had a separate market of its own. The Northern Nigerian goats, particularly the small 'Sokoto Reds', yielded fine skins, unique in quality. These skins were dispatched across the Sahara by camel caravans and sold to European merchants in North African ports, particularly at the ports of Morocco, and so became known to the world as 'Morocco leather' – an injustice to Nigeria since the skins actually produced in North Africa were inferior to those of Sokoto and Kano.

The soap industry existed in many southern districts. There were also flourishing brewing industries in all parts of the country. Palm-wine was tapped from the palm trees, beer brewed from local corn and millet and strong wine brewed from kolanuts. Other minor local industries included basket and mat weaving, and pottery. As a rule most craftsmen also practised a little agriculture on the farm-plots close to their houses, where they grew a few crops for sub-sistence, thus providing the necessary running capital. However, all the craftsman required for his profession were his tools, which were largely produced by him and made of wood and locally forged iron. The quality of the craftsman's product depended on his skill. Except for such industries as canoe building, and fishing and alluvial mining, which were essentially 'open-air' industries, most of the other industries were operated indoors – in the homes. The raw materials and the tools usually belonged to the craftsman, and labour was provided by him and his family. This was the kind of 'domestic system' of production which prevailed in all the local industries of Nigeria.

The local industries produced different kinds of skilled craftsmen who formed themselves into various organizations, which could be called craft gilds. In most villages and towns each craft had its own gild. Notable among them were the blacksmiths, brass and silver-smiths, builders, brewers, weavers and carvers. There were three main factors which determined the strength and influence of

[1] G. J. A. Ojo, *Yoruba Palaces.*

each gild: first, the nature of the production technique, and the degree of co-operation necessary in the process of production, tended to bring some craftsmen together; secondly, the special skill and experience involved in the production technique forced craftsmen to associate in order to maintain their jealously guarded trade secrets; thirdly, the high demand for the goods produced by an industry, and thus its economic success, inevitably led to the formation of gilds which could effectively control output, and entry into the trade.

An apprenticeship system existed in all the crafts of Nigeria. The period of apprenticeship varied from district to district, and from craft to craft. However, it took into account the time it would normally take to master the craft, and the age of the apprentice, as young children who started at an early age spent more time than the adult apprentice. Also an apprentice who came to the master through the 'pawn' system could spend more time than necessary with the master unless the loan for which he was a 'pawn' was repaid promptly.[1]

After an appreciable period of training the master would entrust the production of certain goods to the apprentice in order to test the level of his skill. The apprentice had to pay the master for his training by providing regular services on the master's farm throughout the period of apprenticeship. Upon the satisfactory completion of his period of training, the apprentice was fully initiated into the gild and might, if he chose, establish himself in business or associate with his former master or another master as a journeyman. As a journeyman, he would receive wages, paid in kind and later partly in kind and partly in commodity-currency. However, it was customary for the newly qualified gildman to spend a few months in employment as journeyman. It was customary for journeymen and particularly the apprentices to live in the master's house, where meals were provided for them. They were subject to the master's control in matters of everyday behaviour as well as of the craft.

---

[1] Under the pressure of unexpected or obligatory heavy expenses, the people might have recourse to pawning one member of the family to procure a 'money' loan. This was different from slavery in that pawning was, at least in theory, regarded as a purely temporary mutual arrangement. See O. Johnson (ed.), *History of the Yorubas*, Lagos, 1937; Nadel, op. cit., pp. 311–13; and R. O. Ekundare, *Marriage and Divorce under Yoruba Customary Law*, p. 66.

THE PROBLEMS OF EXCHANGE

Subsistence economy prevailed in most parts of Nigeria. However, the exchange of a limited number of goods based on a simple system of barter was of long standing in the country. The early exchanges were the results of surplus production over and above the subsistence need. The amount of produce a family could offer and the goods it required in exchange were often small in quantity and value. The cumbersome nature of the system of exchange by barter, and the inadequate transport and communication systems, provided the major hindrances in the development of an exchange economy.

TRANSPORT AND COMMUNICATION

Nigeria depended largely on the natural waterways – the rivers – for the transportation of goods and people. The waterways which provided the easiest routes for the early explorers, traders and missionaries were confined mainly to the southern half of the country, and to a few areas in the north along the Niger and the Benue. People in many other parts of the interior had to travel several miles on foot before they could reach the waterways. The rivers were often affected by the tropical rain and thunderstorms which caused sand to block their openings on the coast, and caused uprooted trees to obstruct free movement of canoes.

With the practical limitations of the waterways, footpaths or bush tracks were extensively used in all areas. In the dense forest districts, the footpaths were too narrow for animal haulage, consequently the easiest and most practicable means of transporting goods was by head-loading. There are limits to the carrying capacity of any human being, and the distance he or she can cover at a given time with a heavy load on the head. The intense heat of the sun and the torrential rain added more problems to what was already a hazardous system of transport. The bush paths of the southern districts of Nigeria found their counterparts in the northern territories in the camel and donkey tracks. Animal haulage was affected by the tsetse fly and animal disease, thus increasing the rate of mortality among the beasts of burden, which often resulted in the complete paralysis of this form of transport. Lack of pasture also limited the effective use of animal haulage. It was therefore a problem to provide adequate pasture and to keep a sufficient number of animals free from diseases. The short supply of such animals in relation to the demand for them resulted in animal haulage remaining in the hands of a few rich people.

Nigerians had long developed various means of communication. Talking-drums made of animal skins were used to send messages to nearby villages, though only on rare and important occasions: for example, the sound of a war-drum would notify the people that an inter-tribal war had started or was imminent. Another important means of communication was the flute.[1] This was made from either a wooden or bamboo pipe, or small round calabashes of a special type, and had holes stopped by fingers or key, and a blow-hole inside or on top for wooden pipe or calabash respectively. The notes sounded on such flutes carried messages for distances of up to a mile. The fact that villages and farms were isolated and that life was generally quiet in them made the flute an effective means of communication.

Another form of indigenous communication was that of sending certain objects or materials which could be identified with certain messages. Generally, the objects or materials used for communication were easy to recognize, but there were instances when the ordinary use of the object could not give sufficient indication of the intended message. In such cases, metaphoric meanings were employed to read the messages. For example, in some Yoruba areas it was customary to send pepper to a person to signify that he had been bereaved. When a child was born, the usual message was a new bathing-sponge sent to the father or to the relatives. If there was famine in any area, the distress message was the chaff. 'Object-messages' could only be used effectively for common and anticipated news or events. It was sometimes difficult to understand some messages. For instance, it would be difficult to understand the exact message when pepper and bathing-sponge were sent together to the same person. It could mean that while a child had been born another person had died in the family; it could also be interpreted to mean that the mother of the new baby had since died, or that a child had been born but died shortly after birth. Such was the crude communication system which was maintained by special messengers

[1] The talking-drums and flutes were used mainly in Southern Nigeria.

who had a good knowledge of the bush tracks connecting the villages.

COMMODITY-CURRENCIES

The people of Nigeria had adopted the barter system of exchange long ago; it suited the predominantly subsistence economy of the country before the advent of foreign traders. With the gradual growth of the economy – the growth of indigenous crafts and industries – some degree of specialization was achieved, thus making exchange by barter cumbersome and unsatisfactory, particularly in the big towns. However, as a result of the increasing foreign contact with North Africa through the trans-Saharan trade, and along the coastal areas with European traders, a number of commodity-currencies and foreign coins found their way into Nigeria. By 1860 the most widely adopted money was the commodity-currency. As well as the manilla and the cowry, which were popularized by the Portuguese, a number of other items were adopted as monies. The adoption of commodity-currencies differed from the barter system in that any commodity adopted as currency was known to be generally accepted, and so came to be employed extensively for exchange rather than for consumption. In Nigeria, the cowry was the most generally accepted currency; the adoption of other commodity-currencies was restricted to local areas: for example, in the south-east of Bornu there was a local currency consisting of thin plates of iron, shaped like the tip used for shoeing racehorses; these were made into parcels, according to their weights, representing certain units of money. The different types of iron currencies varied in size, thus creating great disparity between the intrinsic and the face values. The prices of cowries, iron bars and manillas varied widely according to the supply and demand for each of them.[1] For example, in the Oil River States an iron bar currency was valued at 2s. 6d. in 1820 but fell to 7d. in 1854.[2] In Lagos 2,000 cowries were valued in 1850 and 1859 at 4s. and 1s. 6d. respectively.[3] Another popular form of currency were strips of cotton cloth, which had different names in different areas. They

[1] K. G. Davies, op. cit., p. 357.
[2] Jones, op. cit., p. 93.
[3] Johnson, op. cit., p. 340.

were known as *gubaka* in Bornu and as *leppi* in Adamawa.[1] The strips of cloth were woven locally and then standardized as currencies. Other early commodity-currencies included salt, brass rods and slaves.

In addition to these commodity-currencies, there were a number of foreign coins which were real currencies in their respective countries. The growth of legitimate trade with Nigeria following the abolition of the slave trade increased the volumes and the circulation of such coins. British gold and silver coins were in circulation at their face values. Spanish and South American doubloons were in circulation, and so were French francs and Portuguese 'Isabel'. The values of these coins varied, depending largely on the supply and demand for them as dictated by commercial transactions.

An attempt to organize a reliable monetary system for Nigeria was made in 1858, when McGregor Laird issued small copper coins, each of the value of one-eighth of a penny, to be used in Nigeria and in the other British settlements in West Africa. The coins became popular with the indigenous people in those areas along the coast where they were introduced. However, the coins were withdrawn from circulation because the issue was held by the British government to be an infringement of the Royal Prerogative.[2]

LOCAL TRADE

The exchange of goods (but not of services) in various parts of Nigeria has been of long standing. As one would expect, most early exchanges were the results of surplus production over and above the subsistence level. The amount of produce a family could offer and the goods it required in exchange were often small in quantity and value. The people could not afford the trouble and expense of sending small parcels of goods very far, nor to travel far either to sell them or to make their small purchases. Another limiting factor to the rapid growth of an exchange economy was the limited complementarity between the natural resources and products of the different villages and towns within easy reach of

[1] K. Yeboa Daaku, 'Pre-European Currencies of West Africa and Western Sudan', p. 13.
[2] Burns, op. cit., p. 133.

one another. Hence, local markets were organized at regular intervals of three, five or seven days, and occasionally fortnightly, for the exchange of products.[1] In fixing the local market days, the distances to be covered by those attending the market from the neighbouring villages, and the number of participating villages in a particular district or chiefdom were taken into account, as each village acted as host-village on market days in rotation. In large districts markets were often held simultaneously in two or more villages on a particular day. The organization of such markets gave the people the opportunity to sell local products at regular intervals. A sense of specialization soon grew: each village specialized in supplying particular local foodstuffs and industrial products, and thus the people knew which village market to visit for their rare but special purchases. Items of local exchange included foodstuffs, and household materials such as mats, pottery and soap. These markets also developed as the central markets for local products such as palm oil, which had begun to attract the European merchants.

FOREIGN TRADE

Apart from the slave trade, the foreign trade of Nigeria before 1860 was of little significance. Until the middle of the nineteenth century, the West African countries were generally grouped together by the Europeans for trading purposes. However, from the trade figures available (some of which may not be accurately recorded) it can be seen that the foreign trade of West Africa began to increase after the abolition of the slave trade – though one has to make some allowance for occasional trade fluctuations caused by a number of civil wars which plagued many parts of West Africa in the first half of the nineteenth century.

The main agricultural export of West Africa was palm oil. The ultimate success of stopping the slave trade can be linked with the demand for candles and soaps in Europe,[2] which in turn increased the demand for West African oil at the expense of the slave trade.[3]

[1] B. W. Hodder and V. I. Ukwu, *Markets in West Africa.*
[2] A comprehensive history of the soap industry in England is given by Charles Wilson, *A History of Unilever.*
[3] 'Buy our candles – and help to stop the slave trade – a typical Victorian combination of good business and good morality': McPhee, op. cit., p. 28.

Palm oil was produced largely by the farmers using primitive methods, and involved minimal costs of production as it merely entailed the collection of fresh palm fruits which in the past were left to rot after the immediate family needs had been met. The trade in palm oil, like the other trades of this period, was for a long time confined to the coastal areas, particularly the areas of the Niger Delta.[1] Table 3.1 below shows the volume of palm oil exported to

TABLE 3.1   *Export of palm oil to Britain from West Africa, 1831–50*

Year	Volume (cwt)	Year	Volume (cwt)
1831	163,288	1841	397,073
1832	217,804	1842	420,171
1833	266,990	1843	407,884
1834	269,907	1844	414,570
1835	256,337	1845	500,833
1836	276,635	1846	360,452
1837	223,292	1847	469,348
1838	281,372	1848	499,719
1839	343,449	1849	475,364
1840	315,458	1850	434,450

Sources: *Accounts and Papers*, P.P., XXXIX, 3 February to
      12 August 1842; and *Accounts and Papers*,
      P.P., III, 12 December 1854 to 14 August 1855.

Britain from West Africa for the period 1831–50. It can be seen that the export of palm oil fluctuated widely: there were a few years of marked increased exports, e.g. in 1833, 1838–9 and 1845; and there were also some years of sharp falls in the volume of export, e.g. in 1837, 1840 and 1846. The fact that the slave trade still continued in some areas and the prevalence of civil wars must account for these fluctuations: the years of increased exports can be associated with years of relative peace, while the less peaceful years are reflected in the decline of exports.

Palm oil was not the only export of West Africa to Europe. It is

[1] Dike, op. cit., and Jones, op. cit.

known that as early as 1850, raw cotton was exported to Britain,[1] and that, in order to increase the supply of raw cotton from Nigeria, the Manchester Cotton Supply Association sent out two tons of

TABLE 3.2   *Imports from Britain to West Africa, 1831–50*

Year	Cotton manufactures		Salt	
	Volume (yards)	Value (£)	Volume (bushels)	Value (£)
1831	2,384,000	75,058	195,240	3,872
1832	3,878,034	97,642	261,900	4,783
1833	4,964,666	118,872	330,310	5,972
1834	4,975,433	129,584	216,480	3,857
1835	3,905,158	124,777	214,047	4,226
1836	7,706,053	209,609	314,132	8,094
1837	4,973,412	135,323	180,119	4,333
1838	7,368,526	187,101	275,040	7,217
1839	9,184,772	232,801	389,574	9,318
1840	10,488,479	261,297	344,740	6,620
1841	8,389,266	183,623	387,150	7,951
1842	12,014,239	220,564	331,010	7,235
1843	16,563,895	300,133	420,711	7,198
1844	9,992,382	193,778	374,452	5,484
1845	11,654,703	222,335	357,444	5,623
1846	9,497,986	173,219	295,574	4,947
1847	12,495,665	228,149	380,862	5,970
1848	14,641,068	233,957	497,598	7,479
1849	17,285,544	266,344	411,473	6,337
1850	16,929,026	270,069	469,207	7,738

Sources: *Accounts and Papers,* P.P., XXXIX, 3 February to 12 August 1842; and *Accounts and Papers,* P.P., III, 12 December 1854 to 14 August 1855.

cotton seeds to the British Consul in Nigeria in 1858 for distribution to indigenous farmers.[2] Other items of export included limited amounts of mahogany, elephants' teeth, ginger, hides and pepper. Some other important items of local consumption, such as baskets, calabashes, egusi and mats, were also exported, particularly

[1] In that year 347 lb of cotton was exported to England from Nigeria: Talbot, op. cit., p. 51.
[2] Talbot, op. cit., p. 109.

to Brazil. It is reasonable to assume that the export of such indigenous products to Brazil was to satisfy the needs of the African slaves in that country.

The early European traders faced a big problem in creating demand for their products, because the indigenous people could spin their own thread, weave their own garments, provide their own foodstuffs and even, when the necessity arose, forge their own tools. The people felt no urgency in buying the European goods. The early imports, therefore, included many luxury articles which were designed mainly to attract local interest, such as looking-glasses, toys, beads, alcoholic drinks, cotton goods, guns, gunpowder and salt. Undoubtedly the most important of these items were cotton goods and salt, which were supplied by Britain.

Before 1860 the European merchants who had been trading in Nigeria were largely individuals, trading on their own account. There were also a few trading companies. After the abolition of the slave trade, many of them withdrew from the Nigerian trade as it became less profitable at the initial stage, while some remained to promote 'legitimate' trade. Among those who remained were the British, the Germans, the French and the Brazilians. Occasionally, when foreign traders tried to explore the interior they met with hostile middlemen and chiefs who had vested interests in the coastal trade. The middlemen were reluctant to encourage foreign traders as it could result in the loss of their incomes. The chiefs were also against the intruders, partly for the same reason and partly because the natives were horrified at the presence of white men.[1] In areas where the chiefs took kindly to foreign traders, commercial transactions were often held up abruptly in order to exploit concessions from the foreigners, who had to bribe such chiefs before trade could be resumed. In some cases, the foreign traders had to enlist the help of local secret societies in enforcing the payment of debts which had arisen from commercial transactions. For example, the old Calabar towns were governed by Egbo, an Efik word for leopard. The Egbo or leopard association was a very clever and effective means of government. Its main object was to protect the

[1] The chiefs and peoples (of Ijebu-Ode) appeared horrified at the presence of white men in their country and sacrificed goats, dogs, fowls, etc., at Ode, and all villages through which the mission passed, to avert any evil which the white man's presence might cause: Talbot, op. cit., p. 221.

interests of the merchants of these towns. An example of an Egbo agreement reads: 'I, Prince James Egamba V, hereby agree and promise that at anytime at the request of George Watt or his agent – to compel the said calabar man pay his just debts.'[1] To 'blow Egbo' was to sound the Egbo horn outside the debtor's house, an act which confined him to his house until he had paid up. It was also possible for European traders to acquire for themselves the powers of Egbo, but the merchants made sure that fees for entry to the top or ruling grades of Egbo were high enough to keep the power and the bulk of the commercial transactions in the hands of the wealthiest among them.

[1] *Merchant Adventure: The History of John Holt*, Liverpool, John Holt & Co. Ltd, pp. 31–2.

Part 2 The first British foothold 1860–1900

4 General survey

Although the few available indicators of economic growth in the nineteenth century are not absolutely reliable,[1] the main features of the process of growth and the main constraints upon growth can be established from them. For example, the Lagos population was given as 25,083, 41,236, 62,000 and 86,000, in 1866, 1870, 1880 and 1895 respectively.[2] The increase in the population of Lagos from 1866 to 1870 was 64 per cent, i.e. an average annual increase of 16 per cent, which can be attributed mainly to the movement of population from the interior to Lagos, rather than any spectacular increase in births or decrease in the death rate. In fact, there were no modern medical facilities in Lagos until 1896, when the first hospital was built. The increase in the population of Lagos from 1870 to 1880 represents an average annual increase of about 5·2 per cent, while the increase from 1880 to 1895 represents an average annual increase of 2·6 per cent. Lagos, which was the site of the first organized modern government, attracted a large number of people who sought refuge from the Yoruba civil wars.[3] Another city which showed a remarkable increase in population was Ibadan. The population of Ibadan was estimated at 60,000 and 200,000 in 1851 and 1890 respectively.[4] This sharp increase can be attributed mainly to the influx of people to Ibadan as it was one of the major war camps of the Yoruba civil wars.

The official occupational distribution of the population of Lagos

[1] Official colonial statistics relating to Nigeria began with the *Lagos Blue Books*, CO151/1–37, in 1862; and these concentrated on providing statistics on government revenue and expenditure, and on exports and imports.

[2] *Lagos Blue Books*, 1866–95.

[3] Ajayi and Smith, op. cit.

[4] Talbot, op. cit., pp. 298 and 312.

indicates that the number of people engaged in agriculture increased from 789 in 1866, to 7,785 in 1888 and to 15,911 in 1895; and those who were engaged in commerce numbered 2,540 and 19,977 in 1866 and 1895 respectively. The bulk of those in commerce were petty traders handling small units of imported items such as salt, matches and lamp oil (kerosene). For the country as a whole, the bulk of the working population were farmers, while some people were engaged in local industries and crafts. On occasions, particularly during civil wars, most economic activities were brought under the direct control of the paramount chief (Oba or Emir), i.e. nationalized in modern terms, in order to ensure adequate and regular supplies of food, war implements and other essential materials. Although there are no statistics to show the volume of local industrial production, the reports of a number of European explorers indicate that local industries prospered in the nineteenth century as they provided the basic everyday needs of the people before the advent of modern commerce.

Another indicator of growth can be found in the structure of government revenue and expenditure. For example, the total revenue of Lagos increased from £7,000 in 1862, to £48,000 in 1880 and to £192,000 in 1899.[1] The extent to which the revenue increased is better illustrated by considering the fact that, in 1862, customs duties accounted for 43 per cent of the total revenue, while this proportion increased to 85·4 per cent in 1880 and to 91·7 per cent in 1899. A similar pattern is shown in the revenue of the Niger Coast Protectorate, where the total revenues for 1896–7 and 1899–1900 were £122,000 and £164,000, of which customs duties accounted for £107,000 (87·7 per cent), and £151,000 (92 per cent) respectively.[2] Similarly, the expenditure of the Lagos government increased from £7,000 in 1862, to £55,000 in 1880 and to £223,000 in 1899. Because the annual government expenditure on civil establishment exceeded half of the annual total expenditure, only a few social and economic development projects could be undertaken.

The high proportion of revenue from customs duties reflected the rapid growth in foreign trade, as nearly all the duties were derived from imports. The export of palm products – oil and

[1] *Lagos Blue Books*, 1862–99.
[2] *Niger Coast Protectorate Blue Books*, 1896–1900, CO464/1–4.

kernels – increased considerably. Lagos exported the palm oil tonnage of 6,024 and 10,669 in 1881 and 1890 respectively. However, the bulk of Nigerian palm oil came from the Niger Coast Protectorate, where about 37,844 tons were exported in 1897–8. The most important single item of import was cotton goods. Lagos imported cotton goods to the value of £242,000 and £305,000 in 1875 and 1899, which represented 53 per cent and 32 per cent of the value of total imports respectively. The rapid growth of foreign trade reflected the gradual restoration of law and order following the penetration of British influence into the interior of the country.

Throughout the nineteenth century there were a number of constraints upon growth. The slave trade, which was officially abolished by the British early in the century, continued to flourish until the 1850s. The inter-tribal wars among the various tribes of the country could not be completely halted until the last quarter of the century; and as such the process of economic growth was retarded. Even though commercial transactions expanded steadily, an important constraint to greater economic activity was the absence of any one nationally accepted currency. In addition, the transport system remained largely undeveloped and could only handle a limited amount of goods traffic at one time.

The transition from the slave trade era to that of colonial rule did not achieve much in stimulating direct economic development. It was too soon to expect Nigerians to respond easily and favourably to modern economic growth after the experience of the slave trade, especially as they had to contend with the new fear of British domination. On the British side, the colonial experience in Africa was too short and hence little positive thinking in terms of economic development ever took place. The British government's efforts to establish good and orderly government in Nigeria in order to make it easier to exploit the country's natural resources took precedence over other economic considerations. However, by the end of the nineteenth century a rough basis for economic development had been initiated, as export production was being encouraged, and real attempts to build up the social and economic infrastructure of the country had begun.

POLITICAL DEVELOPMENTS

The most significant single factor which influenced the economic history of Nigeria was the political and economic rivalry among the European nations – rivalry in Europe as well as in Africa – which led to increasing British influence in Nigeria and subsequently to the complete domination of the country by the United Kingdom. The British government's influence in Nigeria started in 1851, when the British attacked Lagos in an attempt to force Kosoko (King of Lagos) to abandon the slave trade.[1] After this incident, the British government still had no immediate plan to administer Lagos as a colony; however, the refusal of the King of Lagos to stop the slave trade in his area forced them to take over the administration in 1861. Even at that stage there was a strong movement of public opinion against the establishment of British colonies in West Africa. Four years later a Select Committee of the House of Commons investigated and reported on the state of British establishments in West Africa.[2] The committee advised strongly against extending British territory there or making fresh treaties offering any protection to native tribes. It realized that it would be impossible to withdraw British administration wholly or immediately from any settlements or engagements on the West African coast; but it recommended that British policy should be to encourage the natives in the exercise of those qualities which should render it possible to transfer the ultimate administration of all the territories to the natives. The recommendations of the committee were in the main wholly ignored by the British government, as the informal empire which had been created by British merchants had become unremovable. However, it was decided on the basis of the committee's report that Sierra Leone should become the seat of government for all the West African dependencies of Great Britain. Thus Lagos was administered with the rest of the British West African territories from 1866 to 1874, and with the Gold Coast from 1874 to 1886.

[1] A very good but brief account of the capture of Lagos and the events which led to its annexation is given by W. N. M. Geary in *Nigeria under British Rule*; also see F. J. A. Ajayi in 'The British Occupation of Lagos 1851–61', pp. 96–105.

[2] *Report of Select Committee on State of British Settlements on the West Coast of Africa*, P.P., V (412), 1865.

After the abolition of the slave trade and before 1870, the other major European countries were less interested in West Africa. Portugal, Holland, France and Denmark, like Britain, had been chiefly attracted to West Africa before the nineteenth century by the slave trade. When this was abolished early in the century, they, unlike Britain, took very little part in putting it down; and they had very little interest in any other kind of commerce. Many of the European nations sold their forts in West Africa to the British as the territories were no longer considered valuable. Even in England a section of public opinion wished the government to follow the example of the other European countries and abandon West Africa, which was considered unhealthy and expensive for the British taxpayers. However, by 1875 the governments of many European countries had become more interested in West Africa. The change of attitude was chiefly due to industrialization and the greater knowledge of the interior of Africa, as a result of the work of explorers. The impact of the industrial revolution began to be felt in England early in the nineteenth century, and during the years that followed Britain changed from mainly an agricultural country to a country chiefly engaged in industry and trade. From Britain the industrial revolution spread to other countries; but many of the European countries were unable to take immediate advantage of it because almost all were at war between 1792 and 1815, after which they also suffered from political revolutions, which led to serious risings and civil wars. For example, it was not until the end of the Franco-German war in 1871 that Germany was unified under a central government authority capable of extending to industry such regulations and protection as it required. For Germany, the end of the war marked the inauguration of a comprehensive, co-ordinated national development policy. She received from France a war indemnity of 5 million francs, which meant some increase of capital available for industrial development; the ultimate result was that France wanted to make up elsewhere for her economic loss with Germany, while Germany, on the other hand, wanted markets for her new manufactures. They both looked towards Africa for the fulfilment of their economic hopes. For example, the ambition of the French was to link their protectorates of North Africa with the West Coast, and, indeed, to extend their territory as far south as Cape Horn. Thus the British companies which had been struggling to establish themselves on the west coast had another force to contend with – competition from the other European countries.

Just at the time when competition from the French and the Germans was proving difficult for the British traders, Captain Goldie-Taubman arrived on the Niger in 1877. He was not only aware of the difficulties presented to the British traders by the series of inter-tribal wars which went on in most parts of the country, and the absence of orderly governments in most areas, but he was also convinced that unhealthy competition among the British traders helped the other foreign traders to capture British markets. He decided, therefore, to compaign for the unification of all British trading interests in Nigeria. He succeeded in 1879, when all the British traders united to form the United African Company. However, his main ambition was to add the region of the Niger to the British Empire.[1] The French were quick to react to the new British monopoly: they established their own company up the river Niger which had as much strength as the United African Company.

Goldie believed that only a royal charter, conferring on his company the full support of the government in relation to the whole valley of the Niger, could enable him to fulfil his task.[2] His first application for a royal charter in 1881 was refused by the British government on the grounds that the United African Company did not command the necessary capital. He thereupon launched the National African Company in 1882 with a capital of £1 million sterling. Meanwhile, Goldie proceeded to conclude a number of trading treaties with some Nigerian rulers. The Germans also made some unsuccessful attempts to establish trading posts in Nigeria, particularly through the efforts of G. L. Gaiser, the founder of the well-known German company.[3]

The raw materials in Africa, and the market which the continent offered to manufactured goods, became increasingly important to the growing industries in Europe. The commercial interests of some of the European nations were very strong, and led to political claims on some territories with which they had established trade or treaty: for example, in 1884 the Germans declared a protectorate over the Cameroons. It was clear that the principal incentive to colonization

[1] C. H. Currey, *The British Commonwealth since 1815*, p. 49.
[2] Wilson, op. cit., p. 251.
[3] Geary, op. cit., pp. 46–8.

was the acquisition of wealth, though the political ambitions of the European nations in acquiring African territories were of great importance. However, the scramble for African territories was set in motion, and it reached its climax in the Berlin Conference of 1885, when the major European nations decided on the partition of Africa.[1] Germany insisted that only the areas which were effectively occupied could be claimed. As a result of the several treaties which Goldie had concluded with many indigenous rulers, the British had no difficulty in claiming the area around the Niger.[2] The mania for colonization in Africa with which a number of the European nations were seized proceeded largely from a desire to provide outlets for surplus home products, much more so than for surplus population.[3] Nigeria did provide a market for some European manufactures, but its real source of profit lay in its own products: there was a much greater contribution to economic growth to be made in the purchase of Nigerian rubber, palm oil and palm kernels than by the sale of gin and cotton goods to the people of Africa. However, it is very difficult to give any definite account of the mixture of motives which led to the partition of Africa. From the accounts of the abolition of the slave trade and the growth of European trading interests in Africa, the motives varied from the one extreme of economic exploitation of the weak to the other which stressed only the restoration of law and order, making possible the development of peaceful trade.[4]

The Berlin Conference of 1885 left Britain much in command of the areas around Lagos, even though her influence was still confined largely to the coastal areas. In order to extend the British influence in Nigeria, a number of treaties were signed with the natural rulers in the interior by which the British government offered protection to the people.

During the period between 1861 and 1900, the law administered in Lagos and in the Protectorate of Southern Nigeria was based on the ordinance of the local legislature,[5] which required the assent

[1] J. D. Hargreaves, *Prelude to the Partition of West Africa*.
[2] Mockler-Ferryman, op. cit.; C. W. J. Orr, op. cit., pp. 18–50; and Dorothy Wellesley, *Sir George Goldie*.
[3] J. W. Root, 'British Trade with West Africa', pp. 40–63.
[4] Leonard Woolf, *Empire and Commerce in Africa*, p. 14.
[5] The Legislative Council based in Lagos.

of the British government to be effective; the native laws and customs; and the common law, the doctrine of equity and the statutes of general application in force in England. The local legislative council was given power to legislate on minor issues, especially on those which had no effect on the constitution of the colony. In the main, the British government was responsible for passing major legislation relating to Nigeria. In addition to the acts of British parliament, Nigeria, like any other British colony, was bound by the obligations and trading treaties concluded by Britain with other nations. This meant that legislation affecting all economic activity, even if initiated by the colonial governors, had to be approved by Britain; and such approvals were based largely on British political and economic interests.

THE CHURCH MISSIONS AND EDUCATION

It is important to mention very briefly the activities of the Christian missionaries in Nigeria.[1] The Church of Scotland mission established its headquarters at Calabar; the Church Missionary Society established missions in the Niger Delta and up the Niger, and in the Yoruba land where it was most successful. The Baptists also established missions in the Yoruba areas. A number of Europeans were prominent in the evangelization of Nigeria, and among these were the Reverend J. F. Schon, Henry Townsend and Thomas Birch Freeman. However, a number of freed slaves were also prominent in evangelistic work. The Christian work of Ajayi Crowther cannot be over-emphasized in this respect: he travelled extensively in most parts of Nigeria helping to lay the foundations of modern Christianity. Closely related to such evangelistic work was the introduction of education by the missionaries. They encouraged many people to send their children to school to be educated, free of charge. At first, these schools received little response from the people, as many parents were unwilling to release their children from farm labour. After long persuasion and campaign some parents agreed to allow one child to attend school, but they reserved the right to

[1] The activities of the Christian missionaries are covered in a number of books, but the following are directly relevant to Nigeria: J. F. A. Ajayi, *Christian Missions in Nigeria 1841–1891*, and E. A. Ayandele, *The Missionary Impact on Modern Nigeria 1842–1914*.

withdraw him at any time he was needed for domestic and farm work.[1] Attendance at schools was very irregular. For a considerable period, girls' education was not favoured by many parents; however, towards the close of the nineteenth century a few, mostly in the Lagos area, allowed their daughters to attend school. The missionaries were more successful in opening schools in the Southern Provinces than in the north, where most children devoted much time to Arabic lessons.

The immediate economic aspect of the missionary work was the increase in the demand for a number of goods. The building and furnishing of the churches brought about increases in the demand for building materials. The few schools which were established needed reading and writing materials, the demand for which increased steadily. Above all, the few people who were educated gradually acquired a new but foreign culture, which in turn modified the mode of life and began to create a new social class – the educated – in Nigeria.[2] Most of the early educated Nigerians found employment as elementary school teachers – the most popular and 'dignified' profession – and a few of those who were ambitious later trained as pastors. The rest of the educated few settled for the 'less important' job of clerical officer in the civil service or with the commercial firms.

THE FISCAL SYSTEM

With the advent of the British administration, it became the turn of Nigerians to pay for the administration of the government set up by the British government, and at the same time they had to maintain their indigenous local governments under the Obas, Emirs, Obis, etc., which functioned as part of the political administration of the country. In fact, the British government's policy of raising enough revenue to develop the country was based on the old principle laid down by Earl Grey in 1852, 'that the surest test for the soundness of measures for the improvement of an uncivilised people is that they should be self-supporting'.[3] In other words, the

[1] In 1862 there were 406 pupils (252 males and 154 females) in all schools in Lagos: *Lagos Blue Book*, 1862, CO151/1.
[2] Ayandele, op. cit., pp. 283–304; Crowder, *Story of Nigeria*, pp. 148–9.
[3] M. Perham (ed.), *Mining, Commerce and Finance in Nigeria*, p. 226.

policy was that of economic self-determination under the supervision of the British government. This policy seemed to suit Nigeria
where native or local authorities capable of running the affairs of
the country already existed. Indeed, it led to the indirect-rule policy
which operated in Nigeria probably more than anywhere else in
the British Colonial Empire.

The main fiscal policy was eventually based on raising revenue
by the easiest means, while taking due regard of the probable
reaction of the people to different forms of taxation. The British
government discovered that the most attractive source of revenue
was the customs duty, particularly on imported goods, as this was
unlikely to disrupt the indigenous social and economic systems
since the incidence of customs duties would not directly affect the
average Nigerian. Because the revenue was raised through customs
duties, the annual budgeting had to be approached from the revenue
collected. Any fluctuation in the volume of foreign trade directly
affected the revenue which accrued to the government. On a
number of occasions, the British government had to supplement the
Nigerian revenue by direct grants: the British parliamentary grant
to Lagos (Colony) was about £5,000 in 1862. However, public
opinion in England against the spreading of British influence in
West Africa forced the British government to reconsider helping

TABLE 4.1   *Revenue and expenditure of Lagos: selected years, 1862–99*

Year	(a) Total revenue (£000)	(b) Revenue from customs duties (£000)	(c) Percentage (b) over (a)	(d) Total expenditure (£000)
1862	7	3	43·0	7
1865	24	17	70·8	24
1870	43	32	74·4	42
1875	43	39	90·7	44
1880	48	41	85·4	55
1885	64	56	87·5	40
1890	56	47	83·9	64
1895	142	128	90·1	144
1899	192	176	91·7	223

Source: *Colonial Annual Reports*, Lagos, 1862–99.

Nigeria with annual grants. In 1863 Lagos received a £2,000 grant from Britain; this was reduced to £1,000 in 1865 and then it was dropped altogether. In addition to these grants, the salaries of the governors in Nigeria continued to be defrayed by the British government throughout the 1870s. After the grants-in-aid were discontinued it became necessary to devise new ways of raising revenue. There already existed certain taxes levied by the native or local governments – the governments of the chiefs and Emirs – such as the cattle tax, death duties, horse tax, etc. The colonial fiscal policy began to affect the ordinary people in 1866 when boats and canoes in the Settlement of Lagos had to carry licences costing 10s. each per annum.[1] This measure was taken because of the increasing use of canoes on the inland waterways; it was a good tax from the government viewpoint because it brought a steady, but small, revenue, since one of the few reliable means of communication at that time was through the inland waterways. Another source of revenue was created in 1869, when traders using government-built market stalls or sheds were charged certain fees every month.

Meanwhile, the civil wars which continued in many parts of the country prevented the regular flow of trade, which resulted in fluctuating revenues. For example, in 1873 the loss of revenue due to the inter-tribal wars around Lagos forced the government of Lagos to raise what then amounted to a substantial loan.[2] From the total revenue of about £52,000 for 1873, about £21,000 was raised in loans – £15,000 from the British government, £3,000 from the Sierra Leone government and £2,500 from the Gold Coast government.

The *laissez-faire* view to which the British government was committed in the nineteenth century necessarily involved it in a too restrictive view of its economic functions towards its colonies.[3] The result was that it undertook very little by way of direct economic expenditure. A colony had to finance its development, however urgently required, out of its own revenue. The Lagos government recognized the need to encourage economic and social developments even though it undertook no direct major projects; it exempted from import duties items such as salt, building materials,

[1] Ordinance no. 3 of 3 February 1866, CO151/4.
[2] CO151/11.
[3] N. A. W. Cox-George, *Finance and Development in West Africa*, p. 151.

educational books and materials, and some other items used by the government and the administrative officers in the course of administration. In 1875 wholesale and retail licences were introduced for the sale of spirits in order to boost the revenue with whatever amount was collected through these sources.

In order to bridge the financial gap created by the discontinuation of grants-in-aid, the British governments provided loans for the colonies through the Colonial Stock Acts; but these again depended on the ability of the colony to pay the interest out of revenue. The first Colonial Stock Act was passed in 1877, and authorized investments in colonial stocks, which were raised for various development projects. Though section 19 provides that 'the Consolidated fund of the United Kingdom and the Commissioners of H.M. Treasury are not directly or indirectly liable or responsible for the payments of the stock or of the dividends thereon', the view was widely held that any British government would go to great lengths to prevent any default. The Act also empowered trustees (unless expressly forbidden by their trusts) to invest their trust funds in colonial stocks. It therefore encouraged British private investors to invest in the colonies. However, no substantial colonial stocks were raised in Nigeria until the railway construction project started early in the 1890s. Indeed, the guarantees of loans provided for by the Act applied only to the colonies and not to the protectorates. It has been said that the British government policy on the Colonial Stock Acts was a misguided one, in that 'it puts the cart before the horse, for the amounts of a colony's revenue depends entirely on the development of its natural resources'.[1]

Meanwhile the Lagos government continued to rely heavily on import duties for its revenue; significantly, the bulk of the revenue collected was on two main items – cotton goods and trade spirits (i.e. gin and rum). In 1885, when the total revenue was about £64,000, £56,000 came from customs duties, of which about £8,000 and £33,000 were derived from imported cotton goods and trade spirits respectively. This pattern was typical of the structure of revenues for the years between 1863 and 1890.

The bulk of the revenue was spent on civil establishment, i.e. expenditure on administration, including the payment of salaries to the British officers and the few indigenous civil servants, and

[1] G. Guggisberg, *The Gold Coast (1920–1926)*, p. 66.

expenditure on police and military forces. Between 1860 and 1890, the annual expenditure on civil establishment exceeded 50 per cent of the annual total expenditure. A few development projects were undertaken in Lagos, and these concentrated on making Lagos a more habitable town, especially for the British officers. Such developments, which took place in the 1890s, included the drainage of streets, the construction of a few bridges, the building of a few hospitals and dispensaries, and the installation of electricity.

For the greater part of the period before 1900, the British government did not contribute significantly towards financing social and economic development projects in Nigeria. However, towards the close of the nineteenth century the policy of the British government was modified through the influence of Joseph Chamberlain, who introduced a new policy of 'constructive imperialism' in 1895. Chamberlain believed in offering direct financial aid to the colonies in order to raise the standard of living of their peoples. It was realized that a higher rate of social and economic development could be achieved if the revenues of the colonies could be supplemented by external borrowing. In this respect, Chamberlain meant 'the judicious investment of British money'[1] in the colonies. The major development project which led to large external borrowing by Nigeria was the construction of the railway system, for which a series of loans were raised through the Crown Agents in London.

[1] McPhee, op. cit., p. 19.

5 The foundation of modern commerce

The transport system of Nigeria by the middle of the nineteenth century was very backward; most of the country, particularly the interior, remained in almost complete darkness to the outside world, except for the few foreign contacts along the coastal areas, and in the extreme north where the caravan trade with North Africa already existed. Undoubtedly, a good transport system was necessary for spreading British influence and for opening up the country for modern commerce, which was an essential factor for growth. The political and economic implications of the backward systems of transport and communications in the country were spotlighted in 1862 in a dispatch by the Governor of Lagos to the Duke of Newcastle, who was then the Principal Secretary of State for Colonial Affairs. He said:

> The existing wars in the interior have greatly paralysed the trade of this place which had been rapidly increasing up to the date of their commencements. . . . I have not a doubt that these wars could be speedily terminated if a communication could be opened with some of the principal towns situated on the surrounding Lagoons and River. . . . When once navigation of these rivers and lagoons has commenced, private speculators will establish small trading steamers, the commerce of Lagos will then rapidly increase, and the facility of communication will enable the Governor of this Colony to use his influence in keeping the various tribes of the interior at peace with one another.[1]

The Lagos government, as well as the British government, realized that the transport system of the country had to improve

[1] Letter from Freeman dated 10 February 1862: CO147/1.

before peace and any kind of commercial progress could be achieved. However, it did not improve appreciably between 1860 and 1900: the inland waterways continued to provide the only effective means of transport and communication round the coastal areas and further along the routes of the rivers Niger and Benue. In addition to these, there were a number of rivers which were navigable for some distances. The inland waterways were used by the British administrative officers in the course of their duties, and a few traders also found them useful in transporting bulky export products (e.g. palm products) down to the coast, and in supplying imported goods to the people of the interior. The missionaries found the waterways very helpful in their task of spreading the Christian faith. From about 1880 a number of steam launches were being operated; for example, the Royal Niger Company operated a number of steam launches on the river Niger, connecting the northern portion of the country with the coast. The number of canoes plying the waterways also increased as a result of growing commercial activities, particularly towards the end of the nineteenth century.

Roads

The footpaths or bush tracks of Nigeria provided the major links between towns and villages in the interior where waterways were not accessible. They became increasingly important to the Nigerian traders, who were becoming enthusiastic about exchanging Nigerian produce for European manufactures, and who organized the head-loading system. By this system, a Nigerian trader would engage some strong men, the number varying with the volume of the loads to be carried and the carrying-capacity of each man. Women were also employed as carriers, but were made to operate along shorter routes. In the early stages, carriers were usually people of the same village or town as the trader (hirer) himself. However, at a later stage, it was quite usual to find people from different areas seeking to be employed as carriers. There were different ways in which a trader could contract with the carriers: he could agree with the carriers on the rate of pay per mile of the journey; he could also agree to feed the carriers throughout the journey, in which case he would pay a reduced rate per mile; or, on the other hand, the carriers could charge a lump sum for the entire journey.

These negotiations were often made between the trader or hirer and the head (master) carrier, whose business it was to supply carriers to those who might need them. It often happened that the master carrier was in no physical condition to carry any loads himself, but his organizing ability and perhaps his social status gave him control over the carriers. In the areas where the palm oil trade flourished, particularly in the delta area, barrel-rolling became important. The palm oil was stored in carefully prepared wooden barrels or casks which were brought down to the coast by rolling them along the footpaths. A number of porters were engaged for barrel-rolling in the same way as the head carriers were engaged. All the footpaths were constructed and maintained by community efforts under the supervision of the chiefs. On big rivers, hammock bridges were constructed; the bridges on narrow rivers were constructed by felling huge trees across them.

The Lagos government did not take any positive measure to develop the roads until 1885, when an ordinance was passed 'to provide for the construction of roads and public works and for the performance of labour required for the better defence of the Colony and Protectorate'.[1] The delay in the development of roads was caused mainly by the lack of funds, by the inter-tribal wars and by the opposition of chiefs to the infiltration of Europeans into the interior. Following the passing of this ordinance, a few roads were constructed and maintained by the chiefs. By 1889 about 250 miles of laterite roads were constructed around Lagos under government supervision.[2] In the last decade of the nineteenth century, when the government decided to embark on more road building, there was a scarcity of unskilled labour, due mainly to the attraction which farming offered because of the introduction of a few cash-crops, namely cocoa, rubber and groundnuts. The camel and donkey tracks continued to serve the semi-desert and desert areas of the north. The trans-Saharan trade continued, though on a much reduced scale than in the previous centuries. Camels and donkeys were also used to promote a limited volume of local trade in Northern Nigeria.

[1] Ordinance no. 2 of 1883, *Lagos Blue Book*, CO151/21.
[2] *Lagos Blue Book*, 1889, CO151/27.

Railways

A number of British companies were interested in the construction of the railways in West Africa long before work actually began on the Nigerian railways. The success of railway construction in North America stimulated interest in similar projects in West Africa. There was also the strong urge to export the natural resources of West Africa, which could be made easier by having an effective transport system stretching into the interior. In addition, it was argued that the construction of railways would bring civilization and Christianity into the hinterland. A number of proposals were put forward for railways projects. For example, John Whitford, who travelled extensively in West Africa between 1853 and 1875, published an account of his travels in which he suggested the construction of a railway from Lagos to Lokoja.[1] However, it is not known whether his proposals were communicated to the Colonial Office. Between 1870 and 1893, applications from a number of British firms for concessions to construct railways in Nigeria (and the other British West African possessions) were received by the British Colonial Office in London. One such application came from Messrs Frederick Fitzgerland and William Mercer in 1879, offering to construct three lines in Ghana and one in Nigeria in return for land concessions on each side of the tracks, and monopolies of quarrying, waterways and forests therein. Another application came in 1880 from Frederick Barry, a London businessman, for permission to build a line from Lagos to Abeokuta. However, the British colonial policy was against any involvement in the affairs of the Yorubaland.[2] In fact, the British government was undecided on its political commitments and economic role towards West Africa until 1884–5, when the Berlin Conference was held. The Colonial Office also insisted that before such major development projects could start, the people of West Africa should show sufficient interest. This could be taken to mean that the colonies should raise adequate revenue of their own to finance the railway projects, rather than rely on the guarantee of capital loans by the British government. However, the Colonial Office continued to receive deputations from British traders and chambers of commerce plead-

[1] John Whitford, *Trading Life in Western and Central Africa.*
[2] See C. W. Newbury, *The Western Slave Coast and its Rulers*, pp. 89–92.

ing for the construction of railway lines in West Africa. In the early 1890s the British government began to realize, more than ever before, the importance of railways in order to develop the latent resources of the country and expedite effective administration.

> Although the reasons for the construction of the railways have been primarily economic, other factors such as strategic and military considerations undoubtedly influenced the project. It was sufficiently apparent that a railway traversing the country between Lagos and the Niger would strengthen considerably the British position both from the military and economic points of view.[1]

From January to April 1893, Sir Gilbert Carter, the Governor of Lagos, undertook a tour of the interior of Nigeria, paying special attention to the prospect of railway construction. He visited a number of Yoruba towns, and went as far north as Ilorin. After the tour he reported to the British government in favour of constructing railways through the interior of the country. The British government, acting on Governor Carter's report, instructed William Shelford of Messrs Shelford (consulting engineers) to survey possible routes. Shelford conducted his survey during the dry season of 1894-5, and made reconnaissances of several routes including Lagos to Ilaro via Otta, Ilaro to Abeokuta, Otta to Ibadan, Abeokuta to Ibadan, Ijebu-Ode to Ibadan, Ede to Ijebu-Ode, Ejirin to Ijebu-Ode and Ikorodu to Lagos. The cost and traffic prospects of each route were fully considered in the report which Shelford submitted in October 1895. The British government, in considering the possibility of extending the railway to the river Niger area, thus linking the railway with the great waterway provided by the Niger, suggested that Warri or Sapele or some place on the Niger itself, such as Asaba, might be more suitable than Lagos for the starting point. After much deliberation and many arguments about the costs and the comparative ease of construction work on the proposed routes, Lagos was finally chosen as the terminus.

In December 1895 the construction of the first Nigerian railway between Lagos and Otta (20 miles) was authorized, but the work did not start until 1898. A number of factors were responsible for

[1] *Handbook of Railways in Africa*, CB 910, vol. 1, pp. 339-417.

the delay: first, it was difficult to raise enough foreign capital to supplement local revenues for the finance of the railway project; secondly, there was the problem of transporting the rail equipment to Nigeria, as shipping to and from West Africa took time; thirdly, it was difficult to recruit skilled labour in the United Kingdom for the supervision of the construction work. However, by the close of the nineteenth century the railway construction, on a gauge of 3 feet 6 inches, had progressed steadily along the Lagos–Ibadan route. In fact, by 30 September 1899, 60 miles of the Nigerian railway costing £398,725 had already been opened to traffic.[1]

Ocean shipping

In 1868, the British & African Steam Navigation Company was formed, and it joined the African Shipping Company already in operation in providing shipping services to Nigeria.[2] In that year these two companies had between them 34 steamers of a total tonnage of 53,000 – a considerable improvement on the previous regular shipping facilities available to West Africa.[3] Also in 1868, the company of John Holt established a shipping subsidiary of John Holt Line Ltd serving the West African coast.[4] Despite the increasing use of steamers in the second half of the nineteenth century, sailing vessels continued to be used for ocean shipping. For example, in 1880 about 270 steamers and 96 sailing vessels visited Lagos, but by 1900 526 vessels visited Lagos of which only one was a sailing ship. The bulk of the vessels which visited Nigeria were from Britain, Germany and Brazil, with Britain having the greatest number. In 1890 the management of the two main British shipping companies in West Africa came under the new management of Elder Dempster & Company, which later became widely known as Elder Dempster Lines Ltd.[5] Elder Dempster & Company were the first to run regular mail and passenger services to and from West Africa. About the same period, another important steamship service was that of the Woerman Line (a German company), running direct from Hamburg, Rotterdam and Antwerp to the ports on the West Coast of

[1] *Lagos Blue Book*, CO151/37.
[2] See Chapter 2.
[3] Talbot, op. cit., p. 64.
[4] *Merchant Adventure*, op. cit., p. 67.
[5] McPhee, op. cit., p. 71.

TABLE 5.1   *Vessels entering the port
of Lagos, 1863–1900*

Year	Total number of vessels	Total tonnage of vessels
1863	97	29,591
1870	—	99,795
1880	366	170,740
1890	409	272,423
1900	526	531,871

Sources: *Lagos Blue Books*, and Talbot, op. cit., p. 64.

Africa until 1899;[1] later, in April 1900, Southampton was included as a port of call.

Postal and telegraphic systems

The modern system of communication – the postal system, telegraph and telephone – was introduced into Nigeria by the British administration. At the initial stage the British found it difficult to organize any kind of communication system, due partly to the lack of orderly government and partly to lack of funds. Again, the fact that the bulk of the population was illiterate did not encourage such a development. In the first twenty years of British administration in Nigeria overseas mails, particularly those from the United Kingdom, used to arrive at the government house in Lagos, where British officers stationed in and around Lagos collected their mails, both official and private. The mails of the British officers serving in other parts of the country were dispatched by special canoes where and when available, or carried by special messengers on the footpaths.

By 1886 a general post office was established in Lagos. The extensive use of canoes in the coastal areas and on the inland waterways, the development of government-built roads which began in 1883 and the construction of the railways which started in 1898 – all contributed to the gradual development of the postal system. As the railways extended slowly into the interior, post offices were established along the route, but only in important centres. The

[1] *The West African Yearbook*, 1901, pp. 86–9.

inland waterways also helped to carry mails to the few post offices. In 1899–1900, the postal services in Southern Nigeria were handled by 16 post offices, namely the general post offices at Lagos and Old Calabar, 8 district post offices, 4 sub-post offices (performing only postal work) and 2 postal agencies.[1] The number of letters handled by the post offices is not known. From 1 January 1900, when Northern Nigeria came under the administration of the British

TABLE 5.2   *Post Office Savings Bank deposits, Lagos 1889–99*

Year	Amount deposited (to nearest £)
1889	3,423
1890	5,360
1891	5,195
1892	6,233
1893	6,433
1894	7,681
1895	7,157
1896	7,157
1897	7,957
1898	8,317
1899	10,488

Source: *Lagos Blue Books.*

government, it was found necessary to run a postal launch between Forcados (in the south) and Idah (in the north) to coincide with the arrival and departure of the fornightly mail steamers from Lagos. This service was run with great difficulty. During certain weeks of the year the launch could not proceed beyond Asaba owing to the lowness of the water in the Niger, and the mails consequently had to be conveyed in canoes from there to Idah. This naturally caused great delay, and more delays continually occurred through the launch grounding on sandbanks.

The spread of education, largely by the missionaries, helped to introduce letter-writing and thus the habit of posting letters. In 1899 penny postage was introduced in Nigeria. By modern standards

[1] *Colonial Annual Report*, no. 315, Southern Nigeria, 1899–1900.

this is a low charge, but at the time only a few educated and rich people could afford it. The official exchange rate of the cowry, which was being widely adopted as currency then, was 300 cowries to 1*d.*, and 300 cowries could feed a family of 6 for between 2 to 3 days. Until 1894, when the first commercial bank was formally established, the post office was the only institution which provided modern savings facilities. The absence of a proper money economy limited the number of people who patronized the post office. The bulk of the depositors were educated businessmen and civil servants.

Towards the end of the nineteenth century a few telegraph offices were opened in Nigeria. As the railway line moved gradually into the interior, more telegraph offices were opened to connect important administrative centres. As one would expect, the early telegraph services were used by British officials in running the railway system and in transmitting important administrative messages. By 1900, telegraph offices had been established at Lagos, Lokoja, Bonny, Zungeru and Ibadan. A report in 1900 describes how telegraphic messages were handled in some parts of Southern Nigeria:

> As matters stand now the only way in which Telegrams can be despatched from Bonny (the telegraph head) to Old Calabar is by means of the mail steamers which call at Bonny once a fort-night. Telegrams can also be sent via Opobo to Eket, but this method is not at all satisfactory. The telegrams have first to be sent from Bonny to Opobo, and from Opobo to Eket by canoe. This takes at least 36 hours. From Eket they are sent by land to Jamestown on the right bank of the Cross River, a distance of about 30 miles, the journey taking as a rule from one-and-a-half days to two days. The messenger then proceeds by canoe to Old Calabar, and very often, especially in the rains, the water at the mouth of the river is too rough to allow a canoe to be navigable, and consequently there is sometimes a delay of two or three days at Jamestown. . . .[1]

The above quotation summarizes the unsatisfactory system of telegraphic communication which existed in the country at the turn of the century and for a considerable period thereafter.

[1] Ibid., p. 21.

AGRICULTURE AND MINING

Agriculture

The most obvious characteristic of the Nigerian economy in the second half of the nineteenth century was the gradual prominence which agricultural production for export assumed. A few of the important agricultural products which were of commercial interest deserve mention.

Palm products   Palm products, which were the first major items of 'legitimate' trade with Europe, became more important with the spread of the industrial revolution in Europe. Palm trees grew most luxuriantly in Nigeria, and in the absence of milk and butter, palm oil provided the people with the vegetable oil needed: it was, therefore, a basic food necessity. In Europe it was realized that the intrinsic qualities of palm oil placed it at the head of the vegetable fats, and that no other oil was capable of being put to such a variety of uses. Besides its value in the soap and candle industries, palm oil found a large application in the manufacture of tin plate. It was, therefore, necessary to increase the production of palm oil in order to cater for both internal consumption in Nigeria and the industrial demand in Europe. As for palm kernels, the internal demand in Nigeria was very small, and the demand came mainly from Europe, particularly from Germany. Towards the end of the nineteenth century, the Germans discovered that palm kernels made very good feeding cakes for cows. They also discovered that feeding cake given to milking cows helped to increase the butter fat in the milk. In addition, it was realized that the kernel oil was much more valuable for making nut butters. These discoveries led to increased demand from Germany for palm kernels. The volume of palm products in Nigeria depended largely on extra efforts in collecting the palm nuts in the bush. Firstly, palm oil was extracted by the process consisting of burying the fruits for a few weeks to allow partial decomposition, then pounding in vats, and finally boiling. The second stage involved the cracking of the palm nuts discarded (after producing the oil) for producing palm kernels. The only notable effort made towards increasing the volume of palm kernels by adopting a better method was in 1877, when the first power-driven machinery for cracking palm nuts was introduced into

Nigeria by C. A. Moore of Liverpool.[1] Little use was made of
the machine, as farmers were content to continue with their old
methods of hand-production.

TABLE 5.3   *Palm oil production estimates, and palm oil
and palm kernel exports, Lagos 1865–89 (tons)*

Year	Total production (estimated): Palm oil	Total exports: Palm oil	Palm kernels
1865–9	10,552	5,288	11,871
1870–4	18,443	4,791	20,748
1875–9	25,270	7,502	28,430
1880–4	23,937	6,865	26,929
1885–9	31,580	8,718	35,528

Notes:
1. Figures averaged for each quinquennium.
2. Palm oil production estimate is based on the assumptions that all palm
   kernels produced were exported, and that the proportion of palm kernels
   to palm oil is 9 to 8.
Source: *Colonial Report*, no. 58, Lagos, 1891.

Table 5.3 above shows an estimate of total palm oil production
based on the figures for Lagos (1865–89). It was suggested that the
ratio of palm kernel production to palm oil production was about
27 to 25.[2] However, this has been modified to the ratio 9 to 8
because palm kernels were also obtained from palm nuts which did
not yield any palm oil. These were fruits blown down by the wind
and hand-picked to produce palm kernels. It can be seen, therefore,
that total palm oil production increased at a greater rate than total
palm oil exports. This was due primarily to increased local consumption. On the other hand, the total export of palm kernels
increased almost at the same rate as the production of palm oil,
because local demands for palm kernels were negligible.

Cocoa   The most important agricultural product introduced into
Nigeria in the nineteenth century was cocoa. There are conflicting

[1] *West Africa* (weekly), 22 September 1917, p. 575.
[2] J. R. Mackie, *Papers on Nigerian Agriculture 1939–1945*: Afr. S. 823(i),
Rhodes House, Oxford.

accounts about how and when cocoa came to be introduced. According to Howes, it is said to have been introduced into Eastern Nigeria from Fernando Po in 1874, by a chief, Squiss Benego, who established a plantation in the vicinity of Bonny.[1] Another version given by Allan McPhee states that a native chief named David Henshaw introduced cocoa seeds from Fernando Po in 1880 and established a plantation near Calabar.[2] The introduction of the crop into Nigeria was prompted by the knowledge that it was in demand in Europe and that, if produced, it could be a reliable source

TABLE 5.4   *Exports of cocoa, Lagos 1886–99*

Year	Volume tons	cwt	Year	Volume tons	cwt
1886	1	5	1893	8	1
1887	1	6	1894	17	10
1888	1	13	1895	21	10
1889	1	7	1896	12	10
1890	6	2	1897	45	3
1891	6	16	1898	34	6
1892	7	1	1899	70	8

Source: *Lagos Blue Books.*

of income to farmers who were being guided into a cash economy. The government in Lagos encouraged the spread of the cocoa culture by establishing a botanical garden for cocoa-seedlings in 1887, and from where cocoa-seedlings were distributed free to farmers. It is also known that the Christian missionaries encouraged cocoa cultivation in West Nigeria.[3]

In 1886 only 25 cwt was exported from Lagos. However, by 1896 cocoa production had increased in Southern Nigeria: in 1897 Lagos[4] and the Niger Coast Protectorate[5] exported 70 tons and

[1] The UAC Ltd, *Statistical and Economic Review*, no. 18, September 1956.
[2] McPhee, op. cit., p. 44.
[3] J. B. Webster, 'The Bible and the Plough', pp. 418–34; and S. S. Berry, 'Christianity and the Rise of Cocoa-Growing in Ibadan and Ondo', pp. 439–51.
[4] *Lagos Blue Book*, 1897, CO151/35.
[5] *Niger Coast Protectorate Blue Book*, 1897–8, CO464/2.

54 tons respectively. Until 1897 cocoa production in Nigeria exceeded that of Ghana, which later became the world's major producing country.[1] Cocoa planting proceeded more rapidly in Ghana than in Nigeria, and by 1900 Ghana exported 536 tons as against Nigeria's 202 tons. There was no local demand for cocoa, consequently total volume of export represented total production.

Rubber The development of transport in Europe resulted in an increasing demand for rubber. Before the railway age, i.e. before 1825, rubber was used in Europe to provide waterproof outerwear, including footwear for exposed travellers, and in the railway age it was used for springs to increase the comfort of travel by reduction of jolting. With the development of the bicycle and the motor car towards the end of the nineteenth century, the demand for rubber rose sharply. In the years between 1870 and 1890 bicycle tyres of various types made from rubber were being produced. In 1895 Michelin's first motor tyre appeared, and this was followed in 1900 by Dunlop's motor tyre. Rubber was also demanded in the electrical industry, where it was used mainly in the insulation of cable.[2]

At first, the rubber forests of Brazil furnished the European markets with the bulk of their supplies. The Brazilians, however, were said to be reckless in their methods of tapping the trees and consequently their supplies were exhausted within a short period. The attention of the European traders was then directed to West Africa, where the rubber was of prolific growth,[3] and it was the turn of Nigeria to experience the reckless tapping of rubber trees which checked abruptly the prosperity of the rubber trade. 'The wholesale destruction of the wild "rubber" trees was unfortunate since at least 8 million lb (about 3,571 tons) of rubber would have been available yearly if better tapping techniques had been known and accepted.'[4] Before 1894 attempts were made by Nigeria to obtain skilled rubber collectors from Ghana, where rubber production was better handled, but it was impossible to secure the services of expert men. However, in 1894, a Fanti (Ghana) chief

[1] W. Arthur Lewis (ed.), *Tropical Development 1880–1913*, p. 158.
[2] T. K. Derry and T. I. Williams, *A Short History of Technology*, pp. 528–9.
[3] For example, by 1890 Ghana had become the third largest producer of rubber in the world: Boahen, *Topics in West African History*, p. 124.
[4] Lewis, op. cit., p. 156.

named Quamina Atcheri, who had been deported to Lagos as a political prisoner, was allowed to return to his country; as a mark of his gratitude he sent some of his people to Lagos, and they undertook the collection of rubber and also helped to train local collectors.[1] In spite of this, the tapping methods did not improve. In fact, in 1896, the Governor of Lagos entertained grave fears 'that the production [of rubber] would fall off in consequence of the bad treatment received by the trees in the hands of the natives'.[2] It was reported that by 1899 about 75 per cent of the rubber trees had died.[3] The predominantly reckless tapping of rubber trees, competition from Malayan rubber in the world market and finally the establishment of the cocoa industry, were jointly responsible for the decline of commercial interest in the rubber industry. Within a period of four years, the export of rubber from Lagos declined from 2,894 tons in 1896 to 890 tons in 1899. However, the production and export of rubber in the Niger Coast Protectorate increased from about 260 tons in 1897 to about 440 tons in 1899. This was the result of planting more rubber trees.

Mineral production

Tin was the first mineral deposit to attract any commercial interest in Nigeria, even though the industry was slow to develop. It is known that William Wallace, when opening up the river Benue to trade for the Royal Niger Company in 1885, discovered that tin mining was being operated by the people in the Bauchi area. 'Before 1900, the Royal Niger Company had been buying small quantities of smelted tin in fagot form and of 98 per cent purity. . . .'[4] The development of the tin-mining industry had to wait until several years later, because two major factors militated against its immediate exploitation. First, such an industry could not be developed until a stable government had been assured, and this was not achieved until several years after the discovery of tin deposits; secondly, foreign investors who were interested in its exploitation were too conscious of the great risks involved in sinking capital in a new industry in a country which was largely economically and com-

[1] Sir George Denton, 'Twenty-three years in Lagos and the Gambia', p. 130.
[2] *Lagos Blue Book*, 1896, CO151/34.
[3] Geary, op. cit., pp. 56-8.
[4] Laws, op. cit., p. 1.

mercially undeveloped. There was no official export production of tin in the nineteenth century.

Money and currency

The first step towards a uniform currency system, if it could be regarded as such, was taken in 1880, when an ordinance was passed providing for the demonetization of certain coins.[1] The ordinance enacted that only certain coins were to be deemed and taken as legal tender:

1. All gold and silver British sterling.
2. Gold coins (foreign) as follows:

> Spanish and South American doubloon at £3. 4s.
> American 'double eagle' at £4. 2s. 2d. (subdivisions in proportion).
> French twenty franc at 15s. 10d.
> Gold dust and nuggets at £3. 12s. 10d. per dozen.

For cowries, which were also in circulation, the following rates were given: 'One bag equals 10 heads or 20,000 cowries, value between 8s. to 10s. One head equals 2,000 cowries, value between $9\frac{3}{4}d.$ to 1s. Fifty strings equal one head or 2,000 cowries, value between $9\frac{3}{4}d.$ to 1s. One string equals 40 cowries, value about $\frac{3}{8}d.$'

Some other commodity currencies which were adopted in the country had their exchange values regulated: for example, one brass rod exchanged for $2\frac{1}{2}d.$, one manilla exchanged for $1\frac{1}{4}d.$, and one copper wire (Cheethams) exchanged for $\frac{1}{8}d.$[2]

By 1884 a few Bank of England currency notes had been in circulation in Nigeria.[3] These were brought into the country by British officials and traders. It is not known to what extent the notes were used, but it is certain they could not have been popular with the indigenous people, who had no regard for 'mere paper' as a form of currency.

Towards the end of the nineteenth century, the British ad-

[1] Ordinance no. 2 of 1880, *Lagos Blue Book*, 1880, CO151/18: this applied to the Lagos colony only.

[2] *Niger Coast Protectorate Blue Book*, 1897–8, CO462/2.

[3] *Lagos Blue Book*, 1884, CO151/22.

ministration made strong efforts to introduce British coin currency into Nigeria and other British possessions in West Africa, but only met with partial success.[1] The commodity-currencies remained popular with the people, who regarded the British coin units or denominations as too big for the small transactions which they made. The Maria Theresa dollars, the cowries and the manillas, among several commodity-currencies which existed in various parts of the country, together with a few foreign coins (French five-franc pieces and Spanish dollars), continued to be widely adopted for exchange. However, in South-West Nigeria, the predominantly Yoruba land, trade by barter declined and there was an increasing use of British silver coins.[2] By the 1890s it became clear that the people in other areas would not readily adopt the British coins. The British government then began to think in terms of positive action rather than mere persuasion for reorganizing the monetary system.

Meanwhile, the increased importation of British coins into West Africa[3] led to speculation in these territories as to whether they (the colonies) could share in the contingent profit accruing to the British Treasury in the United Kingdom from the issue of silver coins from the Royal Mint. The contingent profit was the seignorage – the difference between the metal value of coins and their face value – less the cost of coining, the cost of transport to and from the colonies, administrative costs and some other expenses that might be incurred before the coins finally reached the hands of the people.[4] The governors of the West African territories considered the sharing

[1] It was reported in 1890 that: 'Another reason for the decrease (in imports) is also to be found, to a certain extent, in the introduction of the cash system which previous to 1886 was almost unknown in the Colony. Now all the kernels, and no inconsiderable a proportion of the oil, are bought for cash, and day by day, the old custom of bartering merchandise for produce is less resorted to. . . . The change in system has undoubtedly been temporarily prejudicial to the interests of the Colony. . . .' *Colonial Annual Reports*, no. 32, Lagos, 1890, pp. 18–19.

[2] A. H. M. Kirk-Greene, 'The Major Currencies in Nigerian History', pp. 132–50; A. G. Hopkins, 'The Currency Revolution in South-West Nigeria in the Late Nineteenth Century', pp. 471–83.

[3] British sterling silver issued for circulation in West Africa (i.e. The Gambia, Sierra Leone, Ghana and Nigeria) averaged £24,426 for 1886–90, £116,323 for 1891–5, and £257,090 for 1896–1900: *Report of the West African Currency Committee*, 1912.

[4] Perham (ed.), *Mining, Commerce and Finance in Nigeria*, p. 178.

of such profits a good source of funds from which development projects could be financed. They pressed their claims to share in the profits, but these were turned down because the British government feared that, in the long run, such coins could be repatriated to the United Kingdom, thus causing inflation. However, in 1898 Mr Chamberlain, the British Secretary of State for the Colonies, intervened and suggested that the British Treasury should agree to share the seignorage profit with the West African countries, or as an alternative that a new currency system be created for the colonies.[1] In the event of the creation of a new currency system, the West African colonies were to bear the risk of the issue of the currency, and all profits resulting from the supply were to accrue to them. Chamberlain favoured the profit-sharing scheme. He also realized that a special West African currency would find favour among the indigenous people, and by that commercial activity would be stimulated, thus bringing about the rapid growth of a money economy.

The proposal for a new currency was drawn up in July 1898, when Chamberlain notified the British Treasury of his intention to appoint a committee to collect information and report on the currency of the British West African territories. Sir David Barbour was appointed the president of the committee. The report of the Barbour Committee favoured the creation of a new currency, and it considered the sharing of seignorage profits and the problem of the convertibility of the new currency. It came out strongly in support of sharing seignorage profits with Britain as an interim measure. However, the British Treasury, reinstating its previous objections, rejected the idea and decided to look into the currency problem again at a later date. Thus at the end of the nineteenth century Nigeria had no currency of her own.

Commercial banking

A reliable coin currency is a *sine qua non* of modern banking, and since there was no uniform currency in Nigeria before the twentieth century, commercial banking had a shaky start. The first commercial bank to become established in Nigeria was the African Banking Corporation (a British company), which had been the

[1] A. G. Hopkins, 'The Creation of a Colonial Monetary System: The Origins of the West African Currency Board'.

sole distributor of British silver coins in Lagos and also the sole repatriating agent since 1872. The corporation started a banking business in Lagos in 1891. It was privately owned and received no government assistance for its operations. As a pioneer business in a country where a money economy was yet to develop, the bank faced many problems, the most important of which was lack of patronage. The business ran at a loss for a period of about twelve months, after which it decided to close down. The most prominent figure among the businessmen who made efforts to rescue the bank was Sir Alfred Jones,[1] a shipping magnate of Elder Dempster & Company.[2] His business agent in Lagos, G. W. Neville, had persuaded him to buy the business of the African Banking Corporation, and Sir Alfred eventually agreed to the takeover, believing that by extending credit facilities to smaller merchants his shipping business would continue to expand.[3] The bank, therefore, continued to operate under him as a private concern, depending almost exclusively on the shipping trade.

After the bank had operated under its new proprietor for a year, the British government requested that it should be made a joint-stock bank. An agreement was reached, and on 31 May 1894 the business was registered in England as a limited liability company under the new name of the Bank of British West Africa. The British administration in Nigeria had, in 1892, transferred its account into the Lagos branch of the African Banking Corporation, and it continued to keep its account with the new bank. It was reported in 1896 that the bank had benefited Lagos in many ways, and had supplied a want which was much felt in the past.[4] It was also said that the bank was fairly successful in its transactions, and, by advancing money against produce on reasonable terms, had considerably improved the position of the small traders.

The banking monopoly of the BBWA was challenged in 1899, when a number of British firms – including the Niger Company, the African Association, Miller Brothers and John Holt – backed the establishment of the Bank of Nigeria. This bank also received great

[1] For the details of his commercial activity, see A. H. Milne, *Sir Alfred Lewis Jones. A Story of Energy and Success.*
[2] McPhee, op. cit., chapter 6.
[3] A. G. Hopkins, 'The Creation of a Colonial Monetary System', p. 110.
[4] *Colonial Annual Reports*, no. 219, Lagos, 1896, p. 9.

support from indigenous traders, who regarded its establishment as a kind of salvation from the monopoly of the BBWA. Thus, at the close of the nineteenth century, Nigeria had two commercial banks. They had no powers to issue any currency, but merely performed the ordinary banking business, accepting money from their customers for safe-keeping and helping to transfer money from one person or institution to another by the use of cheques. The commercial banks drew their customers mainly from traders, to whom they extended credit facilities to finance imports and exports.

FOREIGN TRADE

The 'legitimate' trade of Nigeria was slow to develop owing to a number of factors. The inter-tribal wars in most parts of the country blocked the way to commercial progress. The powerful chiefs and Emirs continued to dominate the political as well as the economic life of the people until the British began to intervene.[1] The efforts of the British government for most of the second half of the nineteenth century were therefore concentrated on establishing peace and good government in Nigeria, which was a prerequisite to the growth of modern commerce. The productive efforts of Nigerians themselves were limited for a number of reasons. Even though the palm oil trade had been in existence for some time, most people were still unaware of the benefits of export production as a source of income and as a means of improving their standard of living. Apart from the unsettled political conditions, this may be explained by the absence of a proper money economy, bad transport and communication systems and the ignorance and poverty of the people. Nigerians continued to produce most of their essential needs, consequently they had limited interests in the import trade.

However, in the last quarter of the nineteenth century, when some trade became possible, some fresh problems arose. Many of the

[1] 'Trade with the interior prospered, though Kosoko proved a major problem through his constant interference with trading canoes plying between Lagos and Abeokuta': Crowder, *Story of Nigeria*, p. 166. Also in the Oil River State, Jaja of Opobo 'was a bitter opponent of free trade, preventing any European trader dealing directly with his sources of supply': Crowder, ibid., p. 196. Also see Dike, op. cit., p. 193.

early Europeans assumed, in establishing trade contacts, that Nigerians would buy anything they offered to sell. The people were fascinated by the luxury and flashiness of goods which were imported in order to entice and lure them to trade; but they frowned on and rejected some essential goods, particularly cotton goods which were considered inferior to locally-manufactured products.[1] In some areas, the European traders resorted to force in order to get customers, as well as to protect themselves against hostile people. An example of this took place in 1879, when the HMS *Pioneer*, a British warship, carried some British traders to Onitsha, and later bombarded the town because the people were hostile to the traders.[2] On the export side, the few export products of Nigeria were bought by weight, and so many producers were tempted to adulterate the crops in order to increase their volume and claim more money. For example, rubber was wrapped round stones and extraneous matter was mixed up with palm products in order to increase their weight.[3] There was also the short-weight trick of palm oil casks.[4] The Lagos government was soon aware of the bad reputation which Nigerian export products had earned in the world market, and it finally took steps against the adulteration of produce by passing the Native Trade Law in 1896, which was followed by the Adulteration of Produce Ordinance of March 1897.[5] These laws were designed to eliminate malpractices in the export of agricultural products. However, there was no provision for any kind of inspection system which could ensure the enforcement of the law. Consequently, the agricultural producers continued to adulterate their produce, though on a smaller scale than before.

Trade competition

The foreign trading companies, particularly the British, played a significant part in the development of the foreign trade of Nigeria. The role of the indigenous trader was confined almost exclusively to the collection of export products from the interior for transporta-

[1] *Colonial Annual Reports*, no. 32, Lagos, 1890, p. 18.
[2] Dike, op. cit., p. 207.
[3] A number of complaints were received from Europe about the bad quality of Nigerian products: *Lagos Blue Book*, 1896, CO151/34.
[4] *Merchant Adventure*, op. cit., p. 28.
[5] *Niger Coast Protectorate Blue Book*, 1896–7, CO464/1.

tion to the coastal areas – where such products were sold to European traders and exporting companies – and to the distribution of the imported goods. However, a few Nigerians had some direct trading contacts with England. There was the exceptional case of the direct export of palm oil to Europe by Jaja of Opobo. Some of the Nigerians who were educated in the early mission schools organized direct importation of goods from Europe through parcel posts. Such trading activities were not to be compared with those of the established European traders, who commanded greater capital funds and commercial experience. The European firms handled the wholesale trade of imported goods and bought local produce in bulk for export. Most Nigerians, on the other hand, concentrated on the retail trade and operated as middlemen or agents for purchasing local produce for export. They operated on small capitals and their turnovers and stocks were relatively small too, but they were able to provide the essential link in the commercial progress of the country. So powerful were these groups of Nigerians that an adventurous European trader trying to break new territory might well lose his entire stocks – and perhaps his life into the bargain – if the local people disliked his rate of exchange.[1]

From about the period of the 1850s, there was an influx of British traders into Nigeria as a result of two important developments. First, the regular appearance of steamships in Nigeria provided cheap freights, which helped to lower the costs of European trading expeditions. The second inducement to British traders was the reorganization of business units in England, which allowed for limited liability companies to be formed. By the Limited Liability Act of 1862 (United Kingdom), all that was required of a limited company was seven signatures on a Memorandum of Association, and a registration fee. It meant that as many as possible could pool their resources, thereby increasing their trading activities and spreading possible losses on a number of traders.

Two groups of foreign traders soon identified themselves. There were the old companies which had already acquired some monopoly in the trade; and there were still some visiting traders, who transacted their business on the steamers on which they came. The number of the latter group diminished gradually as the foreign trade grew to be more competitive and as it became more expensive to

[1] *Merchant Adventure*, op. cit., p. 11.

hold trading stocks. Besides the lavish gifts often made to customers in the form of gin, rum, gunpowder, toys and other attractive luxuries, some of the foreign traders provided the kind of credit facility known as the 'trust'.[1] The 'trust' was a peculiar form of credit by which goods were entrusted to the local middlemen by foreign merchants for periods varying from six months to a year or, in some cases, to two years, during which time the middlemen were required to exchange imported goods for local produce and pay back their European 'principals' the equivalent in palm products, ivory, timber, etc. The important English trading companies which were in operation included the River Niger Navigation & Trading Company, the Company of African Merchants, the Anglo-African Company, the African Merchants of Bristol, the Merchants of London–Liverpool trading to the West Coast of Africa and the United African Company.[2] The United African Company, which was the biggest and the most important company, was formed through the efforts of Goldie in 1879, following the amalgamation of three big firms – the West African Company, the Central African Company and the Miller Brothers – in order to eliminate unhealthy competition and to pull capital resources together. Some French and German merchants also competed with the British for shares in Nigeria's foreign trade, but were unsuccessful in challenging the relatively stronger position of the British.

The foreign traders struggled for survival, and in the process many of them adopted the policy of price-cutting in order to fight their competitors. Some firms which were unable to withstand the cut-throat competition incurred great losses and were forced to cease operations, while some other companies found no alternative but to amalgamate with the big and financially strong firms. 'Of the twelve European firms which were established in Lagos in 1888 only five remained in 1892, and by then two of these were present in name only.'[3] In some areas, particularly in the Niger Delta, foreign traders in collaboration with the local rulers devised methods of protecting their trading interests, particularly that of the enforcement of business contracts. They established 'trade' courts

[1] Dike, op. cit., pp. 108–27.
[2] Dike, op. cit., p. 178n.
[3] A. G. Hopkins, 'Economic Imperialism in West Africa: Lagos, 1880–1892', p. 595.

known as Courts of Equity.[1] These were composed of the agents of
the various trading companies, and were presided over in turn by
each of the members in order that no one should obtain, as president,
undue influence among the inhabitants to the detriment of his
trade rivals, or should cause the displeasure of the powerful chiefs by
being the regular mouthpiece of the court, which did not always
decide in favour of the Nigerian litigant.

Towards the end of the nineteenth century, the British government became unhappy about the trade rivalry of the Germans, who
were bringing large quantities of geneva and rum (trade spirits)
into Nigeria: it feared that the increasing importation of trade
spirits would result in decreasing demand for British goods, particularly cotton goods. It argued, therefore, that the importation of
geneva and rum did more social harm than good to the people,
but it was unable to adopt a direct policy to prohibit their importation because Lagos derived the bulk of its revenue from import
duties on them. The British government urged the Lagos government to impose heavy import duties on geneva and rum in order
to discourage the consumption of these items. In 1896, in a dispatch to Chamberlain, the Secretary of State for the Colonies,
McCallum, the Governor of Lagos, said:

> That vexed question, the harm done to the natives of the interior,
> by the spirit trade, still remains under discussion. . . . I have
> during a service of over nine years in Lagos travelled a great deal
> along the Lagoon, and in the interior countries, and I am bound
> to say that drunken people are but rarely met with and that the
> representations on the subject are much exaggerated. . . . No
> one is more anxious than myself to prevent the introduction into
> the Hinterland of ardent spirits in undue quantities, and as the
> surest means of checking the trade I should like to see the duty on
> them raised, if an international agreement on the point can be
> arrived at, but it would be useless for Lagos to follow this course
> alone as the only result would be a great influx of spirits from
> Dahomey which would cause loss of revenue to the colony
> (Lagos) and do no good to the people whom it is desired to
> benefit.[2]

[1] Dike, op. cit., p. 126; Burns, op. cit., p. 132; and Jones, op. cit., pp. 77–83.
[2] *Colonial Annual Reports*, no. 219, Lagos, 1896, p. 15.

The problem of the increasing importation of 'trade spirits' remained unsolved before the close of the nineteenth century.

Pattern of trade

Until 1900 there were no trade statistics available for the whole country. Records for Lagos began in 1862, while those for the Niger Coast Protectorate were kept after 1893. However, the trade statistics for Lagos provide reliable indicators of the trend and pattern of Nigeria's foreign trade. Between the period 1860 and 1890, Nigeria's foreign trade[1] fluctuated widely because of the civil wars, the relatively backward conditions of transport and communications, the absence of an accepted coin currency and economic fluctuations in Europe, particularly in Britain – Nigeria's most important customer. For example, the value of the total foreign trade for Lagos, which was about £1·1 million in 1862 fell to £0·8 million in 1881 but went up again to £1·1 in 1890. However,

TABLE 5.5   *Values of total imports and exports,*
            Lagos 1865–99 (£000)

Year	Total imports	Total exports
1865–9	283	428
1870–4	353	501
1875–9	512	621
1880–4	438	577
1885–9	445	522
1890–4	625	710
1895–9	873	914

Note: Figures averaged for each quinquennium.
Source: *Lagos Blue Books*, 1865–99.

the position changed in the last decade of the nineteenth century as there were steady increases in both the imports and exports of Nigeria. The value of the total trade of Lagos increased from £1,096,021 in 1890 to £1,801,401 in 1895 and to £1,882,529 in 1899. Similarly, the value of the total trade of the Niger Coast Protectorate increased from £1,440,533 in 1896 to £1,614,753 in

[1] Patrick Manning, 'Some Export Statistics for Nigeria 1880–1905'.

1899.[1] The increasing demand for Nigerian products in Europe and the gradual acceptance of European manufactures, particularly those of the British, influenced the pattern of Nigeria's trade.

Palm products were the most important items of export. The average annual value of total exports of palm products was about 75 per cent of exports. Nigerian palm oil found a growing market in Europe until about the 1860s, when petroleum was tapped in the United States of America. When American petroleum flooded

TABLE 5.6 *Total volume of exports and average prices for palm oil and palm kernels, Lagos 1881–90*

	Palm oil		Palm kernels	
Year	Total export (tons)	Price per ton (to nearest £)	Total export (tons)	Price per ton (to nearest £)
1881	6,024	30	20,801	12
1882	8,791	33	28,591	12
1883	6,571	39	25,820	15
1884	7,942	35	29,802	14
1885	8,859	28	30,805	12
1886	10,322	22	34,812	10
1887	8,354	22	35,784	10
1888	8,225	20	43,524	10
1889	7,830	23	32,715	10
1890	10,669	25	38,829	12

Sources: *Colonial Annual Reports*, nos. 32 and 58, Lagos, 1890 and 1891.

Europe the demand for the Nigerian palm oil fell, as did the prices.[2] Besides this decline, it is important to add that the volume of export of palm oil depended on total supply on the one hand – which was often affected by inter-tribal wars – and the level of internal consumption on the other. At the time the demand for palm oil was declining, it was discovered that the palm kernel, a by-product, could provide oil which was good for the manufacture of margarine. However, the price of palm products, particularly that of palm oil, fluctuated from time to time.

[1] *Niger Coast Protectorate Blue Books*, CO464/1–4.
[2] McPhee, op. cit., p. 33.

The bulk of Nigerian palm kernels were exported to Europe, with Germany taking an average of more than 70 per cent of the annual export in each year of the period 1862–99. The United Kingdom, on the other hand, was the main consumer of Nigerian palm oil, as she bought a yearly average of about 50 per cent of the total export in each year of the same period. The export of raw cotton fluctuated widely because of the changing home demands for it, and because of the disparity in the prices offered for cotton, other export crops and the local food crops, which influenced the

TABLE 5.7   *Values of cotton goods imported into Lagos: selected years, 1862–99 (to nearest £)*

Year	United Kingdom	Germany	Other countries	All countries
1862	21,587	392	504	22,483
1865	19,336	4	4,724	24,064
1870	201,173	7,088	3,043	211,304
1875	240,600	570	626	241,796
1880	131,958	3,910	3,441	135,309
1885	183,557	2,337	1,775	187,669
1890	178,234	12,526	3,562	194,322
1895	234,619	19,980	450	255,059
1899	303,144	2,058	236	305,438

Source: *Lagos Blue Books*, 1862–99.

farmers' decision on which of these to grow. However, the bulk of the Nigerian cotton was exported to the United Kingdom. In the last decade of the nineteenth century, exports of groundnuts and rubber also increased. Cocoa, which had just been introduced into Nigeria, began to appear as an item of export after 1886. Others included benniseed, hides, maize and mahogany.

The early imports to Nigeria included a large number of luxury articles for which Nigerians gradually cultivated a taste, such as looking-glasses, beads, scissors, combs, bracelets and handkerchiefs. Some other import items were also introduced as substitutes for similar locally-produced goods: these included wine, gin, rum, cutlery, matches, salt, lamp oil (kerosene), medicine, boats, canoes, needles, guns, gunpowder and cotton goods. The most important single item of import was cotton goods, the value of which varied, averaging annually between 35 and 50 per cent of the total imports of Nigeria. The presence of some Europeans in Nigeria, particularly the British officers, brought about gradual increases in the importation of items such as butter, bread, vegetables, cigars and cutlery. The government in Nigeria also imported medicines for their officers, as did the missionaries, who discovered that the use of modern medicines for sick Nigerians was helpful in bringing more people into the Christian fold. The missionaries' work on education also increased the demand for books, writing materials and a number of other school materials. The Nigerian government imported a number of building materials, e.g. cement, nails, bricks and plain glasses, for administrative offices, staff quarters and for some public works. The importation of iron and steel increased considerably towards the end of the nineteenth century as work started on the construction of the railways and bridges.

TABLE 5.8   *Percentage of total imports and exports of Lagos with principal countries: selected years, 1865–99*

Year	United Kingdom		Germany	
	Imports	Exports	Imports	Exports
1865	51·8	52·3	12·3	1·1
1870	68·0	52·0	10·2	9·9
1875	71·9	52·3	12·6	26·3
1881	47·9	34·8	31·1	25·2
1885	53·9	31·8	34·9	34·4
1890	67·3	35·3	26·1	41·7
1895	74·1	44·7	21·6	36·5
1899	81·6	36·2	12·7	48·7

Source: *Lagos Blue Books*, 1865–99.

From the inception of British rule in Nigeria and up to 1899, imports from the United Kingdom exceeded 50 per cent of the country's total annual imports. The main item was cotton goods, which represented, annually, about 50 per cent of Nigeria's total imports from Britain. Germany made some efforts to sell cotton goods in Nigeria, particularly towards the close of the nineteenth century, but she was unable to catch up with the lead already established in this trade by the United Kingdom. Other imports from the United Kingdom included salt, books, iron, steel, matches, and a host of other small items. Imports from Germany were dominated by geneva (trade spirits), which, put together in each year between 1860 and 1899, accounted for more than 50 per cent of Nigeria's total imports from Germany. Some items of imported goods came from a few other countries, including Zanzibar and Mozambique, both of which supplied large quantities of cowries for use as currency; Portugal, Holland and Belgium, which supplied Nigeria with some wine, gin and rum; and the United States of America, a relative newcomer to the Nigerian trade, which supplied tobacco and lamp oil.

Conclusion

The British met in Nigeria a basically free enterprise economic system under the supervision of the Obas, Emirs and chiefs. Of course the British economy had operated on the same system for centuries. The colonial government expected private enterprise to contribute substantially to the process of economic growth in the colonies. The private sector of the Nigerian economy was made up largely of indigenous farmers, traders, craftsmen and a small but important group of foreign merchants. An orderly government was a necessary condition for the efficient operation of the mechanism of a free enterprise economy. The extent to which the private sector, particularly the foreign firms, could contribute to economic growth depended a great deal on the government's offer of protection to the people and their property. By 1900 the British had succeeded in establishing peace and a stable government in Southern Nigeria, but some resistance to the British still existed in certain parts of the north.

The free enterprise philosophy affected the colonial government's policy towards economic development. There was no deliberate government planning for the social and economic development of the country. The bulk of the government's revenue – derived mainly from customs duties – was devoted to financing the civil establishment, leaving very little, if any, for social and economic projects. Apart from the hesitation of the British government about whether or not to invest in the economic development of Nigeria, the possible political implications of disrupting the indigenous social and economic system (the land tenure system, for example) made it difficult for the government to grant land concessions to foreign private enterprise for any kind of development. The classic example was that of the railway project. By 1900, therefore, direct private investment was in the form of community efforts in constructing and maintaining bush paths and a few roads, while the only notable public investment was on the railway project which began in 1898.

Farming was the main occupation of the people, and agricultural production remained in the hands of peasants, who began to respond to the monetary incentives created by the introduction of new crops, e.g. cocoa and rubber, towards the end of the century. Agricultural production for export began to increase and so did the farmers' incomes. During this period, capital formation included new mud-houses, a few of which were roofed with iron sheets, particularly in Southern Nigeria; new farms and new crops; farm implements such as cutlasses; and guns and gunpowder for the hunters. In the last decade of the nineteenth century, agricultural prosperity in Southern Nigeria encouraged urbanization.

A few of the prosperous farmers and traders began to invest in the education of their children. At first, the mission schools provided free tuition; but parents bore other expenses, such as clothing, books and writing materials, and, above all, the loss of the services of their children on the farm. Thus began the process of training the first group of Nigerian manpower, but the kind of education offered only catered for the training of teachers and pastors. Technical education, which was much more relevant to economic growth, was neglected. The manpower which emerged at the end of the nineteenth century was ill-equipped to accept the challenge of modern economic development.

The foreign trade of Nigeria remained largely in the hands of expatriate merchants who could afford the necessary capital to finance imports and exports. Ocean shipping, on which foreign trade depended, was also managed almost exclusively by foreign firms. Undoubtedly, the absence of a national currency limited the volume of commercial transactions, particularly local trade, as people could only trade in the kind of currency with which they were familiar. While the manilla was current in the south-east, it was not accepted as money in the south-west where the cowry was most popular. However, Nigeria's foreign trade continued to increase despite this major drawback. The very limited banking facilities provided by the BBWA and the Bank of Nigeria were grossly inadequate to cope with the rapidly expanding commerce of the country.

By 1900 the British government had decided to take some positive measures to develop the Nigerian economy. The railway project had begun, and plans were being formulated to introduce a proper money economy. Apart from these, all other developments, social and economic, were 'by-products' of political administration. The one factor of significance to economic development was the growth of rural capitalism – investments in farming – which laid the foundation for the rapid expansion of the economy in the twentieth century.

Part 3 The colonial period to 1945

6   General survey

Between 1900 and 1945, two world wars and a world-wide economic depression inevitably had their effects on the economic, social and political developments of Nigeria.[1] Although the colonial government did not adopt economic planning as a policy, the Nigerian economy grew rapidly. Both the government and private enterprise (foreign and indigenous) increased their economic activities as a direct result of the establishment of peace and a stable government.

The major indicators of growth, which are discussed fully in other chapters, included the development of the infrastructure, expansion of peasant agriculture, introduction of a modern money economy, and the increase in foreign trade. In absolute terms, the growth rates of the various sectors were spectacular. For example, the railway mileage increased from 124 in 1905 to 1,903 in 1945. Again, the mileage of roads maintained by the Public Works Department of the government increased from 2,800 in 1925 to 6,225 in 1945. It must be added that the population of Nigeria increased from an estimated 16·8 million in 1900 to 27·4 million in 1945. The value of total foreign trade also increased from £3·9 million (4s. per head) in 1900, to £35·2 million (£1. 6s. per head) in 1945. The total value of imports increased from £1·9 million (2s. per head) in 1900 to £15·9 million (10s. 6d. per head) in 1945. Similarly, the total value of exports increased from £2 million (2s. per head) to £19 million (15s. per head) in 1945. The Nigerian government revenue also increased from £2·7 million in 1900, to £13·2 million in 1945. In relative terms, however, these and other

[1] G. K. Helleiner has referred to part of this period (1929–45) as the period of interrupted growth: *Peasant Agriculture, Government and Economic Growth in Nigeria*: also Michael Crowder, *West Africa under Colonial Rule*, pp. 345–53.

similar rates of growth were inadequate for a country with the size and population of Nigeria. The major constraint upon growth was inadequate government revenue, which limited the number and the extent of economic and social development projects the government could undertake. Although private investment on agricultural export production, motor transport and export marketing increased, the general economic conditions, e.g. fluctuations in export prices, limited the contribution which the private sector could have made to economic growth.

POLITICAL DEVELOPMENTS

In 1899, the British government decided to withdraw the charter of the Royal Niger Company which had administered Northern Nigeria since 1886. There were a number of reasons for this measure. The company had already been at war with the northern Emirs in its efforts to stop the slave trade and slavery. Contrary to the provisions of its charter, the company used its authority to monopolize trade. There was also the danger of war with the French, who were determined to occupy some areas already claimed by the British. The British government, 'anxious to remove any source of irritation which might imperil the success of the Anglo-French Convention of 1899, decided that the administrative functions of the company must be separated from its commercial activities'.[1] It was also considered that any wars that might be necessary in that part of Nigeria would be more successfully fought under the British government's administration. In January 1900, therefore, the British government proclaimed Northern Nigeria a protectorate: the country was now in fragments of protectorates.

The first step towards political unification in Nigeria was taken in 1906, when the Southern Nigeria Protectorate and the Lagos Colony amalgamated under the name of the Colony and Protectorate of Southern Nigeria. The complete political unification of Nigeria was achieved in 1914, when the Protectorate of Northern Nigeria and the Colony and Protectorate of Southern Nigeria were amalgamated and came under a central administration based in Lagos. The unification was considered desirable and expedient in order to centralize the administrative control of the country and

[1] Wilson, op. cit., p. 252.

thus facilitate better utilization of resources and co-ordination of social and economic development projects.

Sir F. D. Lugard had argued since 1902 that the amalgamation should take place at least on a fiscal basis.[1] It was not surprising, therefore, that on becoming the country's first governor-general he justified the amalgamation on economic grounds. First, he argued that while the material prosperity (derived mainly from customs duties) of the South had increased with 'astonishing rapidity', the North depended on the annual grants from the Imperial government. The North 'was barely able to balance its budget with the most parsimonious economy, and was starved of the necessary staff, and unable to find funds to house its officers properly'.[2] Secondly, the distance of the North from the coast (about 250 miles) rendered the expansion of trade difficult, thus limiting its revenue-earning capacity.

> Thus the anomaly was presented of a country with an aggregate revenue practically equal to its needs, but divided into two by an arbitrary line of latitude. The portion was dependent on a grant paid by the British taxpayer, which in the year before amalgamation stood at £136,000 and had averaged £314,000 for the eleven years ending March 1912.[3]

Lastly, Lugard argued that before amalgamation no single railway policy for the whole country had been possible, and that the two outlets to the sea (rail from Lagos and river via the Niger) were in acute competition, which resulted in extravagance.

Another important political event took place at the end of the first world war, when the former German colony of the Cameroons was handed over to the British government as a trust territory in 1922, and was administered as part of Nigeria.

[1] A. O. Anjorin, 'The Background to the Amalgamation of Nigeria in 1914', pp. 72–86.
[2] *Amalgamation of Northern and Southern Nigeria, and Administration. 1912–1919*, Cmd. 468, HMSO, 1919.
[3] Ibid., p. 7.

FISCAL POLICY

At the turn of the century, Nigeria continued to derive most of her revenue from customs duties. The British government held on to its cautious approach to the problem of introducing direct taxation. The indigenous fiscal systems continued to operate in the country. The evolution of direct taxation in Nigeria is directly connected with the administration of Northern Nigeria under Lugard. In 1902, commenting on the indigenous (Fulani) fiscal system in Northern Nigeria, he said:

> Greed was one of the chief characteristics of the new dynasty, and tax after tax was enforced upon the people, so that at the present day there is no conceivable trade and no profession which has not its own special tax. Every form of handicraft, the dyers, weavers, blacksmiths, etc., was taxed. Even the collectors of honey in the woods paid their dole to the chiefs. . . .'[1]

On the introduction of a new form of taxation by the government, he commented: 'I am opposed to direct taxation by government upon individuals because (1) I think it premature until individual property in land has been recognized, and (2) Until the system of serfdom has given place to one of independent agricultural labour, and (3) Until a currency has obtained a footing so as to obviate too frequent a payment in kind.'[2] However, he favoured an income or profits tax,[3] because he hoped that the enforcement of such a tax would put an end to the idleness and apathy which existed in some parts of Northern Nigeria and induce the people to cultivate their land.[4]

The government found it difficult to ignore or postpone any longer the problems of tax reforms, particularly in Northern Nigeria. According to Lugard,

> . . . the decadence of the Fulani rule had at the time that government assumed charge of the country led to revolt in many pro-

---

[1] *Colonial Annual Reports*, no. 409, Northern Nigeria, 1902, p. 20.
[2] Ibid., p. 54.
[3] Lord Lugard, *The Dual Mandate in British Tropical Africa*, p. 237. Also see Hailey, op. cit., pp. 733–4.
[4] *Colonial Annual Reports*, no. 409, Northern Nigeria, 1902, pp. 47–8.

vinces, and the enforcement of taxation was marked by continual wars or raids, while those who continued to pay were driven to sullen discontent by ceaseless extortions. The advent of the British and the overthrow of the Fulani domination were heralded by the peasantry as an excuse for the repudiation of any obligation to pay taxes, even in a province so well organized as Kano – the very centre of Fulani rule.[1]

Under the new British regime the native chiefs had lost the income they used to derive from slave-raiding and from taxes on traders, consequently it became the more urgent to assure them of a regular income from the tribute of the peasantry. In 1904 the government of Northern Nigeria passed the Northern Nigeria Land Revenue Ordinance, which gave legal effect to the indigenous, pre-British, system of taxation. The Emirs and the chiefs continued to collect the taxes, and they were required to pay one-fourth of this revenue to the government. However,

> the absence of a fixed scale of emoluments for public servants is always the weak point of native government, [and] Northern Nigeria was no exception to the rule. The proportion of the taxes actually collected which eventually found its way into the so-called Public Treasury was used by the Emir with small regard to the public interest and with a great deal for his own.[2]

It was necessary therefore to improve on the new tax system in order to ensure equitable assessment and the fairly reliable revenue necessary for the running of native administrations. The reform was introduced under the Native Revenue Proclamation of 1906. Under the proclamation, the Emirs and the chiefs were to surrender to the protectorate administration one-quarter of the total amount of revenue collected, while the remaining three-fourths were divided between a fixed amount representing their personal income and a further amount representing provision for expenditure on public projects. This marked the creation of the native authority treasury system in Northern Nigeria.[3] The unit of tax assessment under the new system was the village or group of villages, and their

---

[1] *Colonial Annual Reports*, no. 476, Northern Nigeria, 1904.
[2] E. D. Morel, *Nigeria: its Peoples and its Problems*, p. 147.
[3] Hailey, op. cit., p. 454.

resources were examined and assessed by an administrative officer, who, from an estimate of the average yield of the land under cultivation and the yield from other sources (such as livestock or wage-earning), assigned a cash value to the gross resources of the unit.[1] '*This . . . introduces the important principle that the tax is not an income tax pure and simple, but a tax on potential profits* – viz. profits realizable by the expenditure of ordinary and normal industry and effort. . . .'[2] The 'lump sum' payable by each unit was apportioned among the inhabitants by the headman according to their ability to pay.

The system of tax assessment which finally emerged represented a pioneer attempt to adjust taxation to the resources of the community. In the process of administering the new system, British administrative officers were brought into close touch and relations with the peasantry (the taxpayers) and with the ruling classes (the Emirs and the chiefs). These officers, therefore, had the opportunity to discuss the incidence of tax assessments. Various standards of living existed in most parts of Northern Nigeria, consequently the incidence of taxation was liable to be affected by the competence shown by the British officers in the assessment of income; indeed in some very backward areas, the tax system continued to be in the form of a poll tax at a flat rate. Again, in the semi-nomadic pastoral areas, the Jangali – a cattle tax – was one of the main sources of revenue to the native treasuries.[3]

Until the outbreak of the first world war, Southern Nigeria continued to derive most of its revenue from customs duties, and there was no immediate problem of finding alternative sources of revenue. It is important to add that there was at that period no reliable procedure for direct taxation in force, hence it was difficult to introduce a similar tax system to that already in force in Northern Nigeria. The administration in Southern Nigeria was afraid to introduce taxation because it feared possible riots and demonstrations in protest against it.[4] Meanwhile, the Obas held on to their arbitrary and irregular indigenous fiscal system.

[1] Ibid., pp. 662–3.
[2] Lugard, op. cit., pp. 238–9.
[3] M. Perham, *Native Administration in Nigeria*, London, Oxford University Press, 1937, pp. 105–6.
[4] G. O. Orewa, *Taxation in Western Nigeria*, p. 3.

The first world war brought a considerable falling off in quantity of the imported spirits from which Southern Nigeria derived most of its revenue.[1] In 1913, 1,800,000 gallons of spirits were imported, bringing in a revenue of £1,140,000; in 1914 it was 1,427,000 gallons, bringing in a revenue of £924,000; in 1915 it was 768,000 gallons with a revenue of £728,000; and in 1916 it fell again to 394,000 gallons, bringing in a revenue of £373,000.[2] Export duties on products such as cocoa, palm oil and palm kernels, were introduced during the first world war, partly to raise additional revenue and partly to divert trade in these products to Britain.[3] The export duties inevitably increased the revenues of Nigeria, but even then the country was still short of funds for basic development projects, and some additional sources of revenue had to be found. The loss of revenue during and immediately after the first world war forced the British administration to decide on the gradual introduction of a permanent and modern income tax system. 'It was not till 1916 that the Obas (in the South-West) were persuaded to surrender their quasi-independent status and the native authority system prevailing in the North was formally extended to Yorubaland by an ordinance of that year.'[4]

The Oyo province of South-Western Nigeria was the first to adopt direct taxation in 1918 under the Native Revenue (Southern Provinces) Ordinance, no. 29 of 1918. The tax was called an income tax, but in practice became a poll tax for the masses, with additions for the obviously wealthier people. The flat rate was calculated on a basis of 2·5 per cent of the gross income of the ordinary farmer, with special rates for the various trades and professions or for those possessing special types of property.[5] By 1922, this system had been extended to most provinces of South-Western Nigeria.

The first attempt at a titular income tax system (as distinct from a direct taxation system) in Nigeria was made in 1927 when the

[1] Imported spirits into Nigeria came mainly from Germany, who ceased to trade with Nigeria at the outbreak of war in 1914.
[2] *West Africa*, 28 July 1917, p. 435.
[3] 120, *House of Commons Debate*, Col. 668, 1919.
[4] Hailey, op. cit., pp. 460–1.
[5] For example there was a tax on cocoa trees in Ilesha: Perham (ed.), *Mining, Commerce and Finance in Nigeria*, p. 177.

Income Tax (Colony) Ordinance was enacted to cover what was then the Lagos and Colony area.[1] The provisions of this ordinance were later adopted for all the Yoruba-speaking areas of Southern Nigeria. The rates laid down were: a flat-rate assessment for incomes under £50; 10s. for all incomes from £50 to £100; £1 for incomes from £100 to £200; £2 for incomes from £200 to £300; and £1 for every additional income of £100 per annum. Since it was very difficult to assess the incomes of individuals, most taxable adults paid the flat rate. The same ordinance formally introduced business and trade taxes, which affected such self-employed people as the goldsmiths, shoemakers, artisans, auctioneers and public letter-writers.

The introduction of direct taxation into the South-Eastern Provinces of Nigeria met with considerable opposition. The main problems were that 'political evolution had not advanced beyond the local community and sub-tribal stage, and there was no previous system of taxation or even of tribute'.[2] By 1927, preparations had been completed for the extension of the native authority system into South-Eastern Nigeria, and for introducing direct taxation in order to finance native treasuries under the new system.[3] In 1928, direct taxes were collected for the first time throughout the South-Eastern Provinces of Nigeria, largely with the aid of the warrant chiefs. Taxes were collected with some difficulty, but without any of the serious disturbances in anticipation of which 500 additional police had been enrolled.[4] However, anti-tax riots and demonstrations broke out in many provinces of South-Eastern Nigeria during the following year.

One significant feature of the anti-tax riot was that it was almost totally confined to women. It was officially stated that the disturbances arose from tax reassessments in certain districts involving the counting of women, thus encouraging the erroneous belief that women were to be taxed.[5] The tax reassessment was found

[1] Income Tax (Colony) Ordinance, no. 23 of 1927; and *Colonial Report*, no. 1384, Nigeria, 1927, p. 26.
[2] Perham (ed.), *Mining, Commerce and Finance in Nigeria*, p. 229.
[3] *Colonial Annual Reports*, no. 1384, Nigeria, 1927, p. 8; and Hailey, op. cit., p. 466.
[4] Perham, *Native Administration in Nigeria*, pp. 204–5.
[5] *Colonial Annual Reports*, no. 1493, Nigeria, 1929, p. 8.

necessary because of the fall in the prices of agricultural products. However, a commission of inquiry into the origin of the disturbances found that discontent with the warrant chiefs was a contributing factor.[1] Some were alleged to have proposed taxes on women in order to boost their revenues. The women resorted to rioting because, as they said, 'we depend upon our husbands, we cannot buy food or clothes ourselves and how shall we get money to pay tax?'[2] In a dispatch to the Officer Administering the Government of Nigeria, the Secretary of State for the Colonies, commenting on the Report of the Commission of Inquiry into the Disturbances at Aba and other places in South-Eastern Nigeria, wrote:

> In the circumstances of the districts concerned, it would probably have been better, on the first introduction of direct taxation, to have started with lower rates of tax. It was also, no doubt, the case that the people in various places would have been more reconciled to this taxation if they could have seen some immediate results in the way of local services or local improvements. It is further to be remembered that neither the government nor anyone else could have foreseen the fall in the price of local produce, which, naturally, would increase the irksomeness of any tax on a population living mainly by the sale of such produce. . . . But the one thing which is plain is that direct taxation was introduced among a population of whom comparatively little was known, in contrast with the Northern and South-Western Provinces, and that the subsequent unhappy events depended on the first step.[3]

By 1930 direct taxation had been introduced throughout the country, and table 6.1 shows that from that year there was a steady increase in its contribution to total revenue.

As a direct result of the tax riots, and because of the fall in the prices of agricultural products due to the general economic depression of the early thirties, tax assessments were reviewed in a number of provinces throughout the country and the levels of taxes reduced. Adult women in Ijebu and Abeokuta provinces of Southern Nigeria

[1] Sessional Papers of the Nigerian Legislative Council, nos. 12 and 28 of 1930.
[2] Sessional Paper of the Nigerian Legislative Council, no. 28 of 1930, para. 32, p. 12.
[3] Cmd. 3784, HMSO, 1931.

were made to pay a flat-rate tax, 'but the combined rate of tax on adult males and females [in these provinces] is much the same as that on adult males only in the neighbouring provinces'.[1]

TABLE 6.1   *Nigerian government revenue and expenditure, 1929–45 (£000)*

Fiscal year ending 31 March	Total revenue *	Total customs revenue	Percentage of total revenue	Total direct tax revenue	Percentage of total revenue	Total expenditure
1930	6,045	3,360	55·6	848	14·0	6,987
1931	5,622	2,981	53·0	810	14·4	6,330
1932	4,858	2,110	43·2	770	15·9	6,188
1933	4,985	2,414	48·4	773	15·5	4,984
1934	4,887	2,164	44·3	808	16·5	5,036
1935	4,961	2,069	41·7	808	16·3	4,837
1936	5,996	2,912	48·6	829	13·8	5,757
1937	6,260	3,624	57·9	852	13·6	6,061
1938	7,342	3,505	47·7	854	11·5	7,376
1939	5,811	2,472	42·4	853	14·7	6,867
1940	6,113	2,487	40·7	938	15·3	6,499
1941	7,273	2,433	33·5	1,138	15·6	7,254
1942	7,955	3,085	38·8	1,451	18·3	7,027
1943	9,034	3,622	40·1	1,756	17·2	8,999
1944	10,913	4,897	44·8	2,383	21·8	9,977
1945	11,445	5,242	45·8	2,205	19·3	10,133

* Excluding railway revenue.
Sources: *Reports on the Accounts and Finances, 1935–6 to 1938–9*, Lagos, Government Printer, and *Annual Report*, Nigeria, 1945–6, HMSO.

In the thirties, a number of modifications were made to the existing ordinances on direct taxation, in order to broaden the base of the tax system. In 1931 the Non-Natives Income Tax (Protectorate) Ordinance was passed,[2] extending income tax to

[1] Women in the two provinces were said to be very enterprising and rich enough to bear the burden of a tax: *Colonial Report*, no. 1569, Nigeria, 1931, pp. 57 and 60.
[2] Non-Natives Income Tax (Protectorate) Ordinance, no. 21 of 1931.

non-natives in the protectorate at the rates imposed by the Income Tax (Colony) Ordinance of 1927, which has already been mentioned. Again, the Income Tax (Colony) (Amendment) Ordinance, no. 22 of 1931, brought the provisions of the Income Tax (Colony) Ordinance into line with those of the Non-Natives Income Tax (Protectorate) Ordinance. The position was that by 1931 an income tax of 1 per cent was levied on the incomes of all non-natives throughout the colony and protectorate, while a graduated income tax not exceeding 1 per cent was levied on the incomes of Africans residing in the colony. The natives of the Northern and Southern Provinces paid direct taxes per adult male (and female in Ijebu and Abeokuta).

It was not until 1936 that the government enacted for the first time a law directed against tax evasion. The Income Tax (Colony) (Amendment no. 1) Ordinance, no. 17 of 1936, made it an offence for a person to neglect or refuse to pay tax, and this was extended to cover the protectorate by the Non-Natives Income Tax (Protectorate) (Amendment) Ordinance, no. 23 of 1936. By 1936 the rates of taxes had been increased in a number of provinces, owing to improvements in the prices of agricultural products.

The 1927 Income Tax Ordinance was amended in 1937 and framed generally on British lines, except that the Nigerian ordinance did not provide for company taxation, and adults with incomes under £30 per annum were exempted. Further innovations and modifications were made in 1939: first, the government introduced a tax of 2s. 6d. in the £ on company profits;[1] secondly, as regards income tax, the local rate was increased from 1 per cent to 1½ per cent in the case of all incomes of £50 or over; thirdly, non-native females were no longer exempted from taxation; and lastly, all incomes derived from Nigeria were taxed, whether the recipient was resident in the country or not.

The export duties which had been introduced during the period of the first world war were reviewed from time to time to meet revenue requirements, and also as the result of changes in the export trade. During the depression years, the Nigerian government reduced duties on the principal export products – cocoa, palm oil, palm kernels and groundnuts – in order to stimulate more exports.

[1] 'An Ordinance to impose an Income Tax upon Companies and to regulate the collection thereof': Ordinance no. 14 of 1939.

Where this failed, some of the duties were abolished altogether, only to be reimposed at the start of the second world war.[1] Later additions to the list of export duties were levies on fresh and dried bananas and on rubber. Excise duties on locally manufactured products were first introduced in 1939 on the cigarette industry, which had started production in 1933. The distinction between revenue and protective duties is a fine one, and as the home production of some commodities, such as dried fish and cigarettes – which were also being imported – developed, the revenue duties automatically became protective duties.

The process of introducing a modern income tax system reached its final stage during the second world war. The expected hazards of war reduced the flow of Nigerian trade; consequently the country's revenue, which was derived largely from customs duties, fell drastically. It became clear once again that a more stable and permanent form of taxation had to be introduced to supplement revenue from other sources. It was also felt that income tax should be introduced as a wartime economy measure, in order to reduce the purchasing power of the public, particularly when less imported goods were available, and thus check a possible inflationary pressure.

In 1940 two important ordinances were enacted. The Income Tax Ordinance, no. 3 of 1940, introduced into Nigeria a modern progressive income tax. It applied to the whole country but exempted natives taxable under the second ordinance – the Direct Tax Ordinance, no. 4 of 1940 – which also covered the whole country except non-natives and people in the township of Lagos.[2] These ordinances remained in force in 1945, by which time two forms of direct taxation had emerged in Nigeria, income tax and native authority tax. The income tax applied to non-Nigerians throughout Nigeria, and Nigerians in the township of Lagos, and provided for the payment of a graduated income tax. The rate of tax laid down prescribed a fixed sum of 5s. for all incomes up to £24, thus abolishing the exemptions for incomes under £30 which

[1] For example, the export duty on groundnuts was reintroduced in 1939.
[2] Income Tax Ordinance no. 3 of 1940 was replaced by Income Tax Ordinance no. 29 of 1943, and subsequently amended by Income Tax Ordinances no. 36 of 1944 and no. 23 of 1945. Also, Direct Tax Ordinance no. 4 of 1940 was amended by Direct Tax Ordinance no. 2 of 1943.

had been introduced in 1937. It also provided for a fixed tax of 3*d*. in the £ for incomes from £25 to £50; 4½*d*. in the £ on incomes up to £150 and thereafter on a progressive scale with substantial personal reliefs. All companies had to pay a flat-rate tax of 5*s*. in the £. Nigerians outside the township of Lagos paid the native authority tax in accordance with various forms of assessment. The political, social and economic conditions prevailing in each locality were so diverse that a variety of assessment methods were unavoidable, ranging from the individual assessments of wealthy traders and professional men in large towns to a flat rate in backward areas.

Even though the British administration in Nigeria hesitated for a number of years before introducing the new tax system, the events that followed indicate clearly that the opportunity to study the economic and social conditions of the people was not taken. Belatedly, after the great disturbances in the South-Eastern Provinces a number of researches into the tribal organizations in many provinces were pursued. It was clear that a cautious approach was needed if the 'natural rulers' were to be deprived of part or all of the taxes they had enjoyed for centuries.

Again, the fact that a money economy was slow to develop handicapped the early introduction of a modern income tax system. For many years after the establishment of British rule, barter exchange prevailed in parts of Nigeria, and the adoption of commodity-currencies was widespread. Indeed, it was not until 1949 that Nigeria finally ousted the last of her main commodity-currencies, the manilla.[1] For a considerable period after the establishment of the West African Currency Board in 1912, it remained difficult to introduce any direct taxation which would avoid payment in kind.

It must be added that the general pace of the economic development of Nigeria was slow. The land tenure system gave little room for individual ownership in land, and subsistence farming was predominant. Even with the introduction of the cash-crops – cocoa, cotton, groundnuts, etc. – the position did not change significantly because the efforts made to grow and harvest cash-crops were dictated by the immediate social and economic needs of the farmers. There was, therefore, no reliable basis for tax assessments.

[1] *Colonial Annual Report*, Nigeria, 1948. See also UAC Ltd, *Statistical and Economic Review*, no. 3, March 1949.

Direct progressive taxation of individuals engaged mainly in production on their own account is not easy to organize effectively in any country. It raises formidable problems where the general level of money incomes is low and where ordinary standards of commercial accounting are unfamiliar to the producer. In these circumstances, everything depends on the quality of the personal contact between tax officials and the people . . . and on the possibility of devising simple and acceptable criteria of relative wealth which can be generally applied.[1]

The development of the railways did absorb some workers, and the civil service and missionaries also provided employment for the educated few. But by the early thirties, the railway projects had been completed and the rate of expansion of employment opportunities in the civil service became very low. The result was that most of the taxable adults had unascertainable incomes on which no modern income tax system could effectively be raised.

Another problem which often arises, and which is usually difficult to solve under any fiscal system, is that of tax evasion. In Nigeria it was particularly difficult. To start with, there was the problem of defining 'a taxable adult' since there was no registration of births, except in Lagos. Again, in a country with backward transport and communication systems many people could not be covered by the tax system, while those who were covered could easily evade payment by escaping into the bush. It was also the practice of a number of people to understate their incomes in order to evade full payment of tax.

It must be mentioned that expenditure on civil establishment, i.e. the cost of administering the government, accounted for an annual average of between 30 and 40 per cent of total revenue, thus leaving little surplus for any major development projects. Throughout this period the government did not allocate any funds for the development of commerce and industry. The expenditure on public works, i.e. the maintenance of roads, bridges, waterworks and electricity, increased during the period of the first world war and reached its peak in the financial year 1943–4 when it accounted for about 10 per cent of total expenditure. Expenditures on agriculture

[1] Hailey, op. cit., p. 1312.

and education also reached their highest in the financial year 1944–5 when each took about 5 per cent of total expenditure.

ECONOMIC CONDITIONS AND POLICY

Immediately after the first world war it seemed that economic conditions in Nigeria would improve: industrial activity increased in Europe, leading to greater demand for Nigerian products which began to fetch higher prices. There was a short-lived boom which collapsed in 1921. In that year the level of prices for export products, e.g. cocoa, cotton, groundnuts, palm oil and palm kernels, fell in many of the European countries and in the United States of America. The fall in the prices of export products and the general economic depression, though spread over the whole period of the 1920s, were neither continuous nor evenly distributed over the different commodities and industrial activities. Some efforts were made to advertise and to sell more Nigerian products in a number of world markets, particularly in Europe and in North America. For example, Nigeria participated with the other former West African British colonies (Gambia, Sierra Leone and Ghana) in the Canadian National Exhibition in Toronto in 1928, when all the major West African products were on display for Canadian manufacturers.[1] 'It is interesting to note that whereas in 1929, 23,454 cwt of West African cocoa was imported into Canada this was increased in 1930 to 40,626 cwt.'[2] It must be realized that no preference was given to West African cocoa, and the increase took place without any diminishing quantities coming to Canada from the West Indies, which had a distinct advantage over West African cocoa owing to the trade agreement between the West Indies and Canada.

Also, in 1930, on the occasion of the International Maritime and Colonial Exhibition at Antwerp in celebration of the centenary of Belgium's independence, there was a very earnest undertaking on the part of the Nigerian government to provide exhibits which were really comprehensive of the resources of the country.[3] The

[1] *Annual Report on the Agricultural Department, 1929*, Lagos, Government Printer, p. 15. *The Gold Coast Independent* (Christmas Number), Accra, 1928, p. 29.
[2] *The Gold Coast Independent* (Christmas Number), Accra, 1930, p. 27.
[3] Ibid.

Nigerian exhibits were staged on the British pavilion. The main object of participating in the exhibition was to take advantage of the opportunity of putting before continental manufacturers the variety of raw materials available in Nigeria. The main exhibits were cocoa, beans, palm kernels, palm oil, copra, coconut oil, cotton and cottonseed; and a few minor agricultural products including kolanuts, benniseed and maize. There were exhibits of various qualities of mahogany and samples of such Nigerian woods as iroko and ebony. Some exhibits of mineral resources were also on display: these included tin ore, refined tin ore and samples of coal from the coalfields of Enugu.

Nigeria's participation in the exhibitions at Toronto and Antwerp reflected the rapid growth of cash-crops and their importance to the economy of the country. It also indicated the desire of the government to expand trade which was the main source of revenue. The exhibition of mineral products also indicated the gradual growth of the extractive industries in Nigeria.

Towards the end of the twenties, particularly in 1927 and 1928, the prices of some agricultural export products rose slightly, and there was a token revival of economic activity. However, the severest effect of the economic depression was felt in the early thirties. For example, the average market price of palm oil fell from £35 per ton in 1928, to £26 per ton in 1930, and to £12 per ton in 1934; while that of palm kernels fell from £21 per ton in 1929, to £14 per ton in 1930, and £7 per ton in 1934. The prices of the principal imported goods in the same period did not fall as drastically as the export prices. For example, the average price of cement was £3. 7s. per ton in 1928, £2. 4s. per ton in 1930 and £2. 6s. per ton in 1934; the average price for cotton piece goods per square yard was 7d. in 1928, 6½d. in 1930 and 4d. in 1934; and the average price for salt per cwt was 19s. 7d. in 1928, 17s. 1d. in 1930, and £1. 13s. 5d. in 1934. As a result of these price fluctuations, the average income of the farmers fell, while the prices of the basic imported goods, on which they spent the bulk of their income, remained relatively high.

The general trade depression which was experienced in most parts of the world was aggravated by the financial crisis in Europe and America and by the collapse of some national currencies, particularly in Europe. The depression was also reflected in the

TABLE 6.2 *Index numbers of import, export and domestic prices, 1926–40*

(1) Year	(2) Import price indices	(3) Export price indices	(4) Export/ import price indices: (3) over (2)	(5) Weighted index numbers of Lagos: retail prices of imported goods	(6) Weighted index numbers of Lagos: retail prices of domestic goods
1926	100·0	100·0	1·0	1·0	1·0
1927	91·6	98·3	1·1	1·1	1·5
1928	84·2	97·4	1·2	1·2	1·2
1929	90·2	87·6	0·9	1·2	1·2
1930	80·8	74·5	0·9	1·2	0·9
1931	73·3	47·2	0·6	1·2	0·9
1932	66·3	50·0	0·7	1·1	0·8
1933	61·4	47·3	0·8	1·2	0·7
1934	58·8	41·7	0·7	1·1	0·6
1935	68·2	51·7	0·7	1·1	0·7
1936	62·3	58·6	0·9	1·1	0·7
1937	56·4	50·7	0·9	0·9	0·6
1938	65·0	44·8	0·7	0·9	0·6
1939	61·0	41·3	0·7	—	—
1940	61·5	37·8	0·6	—	—

Notes:

Col. 2 is based on wholesale prices at port of entry of 52 imported commodities whose value in 1926 and 1936 amounted to about two-thirds of total imports, using as weights average value of imports in 1926 and 1936, which appeared to be normal years.

Col. 3 is based on prices of 18 exported domestic products whose value in 1926 and 1936 amounted on an average to 81 per cent of total exports, using as weights average value of exports in 1926 and 1936.

Source: *Nigerian Trade Reports.*

Col. 5 includes wheat bread, evaporated milk, butter, rice, coffee, cocoa, tea, sugar, salt, brandy, beer, kerosene, soap, stockfish.

Source of weight: *Report of Cost of Living Committee*, Lagos, 1942.

Source of prices: *Nigerian Blue Book.*

Col. 6 includes eggs, beef, mutton, native tobacco, maize, yams, plantains, bananas, fowls, ducks, Nigerian stockfish, palm oil, and gari. Source of weights and prices: as for Col. 5.

Source: Perham (ed.), *Mining, Commerce and Finance in Nigeria.*

international payments agreement which became unreliable and disrupted, as many countries abandoned the gold standard, the basis of the agreement. In 1931, sterling, with which the West African currency had been linked since its inception in 1912, also left the gold standard 'ring'. The abandonment of the link with gold, and the depreciation of the pound sterling in terms of gold, by all countries which had kept their currencies allied to sterling, led to the birth of the sterling area, or the sterling block as it is sometimes called.

It was in the period between the first world war and the depression years that the British government realized, more than ever before, the part she should play in the economic and social developments of her dependencies all over the world. Hitherto, it had been the accepted view in Britain that a dependency should only have the communications, social services and so forth which it could afford out of its own revenue, and that economic development was properly the function of private enterprise. Nigeria, though with rich natural resources, could not achieve progress along these lines because there was an inadequate number of indigenous private enterprises capable of tapping most of the resources.

It was true that many Nigerians engaged in the cultivation of cash-crops, but only small-scale farms existed, and farming was not regarded as a business as such. Most incomes derived from the sales of cash-crops were not reinvested in agriculture. There was also a large group of Nigerians who were engaged in the distributive trade. Most of the people in these groups were just able to make ends meet and could not accumulate sufficient wealth from which to finance further production. Nigeria, therefore, did not have a strong capitalist element in society which could speed up the rate of economic growth. Again, a number of Lebanese and Syrians helped in the marketing of export products, and opened shops in the large towns where they sold imported goods, particularly cotton goods. These traders, though important in the commercial life of the country, did not make much direct capital investment in Nigeria. Few invested in the mining industry – gold and tin – and their direct contribution to the economic growth of Nigeria is not as great as some writers would want us to accept.[1] Even foreign private enterprises which ventured into pioneer trading activities here did not

[1] Crowder, *West Africa under Colonial Rule*, pp. 293–305.

find the business climate entirely favourable. Considerable progress still had to be made in the provision of primary economic and social services – good roads, communications, banking facilities and better health conditions – on which to lay the foundations of a strong economy.

TABLE 6.3   *Colonial Development Fund for Nigeria, 1932**

Schemes	Amount ($£$)
Dietetics research	3,750
Veterinary scholarships	920
Tsetse fly investigation	1,500
Public health improvements	50,200
Relaying Minna–Kaduna railway: interest for seven years on £326,000 (approximate figures) at 5 per cent per annum	114,000
Total	£170,370

* Amount received was £28,016 and amount approved for further projects was £142,354.
Source: *An Economic Survey of the Colonial Empire, 1932*, Col. no. 95.

The British government realized that economic growth should not be impeded and that it was its duty to develop the vast economic potentialities of Africa which had been lying fallow. In order to achieve this, the government admitted that its methods should be evolutionary rather than revolutionary. In 1929 the financial assistance from the United Kingdom Exchequer to the colonies, which had been in the form of grants-in-aid, was further extended by the Colonial Development Act, which established a fund of £1 million a year for schemes of economic development. The object was 'to promote commerce with, relieve economic depression in the United Kingdom and to stimulate agricultural and industrial activity in the colonial territories'.[1] The small funds which were made available to Nigeria were expended on a variety of projects

[1] *The United Kingdom Colonial Development and Welfare Acts*, COI Reference Paper, no. RFP 3400, August 1956.

which included dietetic research, veterinary schemes and scholar-ships, tsetse fly investigation, public health improvements, railway developments and communications. By 1939, however, it had become clear that far greater financial provision, supplementing local resources, and a far more imaginative handling of the problems of development of the colonial territories, were needed to create the conditions of life which would lead to the social and economic progress necessary for the establishment of self-government, which was gradually becoming prominent in the minds of educated Africans.

At the outbreak of the second world war, the most important task for the British government was to mobilize economic and man-power resources. The task was one of great magnitude because the whole range of economic life had to be reorganized both in Britain and in the colonial territories to meet the war emergency. Although the various aspects of economic control introduced assumed different stages of the war, the main targets set for the colonies included the following: the participation in general blockade measures against Germany; the increase of exports of foodstuffs and raw materials to Britain and her allies; the organization of import controls and shipping programmes on a war basis; the in-crease of local production and other essentials for local consumption in order to meet shortages of imported goods; the adoption of financial measures, including taxation, price control, cost of living allowances, etc., in order to curb possible inflationary pressures; and the adoption of relief measures to meet special difficulties for staple export industries. It was not until after the German advance in Western Europe and the entry of Italy into the war that all these economic controls were brought into play. The sudden rise in the tempo of war activity and increased shipping difficulties had im-mediate effects upon both the import and export trades of Nigeria. The Nigerian government, with the help of the British government, paid more attention to securing the imports essential for carrying on the ordinary life of the people since the supplies from many European countries were reduced considerably.

One other major factor which affected the import trade of Nigeria was the imposition of the currency regulations by the British government. At the outbreak of war, sterling was under considerable pressure, as it was depreciating in terms of the American dollar from the rate of £1 to $4.68 at the end of July, to the rate of £1 to $4.05 on the outbreak of hostilities in September 1939. This fall in the exchange rate of sterling in terms of the dollar, and the financial and political developments that accompanied it, led to the withdrawal of most non-Commonwealth countries from the sterling block. The closer identification of the sterling block with the countries of the Commonwealth was formalized with the introduction of sterling exchange control immediately following the outbreak of war. In connexion with exchange control, the Finance (Defence) Regulations were introduced into Nigeria in 1939. The sterling area became part of the mechanism of exchange control, involving an inevitable element of discrimination. The basic principles of the exchange regulations applied to the sterling area as a whole, but funds were allowed to move freely within it. The broad objective in view was the greatest economy of hard currencies and gold, the resources of which were urgently required to finance essential purchases of munitions and raw materials. Every member of the sterling area, including the colonies, was left to operate its own exchange control. In Nigeria, import licences were introduced and restrictions were placed on capital movements. In the matter of import licensing, all members of the sterling area undertook to save hard currencies by limiting their purchases from hard currency countries to absolute essentials. The agreement to economize hard currencies and dollars was a 'gentlemen's agreement', as members were left to interpret it in the light of their own sense of responsibility. The hard currency reserves of the sterling area were canalized to London and held by the British government in the area's dollar pool. These receipts of dollars and other currencies, which represented savings on imports, were paid for in sterling by the British government and constituted one of the factors in the growth of sterling balances held by the members of the sterling area. By June 1945 West Africa (The Gambia, Sierra Leone, Ghana and Nigeria) had a total of £93 million in sterling balances.[1] The main economic significance of this policy was that Nigeria and many other members of the sterling area were forced to extend credit to Britain on a large scale, by sacrificing their demands for imported capital and consumption goods principally from the hard currency countries. This hampered the normal rate

[1] Paul Bareau, *The Sterling Area*, p. 9.

of economic development and thus reduced the economic welfare of the people.[1]

In spite of the heavy burden imposed on the British government by the day-to-day necessities of war, it was found possible to pay some attention to economic development and to the general improvements of social services in the colonies. In February 1940 a parliamentary paper was published on the British government policy on colonial development and welfare.[2] In the same year, the first Colonial Development and Welfare Act was passed, superseding the 1929 Act, and greatly increasing the sums available and extending their scope to cover the whole field of development, both economic and social. The 1940 act stipulated that United Kingdom assistance was 'for any purpose likely to promote the development of the resources of any colony or welfare of its people'. The general conception of how this policy would meet the needs of the British dependencies was outlined by the Secretary of State for the Colonies, who expressed the view that

> if full and balanced development was to be obtained and if Colonial governments were to be placed in a position to maintain administrative, technical and social services at proper standards, some assistance from outside was necessary at that stage. Few of the colonies had the good fortune to possess substantial mineral wealth, and in comparatively few were there manufacturing industries of any magnitude. The majority were wholly, or almost wholly, dependent on the more limited resources derived from agriculture. The value of agricultural products varied widely from year to year as conditions fluctuated in the world market, with the result that Colonial revenues provided an unreliable basis for a policy of steady development. In some cases, the position was aggravated by a heavy burden of indebtedness.[3] However able the governments, however efficient their economic administration, many colonies could not finance out of their own resources the research and survey work, the schemes

[1] See G. A. Petch, *Economic Development and Modern West Africa*, pp. 190–206.
[2] *Statement of Policy on Colonial Development and Welfare, February 1940*, Cmd. 6175, HMSO, 1940.
[3] In 1936, Nigeria's public debt was about £25 million: *Colonial Annual Reports*, no. 1842, Nigeria, 1936, p. 94.

of major capital enterprise and the expansion of administrative and technical staffs which were necessary for their full and vigorous development.[1]

The Colonial Development and Welfare Act of 1940 empowered the Secretary of State for the Colonies, with the concurrence of the British Treasury, to make schemes for any purpose likely to promote the development of the resources of any colony or the welfare of its people.[2] The sums required for such schemes were to be paid out of money provided by the British parliament. The act prescribed maximum expenditure of £5 million a year, plus £5 million for research, for the ten years 1941–51, and cancelled some £10 million in loans owed by colonial governments to the United Kingdom. It laid down, however, that any money which remained unspent at the end of any year would lapse. By this act, the colonies were encouraged to plan their social and economic development with the technical and financial assistance of Britain to augment their own resources, so that programmes could be launched and natural resources expanded and new and better standards of living made possible. The colonies were allowed to plan development programmes on certain broad lines of policy suggested by the British government: the funds were to be spent on providing greater knowledge of the natural resources of the colonies; improvements in quality, output and uses of their export products; the opening up of the country by new means of communications; new schools, technical colleges and university institutions; and new hospitals, clinics and dispensaries. The war prevented the full implementation of the policy in many colonies. In Nigeria a few development projects were undertaken, touching on transport and communications, public health improvements, tsetse fly investigation, rinderpest investigation, irrigation, geological surveys and general research on the production of primary products. There were also some development projects which were undertaken jointly by the British colonies in West Africa. In 1938 the Agriculture Department of the Ghana government opened a research station at New Tafo to study matters relating to the care and cultivation of cocoa, and to

[1] Cmd. 6175, HMSO, 1940.
[2] See *The United Kingdom Colonial Development and Welfare Acts*, COI, RFP 3400, August 1956.

study the cause and possible remedies of swollen shoot and other prevalent cocoa diseases. Six years later, the station was taken over by the West African Cocoa Research Institute, which was partly financed from the Colonial Development and Welfare Fund.[1] In 1939, the West African Institute of Oil Palm Research was established at Benin in Nigeria. The institute was sustained by funds from the British West African colonial governments and the Colonial Development and Welfare Fund.

The Colonial Development and Welfare Act of 1940 was supplemented by the Colonial Development and Welfare Act of 1945, which provided £120 million for the ten years 1946–56, including £20 million carried forward in commitments under the 1940 Act. It also enabled long-term plans to be made by abolishing the need to surrender unspent annual balances, and provided that the money could be drawn on at any time within the ten years, subject to an upper limit of £17·5 million a year. The full implications of the 1945 act are discussed in Chapter 12.

[1] The institute was jointly financed by The Gambia, Sierra Leone, Ghana and Nigeria.

7 Transport and communications

Improved transport and communications are fundamental to all other types of development. There was no doubt that at the start of the twentieth century transport difficulties were among the most important and urgent problems facing Nigeria. It was necessary for the British government to have effective control over the relatively new district which had been acquired. The movements of the administrative officers up and down the country, and the regularity of effective communications between the administrative centres and the respective local administrative stations, were indispensable to any good government. This could be made possible only with improved and modern systems of transport and communications. As far as the economic development of Nigeria was concerned there was a great need to introduce better transport and communications systems in order to quicken the pace of the transition from a predominantly subsistence economy to a modern exchange economy. Southern Nigeria produced palm oil, palm kernels, rubber and cocoa; and some of the main producing centres were up to 200 miles or more from the coast. Groundnuts, cotton, benniseed, hides and skins were produced in the North, in areas which were at least 600 miles from the coast. Tin, one of the few important mineral export items, was produced in Jos, a distance of about 550 miles from Port Harcourt, its nearest seaport. Similarly, imported goods had to reach the consumers who were scattered over a very wide area. Again, any industrial or commercial establishment would want to make sure that its products could reach the widest markets possible; since production is not complete until the product has been effectively marketed to reach the consumers, the amount of transport available and its overall efficiency limits the volume of economic activity and thus the economic growth of a country.

INLAND WATERWAYS

The development of the inland waterways in Nigeria did not involve any major constructions of canals as such, but was mainly
concerned with improving the major rivers and their tributaries.
The big rivers in Nigeria have certain common characteristics:

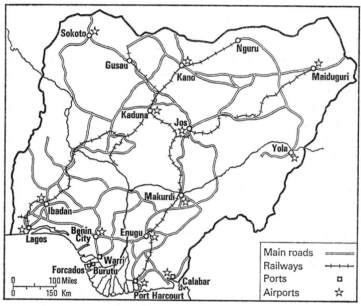

6 Transport and communications

a considerable fall; a swift current; a course impeded by rocks and
rapids; bars and shifting sandbanks formed at the mouth by the
silt of the soft soil through which the rivers run; numerous tributaries; often dry, broad beds; and great variations in volume according to the season of the year. Their development was financed
entirely by the Nigerian government. After 1900, various schemes
were introduced; most concentrated on clearing snags on the waterways and in some cases rivers were deepened and widened. The
regular dredging of some rivers was undertaken and explosives
were often used to clear obstructions. The main rivers and their
tributaries were kept open for navigation. For example, in 1905,

the Sombriero river in the Degema district was cleared of all
obstructions and made navigable by canoe to Ikiri. The Ossiomo
river was also cleared, providing about 155 miles of navigable
waterway. The tributary of the river Nun, a branch of the river
Niger, was cleared of obstructions to launch navigation, and other
rivers which were improved for navigation in the same year included the Ethiope and Moya.[1] Some portions of the Moya and
Aboynia rivers, tributaries of the Cross river, were dug to connect
them with the Calabar and Kwa Ibo rivers. This was one of the
few instances when canals were constructed to help navigation on
the rivers. By 1909 the Imo river had been made safe for navigation to Owerinta, a distance of 103 miles; and the Otamini river
had been opened up nearly as far as Owerri.[2] In 1911 the Koko
canal in the Benin district was widened and deepened; and in the
same year the Ndone creek was cleared, and more clearing was
done on the river Orashi as far as the Oguta Lake. The river Niger
received more attention, especially after the British government
took over the administration of Northern Nigeria in 1900. The
government maintained a clear passage on the river from the coast
as far north as Idah, which was then one of the principal trading posts
of the North. Also in 1911 the Ethiope river was further cleared as
far as Umutu in order to allow timber traffic. In connexion with the
exploitation of the newly discovered coal deposit at Udi in Eastern
Nigeria, the rivers Anambra, Omerum and Manu were surveyed
shortly before the start of the first world war, for the purpose of
ascertaining their possibilities for transporting coal.[3] The development of these rivers was never undertaken. The railway system was
eventually used to transport coal, because it was considered cheaper
and faster under the prevailing conditions.

Between the two world wars, the Nigerian government was
unable to provide adequate funds for any kind of development
project. The unstable world economic conditions affected adversely
Nigeria's foreign trade, from which most of the country's revenue
came. The government could only afford to spend a small sum of
money on the improvement of the inland waterways. In 1925,
clearings were undertaken on the river Niger, the Imo river, Saka

[1] *Southern Nigeria Blue Book*, 1905.
[2] *Colonial Annual Reports*, no. 665, Southern Nigeria, 1909, p. 25.
[3] *Colonial Annual Reports*, no. 735, Southern Nigeria, 1911, p. 26.

creek and the Mungo river in the Cameroons.[1] There was also an attempt to improve navigation around the Bussa Rapids on the river Niger: the work on this project began in 1928, but had to be abandoned in 1931 for lack of funds. Again in 1930, the Okitipupa–Agbabu channel was dredged in an attempt to deepen the waterway from Okitipupa to the terminus of the Ondo–Agbabu road.[2]

GOVERNMENT MARINE SERVICES

Before the first world war, Northern Nigeria was linked with the South only by waterways, mainly by way of the river Niger, and before the advent of the railway, the rivers Niger and Benue provided the channels by which goods and passengers could be transported to and from the North. The government was forced to keep these rivers navigable at all times, not only because of trade but also for the increasing administrative needs, particularly after 1900. For the same reasons, the government improved the rivers Kaduna and Gongola, both flowing southwards joining the rivers Niger and Benue respectively. The opening up of the river Gongola provided access to the cotton-growing area of Bornu and the tin-mining district of Bauchi. In the rainy season, canoes and light vessels were able to reach Genole on the river Gongola, a total distance of some 1,200 miles from the sea: this was claimed as the greatest distance of river navigation from a seaport, uninterrupted by rapids, in Africa.[3]

Until 1903, the river transport services between the South and the North were monopolized by the trading companies, particularly the Niger Company. In order to break the monopoly, the government of Northern Nigeria started mail and cargo services (the Niger and Benue system) to help all merchants alike by conveying a limited quantity of merchandise up the river Niger in government vessels. The rates announced by the government for passengers and consignments of cargo were about half the rates charged by the Niger Company. The merchants responded swiftly to the government services, and in the early stages they were unable to cope with the demand.

[1] *Colonial Annual Reports*, no. 1315, Nigeria, 1925, p. 25.
[2] *Colonial Annual Reports*, no. 1528, Nigeria, 1930, p. 23.
[3] *Colonial Reports*, no. 437, Northern Nigeria, 1903, p. 105.

In 1907, 13,021 passengers and 13,739 tons of cargo were transported, and in 1908 the traffic reached its peak with 13,587 passengers and 20,889 tons of cargo. There are no statistics to show the various items of cargo transported by marine services. It is known, however, that the bulk of the export products of Northern Nigeria, e.g. groundnuts and cotton, were brought down to the coast via the waterways. Imported goods and some local produce, e.g. yams, cassava, kolanuts and rice, were also transported.

After the railways had been extended to connect Northern and Southern Nigeria in 1912, river transport gradually ceased to be the most important means of transport and communication between the two areas. There was a gradual decline in the number of vessels serving the North, as trade was steadily diverted to the railway. In 1911, the government stopped its marine services on the Kaduna waterway, and the volume of trade passing through Lokoja and Idah reduced considerably.[1]

In Southern Nigeria the government maintained marine services on the coast and on navigable rivers from about 1906. The following were the main services undertaken by the Marine Department:

(1) Lagos–Porto Novo. A weekly mail and passenger service, this handled the trade between the two countries and also served the intermediate ports.[2] However, in 1912 it was discontinued and handed over to a French shipping company.[3]

(2) Lagos–Siluko–Sapele. A weekly mail and passenger service which, between 1908 and 1911, carried about 25,000 passengers. It was reorganized in 1912 and incorporated in a single service for the Western Provinces of Nigeria.

(3) Lagos–Ejirin–Epe. This service ran over a shorter distance, and a motor barge was maintained for transporting goods to the famous Ejirin market every nine days. The service was discontinued as a separate operation in 1911.

(4) Forcados–Warri–Sapele and Forcados–Koko–Sapele. Mail launches provided a weekly service on these two routes until 1912, when they were replaced by a bi-weekly one.

---

[1] *Colonial Reports*, no. 738, Northern Nigeria, 1911, p. 23.

[2] Between 1908 and 1911, a total number of 13,168 passengers travelled on this route.

[3] *Colonial Reports*, no. 825, Southern Nigeria, 1913, p. 28.

(5) The Cross River Transport, which began in 1905, ran regularly in Eastern Nigeria, and three of the motor launches used on this service were adapted to navigation in shallow waters.

In addition to the marine services provided by the government and the trading companies, countless numbers of canoes were used by the people, especially those living around the coastal areas and along the rivers, and the traders who were engaged in retail trade in Northern Nigeria. There were a few times when some Nigerians attempted to establish shipping companies. One such instance

TABLE 7.1   *Marine services, Nigeria* 1925–35*

Year	Passenger Government	Public	Cargo Government	Public	Coal traffic (tons)	Total revenue† (£)	Regular African staff employed	Daily average of floating African staff‡
1925	5,431	10,207	3,320	6,889	107,410	377,562	2,225	550
1926	4,927	8,070	3,199	3,251	117,263	355,184	2,241	600
1928	2,908	3,367	938	441	118,353	377,048	2,477	1,000
1929	2,959	2,417	994	1,615	121,802	379,181	2,474	1,400
1930	2,445	2,465	2,276	1,829	125,919	376,165	2,637	1,361
1931	3,170	1,842	2,879	1,331	111,477	323,795	1,698	1,080
1932	2,850	1,528	2,528	407	96,196	299,881	1,053	804
1933	2,350	1,200	1,028	15	87,785	280,299	833	877
1934	2,728	1,211	1,181	17	109,518	344,802	1,455	n.a.
1935	2,696	945	916	12	92,145	285,222§	1,630	n.a.

n.a. Not available.
* Excluding Victoria (Cameroons) division.
† Including paper credit for services to other government departments.
‡ Casual labour on daily paid rates.
§ Cash revenue only.
Source: *Annual Reports on the Marine Department*, Lagos, Government Printer.

deserves mention. In 1911 a group of Nigerian businessmen tried to promote a company to build and buy steamers, launches and barges in order to provide regular shipping and transport facilities for the petty traders up the river Niger. The company was to have had a capital of £20,000 divided into 20,000 shares of £1 each offered to the public; but it was never established because it could not register since the Company's Act had not yet been introduced into the country. This caused great discontent and arguments among the people.

Conditions after the first world war were less favourable to the development of the inland waterways transport system. The development of the railways and road transport led to the gradual decline of inland waterways, and this decline was reflected in the marine services after 1914. Marine services handled the cargo of coal from Udi mines, which began to operate in 1915. The completion of the railway between Port Harcourt and Enugu in 1916 enabled the government to provide coastal steamers for carrying coal from Udi, via Enugu and Port Harcourt, to Lagos. It is important to add that in 1925 the Marine Department introduced ferry services for workers crossing from Lagos to Apapa and back. In 1926, the first full year of its operation, 497,917 passengers travelled on the ferry. This number increased to 1,244,697 in 1929, but fell drastically during the depression years to 505,344 in 1934.[1] However, between 1915 and 1939 most of the marine services were drastically reduced. One of the very few services which remained until 1939 in Northern Nigeria was the weekly mail launch service between Burutu and Baro which was maintained by the Marine Department. A fortnightly mail launch service which ran between Lagos and Sapele, a distance of 227 miles was maintained, and it was connected at Koko with the Burutu–Forcados–Koko service covering another 60 miles. A weekly service between Lagos and Porto Novo was maintained, and some services on the Benue, between Lokoja, Makurdi and Yola were also in operation. There was a mail service between Port Harcourt, Degema and Nembe covering a distance of about 90 miles. During this period, the government partially transferred to the Elder Dempster Lines the services on the Cross river between Itu and Ikom; these were to be used by the company during the high water, but the government retained control during the low water season.[2] During the second world war very few improvements were made on the inland waterways, and they were confined to the key areas on the coast where raw materials vital to the war effort could be obtained. The United Africa Company Limited and John Holt Limited continued to provide

[1] *Annual Reports on the Marine Department, 1925–35*, Lagos, Government Printer.
[2] *Colonial Reports*, Nigeria, 1925–36.

cargo services, mainly between the seaports and the North through the river Niger. The bulk of the passengers and cargoes handled by these firms were for their trading groups and agents.

In addition to transporting passengers and cargo, marine services provided regular employment for a number of Nigerians. For example, between 1925 and 1935 over 20,000 Nigerians were employed as regular staff, among whom were a few clerks, mechanics and draughtsmen; and over 10,000 others were employed as casual labour on daily paid rates. Although the dockyards provided a limited amount of technical training, the government realized that a formal technical education was necessary to enable more Nigerians to take up skilled jobs.[1] In 1925 a class of apprentice masters was established on a part-time basis for a few selected Nigerians who were already in regular employment with the Marine Department. But it was not until 1929, when a technical instructor was employed from Britain, that the technical training scheme began on a permanent basis.[2]

RAILWAYS

In 1900 Messrs Shelford & Sons, the engineering firm responsible for the construction of the Nigerian railway, recommended to the British government that the railway system be extended beyond Ibadan. The British government responded to the recommendation by conducting a new series of surveys and investigations.[3] Sir Frederick Lugard, the Governor of Northern Nigeria, was anxious to see the railway extended to Northern Nigeria, and stressed its economic and military importance in view of the French policy on her territories around Nigeria. He recommended that the Lagos railway be extended to Ilorin and, ultimately, to Kano, and that a new Eastern line be given urgent consideration. After much pressure, the government agreed on the extension of the line to the North, and two possible routes were considered: one from Lagos via Fiditi, Oyo and Ogbomosho, and the other from Lagos via

[1] *Annual Report on the Marine Department, 1923*, Lagos, Government Printer, p. 43.
[2] *Annual Report on the Marine Department, 1929*, Lagos, Government Printer, p. 75.
[3] *Handbook of Railways in Africa*, C B910, vol. I, pp. 346–7.

Oshogbo. The latter was approved, and work began immediately. The progress made on the project was spectacular, considering the natural features of the areas through which the line had to pass, and the time it took to extend the line to important centres: the railway line reached Ibadan in 1901, Oshogbo in 1907 and Jebba (on the river Niger) in 1909. The problem of bridging the Niger remained to be solved; the government, faced with many proposals on this project, finally decided that a permanent bridge should be built. Work on the Jebba bridge took five years to complete and it was opened to traffic in 1914.

Before the Lagos railway was extended to Northern Nigeria, work had already started on some internal lines in the area. The first of these lines was between Zungeru and Kaduna, linking the seat of the Northern government at Zungeru with the river Kaduna, from where goods and passengers could travel via the river Niger to the coast. Work started on this line in 1901, when 12 miles of 2 feet 6 inches gauge tramway was laid. This was extended to cover 22 miles in 1902. Lack of funds held up the work on the Northern railways, and it was not until 1907 that financial arrangements were made whereby money was advanced by Southern Nigeria (Lagos Colony and Southern Nigeria Protectorate) and by Imperial Grant-in-Aid to enable a line to be built from Baro (on the Niger) to Zungeru, Zaria and Kano.[1] The extension work to Kano began in 1907 under two distinct engineering parties, one dealing with the line from Ilorin to Jebba and the other with the Niger bridge and the Jebba–Baro–Kano section. The work progressed with considerable rapidity, and on 1 January 1912 the through route from Lagos to Kano was officially opened. The Bauchi Light Railway, which was authorized to be constructed in 1911, was completed as far as Bukuru in 1914, thus serving the tin-mining area of Northern Nigeria.

On 3 October 1912, the railway of Northern Nigeria was amalgamated with the Southern Nigeria railway. Hitherto, they had been managed by two separate administrative bodies.[2]

Meanwhile, the discovery of coal at Enugu in 1909 encouraged the government to investigate the possibility of an Eastern railway line. The first problem to be solved was that of finding the cheapest

[1] *Colonial Annual Reports*, no. 594, Northern Nigeria, 1907–8.
[2] *Handbook of Railways in Africa*, p. 349.

route by which coal from Enugu could reach the coast: it was proposed that a railway line be constructed from Enugu to Onitsha on the river Niger, where coal could be brought to Lagos by boat. This proposal was later abandoned in favour of a more ambitious and expensive system stretching through Eastern Nigeria and joining the existing Western system in the North – bringing to an end the possibility of a railway line joining the West and the East. Port Harcourt was chosen as the terminus of the Eastern system, and work began on its construction late in 1913. By 1916 the construction work had been completed between Port Harcourt and Enugu. The project was halted temporarily during the first world war, but work was resumed in 1920. The Eastern railway line finally joined the Western line at Kaduna in 1926, and the railway bridge over the river Benue was completed in 1932. Before 1920 the Nigerian government operated a few motor services[1] to serve as feeders and outlets to the railways.

During the period between the two world wars, the government considered a number of surveys and proposals for a further extension of the Nigerian railway. As a result the following lines were constructed:

(a) A new line from Ifo to Idogo (31 miles). It was thought that this line would secure more produce for Lagos.
(b) A line from Zaria, a point between Kano and Kaduna, to Kaura-Namoda in the north-west direction (Kaura-Namoda lies just between Sokoto and Katsina). This was completed in 1929.
(c) The extension of the railway north-eastwards as far as Nguru, in 1930.

After these projects were concluded no further major developments were undertaken, except for the re-grading and re-laying of the Minna–Kaduna junction, for which the Nigerian government obtained an interest-free loan of £420,000 (for seven years) from the Colonial Development Fund.[2]

During the second world war the Nigerian railway handled the war traffic and increased passengers and merchandise. In the financial

[1] See the section on the road transport system.
[2] *Nigerian Railway and Udi Coal Mines: Administrative Report. Year ending 31 March 1931*, Lagos, Government Printer, p. 3.

year 1943–4 the government ordered locomotives, passenger coaches, goods wagons and manufactured spares, to replace the old existing ones. The war prevented their delivery and for a number of years the railway was hard hit by delays caused by overworked and damaged engines.

The construction of the railways was financed entirely by the Nigerian government through loans raised on the London money market. The total cost of construction steadily increased as railway mileage increased, rising from a total of about £6·6 million in 1914 to £15 million in 1925; and by 1938 the total railway mileage of 1,903 miles had cost about £23·4 million. The major expenses included the cost of imported rail construction materials from the United Kingdom, the cost of rolling-stock, and labour costs.

TABLE 7.2 *Nigerian railway: total cost of construction, 1914–38*

Year	Amount (£)
Up to 1914	6,656,476
1915	6,803,103
1919	9,277,041
1920	10,388,318
1924–5*	15,071,109
1926–7	18,014,227
1928–9	20,987,995
1929–30	21,539,646
1930–1	22,021,434
1931–2	22,120,905
1932–3	23,098,424
1936–7	23,113,887
1937–8	23,492,890

* Fiscal year ending 31 March as from 1924.
Source: *Nigerian Blue Book*, 1914–38.

The Nigerian railways provided passenger and cargo services. Passenger accommodation and rates were classified into first, second and third class. Passengers were given limited free allowances for baggage, and any excess baggage was liable to be surcharged. Special concessions were usually made for commercial travellers in respect of luggage and charges for excess luggage. Special rates were also provided for export products such as cocoa, palm oil, palm kernels, groundnuts, cotton and timber. The tonnage of the principal items of goods transported by the Nigerian railway is shown on table 7.3 below.

It was not until the mid-twenties, when about two-thirds of the railway system had been constructed, that many areas began to feel the full economic and social impact of the railways. The number of

TABLE 7.3   *Nigerian railway: goods traffic, 1916–38 ('000 tons)*

Year	Ground-nuts	Tin ore	Kola-nuts	Palm kernels	Palm oil	Cocoa
1916	43	7	—	—	—	—
1917	48	9	—	—	—	—
1918	—	8	—	—	—	—
1919	56	8	—	—	—	—
1920	52	7	—	—	—	—
1 January 1921– 31 March 1922	46	7	6*	—	—	—
1922–3	25	8	7	—	—	—
1923–4	40	9	8	—	—	—
1924–5	101	8	9	76†	35†	31†
1925–6	131	9	10	81	35	28
1926–7	112	11	10	70	31	27
1927–8	96	11	10	73	32	28
1928–9	115	14	10	58	37	34
1929–30	157	15	11	53	35	31
1930–1	132	11	12	51	38	18
1931–2	158	9	12	48	30	18
1932–3	198	5	13	63	30	26
1933–4	206	5	13	46	33	27
1934–5	220	8	19	56	22	30
1935–6	164	11	17	70	36	35
1936–7	285	14	17	72	45	28
1937–8	257	15	24	50	40	34

* No reliable statistics before 1921.
† No reliable statistics before 1924.
Note: Official statistics of the Nigerian railway were not released between 1939 and 1945.
Source: *Nigerian Railway and Udi Coal Mines: Administrative Reports, 1922–38.* Lagos, Government Printer.

passengers who travelled on the railways increased from 1,923,000 in 1924–5 to 3,851,000 in 1929–30; and the tonnage of goods hauled increased from 560,000 in 1924–5 to 1,002,000 in 1927–8. Both passenger and cargo services were affected by the economic

TABLE 7.4   *Nigerian railway: mileage, passenger and goods traffic, 1924–39*

Year	Mileage opened to traffic	Total number of passengers carried ('000)	Total tonnage hauled ('000 tons)
1924–5	1,220	1,923	560
1925–6	1,265	2,413	677
1926–7	1,265	2,621	948
1927–8	1,265	2,831	1,002
1928–9	1,265	3,162	958
1929–30	1,265	3,851	930
1930–1	1,265	3,663	762
1931–2	1,830	2,481	667
1932–3	1,830	2,378	646
1933–4	1,830	5,179	627
1934–5	1,900	5,080	661
1935–6	1,900	7,939	709
1936–7	1,900	8,426	1,162
1937–8	1,903	7,357	1,201
1938–9	1,903	6,707	955

Notes:
1. Official statistics of the Nigerian railway were not released between 1939 and 1945.
2. From 1921–2, financial year ended 31 March.

Sources: *Nigerian Railway and Udi Coal Mines: Administrative Reports, 1925–38*, Lagos, Government Printer, and *Digest of Statistics*, vol. 8, no. 3 (July 1959), Lagos, Government Printer.

depression of the early thirties, but by 1934 the number of passengers who travelled on the railways had increased, and the tonnage of goods hauled also increased.

The revenue of the Nigerian railway was derived from four main sources: coaching, goods traffic, telegraph service and motor-transport services (see table 7.5). However, the bulk of the annual

TABLE 7.5 *Nigerian railway: detailed statement of receipts, 1903–38* (£000)

Year	Coaching	Goods traffic	Telegraph	Sundries and motor services	Total
1903–11	316	985	5	14	1,320
1912	119	377	1	6	503
1913	133	567	1	13	714
1914	150	592	1	21	764
1915	131	466	0·9	25	623
1916	148	619	1	18	786
1917	165	841	2	22	1,031
1918	198	1,016	2	36	1,252
1919	285	1,147	3	31	1,466
1920	393	1,177	4	53	1,627
January–March 1921	97	254	0·7	13	364
1921–2	327	1,056	3	54	1,440
1922–3	290	1,096	3	37	1,426
1923–4	300	1,309	3	42	1,654
1924–5	291	1,736	3	47	2,077
1925–6	309	2,019	3	46	2,377
1926–7	322	2,046	4	49	2,421
1927–8	366	2,046	4	40	2,456
1928–9	394	2,093	4	62	2,553
1929–30	398	2,221	3	93	2,715
1930–1	351	1,758	3	66	2,178
1931–2	253	1,548	3	51	1,855
1932–3	218	1,612	3	54	1,887
1933–4	243	1,583	2	57*	1,885
1934–5	230	1,722	2	73†	2,027
1935–6	262	1,651	2	51‡	1,966
1936–7	308	2,316	2	67	2,693
1937–8	324	2,407	2	121	2,854

* Included levy on salary (£13,000).
† Included levy on salary (£14,000).
‡ Included levy on salary (£300).

Notes:

1. Official statistics of the Nigerian railway were not released between 1939 and 1945.
2. From 1921–2, financial year ended 31 March.

Source: *Nigerian Railway and Udi Coal Mines: Administrative Reports, 1923–38*, Lagos, Government Printer.

revenue came from goods traffic: in 1920, for example, the percentage of the revenue from goods traffic to total revenue was 72·3 per cent. This increased to 81·4 per cent in 1930, and to 83·3 per cent in 1938.

Traffic on the Nigerian railway was usually very slow. All the railway lines were single track – loops were provided in each station for the crossing trains. A great deal of time was wasted in sorting out and in waiting for crossing trains: if two trains started travelling in opposite directions, the time it would take either to reach its destination did not depend only on its speed but also on the speed of the other train and the possibility of being delayed by anything like a damaged engine or track. Most of the railway engines used in Nigeria were secondhand and bought from Britain. They broke down frequently, causing delays to journeys, and the fact that the railways provided no canteen facilities increased the discomfort of the passengers. The railway tracks, which were laid on wood sleepers, were often eaten away by white ants, thus increasing the hazards of travelling by rail. Again, the torrential rain often washed away the railway tracks, halting train journeys for several days. The railways provided limited travelling facilities for those who could afford the charges and for those who were fortunate enough to have the lines running through or near their towns and villages. For the bulk of the remaining travelling population, the railways did not serve them. Many had their homes too far away from the nearest railway station and had to rely on the inland waterways, where they existed, and on the roads, which soon became a serious challenge to the railways.

The railway workshops established at the main termini (in Lagos, Kaduna and Port Harcourt) provided limited facilities for the maintenance of mechanical plants and rolling-stock. Such workshops also provided some technical training for the Nigerians who were employed in them. Generally, the total number of Nigerians employed by the railway steadily increased. By 1925, 12,663 Nigerians were employed, and this rose to 18,086 in 1930, and to 18,844 in 1938. About 60 per cent of those employed were labourers. The Nigerian railway also provided training schemes for its Nigerian staff. The mechanical engineering section was responsible for training a few apprentice-mechanics, and the traffic training school also trained Nigerians for various jobs in the traffic section. By 1938 all station-masters (there were 210 stations by then), firemen, guards and clerical staff were Nigerians; and more than 65 per cent of locomotive drivers were Nigerians.

ROADS AND ROAD TRANSPORT

It was the need to build feeder-roads for the newly constructed railways which began the transformation of roads and road transport in Nigeria. The feeder roads were meant to provide enough passenger and cargo traffic for the new railways. The progress of their development, therefore, followed closely the gradual construction of railway lines. The fact that motor vehicles were introduced into Nigeria in the first decade of this century also helped to quicken their development. Between 1900 and 1915, road transport services were established by the Nigerian railway on the following feeder roads: Ibadan–Oyo (33 miles), Oyo–Iseyin (27 miles), Oshogbo–Ogbomosho (37 miles), Bukuru–Ropp (22 miles) and Zaria–Maska (25 miles). In addition, the government maintained the following cart-roads in Northern Nigeria: Zungeru–Zaria (164 miles), Zaria–Kano (86 miles) and Loko–Keffi (73 miles).

In 1905 the government embarked on road development projects in many areas in the interior bordering the coastal ports. The roads which were constructed in that year, outside the Lagos area, included the Ibadan–Oyo road, which was of great importance both for administrative and commercial purposes, being a feeder road to the railway which passed through Ibadan, and the Ogbomosho–Oyo road, connecting the remoter interior with Oyo. Between 1905 and 1910 the following were constructed: Ikirun–Illa, Oshogbo–Ilesha, Benin–Agbor, Onitsha–Awka, Adukpani–Uwet, Uwet–Itu, Warri–Benin, Awka–Udi, Agba–Okpanan and the Lagos–Agege road. Some road-metalling was also undertaken in Southern Nigeria.[1] The bridges on these roads were constructed with timber materials and concrete. Though they were the best that could be built to meet the urgent needs of the country, they were unreliable, and with the growth of traffic in later years they had to be repaired or replaced frequently.

By 1900 the country already possessed innumerable bush paths,

[1] *Colonial Reports*, Southern Nigeria, 1905–11.

and these were kept open through regular use – the tread of feet – though with great difficulty during the rainy season when bushes grow very fast. The bush paths continued to provide the main links between the coast and the interior, and with the gradual development of trade at the beginning of this century there was an increasing need to improve them. The development of such paths was in the hands of local chiefs. The first improvement made was the widening of the paths by employing communal effort. The roads which grew in this way were dusty and could be kept open only at certain times of the year.

When motor vehicles were introduced into the country between 1907 and 1909,[1] some businessmen provided a few motor transport services. Increasing numbers of bicycles[2] and motor-cycles were also used on the dusty roads. The motor transport services were available only at principal towns in the South and they ran at irregular times, depending on how soon the lorries had enough passengers and loads to carry. Journeys by motor transport were by no means pleasant. Inside the lorry, passengers were made to sit on very narrow planks stretched across with no back-rest. No special provisions were made for storing the loads, consequently passengers frequently incurred losses through damaged goods. The lorry drivers could stop when they felt like it – no consideration was given to time, or, most important of all, the feelings of the passengers. The lorries were usually overcrowded and the untarred roads were slippery and dangerous, particularly during the rainy season. In view of these hazardous conditions, and the fact that not many people could afford to pay the fares, the head-loading system increased with the development of better footpaths.

By about 1909 a means of transporting goods on locally-made four-wheeled 'carts' (built on lorry chassis) was devised. These were owned and managed by Nigerians. One peculiar feature about them was that they had no effective brakes and were therefore liable to cause accidents. They soon increased in number in Lagos and in a few towns in Western Nigeria. An observation made in 1911 revealed that thirteen men carrying goods on two such carts were

[1] Between 1908 and 1909 over 1,200 motor vehicles were imported into Nigeria: *Southern Nigeria Blue Book*, 1908 and 1909.
[2] Total numbers of bicycles imported into Nigeria in 1908 and 1909 were 1,676 and 1,689 respectively: ibid.

doing the job of eighty men or more carrying goods by head-loading.[1] The increasing use of such vehicles reduced the cost of transporting goods within the township, and it also released some labour from head-loading to assist in the development of the forest and agricultural wealth of the country. In the northern portion of the country the conditions were similar. On occasions, when the

TABLE 7.6   *Roads maintained by the Nigerian*
            government outside townships, 1924–38

Financial year ending 31 March	Road mileage	Maintenance cost per mile per annum (£)
1924–5	2,596	17·0
1925–6	2,780	20·0
1926–7	2,950	n.a.
1927–8	3,199	26·0
1928–9	3,453	30·0
1929–30	3,606	41·0
1930–1	3,610	42·0
1931–2	3,670	31·5
1932–3	3,637	27·5
1933–4	3,627	26·5
1934–5	3,595	25·0
1935–6	3,595	25·0
1936–7	3,731	n.a.
1937–8	3,829	n.a.

n.a. Not available.
Source: *Annual Reports of the Public Works Department,*
        1924–38, Lagos, Government Printer.

scarcity of cart-drawing animals made it impossible to use carts on the sandy roads, carriers were employed.

Road construction was much easier in the savannah and semi-desert areas of the North than it was in the forest areas of the South. The local authorities maintained most of the roads through community efforts. In 1914 and 1920 the total mileage of roads maintained by local authorities was about 21,000 and 22,000 respectively

[1] *Lagos Customs and Trade Journal*, vol. I, 18 September 1911.

in Northern Nigeria, and about 1,400 and 3,000 respectively in Southern Nigeria.

The first world war and the economic depression that followed brought a drastic cut in road development projects. However, in 1923 the government renewed its efforts to link more areas with better roads. It was at this time that the roads between Lagos, Ibadan, Ijebu-Ode, Ilesha and Akure to Ondo, Benin and Sapele were constructed on a permanent basis. The Western Provinces were joined with the Eastern Provinces by a road via Asaba to Onitsha. By about 1925 it was possible, though with some difficulty, to motor from Ibadan to Port Harcourt, but there were several ferries which had to be crossed, including the major crossing from Asaba to Onitsha. In the North a road link between Keffi and Wamba was also completed in 1923. By 1926 the government was responsible for some 2,950 miles of road (see table 7.6), which were maintained by the Public Works Department, and it was estimated that between £20 and £40 a mile was spent on them. In that year a fresh plan was drawn to reorganize the road system and to build new roads, including the breaking-down of the road system into trunk 'A' and 'B' and minor roads.

Trunk 'A' roads were mainly those constructed and maintained by the Public Works Department of the government, and comprised the trunk and main produce routes. The surfaces of these roads were of tar-sprayed macadam, tar-sprayed gravel or laterite gravel. Trunk 'B' roads constituted the better-class roads of lightly-gravelled surfaces maintained by the native or local authorities with the help of local rulers. The minor roads were mainly earth roads, which were maintained exclusively by the local chiefs. The bridges and culverts on trunk 'A' roads were of permanent construction made of steel and cement, while those of trunk 'B' roads were of a semi-permanent nature. The bridges on the minor roads were mainly of timber and their culverts were of light construction. After this plan was made, work began on the projects, but the depression of the late twenties and the early thirties forced the government to cut drastically its expenditure on road-building. Between 1930 and 1934 many roads were abandoned and those which continued to be used were badly in need of repairs. During these depression years, some experiments were made on bituminous surface road-building, and the government drew on the experience of other countries which had faced similar road problems.[1] By 1930 only 78 miles of tarred surface road had been laid from Lagos towards Ibadan.

Throughout the twenties and the thirties the motor transport services continued to develop as more people could afford to buy motor lorries, which were used mainly for carrying agricultural export produce from the interior to the coast. The few passenger services that were provided continued to be badly organized. There were very few motor-servicing stations, but the lorry drivers, who had little or no training as mechanics, tackled unexpected break-downs with enormous skill and courage.

TABLE 7.7   *Commercial vehicles registered in Nigeria, 1929–39*

Year	Number	Year	Number
1929	2,940	1934	2,562
1930	3,130	1935	2,800
1931	2,829	1937	1,819
1932	2,718	1938	550
1933	2,855	1939	559

Sources: *Annual Report of the Public Works Department, 1935*, Lagos, Government Printer, and *Digest of Statistics*, vol. 7, no. 4 (October 1958), Lagos, Government Printer.

The first attempt to organize and centralize the motor transport system was made in 1932, when motor-lorry owners formed the Nigerian Motor Transport Union. The union instructed its members to observe all the motor traffic ordinances, and to discourage overloading and over-speeding. Several check-points were established on the roads, and the union maintained its own inspectors who were charged with the enforcement of these objectives. All lorries were tested for roadworthiness from time to time, in order to reduce the number of road accidents caused by mechanical faults. For the first few years of its operation, the union was successful, but as corruption crept in gradually, the inspectors became less insistent on the observation of the union rules.

[1] Gilbert Walker, *Traffic and Transport in Nigeria*, p. 14.

By 1937 the economic depression was partially over and the government resumed road construction on a substantial scale. A road was built from Mamfe to Bamenda in the Southern Cameroons, and another was completed between Port Harcourt and Jos, thus providing a valuable outlet for minerals from the Jos plateau.

During the second world war road construction was undertaken by the government primarily to suit military requirements. One such road extended from Jos to Maiduguri and the Fort Lamy; the last 90 miles were built on a low embankment across a plain of black cotton soil. The road carried a large amount of the military traffic serving the French base at Fort Lamy. Another important road built about the same time was the Funtua–Zungeru road. A number of other roads were built to help in the campaign for increased export production during the war.

RAIL–ROAD COMPETITION

The road transport system soon offered a strong challenge to the railways. The railways could only serve those areas where the lines passed and thus provided a very rigid transport system, whereas the new roads, even though they were not satisfactory, provided a more flexible transport facility. Most of the roads which were developed in Nigeria linked most of the towns which were being served by the railways. The competition between the railways and the roads became a serious problem in the thirties. After the Railway Department had made a series of complaints to the Nigerian government, a committee was set up in 1933 to consider the loss to railway revenue caused by undue competition from motor transport on certain roads, and to make recommendations as to the propriety and practicality of restricting such motor transport by subjecting it to heavier taxation (in accordance with a practice prevalent in certain other colonies in Africa), or by limiting or conditioning licences. The committee, reporting in September 1933,[1] emphasized the fact that motor transport afforded a cheaper means of evacuating the produce in some provinces than was afforded by the railways; also that the exclusion of commercial motor vehicles from roads 'paralleling' the railway would reduce the prices obtained by the

[1] *Report of Committee on Road–Railway Competition*, Sessional Paper no. 21 of 1933.

producers of export crops, and would throw a number of Africans now engaged in the motor industry out of employment. It recommended, among other things, that no steps should be taken to prohibit or restrict the use of motor transport on the roads which were considered to be in competition with the railways, except that in order to assist the railway, the licences for commercial motor vehicles competing with the railway should be doubled. It also recommended that the railway should consider the possibility of attracting tonnage by introducing a reduced rate for traffic in the competitive zone. The recommendations were accepted by the government, and motor licence duties on lorries registered in Lagos, Abeokuta, Ijebu-Ode, Oyo and Ilorin were doubled. The policy was particularly unfair in regard to lorries registered at Ijebu-Ode and Oyo because these areas were not on the same route as the railway: Oyo and Ijebu-Ode are 33 miles and 44 miles respectively from Ibadan, the nearest railway station to both. The lorry owners, however, responded by increasing their fares, and these were extended to cover areas not affected by the increased licence duties. The competition continued despite these measures. The General Manager of the Nigerian railway, commenting on the rail–road competition, said 'There seems to be something amiss with the economics of the matter. . . . The function of most of these lorries is to carry the traffic for which the railway was built from areas which that railway has developed. National motor roads to feed the national railway would produce a more co-ordinated transport and assist the government to meet the interest charges on its railway capitalization.'[1] The government found it necessary to set up a committee in 1936 to examine the problem once again. The new committee reported in 1937 and agreed with the main findings of the previous one:[2] motor licence fees were increased in order to discourage the expansion of the motor transport services, but this was of no avail.

The fact that better vehicles which suited local conditions were being produced in Europe and imported into Nigeria, and that more good roads came into existence while no additional railway lines were built, further encouraged the use of the road transport system in all parts of Nigeria. The Nigerian government continued to

[1] *Railway and Colliery Annual Report. Financial Year ending 31 March 1934*, p.11.
[2] *Interim Report of the Road–Rail Competition Committee, 1936*, Sessional Paper no. 16 of 1937.

bear the annual deficits accruing from the operations of the railway.[1]

AIR TRANSPORT

The first recorded flight of an aeroplane in Nigeria was in 1925, when some Bristol Fighter aircraft of the Royal Air Force of the United Kingdom visited Nigeria from Cairo.[2] The early flights of the RAF were later extended to cover all the West African countries, and such flights became annual events. However, very little was known about civil aviation until the early thirties. In October 1931 a seaplane arrived in Nigeria from England in an attempt by an English company to establish commercial flying in Nigeria and West Africa generally.[3] After a certain number of exhibition flights, the seaplane made visits to Port Harcourt, Calabar and some stations in the Niger Delta. There were no radio aids or even landing grounds, with the result that many of the privately-owned pioneer aircraft had to land on roads and on dry river beds for refuelling. In the early thirties, the Nigerian government, realizing the need for aerodromes, invited a small party of civil engineers from Britain to plan a chain of landing grounds between Kano and Lagos. As a result, landing grounds were established at Lagos, Ilorin, Minna, Jos, Kaduna, Kano, Katsina, Bauchi, Yola and Maiduguri; but ample notice had to be given before any of these could be used, so that necessary preparations and safety measures could be undertaken. At the same time, sites for seaplane bases were provisionally selected at Lagos, Forcados, Calabar, Port Harcourt, Onitsha, Lokoja, Makurdi and Jebba.

At the end of 1935 an Air Services Development Committee was set up by the Nigerian government to look into the possibility of establishing regular air services in the country.[4] Following the recommendations of the committee, six 'all-seasons' aerodromes

---

[1] It was estimated that the Nigerian railway lost £70,000 to parallel road transport in the competitive section during 1935: *Railway and Colliery Annual Report*, 1936, p. 16.

[2] *Colonial Annual Reports*, no. 1315, Nigeria, 1925, p. 9.

[3] *Colonial Annual Reports*, no. 1569, Nigeria, 1931, p. 44.

[4] *An Economic Survey of the Colonial Empire, 1937*, Col. no. 179, p. 151.

were constructed and fully equipped at Lagos (Apapa), Oshogbo, Minna, Kano and Maiduguri.

Also in 1935 plans were made for the Imperial Airways (UK) to start airmail services between the United Kingdom and West Africa as part of a regular service between the United Kingdom and South Africa. The air service was to go via Khartoum to Kano, and then to the other West African countries. By 1936 a weekly air service was established between Khartoum and Lagos. Proposals were also made for a regular weekly service from Lagos to Accra, Takoradi and ultimately Freetown, connecting with the service between Khartoum and Lagos, which would be operated by Imperial Airways and would form part of the Empire Air Mail Scheme.

No further major development took place before the start of the second world war. The war, however, forced the British government to encourage Nigeria and the other West African territories to speed up developments for air transport services, mainly for military reasons. The construction of aerodromes was actively pursued during the war, and the development plan was enlarged to include additional landing grounds. Many of the runways of the existing landing grounds were considerably lengthened as military aircraft required greater lengths for landing and take-off. Wider networks of wireless telegraphy for communications between aircraft and the airports were set up on a military basis throughout Nigeria.

TABLE 7.8   *Aircraft arriving from countries outside Nigeria, 1941–5*

	Arrival			
Year	Lagos	Kano	Other airports	Total
1941	735	22	486	1,243
1942	953	353	38	1,344
1943	809	354	—	1,163
1944	881	238	39	1,158
1945	660	145	—	805

Source: *Digest of Statistics*, vol. 8, no. 3 (July 1959), Lagos, Government Printer.

OCEAN SHIPPING

There was a steady increase in the number of ships visiting Nigeria as the foreign trade of the country began to expand. There were very few natural harbours; the difficulties of entering and leaving the Nigerian coast caused by the frequent existence of bars allowed only a few brave pilots to visit Nigeria; hence high costs of shipment were experienced and the few shipping lines which took the risk of plying the Nigerian coast constituted themselves into a monopoly – a shipping ring. Conditions were similar in the Gambia, Sierra Leone and Ghana. All ships entering West Africa had to anchor on the sea, where cargoes were discharged and loaded and passengers disembarked and embarked. Local canoes and imported boats, lighters and barges were used in the process of loading and off-loading the ships. These operations called for great skill as well as some luck on the part of the pilots: it was not uncommon to find valuable cargoes being lost to the sea. The operations were wasteful in this respect, and they also involved a waste of precious time as well.

Small traders throughout West Africa complained of the inadequate shipping space which was provided by the shipping companies, and the exorbitant costs of shipment which were imposed. The British government, after receiving a number of petitions on alleged malpractices of the shipping companies in British West Africa, appointed a commission of inquiry in 1906 to investigate the complaints.[1] The investigations of the commission substantiated the main charges of the traders as to the high freight rates charged in their trade, but no measures were recommended to combat them, probably because there were no other means of shipment available. The shipping ring in British West Africa, therefore, continued its absolute control, and operated a rebate system in favour of some big trading companies. Except for the harbour facilities which existed on a limited scale in Lagos and Port Harcourt, no attempt to build modern wharves was made until the twenties.

The first world war disrupted ocean shipping in Nigeria and it temporarily eliminated the German ships. The Nigerian government, together with the governments of the other British West African countries, took over ocean shipping, and the operations of

[1] McPhee, op. cit., p. 95.

the shipping ring, including the rebate system, fell into abeyance. The control of shipping was necessary as part of the war economy. It was found necessary to safeguard the movement of ships and to protect them from enemy action. They were also redeployed to carry essential raw materials for Britain and her allies. After the war, many of the German shipping lines which had operated in West Africa were allowed to operate again. The shipping companies in

TABLE 7.9   *Cargo vessels entering Nigerian ports, 1914–38*

	Total		Vessels registered in UK	
Year	Number	Tonnage ('000)	Number	Tonnage ('000)
1914	411	722	284	502
1915	290	548	243	521
1917	253	403	196	386
1918	193	310	155	303
1919	269	435	223	400
1920	343	676	245	565
1921–2*	369	741	215	514
1922–3	484	1,010	288	670
1923–4	449	1,027	254	610
1924–5	471	1,260	279	757
1925–6	542	1,476	293	838
1926–7	597	1,615	309	907
1927–8	784	1,900	370	969
1928–9	795	1,942	373	985
1929–30	775	1,813	399	916
1930–1	664	1,578	325	733
1931–2	561	1,281	282	635
1932–3	583	1,332	290	643
1933–4	652	1,493	291	669
1934–5	786	1,770	351	838
1935–6	777	1,844	388	863
1936–7	870	2,090	357	960
1937–8	732	1,871	317	903

* Financial year ending 31 March
Note: Official shipping returns were not released during the war period 1939–45.
Source: *Nigerian Blue Book*, 1914–38.

West Africa regrouped and reimposed the rebate system in 1922. In 1924 the West African Shipping Ring was formally reconstituted to include the continental lines operating in West Africa.[1]

Just before the economic depression of the late twenties and the early thirties, some efforts were made to provide better harbour facilities in Nigeria. The first modern wharves were built at Apapa, and when they were opened in 1926 they had four berths. Again, in November of the same year work began on ocean wharfage at Port Harcourt, which would provide berths for the largest vessels visiting the port. These new wharves provided additional safety for ships, lighters, barges and boats, and thus lowered considerably the cost of insurance. The new facilities also speeded up the loading and discharging of goods. The number of breakages and amount of lost property was considerably reduced, and the packing costs incurred by companies trading in Nigeria considerably lowered. However, no important developments took place during the depression years.

Shortly before the outbreak of the second world war, the shipping companies operating in Nigeria included the following: the Elder Dempster Lines Limited (British), American West African Line (American), Compagnie fabre et Fressinet (French), Holland West Afrika Liju and allied companies (Dutch), Woerman Linie and allied companies (German) and Navigazione Libera Triestina Line (Italian). Most of these shipping lines provided cargo services mainly, with a limited number of mail and passenger services. However, the Elder Dempster Lines Limited continued to provide regular passenger and mail services between the United Kingdom and Nigeria. In addition to the services provided by these shipping lines, a number of vessels under charter, chiefly by the United Africa Company Ltd (UAC), visited, among other ports, Lagos and Port Harcourt.

In 1939 the German shipping lines withdrew again from Nigeria. All those remaining were requisitioned by the Nigerian government on behalf of the British government. They shared the job of lifting the oilseeds, palm oil, cocoa and other produce required by the Ministry of Food and Ministry of Supply in the United Kingdom for the duration of the war.

[1] Ibid., p. 98. See also P. T. Bauer, *West African Trade*.

COMMUNICATIONS

A number of obstacles hindered the rapid development of a modern postal system in Nigeria. The bulk of the population was illiterate and could neither read nor write: to such people a postal system was useless. Nevertheless, the government continued to open a number of post offices and some postal agencies were also appointed. The spread of education, initiated by the missionaries, helped considerably to introduce letter-writing and thus the habit of sending letters. The services provided by the early post offices varied: some were established for selling stamps, with letter collection boxes provided for posting letters; very few could deal in postal and money orders – by 1913 there were about 20 post offices which dealt with them. The number of post offices increased steadily, and by 1934 Nigeria had about 110 post offices and 42 postal agencies. The business of the Nigerian Post Office also increased (see table 7.10).

After 1934, however, very few post offices were established; indeed, between 1934 and 1940 only one was established. By 1945 there were 113 post offices in Nigeria. The number of postal agencies, on the other hand, increased considerably: from 42 in 1934 to 161 in 1940, and 298 in 1945.[1]

The Post Office Savings Bank facility was extended to cover more towns. The number of post offices which provided such a service increased from 25 in 1919 to 51 in 1930, and to 113 in 1945. With the increasing number of educated Nigerians, and with increases in the number of wage-earners, indigenous traders and businessmen, more people patronized the Post Office Savings Bank. The number of depositors increased from 5,477 in 1915, to 49,200 and 84,130 in 1940 and 1945 respectively. Total deposits also increased from £30,348 in 1915, to £209,749 and £1,184,823 in 1940 and 1945 respectively.[2]

It is important to add that the government also developed the telephone systems in the country. By 1929 the Lagos–Ibadan telephone trunk line was completed and a new telephone exchange was installed at Abeokuta. Telephone exchanges were also installed at

[1] *Digest of Statistics*, vol. 8, no. 2 (April 1959), Lagos, Government Printer.
[2] *Nigerian Blue Books*, 1914–20; and *An Economic Survey of the Colonial Territories, 1951*, vol. III, Col. nos. 281–3, HMSO, 1953.

TABLE 7.10 *Letters, parcels and telegrams handled by the
Nigerian Post Office, 1914–38 ('000)*

Year	Letters*		Parcels		Internal telegrams
	Internal	External	Internal	External	
1914	1,196	1,670	32	99	—
1915	620	1,551	44	71	—
1917	793	1,656	40	64	—
1918	1,207	1,469	50	67	—
1919	982	2,101	53	105	—
1920	1,386	2,523	57	191	575
1921–2	1,758	2,673	48	114	557
1922–3	2,314	2,052	57	120	571
1923–4	2,391	2,344	56	140	608
1924–5	2,604	3,695	52	158	670
1925–6	2,804	2,654	62	149	699
1926–7	3,294	2,828	75	155	756
1927–8	3,957	2,718	84	158	827
1928–9	4,095	2,854	122	162	795
1929–30	4,649	2,710	68	152	813
1930–1	3,478	2,536	54	108	740
1931–2	3,201	2,061	44	95	596
1932–3	3,354	2,027	36	83	573
1933–4	3,729	2,077	33	66	569
1934–5	3,872	2,425	34	67	583
1935–6	5,193	3,136	37	74	675
1936–7	6,994	4,555	35	90	799
1937–8	7,449	4,831	33	79	741

* Including postcards.
Source: *Nigerian Blue Book*, 1914–38.

Aba, Port Harcourt and Bukuru. In addition, the government
undertook some experimental transmission from the Lagos wireless
station, which was receiving foreign news, but this had to be discontinued in 1931 because of shortage of staff. By 1934 there were
21 telephone exchanges in Nigeria. This figure increased to 40 in
1940, and to 59 in 1945. Trunk telephone services were available in
a number of principal centres, including: Lagos–Abeokuta–Ibadan;
Port Harcourt and Aba; Jos and Bukuru; Victoria, Buea and Tiko
in the Cameroons.

8   Agricultural developments

The true significance of the economic history of Nigeria during the period between 1900 and 1945 lies in the growth of the cash economy, which had its foundation in the development of agricultural export products, usually referred to as cash-crops.

The system of agriculture went through a number of transitional stages. In the northern areas of Nigeria, with savannah vegetation, the primary concern of farmers was the production of food and clothing for their own needs; and until transport facilities were extended to these areas, production of crops for export was greatly limited. In the southern areas, where geographical conditions were more favourable to agricultural production, the pressure of needs was not severe, and in consequence food crops were cultivated intensively only in certain localized dry areas or where proximity to larger towns rendered their cultivation highly profitable.

The rapid rise in the value of agricultural export produce and the consequent increase in the purchasing power of the farmers, which were noticed towards the close of the nineteenth century, continued into the twentieth century, before being slowed down by two world wars and the general economic depression. The development of transport facilities and the gradual spread of education naturally led to greater emphasis being given to the financial or pecuniary aspects of agriculture.[1] Production for local sales and for export became the aim of many farmers, and their success in this respect was undoubted as far as the volumes of export products were concerned. However, improvements in the quality of the farmers' work did not keep pace with the increased physical outputs which were achieved. A number of problems on such matters as tillage, cultivation, drainage, protection of crops from wind, pruning, manuring

[1] McPhee, op. cit., p. 264.

and control of pests and diseases received no significant attention from the indigenous peasant farmers; these and other problems had to be tackled by the government and by some interested private enterprises with established businesses in Nigeria. The system and techniques of production remained largely primitive, thus resulting in defective methods in the preparation of crops for export. A

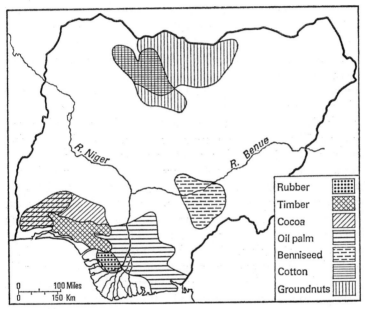

7 Location of main agricultural export products

notable and serious defect of the agricultural system in Nigeria was the absence of any provision for financing the farmer's work, apart from the locally-organized community help and the few agricultural associations and co-operative societies which developed in some areas (particularly in the South) in the twenties and the early thirties.[1] In the event of a serious epidemic of disease in the major crops, such as the swollen shoot and black pod diseases of cocoa, or of a depression in the prices of export produce as experienced in the early thirties, there were no established procedures for providing

[1] *Annual Reports on the Agricultural Department, 1924–34*, Lagos, Government Printer.

immediate relief to the farmers and for financing new enterprises. Most of the agricultural production problems of this period can be considered in relation to the production of each of the major agricultural products. However, there were a number of factors which had a significant impact on agricultural production in general. These included British government policy towards the establishment of foreign-owned agricultural plantations in Nigeria, and the efforts of the Nigerian government towards effecting better systems and techniques of agricultural production in general and in respect of some major products.

It has already been pointed out that land constituted the foundation of the indigenous social and economic systems in Nigeria. It was impossible for a stranger or foreigner to secure absolute ownership of land. The best that could be obtained was the grant of a lease to any foreign individual or firm which desired to use land for any purpose. The British government supported this policy and thus discouraged the establishment of foreign-owned plantations in Nigeria. Lord Lugard, one of the greatest British colonial administrators, realized that an attempt to force a foreign-owned plantation system on the people of Nigeria would disrupt the indigenous social and economic systems of the country, which could have far-reaching political implications. It was obvious to Lugard that the Nigerian economy was largely subsistence in nature, and that the acquisition of land by Europeans would spark off political unrest of wide magnitude which the British government could not afford, both financially and in terms of international politics. It was thought by some foreign businessmen that foreign-owned agricultural plantations, if allowed to operate in Nigeria, would secure the rapid and efficient growth of a cash economy, based on the major agricultural products, such as palm oil, palm kernels and cocoa. Lugard expressed the view that products such as cocoa, improved cotton and coffee should not be grown on plantations owned by Europeans, but that such crops should be introduced to the peasant farmers. The British government should merely encourage the production of such crops by distributing plants and seeds to peasant farmers, and by promising to buy the produce, with the additional incentive of bonuses for good agricultural production results or productivity.[1] However, it was reported that, by 1911, Messrs Miller Brothers & Co. Ltd and

[1] *Colonial Annual Reports*, no. 409, Northern Nigeria, 1902, p. 60.

one James Thomas (a Nigerian) had already concluded private lease agreements with local chiefs in Sapele for the establishment of rubber plantations.[1] The United African Company also acquired long leases of some 12,400 acres for experiments in rubber and oil palm plantations.[2] By 1917, the government had introduced legislation to control agricultural leases. Agricultural leases of Crown lands, which covered the areas of Northern Nigeria and the Colony of Lagos, were limited by statute to 1,200 acres each with a term of 45 years. In the Southern Provinces, leases of lands other than Crown lands could be acquired under the provisions of the law (the Native Lands Acquisition Ordinance, no. 32 of 1917).[3] Mr Ormsby-Gore (the Secretary of State for the Colonies), reporting on his visit to West Africa in 1926,[4] stated that the British government would not support any system of agricultural development (foreign-owned plantations) which could entail compulsory measures or interfere with the native system of land tenure. This became the standard British policy on agricultural production in Nigeria. However, the British government encouraged the establishment of agricultural plantations sponsored or approved by the Nigerian government for the purpose of introducing new crops and for the improvement of existing crops. A number of such plantations, nurseries and experimental farms are mentioned below, in respect of each major crop.

The Nigerian government established a number of institutions for the general advancement of agricultural production. Between 1912 and 1916 it had developed the Moore Plantation at Ibadan as an agricultural experimental station. In 1923 experimental stations were established in Zaria, Umuahia and Benin.[5] An Agricultural Research Station was also established at Vom in Northern Nigeria in 1925. Two years later, the Agricultural School at Ibadan was opened.[6] In 1934 two other institutions were established: the Agricultural

[1] *Lagos Customs and Trade Journal*, vol. 1, no. 1 (18 April 1911).

[2] Hailey, op. cit., p. 732.

[3] Cmd. 468, 1919, p. 36.

[4] *Report by the Hon. W. G. A. Ormsby-Gore M.P. on his visit to West Africa*, Cmd. 2744, HMSO, 1926.

[5] *Annual Report on the Agricultural Department, 1923*, Lagos, Government Printer, p. 1.

[6] *Annual Report on the Agricultural Department, 1927*, Lagos, Government Printer, p. 4.

Station at Samaru and the Veterinary School in Kano.[1] In 1942 the Veterinary School at Vom was established with the aid of the Colonial Development and Welfare Fund. These institutions performed a number of functions: first, the plantations and the agricultural stations provided the basic agricultural research centres for Nigeria; secondly, the agricultural institutions provided training programmes for a number of people who later qualified as agricultural officers of various grades; and thirdly, the institutions encouraged the farmers to improve their systems and techniques of production by disseminating new ideas to the few who were prepared to adopt such new methods. A number of agricultural shows were organized in order to make agriculture more competitive. In addition to these, concentrated efforts were made to improve the production techniques of some of the major crops, e.g. cotton, maize, yams, groundnuts and cocoa. During the depression years of the early thirties, it was thought that a better-organized agricultural system could relieve unemployment. A committee set up by the government in 1935 to look into the problems of unemployment in Lagos and the surrounding districts,[2] recommended that the government should establish farm settlements, which, the committee thought, would not only relieve unemployment but would make possible the introduction of new systems and techniques of agricultural production. There is nothing on record to indicate that the government rejected this recommendation, but at the same time nothing was done to implement it.

One other major aspect of agricultural production in which the Nigerian government was concerned was that of produce inspection. The government found it necessary to improve the quality of agricultural products, particularly those which formed major items of export. The main problem which had to be tackled was that of adulterated produce. At the start of the twentieth century, there were already a few ordinances in force in Lagos and in the Niger Coast Protectorate which prohibited the adulteration of produce and dealing in any adulterated produce.[3] In 1902 a similar ordinance was

[1] *Colonial Annual Reports*, no. 1710, Nigeria, 1934, pp. 44 and 48.
[2] *Report of the Committee appointed by His Excellency the Governor to enquire into the Question of Unemployment*, Sessional Paper no. 46 of 1935, p. 3.
[3] In 1889, the first ordinance to prohibit the adulteration of produce and the dealing in any adulterated produce was enacted in Lagos. This was followed

introduced to cover the Protectorate of Southern Nigeria;[1] and it also provided for the appointment of inspectors who were charged with the responsibility of enforcing the ordinance. The first attempt to control the quality of specific products was made in 1909, when an ordinance forbade the sale or exposure for sale of palm kernels containing more than 5 per cent of shell. Another ordinance, which repealed all previous Nigerian ordinances on adulteration of produce, was made in 1917,[2] and laid down the standards of purity for palm products. The defects of the ordinance were that it was not an offence to buy any produce which did not comply with the required standard of purity, and although it was illegal to possess inferior produce for export, the onus of proof that it did not comply with the prescribed standard of purity lay on the prosecutor, and it was in practice extremely difficult to prove the owner's intention to infringe the law. The regulations established reasonable standards of purity for palm oil and kernels, but the standard established for cocoa was only that it should not contain more than 1 per cent of dirt and foreign matter. It might be wet and contain any proportion of weevil-eaten or mouldy beans and yet conform with the regulations. The ordinance of 1917 was not effective and thus failed to produce any substantial improvement in the quality of the export produce.

However, the government continued to search for an effective system of controlling adulterated produce. In 1928 a new Adulteration of Produce ordinance came into force which introduced compulsory inspection and grading.[3] Produce intended for export was to be exposed for examination and grading at one of the official stations set up for this purpose. The produce inspector or examiner was to ensure that all cocoa or palm kernels, after being graded and passed, were bagged in clean, dry bags sealed and stored in a dry place, and palm oil was to be neatly stored in casks. Produce

---

in 1896 by the Native Trade Law for the Prevention of Sale of Adulterated Produce; and the Adulteration of Produce Ordinance of 1897 (CO151/27 and CO464/1).

[1] *Report of Committee upon the System of Produce Inspection, 1931*, Sessional Paper no. 1 of 1932, pp. 3–4.

[2] Ordinance no. 67 of 1917 repealed the 1909 and other similar ordinances.

[3] This ordinance had been in force in the Lagos district since 1 April 1926: *Report of Committee upon the System of Produce Inspection*, p. 5.

inspectors were trained in the Department of Agriculture. Inspection fees were paid by the exporting firms in order to meet the cost of the scheme. During the cocoa season of 1928–9 the government introduced the system of grading cocoa according to the extent of fermentation carried out. Four main grades were established, varying from Grade I, cocoa which had less than 5 per cent insufficiently fermented or defective or germinated beans, to Grade IV cocoa, which had from 8 per cent to 20 per cent of defective beans. In 1932 the grades were altered to provide for three grades only, as the result of changes made by the United States of America in order to bring its standard of imported beans free from mould or weevils into line with its stringent 'pure food' laws.

PALM PRODUCTS

Palm trees grow wild in Nigeria, and for over a century Nigeria had been supplying Europe with palm oil. The gradual growth of a money economy and increased overseas demand enhanced the economic importance of palm products, and so the Nigerian farmers evolved a system of palm culture which gave them the maximum output with the minimum labour cost.[1]

The system was suitable for working natural palm forests. There were a number of problems, however, on which increased and better productivity depended. Initially, the more accessible palm areas were thoroughly cropped and the immediate rate of expansion depended on the development of transport. In other words, an increase in productivity could only be achieved by extending the system of motor roads or by branch railways. It has already been mentioned that the Nigerian government undertook a number of development projects in connexion with transport in the early years of the twentieth century. Such developments naturally brought more palm areas within cultivation. However, the methods for producing palm oil were extremely wasteful of both produce and labour, and oils of very variable quality were produced. It was, therefore, on the problems of improving the quality of oil while at the same time reducing the product wastage, that attention was urgently required.

The Germans, who were the main consumers of Nigerian palm

[1] Frederick Montague Dyke, *Report on the Oil Palm Industry in British West Africa*, Lagos, Government Printer, 1927.

products early in the twentieth century, took positive steps to secure better production of palm products. In 1901 a prize was awarded by the *Kolonial Wirtschaftlichen Kommittee* of the German *Kolonialgessell-schaft* for a complete set of small machines constructed by the firm of F. Haake in Berlin, and designed to extract palm oil from the palm fruits and also to crack palm nuts to liberate the kernels.[1] The machines were exhibited in Berlin in 1909 and afterwards brought to Nigeria, particularly to the Cameroons, where they were erected for operation. A number of factories were installed with the German machines, and in due course machines designed by other firms, including several machines of British design and construction, found their way to Nigeria. The immediate problem arising from the introduction of oil machines was of ensuring adequate supplies of palm fruits to keep up with the number of existing factories. This in turn depended on the co-operation between the native farmer as the cultivator and collector of palm fruits, and mills erected and operated under the control of European trading concerns in Nigeria. The farmers preferred to keep to their old methods of extracting oil simply because they were familiar, and because they took no account of the value of the time it took to extract oil by the crude indigenous methods.

In the face of new competition from the far Eastern and the Belgian Congo palm products, and under pressure from the joint West African committees of the Liverpool, London and Manchester Chambers of Commerce, the British government set up a committee in 1923 to consider the best means of securing improved and increased production from the West African oil palm.[2] The committee recommended that small factories should be built where efficient methods of extracting oil were to be introduced; it also recommended a better system of oil palm cultivation. These recommendations were accepted, but they were not implemented immediately. The fact that the cocoa industry was not successful in all palm oil producing areas helped to keep up the farmers' interests in palm products. In Eastern Nigeria, where the cocoa culture was less successful, the production of palm oil and palm kernels received

[1] *West Africa*, 22 September 1917, p. 575.
[2] *West Africa, Palm Oil and Palm Kernels. Report of a Committee appointed by the Secretary of State for the Colonies, September 1923, to consider the best means of securing improved and increased production*, Col. no. 10, 1925.

great attention. Even in the South where the cocoa industry was more successful, not all the areas were suitable for cocoa and many farmers had to supplement their earnings with the production of palm oil and palm kernels. The government introduced a number of subsidy schemes to encourage the production of palm oil: one was fixed on a production basis, on the principle that any loss sustained by the factory (oil mill) owners through inadequate supplies of fruits should be made good by the government. This scheme received very little response from both the private enterprises and the farmers. Continuing its policy of 'increased production' the government passed the Cultivated Oil Palm Ordinance in 1935. This provided that if a grower registered his plot with the government and the oil produced by him met the required quality (5 per cent of free fatty acid), he was then to receive a full rebate of the export duty which was in force. The farmer was only allowed to include the oil produced from the registered palms, and if he was unable personally to plant fifteen acres he had to become a member of a palm oil co-operative society.[1] (Registered palms were those from the government experimental farms and supplied to the farmers through the Agricultural Department of the government.) This scheme failed because many of the farmers were unable to produce oil of the requisite standards, as they continued to employ primitive techniques of extracting oil. However, oil production as a whole met the local needs, and there were surpluses for export. Throughout the thirties the government continued its efforts to improve the method of oil extraction. In 1932, the Duchscher press machine, produced by a Luxembourg firm, was introduced into Nigeria.[2] The cost of the machine when first introduced was about £18, which was too high for the Nigerian peasant farmers, with the result that it was not readily adopted. However, a number of native or local authorities in the palm oil producing areas introduced a system whereby they bought the machines from the firm and sold to the farmers on hire purchase. Table 8.1 below shows the number of oil presses in use up to March 1937. It was reported that by 1938 a total of 834 machines were already in the hands of the farmers.

It is important to add that the government encouraged the

[1] M. Perham (ed.), *The Native Economics of Nigeria*, vol. I, p. 235.
[2] *Annual Report on the Agricultural Department, 1932*, Lagos, Government Printer.

TABLE 8.1 *Number of oil presses in use, 1932–7*

Year	Culley, Massa, etc.	Large Duchscher	Small Duchscher	Total
31 December 1932	44	9	5	58
1933	44	22	10	76
1934	50	37	13	100
1935	57	84	39	180
1936	60	205	125	390
31 March 1937	60	253	140	453

Source: *Annual Reports on the Agricultural Department, 1932–7*, Lagos, Government Printer.

establishment of oil palm plantations which were owned and managed by Nigerians. Table 8.2 below shows the areas under oil palm plantation and the number of plantation owners for the period 1928–36. Most of the plantations were found in the Benin

TABLE 8.2 *Oil palm plantations, 1928–36*

Year	Number of owners	Number of acres
31 December 1928	6	21
1929	27	119
1930	53	236
1931	85	352
1932	218	691
1933	382	1,014
1934	704	1,457
1935	1,382	2,498
1936	2,278	4,172

Source: *Annual Reports on the Agricultural Department, 1928–36*, Lagos, Government Printer.

area. There are no production statistics for palm oil and palm kernels in this period. Since local demand for palm kernels was negligible, one can assume that almost its entire production was exported. An estimate of palm oil production is made on table 8.3.

During the second world war the British government encouraged the Nigerian government to produce more palm products for export to Britain and her allies. The Agricultural Department campaigned for greater production.[1] In order to increase production and in support of the British government's policy, the United Africa Company donated 250 handpress oil machines to the Agricultural Department: these were intended for the use of the farmers.

TABLE 8.3   *Palm oil production estimates, and palm oil and palm kernel exports, Nigeria 1900–44 (tons)*

Year	Total production (estimated): Palm oil	Total exports	
		Palm oil	Palm kernels
1900–4	117,358	53,729	120,778
1905–9	115,770	65,177	130,241
1910–14	154,876	77,771	174,236
1915–19	164,060	80,485	184,567
1920–4	180,463	90,352	203,021
1925–9	227,084	124,716	255,469
1930–4	244,070	122,302	274,584
1935–9	296,889	139,000	334,000
1940–4	284,889	134,377	320,613

Notes:

1. Figures averaged for each quinquennium.
2. Palm oil production estimate is based on the assumptions that all palm kernels produced were exported, and that the proportion of palm kernels to palm oil is 9 to 8.

Sources: *Nigerian Handbook, 1936,* and *Nigerian Trade Reports 1939–45,* Lagos, Government Printer.

Increasing numbers of Duchscher presses were also imported and sold by John Holt and the UAC. The increased production of palm products which resulted came from the intensive working of the existing palm trees. The fact that supplies were cut off from capitalized oil palm plantations in Malaya and Sumatra enhanced the importance of the Nigerian palm culture to the British government and its contribution to economic growth in Nigeria.

[1] J. R. Mackie, *Papers on Nigerian Agriculture 1939–1945*: Afr. S. 823 (i), Rhodes House, Oxford.

COCOA[1]

Cocoa was the most revolutionary of exchange cultures in Nigeria. The crop, which was introduced into Nigeria towards the end of the nineteenth century, soon became the main source of money income for most peasant farmers in the South. Cocoa was the first crop in Nigeria to be grown on a plantation system. It was discovered that for cocoa to grow very well, it had to be grown in a reasonably cool area, with sufficient rainfall and sunshine. In addition, adequate space must be allowed between the trees. The methods adopted by farmers for growing cocoa were open to a number of criticisms: plantations were often too thick to allow the crop to flourish reasonably, and little care was generally devoted to measures to protect the trees from diseases.

The economic depression of the late twenties and the early thirties brought a drastic fall in the price of cocoa. This in turn affected the production efforts of the farmers, for many did not consider it worth their while to spend money on improving their farms. Indeed, many cocoa farms were completely neglected by their owners. It was during the depression years that the cocoa industry was hit by another calamity – the swollen shoot disease. Unfortunately, the easiest way for a peasant farmer to store cocoa was to leave it on the trees.[2] When the price of cocoa fell the farmer, hoping for a rise in price, often delayed harvesting until much of his crop had been ruined by black pod disease. The swollen shoot and the black pod diseases which infested Nigerian cocoa from the early thirties onwards first became noticeable in the Ife and Ilesha districts,[3] and can be attributed to the general neglect of cocoa plantations in the depression years. Despite these diseases, and the fact that no immediate steps were taken to get rid of them, cocoa plantation (see table 8.4) in Nigeria in relation to the rest of the world continued to increase. In 1937 Nigeria's share of world production of cocoa was 14 per cent.

The first positive step towards solving the problems of cocoa diseases was made in 1938, when the Agricultural Department of

[1] See R. Galletti *et al.*, *Nigerian Cocoa Farmers*.
[2] *Colonial Annual Reports*, no. 1710, Nigeria, 1934, p. 38.
[3] *Annual Report on the Agricultural Department, 1930*, Lagos, Government Printer.

the Ghana government opened a research station at New Tafo to study them. Nigeria and the other British West African countries relied on the results of this research project until 1944, when the governments of British West Africa, realizing the common problems of cocoa production, decided to pool their resources together to finance a joint research institution and establish the West African Cocoa Research Institute.[1] In the same year a cocoa survey of

TABLE 8.4   *Exports of cocoa,*
1900–44 (tons)

Year	Total cocoa exports
1900–4	305
1905–9	1,167
1910–14	3,857
1915–19	13,887
1920–4	27,276
1925–9	45,483
1930–4	62,978
1935–9	96,000
1940–4	102,379

Note: Figures averaged for each quinquennium.
Sources: *Nigerian Handbook, 1936,* and *Nigerian Trade Reports 1939–45,* Lagos, Government Printer.

Western Nigeria was begun, in order to assess the damage already done by cocoa diseases and to find solutions to the problem thus created.

Another major problem which the cocoa industry faced in Nigeria was that of storage after harvesting.[2] The production of cocoa by peasant farmers necessarily brought with it the problem of collection and storage in central areas from where it could be easily exported. The atmosphere in many central marketing stations is too damp to permit long storage of cocoa without deterioration in

[1] F. M. Bourret, *The Gold Coast 1919–1946,* pp. 178–9.
[2] In Ghana the problem of the storage of cocoa was given great attention: see *Problems Concerning Storage of Cocoa on the Gold Coast. Agricultural Department, Accra,* Accra, Government Printer, 1930. Nigeria drew from the experience of Ghana.

quality. It was realized that the better the preparation of the cocoa beans the longer the period without deterioration in quality. In fact, the Nigerian government introduced grading and inspection systems in order to encourage better quality cocoa. At the Nigerian ports, humidity is low enough to allow the storage of well-prepared cocoa for periods up to fifteen weeks without any serious deterioration in quality. However, long intervals usually elapsed between the harvesting of cocoa and its transportation to the ports. These intervals were the result of a number of intermediate sales and bulk re-drying and re-bagging. It was the common practice for produce buyers to store cocoa under tarpaulins in open spaces. This method was not only unsafe, it usually increased the moisture in the cocoa beans thus making the cocoa mouldy and liable to weevil attack.

COTTON

The Nigerian farmers had been growing cotton for many centuries mainly for local consumption – for the weaving of indigenous cloths. However, the growing of cotton for purely commercial purposes did not begin until the first decade of the twentieth century, when it was encouraged by the British Cotton Growing Association. The history of the BCGA tells the full story of cotton culture in Nigeria during this period, though some trading firms took an interest in its production: for example, Messrs Elder Dempster & Co. brought tons of cotton seeds to Lagos in May 1901, to be distributed to farmers. This company also offered a large reward to the first shipper of 100 tons of cotton, and it tried to engage cotton-growing experts in New Orleans in the United States of America to visit Nigeria and instruct the farmers in the cultivation of cotton.[1] But the efforts of Elder Dempster & Co. were not rewarded; the BCGA was more successful. The BCGA was founded in 1902 with a capital of £50,000, which was increased to £500,000 in 1904.[2] It conducted a number of experiments to discover whether any of the British West African countries could be adapted to cotton growing. The main objective behind such a project was to supply the British market with cotton grown within the British Empire, and thus make Britain independent of America for her raw cotton. A number

[1] *The West African Year Book, 1901*, London, pp. 52–3.
[2] W. H. Himbury, 'Empire Cotton', p. 267, and McPhee, op. cit., p. 44.

of experiments were conducted in Southern and Northern Nigeria, and it was discovered that large areas in Northern Nigeria could be adapted to cotton growing. Indeed, at the initial stages of the BCGA's experiments in Nigeria, numerous plantations were established in Southern Nigeria and cotton ginneries were erected along

TABLE 8.5   *Exports of cotton,*
1900–44 (tons)

Year	Total cotton exports
1900–4	132
1905–9	1,383
1910–14	1,884
1915–19	2,112
1920–4	3,940
1925–9	6,038
1930–4	4,594
1935–9	8,332
1940–4	9,913

Note: Figures averaged for each quinquennium.
Source: *Nigerian Handbook, 1936.*

the railway at Abeokuta, Ibadan, Iwo and Oshogbo. In fact, the Moore Plantations at Ibadan were founded by the BCGA as an experimental farm for cotton growing. The new cocoa culture in Southern Nigeria never gave cotton growing much chance to survive on a large scale. The association soon concentrated its efforts on Northern Nigeria. By 1906 the Chairman was reported as saying:

> We have pursued our enquiries throughout the British Empire and the one place which offers the greatest possibility of providing the millions of bales of cotton which are required is Northern Nigeria, we are absolutely convinced that in Northern Nigeria alone lies the salvation of Lancashire [and the cotton industry]. It is not impossible that at some future date Northern Nigeria will produce at least seven million bales, or sufficient to supply the

whole requirements of Great Britain, and to leave an equal quantity over for other cotton consuming countries.[1]

In their efforts to increase cotton production, the BCGA frequently distributed cotton seeds to farmers.

From 1906 and until the thirties the association engaged in establishing a number of ginneries along the railway lines. Important among the ginnery stations were Ilorin, Zaria, Kano, Kaduna and Sokoto. A new ginnery, with baling press operated by hydraulic power, was introduced which made it possible for bales from Northern Nigeria to be compressed into half their former size, thus facilitating handling in shipping and lessening the cost of freight.

The economic importance of the operations of the BCGA, particularly in Nigeria, lies in the fact that the encouragement of the cotton industry meant the provision of profitable employment for the people in the cotton-growing areas. The farmers were able to add cotton to the list of export 'cash-crops' (see table 8.5) from which they could derive income. In other words, the introduction of cotton helped to diversify agricultural production. The industry also provided additional employment for a number of rich men who engaged in produce-buying for export; it provided freights for the relatively new railway in Northern Nigeria, and cargo for the steamers engaged in international trade. It also supplied one of the most important industries in the United Kingdom with raw materials, thus bringing prosperity to a number of manufacturers.

OTHER PRODUCTS

Some other agricultural products on which the government made efforts to improve production included groundnuts, rice and citrus. Groundnuts were produced mainly in Northern Nigeria.[2] The crop had been grown for hundreds of years for domestic consumption, and it needed just some extra efforts to secure surplus groundnuts for export. In this connexion, the Agricultural Department distributed groundnut seeds free to farmers. However, the groundnut culture had to compete with other cultures, particularly the cotton culture.

[1] *Colonial Annual Reports*, no. 516, Northern Nigeria, 1905–6, p. 65.
[2] Carl K. Eicher and Carl Liedholm (eds), *Growth and Development of the Nigerian Economy*, pp. 30–51.

Nevertheless, increased production was achieved, and this was reflected in the volume exported (see table 8.6).

In 1933 the government invited an Agricultural Officer from Sierra Leone to examine and report on the possibility of growing rice in mangrove swamps in Nigeria, just as it had been successfully done in Sierra Leone. In his report, the officer advised that the first

TABLE 8.6 *Exports of groundnuts,*
1900–44 (tons)

Year	Total groundnuts exports
1900–4	475
1905–9	1,531
1910–14	8,195
1915–19	41,300
1920–4	44,278
1925–9	109,068
1930–4	188,744
1935–9	249,600
1940–4	181,901

Note: Figures averaged for each quinquennium.
Sources: *Nigerian Handbook, 1936*, and *Nigerian Trade Reports 1939–45*, Lagos, Government Printer.

experimental station should be at Warri. As a result, a plot was obtained, and in 1935 the Department of Agriculture experimented with rice growing there and got fairly good results.[1] These encouraged some farmers in the area to take up rice production. However, the increasing home demand for rice did not allow surpluses for export. Early in the thirties, some efforts were also made to develop fruit production in Southern Nigeria. However, the production of fruits and citrus did not succeed beyond meeting local needs, providing very little for export. The production of cocoa, cotton, groundnuts and palm produce, which had already assumed some degree of importance, took most of the efforts of the farmers and thus hindered the production of fruit and citrus, except

[1] *Annual Report on the Agricultural Department, 1935*, Lagos, Government Printer, p. 27.

in the Southern Cameroons where large quantities of bananas were produced and exported to Europe. It must be added that the problem of providing adequate and suitable cool storage accommodation on the voyage to the export markets at a reasonable cost also limited the extent to which fruit and citrus cultivation could be undertaken.[1]

Also in the early thirties, the government encouraged kolanut cultivation in Southern Nigeria, as part of the scheme to help farmers whose cocoa trees had been ruined by the black pod disease. It was also thought that increased cultivation of kolanut trees would go a long way to meeting the increasing home demand for kolanuts, hitherto being met by large imports.[2] The farmers, particularly at Agege, Ijebu-Ode and Abeokuta, responded favourably as more kolanut trees were planted.[3] Increased production in Southern Nigeria was reflected in the volume transported by the Nigerian railway to Northern Nigeria, where demand was highest (see table 7.3).

The production of tobacco was encouraged in Nigeria by the British American Tobacco Company in collaboration with the Department of Agriculture. Even though a number of the farmers in the Western Provinces responded favourably at the initial stage, the cocoa culture which had become important took most of the farmers' efforts and there was little or none left for tobacco.

LIVESTOCK

Livestock could be kept over most of the savannah areas of Nigeria. The most common livestock was cattle. Cattle were not used as farm livestock, as most farm work was done by hand. However, they provided the bulk of meat supplies in Nigeria and some milk was also obtained from them. The prevalence of rinderpest and pleuro-pneumonia (cattle diseases) was, for many years, the greatest obstacle to the development of the cattle-breeding industry in

---

[1] It was discovered that only smaller pineapples than were being produced in Nigeria could be profitably exported: *Annual Report on the Agricultural Department, 1933*, Lagos, Government Printer.

[2] *Colonial Annual Reports*, no. 1710, Nigeria, 1934, p. 42.

[3] *Annual Report on the Agricultural Department, 1932*, Lagos, Government Printer, pp. 35–6.

Nigeria. Each year the diseases took heavy toll of the herds and made impossible the successful rearing of stock. The Nigerian government took steps to combat the menace of these diseases. By 1925 the research laboratory at Vom had successfully produced a reliable anti-rinderpest serum which provided an effective immunity for cattle if properly applied. Rinderpest immunization was, therefore, properly introduced into Nigeria. A veterinary school established in Kano in 1934 provided some training for Nigerians employed at various veterinary inspection stations and at immunization camps.[1] These schemes helped to reduce drastically the incidence of cattle diseases and the consequent loss of cattle.

Livestock population in Nigeria had never been accurately counted. In 1930 an animal census showed that Northern Nigeria had 3 million cattle; 2 million sheep, 5,150,000 goats,[2] 200,000 horses, 550,000 donkeys and 2,500 camels. However, in 1940, an estimate of livestock in Nigeria gave these figures: 5 million cattle, 10 million goats and 4 million sheep.[3] Between 1930 and 1945, Northern Nigeria supplied an annual average of about 100,000 cattle to provide meat in Southern Nigeria.[4]

[1] *Colonial Annual Reports*, no. 1710, Nigeria, 1934, p. 48.
[2] *Colonial Annual Reports*, no. 1569, Nigeria, 1931, p. 28.
[3] Perham (ed.), *Native Economics of Nigeria*, p. 275.
[4] Ibid., p. 277.

9 Modern industrial production

There was no industrial revolution in Nigeria which could be compared, by any standard, with the great industrial revolution in Europe and America. All local industries continued to operate, if only at a much reduced capacity.[1] The increasing importation of foreign goods brought with it new tastes for better, and sometimes cheaper, industrial goods from Europe.[2] For example, the local cloth-weaving industry declined as cheaper and better cotton goods were imported from Britain. Commenting on the impact of foreign goods on local industrial production in Northern Nigeria, Lugard said:

> I foresee with great regret the decline of Kano as a commercial centre when European goods supersede her manufactures, and the exports of other provinces are diverted by more direct routes to the factories of British merchants, instead of passing through the hands of her middlemen and brokers. The cotton of Zaria will then cease to come to the looms of Kano or the skins and hides to her tanneries.[3]

Despite the competition from European goods, a few local industries which catered for special interests, e.g. traditional cloth-weaving, blacksmithing and local breweries, continued to flourish.

The few modern industrial activities which first began in Nigeria were concerned with the primary processing of mineral raw materials. The economy of Nigeria, which remained largely on subsistence level, afforded little or no opportunity for the accumula-

[1] See Chapter 3.
[2] Sir Alan Pim, *The Financial and Economic History of the African Tropical Territories*, p. 57.
[3] *Colonial Annual Reports*, no. 476, Northern Nigeria, 1904, pp. 88–9.

tion of capital which could be invested in modern industrial production. In addition, there was widespread illiteracy. Even with the increased efforts to raise the level of education in the thirties and in the forties, technical education,[1] which is vital to industrial development, received little attention. The early modern industries in Nigeria, therefore, originated from foreign capital and technical knowledge. Foreign capital as well as highly skilled technicians had to be imported at relatively high costs. The growing importance of cash-crops during this period added to the initial problems of industrial development in some areas. At first, many of the people preferred to work comfortably and leisurely on their small farms in order to provide for their basic subsistence, rather than engage in relatively strenuous work in the mines – the only 'big' industry which employed a large labour force. The growth of a money economy, however, soon attracted some labour out of subsistence production, and more people were available for the mines.

THE EXTRACTIVE INDUSTRIES

The growth of the extractive industries in Nigeria was stimulated by foreign interests and concerned the following major minerals: tin, gold, diamonds, coal, salt, petroleum and iron ore. Mining was not foreign to the people of Nigeria as they had engaged in it long before the advent of the British administration.[2] However, in the early years of this century, the Nigerian government began to explore the possibilities of commercial exploitation of the extractive industries. This led to a series of geological surveys conducted by the government in order to locate and to determine the extent of mineral deposits.

Tin

The development of tin mining in Nigeria was slow.[3] As in the other early industries, the indigenous people possessed neither the capital

[1] The first institution which offered any kind of technical education was the Yaba Higher College, which was officially opened in January 1934: *Colonial Annual Reports*, no. 1710, Nigeria, 1934, p. 97.
[2] See Chapter 3.
[3] For a fairly detailed account of the early history of tin-mining in Nigeria, see Perham (ed.), *Mining, Commerce and Finance in Nigeria*.

nor the technical knowledge to develop and modernize the industry[1] – this had to depend on foreign investors. When the Royal Niger Company relinquished its charter in 1900, it concluded an agreement with the British government whereby it retained a half share of the mineral rights over a large area lying to the north of the area between the Niger and Benue rivers. The company then sponsored expeditions to locate a commercial quantity of tin in Bauchi province; the resultant reports confirmed the existence of good quality tin ore in large quantities.[2] In 1906 the Niger Company began its tin-mining operations. However, the tinfield was in an area with inadequate transport facilities, and a number of tin-mining companies had to invest in building roads to link the production centres with the trunk roads[3] and with the railway system. This was one of the very few examples in Nigeria of the development of the infrastructure as a result of industrial development.

The boom in tin mining in Nigeria was begun by the Champion (Nigeria) Tin Fields Company, which abandoned its unproductive gold-prospecting project in Ghana to begin an energetic career dealing with company promotion in London around 1909.[4] Interest increased, and by the end of 1910 over fifty companies had taken up licences to prospect for tin in Nigeria. However, the tin-mining industry had very little hope of survival until the extension of the railway to the mining areas of Bauchi in 1911. By about 1914 a number of good roads had been built by the government in the area,[5] thus lowering transport costs. From 1914 to about 1928 the tin industry enjoyed a considerable prosperity. The general economic depression of the late twenties and the early thirties had its impact on the industry. By 1931 there was great anxiety as to its survival, owing

[1] 'Since the growth of European economic enterprise in Nigeria, native mining has been on the decline because of the *de facto* monopolisation of deposits by Europeans or on account of technical inadequacy or through the competition of European products with the final products of native mineral industries': ibid., p. 4.

[2] W. H. Laws, *Nigerian Tin-Mining Expedition, Canada, 1903*: Afr. S. 888 (1), Rhodes House, Oxford.

[3] It was reported that the Ropp Tin Mines constructed the Bukuru–Ropp road at a cost of £18,000, and that it was taken over by the government without indemnity: *West Africa*, 2 July 1921, p. 569.

[4] McPhee, op. cit., p. 57.

[5] *Nigerian Blue Book*, 1914.

to the accumulation of surplus stocks of the metal during previous years and the general depression in trade. The production of tin became a subject of international control as the result of the economic depression. On 11 July 1929, at a meeting of directors and delegates of tin-producing companies held in London, the Tin Producers Association was formed.[1] At first the association was entirely British, but it was later joined by two great tin-mining and tin-smelting groups in Bolivia, and two great Dutch concerns. The slump which hit the tin-mining industry between 1929 and 1934 forced the association to take steps towards controlling tin prices and production. It first aimed at raising the price of tin by voluntary restriction on the volume of production, but this failed. In April 1930 the association agreed on a new scheme, designed to restrict outputs to 80 per cent of their normal level. In consultation with other tin-producing countries, the International Tin Control Scheme was formed, and charged with imposing compulsory restrictions on tin production. Agreement was reached and each of the producing areas concerned was allocated a standard tonnage based on its contribution to total world output in 1929; thus from 1931, the Nigerian output and export of tin came under an international control. By 1934 the international agreement for the restriction of tin production was renewed, and Nigeria's quota increased. The increasing need for tin during the second world war brought a renewed interest in its mining, and there was a steady increase in its export (see table 9.1).

In 1918 there were 82 tin-mining companies operating in Nigeria with a working capital (i.e. issued capital) of about £2 million.[2] In 1928 the number of companies stood at 83 and their aggregate issued capital was estimated at about £8·4 million (see table 9.2). However, during the depression years the number of companies began to drop, and by 1938 only 31 companies were still operating, with an aggregate issued capital of about £4·9 million. The number of Nigerians employed in the tin mines in 1914 was 21,568.[3] This

[1] For a detailed account of the operations of the Association, see *Papers Relating to the International Tin Control Scheme*, Cmd. 4825, March 1935; and *Papers Relating to the International Tin Control Scheme, Main Control Scheme, Buffer Stock Scheme, Research Scheme*, Cmd. 5879, November 1938.
[2] Allister Macmillan (ed.), *The Red Book of West Africa*, p. 47.
[3] Ibid.

number rose to 28,904 in 1928, but fell drastically during the depression years to 14,911 in 1933. However, by 1938 the number of Nigerians employed had risen to 36,142, following the revival of the industry.[1]

TABLE 9.1   *Exports of tin: selected years, 1907–45*

Year	Volume (tons)	Value (£)
1907	212	25,265
1910	737	77,001
1915	6,535	723,840
1918	8,294	1,770,003
1920	7,913	1,785,724
1925	9,293	1,737,578
1930	12,069	1,373,466
1935	8,949	1,456,753
1940	14,843	2,726,911
1945	15,166	3,129,265

Source: *Nigerian Handbook.*

Gold

Gold was first reported in Nigeria by Dr J. D. Falconer while in charge of the mineral survey of Northern Nigeria instituted by the Colonial Office in 1904.[2] However, the gold-mining industry aroused little commercial interest until many years later.

Gold was discovered at Birnin Gwari in Zaria province in 1911, but it was not until 1921 that any systematic prospecting work was done in this area – by the Naraguta (N) Tin Mines Ltd.[3] Also in 1921, gold was discovered at Rimi in Kano province by Messrs McPharlan and Jeffers, but practically no development was undertaken by the company to determine the value of the deposit.[4] By 1922 gold had been discovered in Nupe, Kotangora, Zaria, Niger and Sokoto

[1] Perham (ed.), *Mining, Commerce and Finance in Nigeria*, pp. 18–19.
[2] *The Nigerian Gold Field*, Sessional Paper no. 17 of 1935.
[3] *Annual Report of the Mines Department, 1932*, Lagos, Government Printer, p. 5.
[4] Ibid., p. 4.

TABLE 9.2 *Number of tin-mining concerns, capital of companies and their relative size*

Fiscal year	Number of individuals	Number of tin companies*	Distribution of companies with issued capital					Estimated aggregate issued capital (£ooo)
			£0–99,999	£100,000–£199,999	£200,000–£299,999	£300,000–£399,999	£400,000 and over	
1926	66	72	45	13	3	3	1	7,059
1927	78	83	48	18	2	3	4	8,359
1928	70	83	48	17	1	4	6	9,881
1929	70	74	36	16	2	3	5	8,701
1930	48	59	25	13	2	3	5	7,598
1931	55	52	24	9	1	1	3	5,539
1932	54	52	27	5	1	1	3	5,300
1933	53	47	25	6	1	1	3	5,182
1934	41	44	23	7	—	—	3	4,881
1935	39	36	24	6	—	—	4	4,742
1936	47	39	23	5	—	—	4	4,635
1937	44	31	22	6	1	—	4	4,69
1938	39	31	18	4	3	—	4	41,856

* A few companies were omitted because their activities and Nigerian assets were negligible in the year in question.
Source: Perham (ed.), *Mining, Commerce and Finance in Nigeria.*

provinces of Northern Nigeria. In the thirties, activities in gold mining increased as a result of the rise in the world price of gold (see table 9.3). For example, at Rimi and Bindim, in the Kano and Sokoto provinces respectively, increased mining activities were undertaken. Again, in the Ilesha and Ile-Ife districts of the Oyo province in Southern Nigeria, a number of Nigerians and Syrians

TABLE 9.3 *Total output of gold, 1914–45*

Fiscal year	Output (oz)	Fiscal year	Output (oz)
1914	350	1930	259
1915	1,396	1931	698
1916	2,422	1932	2,700
1917	2,865	1933	17,715
1918	1,414	1934	37,024
1919	319	1935	38,962
1920	724	1936	23,364
1921	218	1937	26,444
1922	701	1938	24,815
1923	945	1939	25,794
1924	1,441	1940	25,400
1925	1,010	1941	22,636
1926	133	1942	42,410
1927	22	1943	19,928
1928	86	1944	10,709
1929	192	1945	8,021

Sources: *The Nigerian Goldfield*, Sessional Paper no. 17 of 1935;
Perham (ed.), *Mining, Commerce and Finance in Nigeria*;
and *Annual Reports of the Mines Department*.

prospected for gold. In fact, activity in gold mining did much to alleviate the unemployment in the mining industry arising from the restriction of production and export of tin.[1] The average number of Nigerians employed in the gold mines rose from 5,384 in 1933, to 14,235 and 16,694 in 1934 and 1936 respectively. However, by 1938, the number employed had fallen to 8,547.[2] Only a few European

[1] *Annual Report of the Mines Department, 1933*, Lagos, Government Printer, p. 5.
[2] Perham (ed.), *Mining, Commerce and Finance in Nigeria*, pp. 28–9.

companies were involved in prospecting for gold.[1] The main reason for this was that the greater part of the gold output was won from alluvial and detrital deposits by hand methods. It was not worth while for the big European mining companies to sink capital into prospecting for gold which was not a reasonable commercial proposition.

There was a short-lived gold rush at Ilesha and Ile-Ife divisions during the period 1941–2 when Nigeria reached her highest level of gold exports – 42,410 oz troy. In fact, by the end of 1942 the government had prohibited the mining of gold in these areas. The main reason given for the prohibition was to prevent the migration of labour and materials from the tinfields. One can only guess that this was not the only reason, because the tinfields were hundreds of miles away from the gold mines, and there was an adequate supply of labour in the Western Provinces on which the gold mines could draw. It is probably correct to say that tin mining was more important to the war effort than gold mining, hence the action of the government to ensure that there were no distractions from tin production.

Coal

The mining of coal in Nigeria began in 1915 at Udi, near Enugu. The colliery at Udi was administered as part of the Railway Department of the government until 1937, when a separate Colliery Department was established. Most of the coal produced (see table 9.4) was consumed by the Nigerian railway, but a little was exported to Ghana and Sierra Leone.[2] The coal-mining industry in Nigeria had remained, from the very date of its establishment, a government-sponsored project. The extension of the railways to the Eastern Provinces, and to Enugu in particular, helped to reduce the cost of transporting coal from Udi to Lagos and other important railway termini. The coal-mining industry employed a number of Nigerians as clerks, artisans and labourers.

[1] 'During 1938 there were only 19 operating companies which employed on the average a labour force of 130 Africans, while 71 individual operators employed on the average 87 Africans': ibid., p. 30.

[2] Between 1930 and 1937, Nigeria exported an annual average of about 34,687 tons of coal to Ghana: *Annual Reports on the Government Railway and Colliery, 1930–1 to 1936–7.*

TABLE 9.4 *Production and employment in the coal mines, 1924–36*

Fiscal year	Output of coal (tons)	Average number of Nigerians employed (per day)
1924	220,161	n.a.
1925	242,582	1,554
1926	353,274	2,001
1927	345,303	2,401
1928	363,743	2,384
1929	347,115	2,086
1930	327,681	2,108
1931	263,548	1,818
1932	259,860	1,484
1933	234,296	1,537
1934	258,893	1,530
1935	257,287	1,418
1936	310,308	1,634

n.a. Not available.
Source: *Reports on the Government Railway and Colliery, 1924–5 to 1936–7.*

Salt

By about 1905 a salt deposit had been discovered at Muri in Northern Nigeria.[1] After the government had surveyed the extent of the deposit it was considered probable that sufficient salt might be obtained to render Northern Nigeria independent of imported salt. About the same time, salt was being produced at Bauchi; total production there was estimated at about 400 tons per annum in 1906. No further development of the salt industry took place after 1910, because it was considered unprofitable to continue the exploitation of the salt deposits when cheaper salt could be imported.

Petroleum oil

The presence of petroleum oil had been a subject of long speculation in Nigeria. In 1921 two oil exploration licences were issued in the Southern Provinces.[2] The first was to the D'Arcy Exploration

[1] *Colonial Annual Reports*, no. 516, Northern Nigeria, 1905–6, p. 69.
[2] *Annual Report of the Mines Department, 1922*, Lagos, Government Printer, p. 2.

Company (this licence was allowed to lapse in February 1923), for an area west of the river Niger to the Dahomey boundary, and for fifty miles inland from the sea. The second licence was granted to the Whitehall Petroleum Company Limited, for an area which extended from the Akassa mouth of the river Niger, having the Niger as its western boundary, and extending to the eastern boundary of the Cameroons, and from the sea in the south to the 7°N latitude. This latter company allowed its licence to lapse after its geological investigation.

A more serious attempt to explore for oil did not begin until 1937 when the Shell-BP Petroleum Development Company of Nigeria Ltd set up a camp at Owerri in Eastern Nigeria and began some preliminary investigations. The work of the company was interrupted by the outbreak of war, and no significant progress was made until many years later.

Other mineral industries

The other mineral industries in Nigeria included diamonds, silver-lead and columbite. In 1934 a few diamonds were discovered at Sokoto and Zaria provinces.[1] The government decided to retain further prospecting in its own hands, and appointed an agent – the Consolidated African Selection Trust – to investigate the extent of the deposits. However, a year later it was discovered that the diamond deposits were of no commercial importance.[2]

Silver-lead and columbite were also exploited in Nigeria. By 1922 the Union and Rhodesian Trust Ltd had prospected a silver-lead lode near Ameka in Eastern Nigeria.[3] Again a silver-lead industry was operated for a few years at Abakaliki, but production was stopped in 1932. In that year another silver-lead deposit was discovered at Zurak in Adamawa province.[4] This deposit was operated for about five years by the North Nigeria Lead Mines Ltd before it ceased operation in 1937.

Columbite, which is a by-product of tin, developed into an

---

[1] *Annual Report of the Mines Department, 1934*, Lagos, Government Printer, p. 5.
[2] Ibid., *1935*, Lagos, Government Printer, p. 6.
[3] Ibid., *1922*, Lagos, Government Printer, p. 2.
[4] Ibid., *1932*, Lagos, Government Printer, p. 5.

industry of its own after 1933:[1] production of columbite increased steadily, particularly during the second world war. Nigeria was producing the greatest volume of columbite in the world, and the demand for the ore rose as a result of a number of technological developments in Europe and America.

THE NON-EXTRACTIVE INDUSTRIES

The non-extractive industries of this period were concerned with the primary processing of agricultural and forestry materials, including soap, sawmills, breweries and cigarettes. The first company to undertake any organized industrial development (other than minerals) in Nigeria was Miller Brothers. The company established a small sawmill at Koko on the Benin river in 1917, to make use of local timber and supply wood needed for building purposes within the country.[2] The mill was later inherited by the United Africa Company (an amalgamation of Miller Brothers and some other companies), and the site of operation was shifted to Sapele in 1935.

In 1924 Lever Brothers (later Unilever) established the West African Soap Company Ltd at Apapa near Lagos.[3] Among other ingredients the company made use of the locally-produced palm oil; and it specialized in the production of bar soap.

The first cigarette factory was set up at Oshogbo in 1933 by the British American Tobacco Company.[4] At first, cigarettes were manufactured from imported tobacco-leaf as there was no suitable local tobacco. Good quality tobacco was later introduced to the farmers by the company, and, despite the strong challenge of the cocoa industry, some farmers began to grow tobacco, and gradually the quality of locally-grown tobacco-leaf improved.[5] Cigarette production at Oshogbo factory soon proved inadequate, and a new factory was built at Ibadan by the same company in 1936. The

[1] Production of columbite increased from 3·2 tons in 1933 to 67 and 717 tons in 1935 and 1937 respectively.
[2] *UAC Statistical and Economic Review*, no. 10, September 1952, p. 1.
[3] *Colonial Annual Reports*, no. 1315, Nigeria, 1935, p. 18.
[4] Perham (ed.), *Mining, Commerce and Finance in Nigeria*, pp. 51 and 87.
[5] *Colonial Annual Reports*, no. 1763, Nigeria, 1935, pp. 41–2. Earlier experimental work on tobacco growing, particularly at Ilorin, proved unsuccessful: *Annual Report on the Agricultural Department, 1923.*

decision to remove the operations of the company to Ibadan was influenced by the demand for labour in the bigger factory and the enlarged market which the big city of Ibadan offered. The source of power was not considered because there was no electricity in either Oshogbo or Ibadan at that time.

10   Money, currency and banking

MONEY AND CURRENCY[1]

In 1900 Nigeria had no generally accepted currency. A number of foreign coins, including gold and silver sterling, American doubloons, French franc pieces and some locally-adopted commodity-currencies such as cowries, manillas and gold dust were in circulation. In fact, in many areas gin was not used merely for drinking but was employed as a substitute for currency, and large quantities were stored as accumulated wealth. In most parts of the interior, where people were not used to foreign coins, the British coins which the government tried to popularize were regarded with suspicion, and either did not pass current at all or only passed at a depreciated rate. Most exchanges were conducted by the barter system, and for various reasons gin furnished the most convenient standard of value. Its value at a given moment was pretty well ascertained, and as the policy of the government at that time was to increase the duty on gin and thereby increase its retail price, it formed a medium of exchange of which the tendency was to appreciate rather than to depreciate.

A number of measures were taken to control the use of commodity-currencies. In 1902 a government proclamation fixed prices in sterling for manillas and Maria Theresa dollars, and prohibited their further importation. It was much easier for the Nigerian government to control the use of commodity-currencies and foreign coins in areas, particularly along the coast, where people

[1] For a detailed study of money and banking in Nigeria, see R. O. Ekundare, *The Economics of Modern Banking in Nigeria*, University of Durham MA thesis (unpublished), 1959; W. T. Newlyn and D. C. Rowan, *Money and Banking in British Colonial Africa*; and Charles V. Brown, *The Nigerian Banking System*.

adapted themselves more quickly to the use of British coins, but the problem of manillas and of some other commodity-currencies and foreign coins remained to be solved. In 1903 the British government introduced a bronze coinage into Nigeria,[1] but the people showed little inclination for its use since the farthing, which was the smallest unit, was considered too large to act as the smallest unit in Nigeria.

In order to solve the coin currency problems, Lugard proposed in 1905 that a new coinage, common to Southern and Northern Nigeria, be introduced. This was to consist of two denominations, one being one-tenth of a shilling and the other one-hundredth, with an inscription in English on the face and in Arabic on the obverse. The coins were to have circular holes in the centre for stringing, just like the cowries, and were to be without any pictorial design, because of what he called 'the Mohammedan prejudice in Northern Nigeria'.[2] Lugard believed that such coins would easily and speedily oust the commodity-currencies. This proposal did not meet with the complete approval of the colonial government, but some of Lugard's ideas were later adopted.

A more practical step was taken by the government in 1908, when a new local coinage was introduced, consisting of a penny and a tenth of a penny; all had holes in the centre, thereby meeting the local need of the people, who strung the coins together in the same fashion as the cowries. The step marked the first major success for the government in introducing a coinage system. The new coins were minted in the Royal Mint in England; the penny was minted in nickel bronze, and the tenth of a penny was either in nickel bronze or aluminium. In the early stages of the system the government was the greatest importer of coins, which were used for the payment of official salaries and for the wages of indigenous servants employed on government public works.

The first step towards introducing paper money was taken in 1907, when the government announced its plan to introduce paper currency into the country. No thing was done to implement it, but the mere announcement of the plan brought some interesting comments and arguments among foreign traders and businessmen.[3]

[1] McPhee, op. cit., p. 238.
[2] *Colonial Annual Reports*, no. 516, Nigeria, 1905–6, p. 62.
[3] *Lagos Customs and Trade Journal*, 3 July 1911.

Some foreign traders objected strongly on the grounds that the lowest denomination of notes proposed, 10*s.*, was much too high. It was argued that if silver coins of 2*s.* (the highest denomination coin) had no general circulation, except at a few European centres, how much less a paper currency of a higher value. It was contended, therefore, that such paper currency would be useless for general commercial transactions with indigenous people. Other objections were that notes circulating freely from hand to hand in a hot moist climate would prove active sources for the dissemination of the germs of contagious diseases; the notes would not be readily convertible into silver at any place other than that of issue, and would obviously be exchanged at a discount; and notes of great value would, if lost, result in great financial loss to the person holding them.

Two of the points raised above were relevant to the immediate commercial needs of the country. A currency note had no value to the indigenous people, since its intrinsic value is always less than its face value. Also, the use of silver coins had gradually gained popularity among the people in some areas, consequently the tendency would be to exchange silver coins for notes at a discount in these areas. In fact, in some areas coins were still not accepted as money.[1] The sanitary argument was quite ridiculous. The question of losing currency notes was a personal matter, and had nothing to do with the national interest. Despite these objections, many traders favoured the plan to introduce a paper currency since it would provide a substitute to the cumbrous and bulky metals. However, it became clear that in order to achieve rapid economic progress a new and generally acceptable modern currency system was needed in Nigeria.

In 1911, therefore, the British government re-opened the issue of creating a separate currency for her West African colonies by appointing a committee under the chairmanship of Lord Emmott.[2] The committee was to inquire into matters affecting the currency of the British West African colonies and protectorates, and it submitted

---

[1] The District Commissioner for Aba, reporting in 1912, said, 'The nickel coinage does not circulate and is not regarded as money, the natives calling the coins buttons': *Lagos Customs and Trade Journal*, 17 July 1912.

[2] A. G. Hopkins, 'The Creation of a Colonial Monetary System: The Origins of the West African Currency Board'.

its report in October 1912.[1] It recommended the discontinuation of
the existing monetary system in West Africa, in favour of a new
local currency based upon a reserve of gold and securities held in
London under the control of a West African Currency Board. The
board was to be responsible for the supply of currency, and the
holders of such currency notes should have the right to tender them
in West Africa for conversion into sterling. It was also recommended
that the resources and credits of the West African governments
should be the final securities for the discharge of the currency board's
obligations. In order to help the new currency system, the Royal Mint
in England guaranteed the annual absorption of a certain amount of
sterling silver already in circulation; but in the case of any excess over
the agreed amount, the currency board was made responsible for
conversion. The committee also recommended that the seignorage
profits should be put in reserve in the early stages of the board's
operations, in order to provide adequate reserve against the currency
issued. A 100 per cent reserve ratio was recommended for some time
for the new currency system, but the possibility of a fiduciary issue
at a later date was not excluded.

Following these recommendations, the West African Currency
Board was established in November 1912, with its headquarters in
London. The board was to perform a number of functions, including
controlling the supply of currency and ensuring that the currency
was maintained in satisfactory condition; watching over the
interests of the constituent territories so far as currency was concerned; and making all necessary arrangements for the minting of
any special coins authorized for circulation in West Africa.

Between 1912 and 1916 the currency board was mainly concerned
with the supply of silver coins imported from England. The board
created in West Africa a machinery necessary for the proper
management of the new silver coinage, and took steps to secure the
convertibility of the silver into gold. This was done by establishing
one centre in each of the West African countries, where holders of
silver coins were given the legal right to tender them in West Africa
for conversion into gold in London, at a specified rate of exchange
not exceeding the cost of sending specie from West Africa to

[1] *Report of Departmental Committee appointed to inquire into matters affecting the
Currency of the British West African Colonies and Protectorates*, Cmd. 6426,
HMSO, 1912. *Minutes of Evidence*, Cmd. 6427, HMSO, 1912.

London. The Bank of British West Africa[1] was appointed the sole agent of the currency board in West Africa. The British silver coins, which were already in circulation, were gradually withdrawn and replaced by the new West African coins.

The West African governments faced a new and common problem after the new coins had been introduced. People in most areas melted them down, and there was a general hoarding of silver coins. The melted silver was used in manufacturing ornaments such as earrings and necklaces. In view of this, the currency board decided in 1920 to replace the silver coins by alloy coins. Those were of the same denominations (2s., 1s., 6d. and 3d.) as the coins which they replaced. The alloy coinage contained copper, tin and zinc, having the same weight as the silver coins. The importation of silver coins diminished considerably after 1920, and in 1930 it stopped altogether.

No West African currency notes were issued until 1916, when notes of the denominations £5, £1, 10s., 2s. and 1s. were introduced.[2] By ordinances, these notes were made unlimited legal tender in all the West African countries. Notes of small denominations – 2s. and 1s. – were issued because of a shortage in coinage metals. The shortage of coins affected commercial activities by reducing the number of small transactions normally undertaken by the people. At first the use of currency notes was not popular with the public or the trading firms, which considered the denominations too high for local transactions. The hoarding of coins continued, and in many parts of West Africa it was quite usual to exchange a £1 currency note for 17s. or less in coins. The West African currency notes of the denominations of £5, 2s. and 1s. were withdrawn from circulation in 1931. Despite the issue of coins and currency notes by the currency board, commodity-currencies and foreign coins continued to circulate in some parts of Nigeria. The manilla, which after 1911 was no longer a legal tender, continued in circulation in the thickly-populated palm oil belt of South-Eastern Nigeria. Until early in the 1930s, some British coins and currency notes continued to circulate in Nigeria. However, the West African Currency Board's notes and

[1] For the early history of the BBWA, see Chapter 5.

[2] 'The first consignment of West Africa's own notes was despatched to Lagos on June 14th, 1916. This date may hereafter prove not the least important in the history of West Africa, marking as it does the dawn of a new era in commercial life': *West Africa*, 3 February 1917.

coins in circulation increased steadily (see table 10.1). The currency board was responsible for implementing the various defence (finance) regulations which operated during the period of the second world war, and included the operation of an exchange control, and the saving of hard currencies and gold.

BANKING

By 1900 there were two commercial banks in Nigeria: the BBWA, established in 1894 – a foreign bank – and the Bank of Nigeria, which started business in 1899. The business of the Bank of Nigeria expanded rapidly and branches were established at Lagos, Burutu, Onitsha, Calabar, Lokoja, Jebba and Zungeru. In addition to these branches, it had agencies in many parts of the country. The bank received the support of a good number of indigenous traders, and also acted as the bankers to the Southern Nigerian government railway and the Northern Nigeria government. However, the BBWA was the stronger of the two banks, and it exercised a great deal of banking monopoly. In fact, the monopoly of the banking business of the BBWA in Nigeria was completed when, in 1912, it swallowed up its only rival. The purchase of the Bank of Nigeria was not fully disclosed, but it was known that it involved cash transactions which had no effect on the capital of the BBWA.[1]

The next commercial bank to be established in Nigeria was the Anglo-African Bank, which started business in 1901. The bank established three branches in Nigeria – at Old Calabar, Burutu and Lokoja.[2] Very little is known about this bank, which ceased to operate after a few years.

The complete banking monopoly of the BBWA came to an end in 1917, when the Colonial Bank established a branch in Nigeria. The Colonial Bank was first incorporated in 1836, to operate in the West Indies and in British Guiana (now Guyana), but in 1917 it was granted a charter by the British government to carry on its business in any part of the world. The Colonial Bank later adopted the name Barclays Bank (Dominion, Colonial and Overseas, Ltd). However, by 1917 the BBWA had already expanded its business in Nigeria: for example it had about fourteen branch offices in the country. The

[1] *Lagos Customs and Trade Journal*, vol. II, 17 January 1912.
[2] *Colonial Annual Reports*, no. 409, Northern Nigeria, 1902, p. 85.

BBWA and Barclays Bank were the only two commercial banks operating in Nigeria until the early thirties. There was no law prohibiting the establishment of branch banks, consequently they were able to establish a few branches in some important centres of the country. In 1920 the BBWA and Barclays Bank had fourteen and nine bank branch offices respectively in Nigeria.[1] Interest in indigenous commercial banking began in 1929 when the Industrial and Commercial Bank was established;[2] but this bank had an anaemic existence and went into voluntary liquidation in 1930. Its failure caused much distress in Ibadan and the neighbouring district where it had its largest customers,[3] and was attributed by the promoters of the bank to the policy of the expatriate or foreign banks (the BBWA and Barclays Bank), which, it was alleged, was to crush any indigenous banking business. Not much is known about the activities of the bank during its short life, but it is believed that the causes of its liquidation were accounting incompetence and mismanagement. It must be added that the economic depression of that period, which resulted in the reduction of commercial activity, contributed to the failure. In 1931 another indigenous bank was established in Nigeria: the Nigerian Mercantile Bank.[4] Its promoters included a few of the former directors of the Industrial and Commercial Bank. By 1932 it had branch offices at Lagos and Aba; but in 1936, after about five years of unprofitable business, the Mercantile Bank went into voluntary liquidation.

In February 1933, during the life of the Mercantile Bank, the National Bank of Nigeria Ltd was established, and incorporated as a public company.[5] In September of the same year another private company, the Mutual Aids Society, was also incorporated. These two companies were closely linked together. The Mutual Aids Society was founded for the main purpose of running the business of money lending, as the company was registered under the Money Lenders Ordinance of 1929. Three directors of the Nigerian Mercantile Bank were among the promoters of these two new companies. The

[1] *Nigerian Blue Book*, 1920.
[2] Newlyn and Rowan, op. cit., pp. 97–9.
[3] *Colonial Annual Reports*, no. 1569, Nigeria, 1931, p. 62.
[4] *Colonial Annual Reports*, no. 1625, Nigeria, 1932, p. 60.
[5] *Colonial Annual Reports*, no. 1710, Nigeria, 1934, p. 74. Newlyn and Rowan, op. cit., pp. 99–100.

National Bank of Nigeria Ltd operated successfully, despite the allegation that the expatriate banks wanted to destroy the indigenous banking business. At an early stage of its existence the bank faced the problem of inadequate patronage, but this was soon overcome.

During this period there was no central bank in Nigeria. The West African Currency Board did not function as a central bank as it

TABLE 10.1　*Money in circulation: selected years, 1922–45 (£000)*

Year ending 31 March	Silver coins	Alloy coins	Nickel and bronze coins	Currency notes	Total money
1922	n.a.	n.a.	n.a.	n.a.	5,832
1923	2,410	2,174	382	20	4,986
1924	1,667	3,699	361	100	5,827
1925	1,247	5,359	370	100	7,076
1930	149	5,444	447	n.a.	n.a.
1939	—	4,733	874	250	5,857
1940	—	4,289	1,031	228	5,548
1941	—	4,589	1,183	228	6,060
1942	—	5,483	1,440	530	7,453
1943	—	8,378	1,590	1,441	11,409
1944	—	10,152	1,756	1,606	13,514
1945	—	11,208	1,902	2,276	15,386

n.a. Not available.
Sources: *Treasurer's Report, Nigeria 1922–30*, Lagos, Government Printer, and *Colonial Annual Reports*, Nigeria, 1948.

merely helped to convert West African coins and notes on demand into sterling balances in London. The board's main function, therefore, was to supply notes and currencies to the West African countries.

The commercial banks carried on 'ordinary banking business'. The existence of indigenous banks in Nigeria can be attributed to a number of reasons: first, the few Nigerian businessmen who were rich enough took the initiative to venture into the banking business; secondly, some of these businessmen saw the establishment of indigenous banks as a direct challenge to the banking monopoly of the expatriate banks, which, it was alleged, were discriminating in granting credit facilities to indigenous businessmen; thirdly, it was thought that the indigenous banks would relax the conditions of granting credit by relying on personal knowledge rather than by providing adequate securities for loans.

There was no banking law in Nigeria during this period, hence the government had no direct control on the operations of the commercial banks. The banking public was not protected against any fraudulent banking practices.

TABLE 10.2a   *Liabilities of principal banks, 1943–5 (£000)*

Year ending 31 December	Deposits				Other liabilities	Total
	Demand	Time	Savings Bank	Total		
1943	6,138	1,363	673	8,174	817	8,991
1944	7,267	1,759	840	9,866	635	10,501
1945	9,033	1,846	1,034	11,913	872	12,785

Source: *Digest of Statistics*, vol. 7, no. 4 (October 1958), Lagos, Government Printer.

TABLE 10.2b   *Assets of principal banks, 1943–5 (£000)*

Year ending 31 December	Cash	Balance due by other banks		Loans and advances	Investments			Other assets	Total
		Nigeria	Abroad		Nigeria	Other	Total		
1943	889	497	7,126	198	13	20	33	248	8,991
1944	1,074	267	8,547	334	16	30	46	233	10,501
1945	1,016	340	10,427	500	8	30	38	464	12,785

Source: *Digest of Statistics*, vol. 7, no. 4 (October 1958), Lagos, Government Printer.

The expatriate banks, which were the major commercial banks, did not publish any separate accounts of their operations in Nigeria. Indeed, it was difficult to obtain information about their activities.[1] The available published accounts of such banks relate to their overall banking operations in Nigeria and other countries. The first set of commercial banking statistics was published by the government in 1943 (see tables 10.2a and 10.2b). The liabilities of the commercial banks showed that demand deposits represented an annual average of 74·5 per cent of total bank deposits. This meant that the majority

[1] Perham (ed.), *Mining, Commerce and Finance in Nigeria*, p. 185.

of those who patronized the banks did so in order to find a safer place for their money. Only the few educated Nigerians and those engaged in trade on a large scale realized the value of banking: most of the peasants still believed in burying their wealth. The assets of the commercial banks also showed that loans and advances accounted for an annual average of 3·1 per cent of total assets. Most of the banks' assets were held in overseas bank balances. This indicates that the activities of the banks were connected with foreign trade, which was dominated by the expatriate firms. Apart from the National Bank of Nigeria, the commercial banks did very little to help indigenous businessmen. This was probably understandable because the foreign banks possessed very little information, if any, about their credit-worthiness. It was also difficult for most Nigerians to obtain financial help from the banks because they possessed very little 'acceptable' security.

11   Foreign trade

The rapid growth of Nigeria's foreign trade between 1900 and 1945 was made possible by a number of contributory factors. The establishment of peace and a stable government throughout the country contributed towards the growth of commercial activities. The protection offered by the government to the people and their property was necessary if private enterprise was to operate effectively.

One of the main features of the economic growth during this period was the extension and improvement of communications and means of transport, which in turn helped trade to expand, as more areas were linked with principal commercial centres. Farmers found it easier to transport their products, and imported goods reached more markets. By the mid-thirties, when major development projects on transport and communication had been completed, the average distance of a farm from main transport lines had been considerably reduced in many areas (see table 11.1).

The introduction of a proper currency alleviated the problems of exchange. The adoption of an acceptable and uniform currency increased the volume of commercial transactions. Commercial banks were able to function more effectively, and business firms employed their services, particularly for foreign trade transactions.

THE EXPORT TRADE

Farmers were encouraged to grow some of the major primary products which were needed in Europe, e.g. cocoa, cotton, rubber and groundnuts. In some areas growing cash-crops was much easier than in others, because of the competition offered by the growing of local products for foodstuffs. In areas where both export crops and local products could be grown, this phenomenon was significant, and the decision about which to grow depended largely on the relative prices of export products and the local products. Some Nigerian farmers became conscious of commercial farming

TABLE 11.1 *Mean minimum distance of farms from metalled roads, navigable waterways and railways*

Province	Area of province (square miles)	Mileage of metalled roads	Mileage of navigable waterways	Mileage of railways	Total mileage of main transport lines	Mean minimum distance from main transport lines*
Colony	1,381	55·75	142	14	211·75	1·9
Abeokuta	4,266	334·50	—	116	450·50	2·8
Benin	8,622	955·00	90	—	1,045·00	2·4
Calabar	6,331	679·50	433	—	1,112·50	1·7
Cameroons	16,581	330·00	34	—	464·00	10·6
Ijebu	2,456	275·00	10	—	285·00	2·6
Ogoja	7,529	166·00	217	—	383·00	5·8
Ondo	8,211	405·75	62	—	467·75	5·2
Onitsha	4,937	702·00	32	90	824·00	1·8
Owerri	10,374	1,095·25	616	109	1,820·25	1·7
Oyo	14,216	699·00	—	114	783·00	5·4
Warri	5,987	328·00	347	—	675·00	2·6
Adamawa	35,001	425·00	295	—	720·00	14·4
Bauchi	25,977	1,130·50	—	—	1,130·50	6·8
Benue	28,082	313·00	210	117	700·00	11·9
Bornu	45,900	621·00	—	6	627·00	21·7
Ilorin	18,095	301·50	114	88	503·50	10·6
Kabba	10,577	534·00	117	—	711·00	4·4
Kano	17,602	936·00	—	182	1,118·00	4·7
Niger	25,349	1,315·00	121	328	1,764·00	4·3
Plateau	10,977	545·25	—	168	713·25	4·6
Sokoto	39,940	1,142·75	135	66	1,343·75	8·8
Zaria	24,278	1,358·75	—	432	1,790·75	4·0

* Assumes peripheral roads of one-quarter the internal road system.
Note: 'Navigable' waterways means those waterways which can be navigated by a mechanically-propelled craft.
Source: *An Economic Survey of the Colonial Empire, 1932*.

and were largely influenced by the profit-maximizing motive. It became noticeable in many areas that when the export prices rose above the prices of local foodstuffs, the farmers would concentrate on export production, and when the reverse was the case they

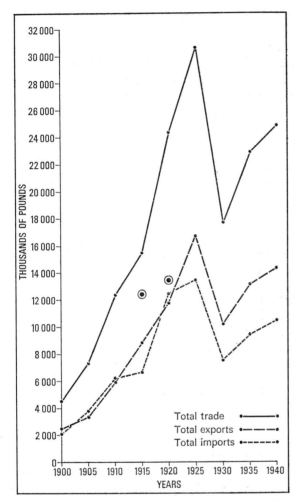

8 Exports and imports, 1900–44

concentrated on home or domestic products. This was clearly indicated as early as 1911 by a report of E. D. Morel in which he said: 'Everywhere the price of foodstuffs is growing. . . . In one part of the Niger province the native farmer now reckons upon getting, I was in formed, £8 to £10 per acre out of yams (local foodstuff). Cotton (which was for export) at 1*d.* per lb. would bring

him £3 to £4.'[1] Also, in an effort to increase export production
during the second world war, it was confirmed that 'in the cases of
palm oil, palm kernels and groundnuts . . . the years of maximum
exports are years of higher prices . . . With a fall in price exports
immediately fell off because it became uneconomic at the ruling
price to transport groundnuts (and other agricultural products) to
railing points from the outlying producing areas.'[2] Under normal
conditions, therefore, supplies responded to price changes.[3]

In some areas, however, export production was not so influenced.
For example, the cocoa culture in the South did not compete
significantly with the production of local foodstuffs. It usually took
five years from the planting of a cocoa tree for it to bear fruit;
consequently the cultivation of local crops continued during the
period. In fact, after a cocoa plantation was fully under production,
local products were grown along with cocoa.

The export trade of Nigeria provided a fitting example of Adam
Smith's argument for international trade. Adam Smith wrote that

> Between whatever places foreign trade is carried on, they all of
> them derive two distinct benefits from it. It carries out that surplus
> part of the produce of their land and labour for which there is no
> demand among them, and brings back in return for it something
> also for which there is demand. It gives a value to their super-
> fluities, by exchanging them for something also, which may
> satisfy a part of their wants, and increase their enjoyments. . . .[4]

The rapid rate of expansion in the export trade of Nigeria was not
due to any changes in the techniques of production which could
have been reflected in a higher productivity.[5] The farmers clung to
the traditional methods of production, and the increases in export
production were achieved merely by bringing more land, hitherto
unused, under cultivation.

[1] *Lagos Customs and Trade Journal*, September 1911, quoting an article written
in the *Manchester Guardian* of 16 August 1911.
[2] J. R. Mackie, *Papers on Nigerian Agriculture 1939–1945*: Afr. S. 823 (i),
Rhodes House, Oxford.
[3] F. J. Pedler, *Economic Geography of West Africa*, p. 60.
[4] A. Smith, *Wealth of Nations*, vol. 1, p. 392.
[5] H. Myint, 'The "Classical Theory" of International Trade and the Under-
developed Countries', p. 324; and Helleiner, op. cit., pp. 44–6.

There were no local demands for cocoa, and the local demands that existed for palm kernels were not of such substantial volume as to affect the size of export. The total production of these products constituted direct surpluses for export. Cotton, groundnuts and palm oil enjoyed very high local demands, and it was in regard to these crops that the surplus argument became more applicable. In order to provide more cotton and groundnuts, more land had to be brought under cultivation, and in order to increase the volume of palm oil production, more attention had to be paid to the wild palm, which had been left unattended for many decades. The farmers continued their old techniques of production, so that there was no question of increasing physical productivity brought about by, say, the introduction of mechanization.[1] With the exception of gold, for which there was some local demand, the entire mineral export products of Nigeria constituted direct surpluses. The surplus nature of the export trade of Nigeria was strengthened by the fact that the country maintained self-sufficiency in basic food crops during this period. International trade did not force the farmers to abandon production for local needs. There were occasional shortages of local crops but these were quickly corrected. Increases in the agricultural labour force were easily achieved, by moving the 'family' labour from purely subsistence production to partly subsistence and partly export production.

The export drive in Nigeria was based on two major factors: first, the British government was determined to make Nigeria one of the main sources of some basic raw materials which were needed in the British factories, and on which the industrial prosperity of Britain partly depended; and secondly, in a developing country like Nigeria where revenues from income tax were not substantial enough to finance any big development projects, revenues from customs duties formed the major source of funds from which to finance economic and social development projects.[2] To the individual farmer, production for export was accepted as an additional cash-raising exercise. A farmer could plant cocoa trees in order to obtain cash, and he could decide to collect more palm fruits than he usually did in order to get more cash from the sale of his palm produce. All

[1] The problem of mechanization was discussed in the *Report of the West African Oilseed Mission*, Col. no. 224, HMSO, 1948.
[2] See Chapter 6.

these could be achieved without any reduction in the production of local foodstuffs. The Nigerian farmers, therefore, regarded the major agricultural export products as 'cash-crops', i.e. the crops that needed to be produced solely for making money. Many farmers, however, developed such a casual attitude to export production that very few of them ever regarded farming as a business. The incomes derived from the sale of export crops were often lavished in ostentatious ceremonies, e.g. marriages, funerals and naming and baptismal ceremonies. In fact, the casual attitude towards export production forced the government to introduce the grading and inspection systems for export crops.[1] The improvements thus achieved in quality did not indicate any change in the traditional techniques and system of production as such, but were merely the result of taking more time and care in the preparation of the crops.

Before 1913 there were no restrictions on the export trade of Nigeria. The United Kingdom was the main consumer of the palm oil produced, buying a yearly average of about 50 per cent of the total export of palm oil. The bulk of the palm kernels went to Germany, who consumed more than 70 per cent of the annual exports. Nigerian cotton was exported to the United Kingdom – a fitting reward for the British Cotton Growing Association, which invested heavily in cotton-growing in Nigeria.[2] The United Kingdom was the main consumer of Nigerian cocoa, although demand gradually built up from the United States of America. The United Kingdom was also the main consumer of Nigerian tin, columbite and gold.

During the first world war, the export trade of Nigeria continued to grow. The United Kingdom's share in it increased considerably as exports to Germany, her chief rival, ceased; and in spite of increased exports to France and America, she continued to dominate in this sphere. The British government realized the great economic benefit which attended the virtual control of the major export products of Nigeria and the other British West African countries, and considered whether it was wise economically to continue a free trade policy, whereby trade with other countries was unrestricted. The West African Produce Committee was appointed in 1916 to look into the pattern of the export trade of West Africa, and to make

[1] Produce inspection for palm oil, palm kernels and cocoa began in 1911.
[2] *Colonial Annual Reports*, no. 437, Northern Nigeria, 1903, p. 133.

recommendations as to how best such trade could be prosecuted.[1] As a result of this investigation, export duties on palm products were introduced.[2] In 1917, however, there was a total prohibition of the export of palm oil from Nigeria except to the United Kingdom, and differentiated export duties were introduced in respect of palm kernels. The Governor-General of Nigeria, addressing the Legislative Council in 1917, explained the export restrictions this way: 'The policy mainly was to divert the trade, especially palm products, from Germany to Britain and her Allies. As a result it was proposed that an export duty of £2 per ton be levied on kernels at the port of export, but a refund should be made on production of a crusher's certificate in England or elsewhere in the Empire.'[3] The issue of West African Trade was also raised in the House of Commons in London: Colonel Wedgwood asked[4] 'whether the governors of the West African Dependencies have been required to prohibit the exports of palm kernels to destinations other than Britain and whether commodities other than palm kernels have been included in these prohibitions, and if so, upon what scale?' The Parliamentary Under-Secretary of State for the Colonies, replying to the question, said

> Yes . . . in order to secure an adequate supply of oil-producing seeds and their products, including margarine, for the next few months the governments [of West Africa] have been requested to prohibit the exportation to destinations outside the British Empire of palm kernels, groundnuts and copra. Licences will be granted to exporters allowing them to export to any lawful destination certain proportions of the commodities mentioned. . . .[5]

It was also asked whether any compensation would be paid to the native producers for the restriction of the markets in which they might sell. To this question, the Under-Secretary replied 'I do not understand that the native producers will lose in any way'. The prohibition of the export of palm products to destinations outside the British Empire was removed immediately after the war, only to be reimposed in 1920 in order to raise additional revenue.

[1] Cmd. 8247 of 1916, and *85 House of Commons Debate*, Cols. 587–93.
[2] The Customs Tariff (Export) Ordinance no. 46 of 1916.
[3] *West Africa*, 31 March 1917: report from the Nigerian Legislative Council.
[4] *120 House of Commons Debate*, Col. 668, 29 October 1919.
[5] Ibid.

In 1922 the British government appointed a Committee on Trade and Taxation for British West Africa to report on the question of the maintenance of export duties on produce and on other matters affecting trade. It examined in detail the tax structure and the pattern of trade in West Africa, and concluded that export duties did not in practice check production, because the high prices for export products which existed at the period had neutralized the likely reduction in production. However, the committee recognized that the danger of these export duties handicapping West African produce, *vis-à-vis* its competitors in the world's markets, was a matter which the government concerned must watch with great care.[1]

While Britain was successful in diverting the trade in palm products to herself, other Nigerian customers were forced to find alternative sources of supply for these products. Germany and the United States of America, for example, increased their home production of vegetable and animal fats; and in order to be less dependent on imported oil, both countries restricted the production of margarine, and duties were imposed on imported oil. The revenue from such duties was used principally to subsidize home production of oil. Holland, another important consumer of Nigerian oil, adopted a similar policy.

Besides the restrictions on the exports of some Nigerian commodities, the export trade faced another big problem, that of price fluctuations. Immediately after the first world war it seemed that economic conditions would brighten up, as industrial activity in Europe increased and prices soared. Then in 1920 and 1921 the 'short' boom collapsed, and prices fell with demoralizing swiftness. The fall in prices and the depression which characterized the twenties and the early thirties were neither continuous nor evenly distributed over the different export commodities. Towards the end of the twenties, export prices rose and there was a token revival of economic activity. However, the severest effect of the depression was felt in the early thirties.

The value of the total exports fell from £17 million in 1928 to approximately £9 million in 1934 (see figure 8). The large decrease in export values was primarily due to poor prices paid for the chief domestic export products. For example, 49,000 tons of cocoa valued

[1] *Report of a Committee on Trade and Taxation for British West Africa*, Cmd. 1600, HMSO.

at £2,421,000 were exported in 1928; but in 1934, with an increased export tonnage of 78,000, the value fell to £1,290,000. Also in 1928, 247,000 tons of palm kernels were exported for the total value of £4,423,000; whereas an increased volume of export of 289,000 tons in 1934 could only fetch £1·6 million. The export of tin fell from 15,070 tons valued at £2.2 million in 1928, to 7,528 tons valued at £1·2 million in 1934. There was also a fall in the physical production

TABLE 11.2   *Exports of principal products, 1928–34*

Year	Cocoa		Palm oil		Palm kernels	
	('ooo tons)	*(£ooo)*	*('ooo tons)*	*(£ooo)*	*('ooo tons)*	*(£ooo)*
1928	49	2,421	127	3,751	247	4,423
1929	55	2,306	132	3,767	251	4,265
1930	52	1,756	136	3,250	260	3,679
1931	53	1,093	118	1,542	254	2,132
1932	71	1,461	116	1,514	309	2,696
1933	61	1,144	128	1,384	260	1,899
1934	68	1,290	113	885	287	1,591

Sources: *Colonial Annual Reports*, Nigeria.

of tin as a result of the quota system introduced by the International Tin Control Scheme.[1] It is important to point out that during and after the depression years export duties were in force in Nigeria on the major export commodities.

The bulk of the population were farmers, and most other people who were not directly involved in practical agriculture earned their incomes from agricultural production, either as produce buyers or motor transport magnates, the latter being responsible for transporting export products from the local markets to the shipping centres on the coast. Fluctuations in the prices of the export products (the cash-crops), therefore, had far-reaching effects on the export trade and the incomes of large numbers of Nigerians.

Violent fluctuations in local prices, panic rumours and unsatisfactory relations between the farmers and the produce buyers, were of too frequent occurrence in the case of the major export crops. The produce buyers, which included the European firms, Lebanese,

[1] See Chapter 9.

Syrians and indigenous people, operated through indigenous middlemen. The middleman was a keen exploiter of the average farmer's ignorance about the market conditions for the main export crops. He also exploited the readiness of the farmer to sell his crop in advance at low prices in order to get ready cash. The eagerness of the farmers to obtain cash was not motivated by any business decision; rather, the bulk of the cash obtained was lavished ostentatiously on social ceremonies. Indebtedness by the farmers to middlemen was widespread. Besides that, many farmers were selling their crops for several years in advance, and many lost their farms, which had been pledged as securities for loans, when they failed to repay their debts.

The produce buyers, however, were worried about the violent price fluctuations of the export products in the world market during the depression years and immediately after. The major problem was the uncertainty in the prices, which frequently involved produce buyers in heavy losses. In 1937 the European firms – the main produce buyers – entered into what were known as the 'Buying Agreements', in order to control cocoa-buying. The agreements were concluded among the large European firms in Ghana and Nigeria, with the exception of the English and Scottish Joint Co-operative Wholesale Society Ltd, and were intended to last for four years with effect from 1 October 1938. The main principles were, first, the division of the total purchase of cocoa by all members and the allocation to each of an agreed proportion based on past experience; and secondly, the payment, subject to certain specially-permitted exceptions, of a uniform 'limit' price by all members, based on the world price ruling from time to time, less an agreed amount to cover costs of transport to the world markets and a reasonable profit for the firms. There was nothing to prevent any individual member overpaying the calculated buying limit, but overpayment was rendered unprofitable by the provision for compulsory transfer, at intervals, of cocoa from firms which overbought to those which did not attain their agreed shares. A formula for calculating the transfer prices was devised and included in the agreement. Two prominent men behind this scheme were Frank Samuel, a director of the UAC Ltd, and John Cadbury of Messrs Cadbury Brothers Ltd.

Coincidentally, the price of cocoa fluctuated more widely at this time, and with the already strained relations between the farmers and the produce buyers, operating through the middlemen, many farmers attributed the cause to the 'buying agreements'. They decided to fight back, first in Ghana and later in Nigeria, by holding up cocoa sales and by boycotting all European imported goods, except necessities such as salt, kerosene and candles. Representations were made by the farmers to the Secretary of State for the Colonies, who agreed to set up a commission to investigate the entire marketing conditions in West Africa. After about six months a truce was declared following the promise of a commission of inquiry; the sale of cocoa began again in April 1938, and at the same time the farmers ended their boycott of European imported goods.

The commission, which was set up under the chairmanship of W. Nowell, studied general marketing conditions in both Ghana and Nigeria; and in its report, published in 1938, it concluded that the continuance of the 'buying agreements' was undesirable.[1] It also concluded that the existing conditions of cocoa marketing were unsatisfactory to the trading firms and the producers alike. The report went on:

> It is essential, in our opinion, that any scheme of reform, alternative to the 'Buying Agreements', must, if it is to be really satisfactory, provide certain requirements. They are as follows . . . the strengthening of the economic position and morale of producers in relation to the buyers, both Europeans and Africans; the recognition of the legitimate interests of both the African Community and the Shippers; the maintenance of free competition in the purchase of cocoa crop; and the avoidance of any unnecessary expenses in marketing.

The commission suggested a number of possible solutions for the marketing of cocoa, but in general it supported the establishment of a statutory body which could arrange for effective and organized marketing. Before the recommendations of the commission could be implemented, the second world war broke out.

The outbreak of war immediately cut off the access of some

---

[1] *Report of Commission on the Marketing of West African Cocoa*, Cmd. 5845, HMSO, 1938. This report is generally referred to as the Nowells Report. It contains detailed accounts of the 'buying agreements' and of the 'boycott' of European imported goods.

important export crops of Nigeria to the major markets in Europe. Cocoa, which was contributing a great deal to Nigeria's revenue, was one of the crops affected. In order to prevent the collapse of the cocoa industry in West Africa, the British government instructed the West African governments to purchase the whole cocoa crop, despite the fact that only part of it could be shipped and sold. The Ministry of Food in the United Kingdom bought the cocoa of the 1939–40 season at the price ruling in West Africa just before the war, and all the trading firms hitherto engaged in the cocoa trade in West Africa acted as the ministry's agents for purchase and sale of cocoa. In 1940 the Ministry of Food in the United Kingdom transferred its responsibility to the West African Cocoa Control Board – an organization set up by the Colonial Office in London for the purpose of selling West African cocoa wherever practicable.[1] From February 1941 the Ministry of Food (UK) bought the cocoa direct from the WACCB on the basis of an annual contract. The board had to destroy many tons of cocoa which could not be shipped because of the war; and it fixed producers' prices for cocoa at levels lower than those that could have been obtained in a free world market. Besides the uncertainty of disposal, many factors commended a policy of low producer prices. Labour was not to be diverted to cocoa production from other crops which were more essential to the war effort, such as rubber and oilseeds; and in view of the shortage of imported goods it seemed desirable to keep down purchasing power in order to avoid or at least control inflation.

The British government also controlled the export of oilseeds and vegetable oils to the United Kingdom, because of the likely shortages of butter and marine oil. From 1939 to 1942 the Ministry of Food organized the bulk purchase of West African oilseeds and palm oil. This arrangement, which was based on the pre-war selling system, was changed in 1942 when purchases from producers, hitherto handled by the trading firms, were transferred to a newly constituted West African Produce Control Board.[2] The new board took over from the WACCB, but the principal object of the change was to give the British government a firmer grip on the West African economies. The intended functions of the WAPCB were: first, to

---

[1] C. Leubuscher, *Bulk-Buying from the Colonies*; also Helleiner, op. cit., p. 154.
[2] See *Report on Cocoa Control in West Africa 1939–1943, and Statement on Future Policy*, Cmd. 6554, HMSO, 1944.

increase the output of agricultural export produce; secondly, to supervise the orderly marketing of the products under its control; and thirdly, to promote economic security in the producing areas by maintaining stable producer prices within each season, as far as possible over a longer period of years. The last function formed the basis of the price equalization policy, which provided a buffer between the producer and the international market, thus protecting the farmer from short-term fluctuations of world prices and ensuring a greater stability of income. The board accumulated or subsidized the differences between the prices paid to the producers, and the world price, allowing for commissions to produce buyers, internal transport costs and shipping costs. Many factors, including shipping difficulties, affected the operation of the board. The price policy did not result in a greater volume of exports, but it safeguarded the possible collapse of the West African export trade and went a long way to ease the tension which could have resulted from wartime inflation.

THE IMPORT TRADE

The additional incomes from export production meant some increases in the consumption of imported goods. Another factor which influenced the growth of the import trade was the changing social structure of Nigeria. This was clearly illustrated by a report of a District Commissioner in 1911.

Reports showed increase in churches (Roman Catholic and C.M.S.) and almost every village has also its mosque. These churches and mosques mean large importation of building materials; corrugated iron, nails, hinges, bolts etc. The district provides its own timber in abundance. At present the churches are provided with wooden shutters instead of windows with glass panes. Probably a trade might be done in church furniture and ornaments, including hassocks or foot-stools which if provided with a strong loop at one end might be carried to and from by individual members of the congregation. There seems also to be room for a trade in musical instruments of good quality. Education is spreading rapidly. A small trade might be done in literature of a useful nature, cheap encyclopaedias, dictionaries, books on 'general knowledge' and on the history of foreign countries. Cheap 'Lives of' Queen Victoria, King Edward VII and King George V would be popular. Books on etiquette and 'polite' letter-writing would have a ready sale, so also would 'ready-reckoners' and similar books with mathematical tables and statistics. Large gaudy coloured portraits of the King and Queen would find purchasers. The town of Ijebu-Ode contains many tailors and many sewing machines and the people are well-dressed, and they have good taste to prefer their own bright-coloured picturesque garments and fashions to the gloomy hues and hideous modes of Europe.[1]

This extract from a typical colonial report indicates sufficiently the trend in import trade as influenced by the spread of education and the missionary work in many areas. The report, however, does not mention the most important single import item – cotton piece goods – which before the first world war came almost exclusively from the United Kingdom.

TABLE 11.3   *Imports of cotton piece goods:*
selected years, 1900–38

Year	Value (£000)	Percentage of total imports
1900	605	31·0
1910	1,323	22·6
1913	1,676	23·3
1920	6,102	29·4
1930	3,045	24·0
1933	1,866	29·4
1938	1,658	19·2

Sources: *Nigerian Administrative Report, 1925,*
CO657/4, and *Trade Reports.*

Indeed, cotton piece goods earned the United Kingdom the bulk of her revenue from Nigeria. The British government was determined, therefore, to ensure the steady growth of imports, and frowned on anything at all which might reduce consumption, either in the form of a substitute or a competitive commodity. The major

[1] *Lagos Customs and Trade Journal*, vol. 1, 1911.

competition to cotton piece goods was from trade spirits, which came mainly from Germany. The importation of trade spirits into Nigeria was criticized in England, because it was thought that they did not contribute to the economic development and welfare of the people, and that they brought many social evils.[1] Even though it was not officially mentioned, the view widely held in business circles in England, particularly among cotton manufacturers, was that money spent on trade spirits meant a reduction in the demand for cotton piece goods. However, in 1909 the British government set up a committee of inquiry into the liquor trade in Southern Nigeria. After hearing the evidence of African and European government officials, missionaries, medical men and local rulers, and after obtaining written statements from others as well, the committee reported that the use of trade spirits was not likely to cause race deterioration or crime.[2] Despite the report, the Nigerian government was encouraged by the British government to increase the import duties on trade spirits.[3]

The main concern of the British government was to secure the bulk of the Nigerian trade, and this policy was reflected in a number of colonial reports. For example, in 1911 Governor H. H. Bell reported that

> I took the occasion of a recent visit to one of our principal markets to inspect personally the stock in trade of a typical native merchant and it was anything but comforting to find that more than half of the various kinds of goods exposed for sale were evidently German manufactures. Though most of the articles were goods of small value and of trumpery quality, the appearance of these foreign manufactures in markets which we are creating at the cost of much money and many lives is neither satisfactory nor encouraging.[4]

[1] The anti-liquor campaign was led by the Empire Resources Development Committee in England. The temperance movement opposed the importation of trade spirits by the colonies from any foreign country, and even from Britain.

[2] *Report of the Committee of Inquiry into the Liquor Trade of Southern Nigeria*, Cmd. 4906, HMSO, 1909. For the influence of the Christian Missions on the liquor trade, see Ayandele, op. cit., pp. 307–27.

[3] The import duty on trade spirits stood at 3*s*. per gallon in 1900. It increased to 3*s*. 6*d*. per gallon in 1905 and increased further to 6*s*. 3*d*. per gallon in 1913.

[4] *Colonial Annual Reports*, no. 704, Northern Nigeria, 1910–11, pp. 6–7.

The main items of import included the following: cotton goods, gin and rum (trade spirits), hats, umbrellas, bicycles, books, building materials (particularly cement), railway materials, motor cars, matches, steam launches, tobacco, salt, kerosene, soap, sewing machines and thread, some electrical goods and medicine.

Cotton goods represented the most important single item of importation. The increased consumption of foreign cotton goods, particularly British cotton, was not a reflection of the better quality of such goods over the indigenous ones,[1] but was due primarily to the cheapness of the foreign cotton as compared with the native cloth. The importation of trade spirits rose sharply between 1900 and 1913, despite the heavy import duties imposed on them.

Building materials, particularly cement, were imported in increasing volumes as the result of the public works projects undertaken by the government, and the building of better private houses to replace the common mud-houses. With the gradual development of roads and the railways the importation of iron and steel increased. Iron and steel materials were also imported for use in the mining industries. Increasing numbers of bicycles were imported, and after 1906 more motor cars were brought into Nigeria. During the first world war, the import trade fell sharply: imports from Germany ceased completely while those from the United Kingdom were considerably reduced.

The persistent agitation against the importation of trade spirits into Nigeria continued during the war and immediately after it. The official attitude towards the pattern of imports, and particularly imports of trade spirits, was clearly reflected in the speech made by the Governor-General of Nigeria to the Nigerian Legislative Council in 1917. He said:

> Are our imports, for the most part, of a nature to promote the commerce and industry of Great Britain and her Allies? Is there any direction in which we can better assist in developing the resources of the Empire? . . . I invite this Council to record its judgement that it would be to the great benefit of the industries of the Empire, if this import [spirits] were replaced by others

[1] 'Native cloth is manufactured in great quantities and competes favourably with Manchester cottons. . . .' *Colonial Annual Reports*, no. 437, Northern Nigeria, 1903, p. 86.

TABLE 11.4 *Imports of certain goods: selected years, 1900–45*

Year	Salt Volume ('000 cwt)	Salt Value (£000)	Trade spirits Volume ('000 galls)	Trade spirits Value (£000)	Soap Volume ('000 galls)	Soap Value (£000)	Kerosene Volume ('000 galls)	Kerosene Value (£000)	Machinery Value (£000)
1900	466	40	—	179	—	13	535	19	—
1905	559	42	1,582	265	—	17	948	29	—
1910	704	49	1,974	463	78	49	2,792	86	50
1915	780	153	768	277	93	89	2,337	70	140
1920	1,063	536	127	341	72	213	3,064	346	447
1925	1,005	309	211	217	81	134	3,991	187	440
1930	1,169	290	186	190	51	74	4,667	207	298
1933	867	205	51	75	22	31	1,961	89	47
1938	1,050	268	106	80	31	33	3,725	89	301
1945	1,131	400	64	95	—	7	4,507	123	296

Sources: *Nigerian Handbook, 1936*, and *Trade Reports*.

which emanate from our own country [Britain] or those of our Allies. . . . I will go further to add – though I am no extremist in this matter – that it would also be to the benefit of Nigeria if these foreign imports of spirits were replaced by articles of more value to the people of this country – articles more calculated to raise their standard of life and comfort, and to increase the output of the industries from which they derive their wealth.[1]

In 1919 an ordinance was passed prohibiting the importation of trade spirits. There were mixed feelings about this: some people in Britain believed that export production would not increase, particularly the output of palm kernels, 'without dangling bottles of gin before the noses of the natives'.[2] This idea probably originated from the fact that the Germans who supplied the bulk of the trade spirits were also the main consumers of Nigerian palm kernels.

Despite the adoption of various policies to secure the import trade exclusively from Britain, imports from other European countries and from the United States of America began to increase after the first world war: for example, the value of total imports from the USA to Nigeria in 1922 and 1927 were £645,000 and £1,292,000 respectively; and imports from Germany into Nigeria for the same period were £380,000 and £1,407,000 respectively. However, the economic depression of the late twenties, which continued till about the mid-thirties, considerably reduced the flow of imports into Nigeria. The values of the imports for the years 1928–34 fell steadily with the exception of 1932; this decline was due to the reduced incomes of the people resulting from the low prices for the major exports – cocoa, groundnuts, palm oil and palm kernels.

One important lesson which the British government learnt during this period, particularly during the depression years, was that the open-door policy or the free trade policy adopted in the colonies would result in gradual loss of trade to other competing countries, particularly to Japan which became a strong competitor of Britain in the importation of cotton goods. A step towards closing the door to some foreign imports was taken in 1932, when the system of imperial preference was extended to cover the British colonies in accordance with the agreement reached at the Imperial Economic

[1] *West Africa*, 31 March 1917: report from the Nigerian Legislative Council.
[2] *House of Commons Debate*, 5th series, 1916, Cols. 556–7.

TABLE 11.5 Percentage of total imports and exports with principal countries: selected years, 1900–38

Country	1900 Imports	1900 Exports	1905 Imports	1905 Exports	1910 Imports	1910 Exports	1915 Imports	1915 Exports	1920 Imports	1920 Exports	1925 Imports	1925 Exports	1930 Imports	1930 Exports	1933 Imports	1933 Exports	1938 Imports	1938 Exports
United Kingdom	70·5	46·2	69·6	50·1	61·2	48·7	83·6	87·3	82·0	91·3	73·8	54·7	68·3	40·2	69·3	39·2	54·6	50·4
Germany	9·8	41·4	11·0	38·2	11·1	47·3	*	*	*	*	8·5	21·8	10·1	27·0	8·3	17·5	8·7	17·1
France	*	3·7	*	1·2	*	*	*	4·4	*	1·5	*	4·5	2·5	5·4	1·3	14·9	*	6·9
USA	*	—	*	—	3·7	—	6·8	4·8	11·5	3·6	6·5	9·6	9·4	13·4	6·3	8·6	8·0	6·9
Others	19·6	8·7	19·4	10·5	24·0	4·0	9·6	3·5	6·5	3·6	11·2	9·4	9·7	14·0	14·8	19·8	28·7	18·7
Total	100	100	100	100	100	100	100	100	100	100	100	100	100	100	100	100	100	100

* Less than 1 per cent.
Sources: *Nigerian Handbook, 1936*, and *Trade Reports*.

Conference at Ottawa, Canada, in 1932. The system was in the nature of tariff alterations and the imposition of quotas on imports. At different times between 1932 and 1934 the quota system was imposed on textiles from Japan entering into Nigeria. The basis chosen for the calculation of the quota – the average imports between 1927 and 1931 – ensured a substantial reduction of imports from Japan.[1] Besides the textile quota, import duties were also imposed on certain manufactured goods from Japan, including galvanized iron sheets, cement, paint, shirts and singlets. The argument in favour of such restrictions was based on three main factors: first, it was considered necessary to impose import duties for revenue purposes; secondly, it was argued that the reciprocal preference treatment enjoyed in the British Empire would be lost by the agricultural countries; and lastly, it was argued that the open-door policy would favour the trade of those countries with low standards of labour costs, to the disadvantage of the trade of other countries with higher labour standards, because the prices of the latter would be less competitive than those of the former. The policy was designed to benefit British manufacturers who were faced with higher labour costs as compared with Japan.

While the imperial preference system was being formulated by the British government, it was obvious that adequate consideration was not given to how it might affect the interests of some African colonies, including Nigeria.[2] When the quota bill was debated in the Nigerian Legislative Council, there were strong protests against the system by some members.[3] The Acting Governor of Nigeria admitted that prices would rise as a result of the measure, but argued that it would reduce the level of spending on imported items and thus Nigerian money would remain in Nigeria.[4] This argument could not be accepted, because any kind of forced savings as anticipated by the Governor would reduce the economic welfare of the people, especially when no reciprocal benefit was forthcoming. Even the protagonists of the system admitted that 'it is only just to recognize that there is a sharing of burdens and an exchange of favours. But it may well be that some colonies, or some section of colonial

[1] Perham (ed.), *Mining, Commerce and Finance in Nigeria*, p. 159.
[2] Ibid., p. 160.
[3] *Legislative Council Debates*, 12 June 1934, p. 47.
[4] Ibid., p. 6.

producers, get more than their fair share of the favours, whereas others bear more than their fair share of the burdens.'[1]

At the outbreak of war in 1939, the British government concentrated on securing the imports essential for carrying on the ordinary life of the people of Nigeria. The supplies of goods from many European countries were reduced considerably. Currency regulations were introduced during the war in order to safeguard the position of sterling and in order to economize on the hard currencies and gold held by the sterling area, which were needed for the purchase of munitions and raw materials. Import licensing was introduced in order to control the types and volume of imported goods, and restrictions were placed on capital movements. The volume of imports showed a consistent decline from 1939 to 1941, after which it began to increase steadily. The direction of the import trade was similar to that of the export trade. Imports from Germany ceased entirely, so did imports from Japan, but the United Kingdom was able to increase her share of the trade. However, owing to the hazards of the war, the volume of imported goods was reduced considerably, and people had to pay high prices for cotton goods, cars, salt, corrugated iron sheets and cycles. Imported cotton goods decreased considerably during the war: in 1937 they amounted to 164 million square yards valued at about £4 million, but this fell in 1941 to 60 million square yards valued at £1·8 million.

COMPETITION IN FOREIGN TRADE

The popular foreign companies which operated in Nigeria during this period included the Niger Company, John Holt & Co., Messrs Miller Brothers & Co., the Kano Trading Company, Lagos Store Ltd, West African Cold Storage Co. Ltd, the African Association Ltd, the British Nigerian Syndicate, British Cotton Growing Association, Elder Dempster & Co., Messrs Siegler & Co., G. L. Gaiser, A. Sachse & Co., Witt & Busch, Oscar Kaiser & Co., Holtman & Co., Jackel & Co. and Messrs W. B. Maelver & Co.

Many of the trading firms continued to provide special services for their customers in order to secure their loyalty. Before 1905 only a few foreign traders had penetrated into the interior, and those who

[1] Hancock, op. cit., p. 312.

had branches in such isolated areas were able to charge high prices for imported goods, and buy export crops from farmers at low prices. After 1906 the pattern of competition began to change, partly because most of the trading firms which survived the cut-throat competition of the last decade of the nineteenth century were British, and partly because of the considerable improvements in the transport system which enabled greater penetration into the interior. Besides the matter of direct 'cut-throat' competition, the number of foreign traders was reduced considerably just before the first world war, primarily as a combined result of the increased capital require-ments for holding stocks of the growing trade, and because of the losses sustained in trade fluctuations. As the number of trading firms grew fewer, imperfect competition increased.

Price war was often resorted to as each trading-group struggled to secure the greater share of the Nigerian trade. At one time the German traders were more successful than the British: this was attributed to the adaptability of German firms to the requirements and pursuit of Nigerian customers; and if the customer could not afford to pay for anything better than shoddy, the German traders would provide him with the most attractive and the cheapest shoddy procurable.[1] The destructive competition among the traders of many European nations continued until the Nigerian market was left almost entirely to the British traders, who were favoured simply because the British government administered the country. Just before the first world war an increasing number of Syrians and Lebanese had been participating in the foreign trade of Nigeria.[2] Most of them began as retailers of imported goods and middlemen in the market-ing of the export crops, and a few prospected for alluvial gold and tin. The most significant feature of the participation of Syrians in the Nigerian trade was the strong spirit of togetherness which existed among them. The rich Syrian assisted his less fortunate brothers to obtain funds and make the right trade contacts. They made efforts to study local languages and customs, with the result that they became more acceptable to the people than the Europeans. With these important qualities, essential for any business success, they made some impact on the Nigerian trade.

There are no quantitative indicators to show the relative import-

[1] *Colonial Annual Reports*, no. 704, Northern Nigeria, 1910–11, p. 7.
[2] Crowder, *West Africa Under Colonial Rule*, p. 345.

ance of participation by indigenous traders, *vis-à-vis* the foreign firms, in Nigeria's foreign trade. Many Nigerian traders had no adequate capital to engage in the import trade, which was characterized by the holding of large stocks for long periods. There were only three commercial banks in Nigeria from which the traders could obtain credit. The BBWA, which was the oldest, and Barclays Bank, which joined it later, preferred to deal with the well-established foreign firms who could provide acceptable securities for loans being sought. The National Bank of Nigeria, which was the only indigenous bank and the youngest of the three, could not afford to operate a generous credit system at a period when it had to struggle for survival. However, some educated Nigerians, particularly in Lagos, operated as export produce merchants and importers. Among them were S. Thomas & Co., The Hon. Samuel Herbert Pearse, J. H. Doherty, W. A. Dawodu & Co. and Adigun Brothers. Almost all the prominent indigenous traders had at one time or another served as clerks or agents under foreign trading firms, where they acquired modern business experience before establishing on their own. It is difficult to know the average size of the business of an indigenous trader: however, it is known that J. H. Doherty started business with a capital of £47, and that when his business expanded a European firm used to extend credit of £4,000 a month to him.[1] In addition, some other rich educated Nigerians imported large quantities of goods, partly for their own personal use and partly for retailing through the medium of the parcel post. These goods were usually ordered from catalogue descriptions, and payment was often made with the order. In the export trade, the efforts of Nigerians were mainly directed towards produce-buying and transportation to shipping centres.

When the first world war broke out, all the German trading firms were closed and wound up by a receiver appointed by the government.[2] The British traders, therefore, had virtually a monopoly in Nigeria. For example, in 1917, there were about 77 European trading firms in Nigeria of which 12 had 10 or more local branches in various parts of the country. After the war some of the German firms were allowed to reopen, and the number of European firms increased considerably: there were 103 European trading firms in

[1] Macmillan (ed.), op. cit., pp. 98–9.
[2] *Nigerian Handbook*, 1917.

Nigeria in 1921.[1] Generally the number varied, especially after 1921, according to the number of liquidations and amalgamations which took place. Between 1921 and 1929, 43 new firms came into existence, while 53 firms were liquidated, and there was only one amalgamation. Between 1929 and 1933, 36 new firms were established, 22 were liquidated and 22 others were amalgamated with some of the big firms.[2]

A few of the major business amalgamations deserve mention. The first amalgamation of some significance took place in 1919, between the Miller Brothers, F. A. Swanzy, the African Association Ltd and a number of small firms. These firms combined to form the African and Eastern Trade Corporation Ltd, which competed effectively with the Niger Company – the principal trading company in Nigeria. In 1920 Lever Brothers Ltd acquired the assets of the Niger Company but made an unsuccessful attempt to buy the assets of the A & ETC. The cut-throat competition which continued among the big firms forced many of the small firms to sell their businesses when on the verge of liquidation. The most significant amalgamation took place in April 1929, when the United Africa Company was formed by the amalgamation of the Niger Company, the A & ETC and some small trading firms.

The economic depression of the late twenties and the early thirties forced a number of trading firms to abandon the Nigerian trade. Only a few big firms remained to handle it, and those which remained in business were faced with reduced profit margins caused mainly by wide price fluctuations. However, between 1934 and 1937 a few firms established the Stape Lines Agreement and the Merchandise Agreement, which allocated import quotas and controlled prices in order to eliminate wasteful competition.[3] The Association of West African Merchants was eventually formed for the same purpose. The agreement among the merchants made provisions for punishment of firms operating against the common policy. These provisions did not stop the price war among the firms, and neither did it eliminate the special services provided by individual firms to some buyers. One of the effects of the imperfect competition on consumers was that on many occasions they could only buy the

[1] *Nigerian Handbook*, 1921.
[2] See Perham (ed.), *Mining, Commerce and Finance in Nigeria*, pp. 49–67.
[3] Bauer, op. cit., p. 79.

available imported goods at prices fixed by the foreign firms. There was nothing to stop the retail traders from charging excessive prices.

Most of the foreign firms engaged in the import trade also handled the bulk of the export trade. During the depression years, these firms faced frequent and wide fluctuations of export prices. Many of the firms thought that the best way to solve the prevailing unstable prices was by trade agreements. The primary producers, on the other hand, had general contempt and resentment for any kind of trade agreement which could result in imperfect competition, and preferred to market their products under free market conditions based on day-to-day negotiations. On many occasions the buying firms resorted to organized oligopsony, in order to eliminate losses caused by the price fluctuations. An example of this was found in the groundnut trade. During the groundnut season of 1927–8, the UAC and some other foreign firms entered into an agreement to stabilize prices and to allocate produce-buying quotas to members of the agreement. The agreement sought to safeguard the parties concerned but did not safeguard them against the competition of newcomers to the trade. Among the many newcomers who competed with the 'agreement' firms was a Syrian trader named S. Raccah. He entered the groundnut trade and competed vigorously with the agreement firms, and he succeeded in increasing his share of the trade at the expense of the firms.[1] Besides the personal organizing ability of Raccah, he was able to fight the agreement firms by offering higher prices for the product and by retaining the loyalty of some producers. He kept his overhead costs down by not attempting to operate on too wide a scale. He had a few out-stations, and he was assisted by some competent middlemen. In the end, Raccah was able to break the organized oligopsony, as the agreement firms released themselves from the price and the tonnage agreements in order to be free to fight a price war with Raccah. The competition which resulted in the groundnut trade continued until the outbreak of the second world war. Another important example of the pattern of competition in the export trade was found in the cocoa trade, when in 1937 the European firms entered into what were known as the 'Buying Agreements'.[2] These were introduced in order to restrict competition

[1] Hancock, op. cit., pp. 215–17.
[2] This has already been discussed in an earlier section of this chapter.

and to control the price of cocoa, but the resentment shown by the West African farmers forced the firms to abandon them.

The policy of bulk-purchase of nearly all the major export crops, adopted by the British government, made deep marks on the Nigerian economy. The effects were evident in the changes in the organization and marketing of export crops, in the position of the primary producers, in the international trading position of Nigeria and also in export production. The bulk-purchase policy led to the establishment of the West African Produce Control Board which eliminated competition in buying among the private commercial firms which handled the pre-war export trade. As the sole buyer of the major export crops, the control board had the power to fix prices which were thought to be reasonable under the prevailing market conditions. The trading firms thus became the agents of the control board. The direct result was that the firms had to buy according to the prices fixed by the control board. They had limited or no freedom as far as the manipulation of the purchase prices was concerned. The primary producers did not object to statutory monopsony, mainly because it provided a better arrangement than that which obtained during the pre-war slump; and in any case, the war emergency gave no room for any protest even if they disliked the policy.

The bulk-purchase scheme also affected the international trading position of Nigeria by its influence on the revenue from exports and thus on the balance of payments, and by its impact on trade relations with countries other than the United Kingdom. The fact that the prices paid to the Nigerian producers were below the world market prices meant a reduction on the credit side of the balance of payments accounts of Nigeria. It meant smaller sterling balances and less income to spend on consumption goods or on investments. Lastly, the scheme prevented the primary producers and the control board from acquiring experience in conducting trade under competitive conditions. It must be added, however, that the intention was to provide better stability of prices, for which a form of control was needed.

Part 4   The modern economic revolution 1946–60

12   General survey

A number of interrelated factors were responsible for the modern economic revolution in Nigeria, which can be associated with the period since 1945. There was a growing feeling of pride and nationalism which soon made some impact on Nigerian politics. Educational facilities improved gradually, and increasing numbers of Nigerians were educated outside the country – particularly in the United Kingdom and in the United States of America. There emerged a new crop of educated and able Nigerians who advocated and participated in both the political and the economic reforms of the country.[1]

The growth of the Nigerian economy during this period was not evenly spaced. Variations of growth depended, naturally, upon the fortunes of the largest single sector of the economy – the agricultural sector – which in turn was dependent upon weather conditions and world market prices for primary products. However, the world-wide shortages of many raw materials experienced immediately after the war resulted in a phenomenal increase in the export trade of Nigeria, which in turn increased the incomes of peasant farmers.[2] The value of total domestic exports increased from £23·7 million in 1946, to £129·8 million and £165·6 million in 1955 and 1960 respectively. The various restrictions on imported goods, which characterized the entire wartime period, were gradually lifted, with a resultant increase in commerce. The value of total imports

[1] 'The great increase in the wealth of the peoples of the European colonies in West Africa in the twentieth century has led to the rise of a class of educated Africans – lawyers, doctors, administrators, schoolmasters and the like – who are anxious to free their countries from European control and to govern them themselves': J. D. Fage, *An Introduction to the History of West Africa*, p. 194.

[2] G. K. Helleiner, *Peasant Agriculture, Government and Economic Growth in Nigeria*, pp. 160–4.

increased from £19·8 million in 1946 to £136·1 million and £215·9 million in 1955 and 1960 respectively. An increasing number of private businesses, foreign and indigenous, were established, even though most of the indigenous businesses were on a small scale. The economic importance of Nigeria, indeed of all the British colonies, which was emphasized during the war, induced the British government to introduce into Nigeria a fresh and more revolutionary economic policy, through the passing of the Colonial Development and Welfare Act of 1945.

POLITICAL CHANGES[1]

By far the most important of the factors affecting the social and economic conditions of Nigeria after 1945 were a number of political reforms. By the 1940s it was evident that the indirect rule with which the British government had administered the country since the early years of the twentieth century was no longer effective in Nigeria, where the people not only accepted European ideas of government but were agitating for increasingly active participation.[2] In 1946 the British government saw that the old Legislative Council, which had been dominated by *ex-officio* members for several decades, needed to be reconstituted in the light of political and economic developments and aspirations in the country. The first stage was the introduction of an unofficial majority in the Legislative Council in 1946 – the Richard's Constitution.[3] Three regional councils were established in the North, West and East, even though the country had not been formally divided into regions. However, in 1951 another constitution was introduced which divided the country into three regions, and which brought elected government into Nigeria.[4]

[1] A number of books have been written on this subject including: L. Franklin Blitz (ed.), *The Politics and Administration of Nigerian Government*; John P. Mackintosh, *Nigerian Government and Politics*; Okoi Arikpo, *The Development of Modern Nigeria*; and I. F. Nicolson, *The Administration of Nigeria 1900–1960*.

[2] Fage, op. cit., p. 179.

[3] The implementation of Sessional Paper no. 4 of 1945, *Political and Constitutional Future of Nigeria*, Lagos, Government Printer, 1945.

[4] *Proceedings of the General Conference on Review of the Constitution. January 1950*, Lagos, Government Printer, 1950. The new constitution which finally

It marked the first step towards self-government. Most of the members of the newly-constituted Houses of Assembly were elected on the platforms of the few political parties which had been created. The most prominent of these were the Action Group, with its headquarters in Western Nigeria; the National Council of Nigeria and the Cameroons;[1] and the Northern People's Congress in the North. The 1951 constitution did not define the relationship between the central and the regional governments, and nothing was said about what might happen if a regional government decided to adopt a different policy from the one laid down by the central government in Lagos. In order to cure this defect, and to move the country further towards independence, a federal constitution was introduced in 1954.[2] This listed the subjects on which the federal government had power to make laws, and they included aviation, banks, censuses, citizenship, copyright, currency, customs, defence, deportation, external relations, certain higher educational institutions, immigration and emigration, mining, police, railways, inter-regional commerce, trunk roads, inter-regional water, weights and measures, radio and television. There was also the concurrent list, which contained a number of subjects on which the regional governments could legislate. The federal government could legislate on subjects included in the concurrent list, but such laws would only apply to a regional government which adopted them. The list included antiquities, bankruptcy, commercial combines, electricity, other higher education, labour, national parks, tourist traffic, surveys, water-power and public safety. A number of other measures were undertaken to bring about the federal structure, including the reorganization of the judiciary and the fiscal system. A major consequence of these changes was that the regional governments were given some degree of autonomy on social and economic

---

emerged was commonly referred to as the Macpherson's Constitution, after the Governor.

[1] 'At its inception, the NCNC was not a political party. It was conceived as a United National Front embracing all nationalist political groups which agitated for self-government': Arikpo, op. cit., p. 61.

[2] The introduction of the new constitution was preceded by two major constitutional conferences. *Report by the Conference on the Nigerian Constitution held in London in July and August 1953*, Cmd. 8934, HMSO, 1953; and *Report by the resumed Conference on the Nigerian Constitution held in Lagos in January and February 1954*, Lagos, Government Printer, 1954.

matters; for example, each region could plan and execute economic development projects of its own.

The increasing participation of Nigerians in the administration of their country brought greater pressure on the British government for complete political independence. Following a number of constitutional conferences[1] the British government granted the governments of the Eastern and Western Regions internal self-government in 1956, as a step towards complete independence. Regional self-government for the Northern Region came in 1959. In 1960 the British government agreed to grant complete political independence to Nigeria, passing the Nigerian Independence Act and authorizing the Queen in Council to draw up a new constitution for an independent Nigeria. The Federation of Nigeria became an independent country within the Commonwealth on 1 October 1960. In the same year, Nigeria's application as a member of the United Nations was also successful.

After the introduction of a federal constitution in 1954, the main problem which the country faced was that of national unity. There was the obvious difficulty of converting a purely personal notion of citizenship – expressed in the duties and obligations owing exclusively to one's own kinship group or local community – into something much more abstract – loyalty and allegiance to a quite impersonal 'state' or 'nation'.[2] All the political parties were associated with different ethnic groups, even though some claimed to be national by name and in policy. The strong political rivalry which developed tended to split the country into several units, and in each unit were numerous groups. It was, therefore, difficult to tackle most issues – social, political and economic – from a national viewpoint.

[1] *Report by the Conference on the Nigerian Constitution held in London in May and June 1957*, Cmd. 207, HMSO, 1957; *Report by the Ad Hoc Meeting on the Nigeria Constitutional Conference held in Lagos in February 1958*, Lagos, Government Printer, 1958; *Report of the resumed Nigerian Constitutional Conference held in London in September and October 1958*, Cmd. 569, HMSO, 1958; and *Report of the Ad Hoc Committee of the Conference on the Nigerian Constitution, Lagos, April 1959*, Lagos, Government Printer, 1959.
[2] Kenneth Little, 'Parliamentary Government and Social Change in West Africa' (unpublished paper), p. 8.

ECONOMIC PLANNING

The general feeling in Nigeria, as well as in the United Kingdom,[1] was that in order to achieve political independence, some degree of rapid economic growth must also be accomplished. It was realized that political development was not the whole story, and that Nigeria should also enjoy a reasonable level of prosperity and a higher standard of living.

The economic prosperity which private enterprise brought to Nigeria was often precarious, as it depended upon the prices obtained on a few export commodities subject to violent price fluctuations in world markets. It was, therefore, necessary to formulate plans which would lead to greater diversification of production. In this respect, private capital and enterprise needed to be supplemented, and in many ways led, by government action. The main object may be said to be to secure an increase in *per capita* income or output of the population of the country over time. Economic growth could not be counted upon to occur spontaneously. Therefore, growth and development had to be planned for by the government. It was no longer realistic to trust the price mechanism of a free market to allocate resources into various productive channels, in such a manner as to guarantee full use of the resources of a developing country such as Nigeria. Some intervention with its working was necessary in order to prevent its undesirable effects, and a certain amount of foresight needed for a proper allocation of economic resources. Experience, particularly in the depression years, had proved unfounded the *laissez-faire* doctrine propounded by Adam Smith regarding the existence of an 'invisible hand' which automatically harmonized private gain with the public good. It was the government which could remove the institutional obstacles to growth, just as the institutional changes favourable to growth could only be made by the government; for example, modernization of land tenure systems, provision of educational and training programmes, direction and control of labour and infrastructural investment (schools, roads, power, communications).

The role of the Nigerian government in the economic development of the country consisted of the expansion of resources available

[1] *Economic Development in the United Kingdom Dependencies*, London, Central Office of Information, 1956, p. 1.

for investment, i.e. provision of infrastructure, training programmes and general services; the allocation of resources, i.e. planning and programming; and direct ownership and management of resources (entrepreneurship).

Planning for economic development may be said to have begun in 1946 when, under the impetus of the scheme for Nigeria contained in the 1945 Colonial Development and Welfare Act, a ten-year plan for development and welfare was inaugurated.[1] It was agreed that the United Kingdom government would contribute £23 million to the total cost of the scheme, estimated at £55 million. The rest of the funds were to be provided from loans raised by the Nigerian government and from the Nigerian revenue. The funds were allocated for a variety of projects ranging from small community improvements to the construction of major health, educational and research facilities. Government policy on economic development was based largely on what could be regarded as pre-industrialization projects: it aimed at providing the infrastructure in the hope that this would induce spontaneous private investment, particularly in industry and agriculture. In 1946 some legislation was passed in connexion with the development programme, the most important being the Development Loan Ordinance no. 3 and the Nigeria (Ten-Year Plan) Local Loan Ordinance no. 10: the former ordinance empowered the Governor of Nigeria to raise a loan of £8 million in England, and the latter empowered him to raise a local loan of £1 million in Nigeria. Loans raised under these ordinances were made a charge upon the general revenue and assets of Nigeria.

The Governor was empowered to establish a Loan Development Board, the resources of which were to be derived from funds appropriated to it by vote or resolution of the Nigerian Legislative Council under the Development Loan Ordinance or any other written law. The board[2] was empowered to make loans or grants, or both, to any authority or co-operative society approved by the Governor in Council, for schemes of development including public works, public utilities and town planning; the promotion of village crafts and industries and industrial development; colonization and

---

[1] *A Ten-Year Plan of Development and Welfare in Nigeria*, Sessional Paper no. 24 of 1945.
[2] *Colonial Annual Reports*, Nigeria, 1946, p. 64.

land settlement and utilization, forest and firewood plantations; experimental undertakings for testing industrial or processing development of any Nigerian produce; and any other scheme of public value authorized by the Governor. Because of the size of the country, which made central planning more difficult, regional development committees were set up to advise the loan board on projects submitted for its consideration.

In 1949 the administration of the Nigerian loan board was decentralized, and the government set up regional production development boards and regional loan boards. The development boards were financed by the marketing board from the funds accruing from sale of produce handled by the latter. They did not make loans to individuals but applied their resources to such purposes as research, the improvement of roads, land settlement and general agricultural development, and the establishment of industries.

The changing social, economic and political conditions in Nigeria soon exposed the difficulties in planning and executing a scheme for a period as long as ten years. The 1945 plan was highly centralized, but the division of the country into regions in 1947 weakened the central mechanism for its implementation. The increasing regional autonomy and responsibility in economic matters led to substantial deviation from the original plan; so the government introduced a revised one for the period 1951–6. The latter plan saw further changes in 1954 when the Federation of Nigeria came into being, and the regional governments assumed responsibility for those parts of the plan coming within their respective territories.

In the meantime, the difficulties which the government faced in its planning forced it to invite the International Bank for Reconstruction and Development, New York, to send a mission to Nigeria to 'assess the resources available for future development, to study the possibilities for development of the major sectors of the economy and make written recommendations for practical steps to be taken, including the timing and co-ordination of departmental activities'. The mission's report was published in September 1954, and contains a number of recommendations covering a wide range of economic, social and technical subjects.[1] A major criticism concerns the

[1] *The Economic Development of Nigeria*, Baltimore, Md., Johns Hopkins Press, and London, OUP, 1955.

multiplicity of the development boards then in existence, and their ill-defined and overlapping functions; the government reacted by creating the Federal Loans Board, the Western Region Finance Corporation and three development corporations, one in each region. The findings and recommendations of the mission played a considerable part in the framing of Nigeria's future plans for development.

In 1955, when the original ten-year development scheme expired, the United Kingdom government announced the extension of the colonial development and welfare scheme for a further five years to 31 March 1960.[1]

It is important, at this stage, to mention the National Economic Council. The creation of the council followed the recommendations of the IBRD mission; it was agreed that it would be extremely valuable for Nigeria to have a forum in which representatives of each government might meet to discuss economic problems common or peculiar to the regions. The council, which was established in 1955, met twice annually under the chairmanship of the Governor-General of the Federation, and it comprised four ministerial representatives from each of the federal and regional governments and two from the Southern Cameroons government.[2] It was essentially a consultative body, designed to give maximum encouragement to the development of national economic and social policies, and to maintain close co-operation between the federal and regional governments. In order to make its work more effective, a Joint Planning Committee was established in September 1958, to act in an advisory capacity to the council. The committee consisted of two officials from each of the federal and regional governments and one from the Southern Cameroons government, with the Governor of the Central Bank of Nigeria[3] as chairman. It was empowered to co-opt experts in various fields, both from inside and outside the public service, to its meetings; for example, members of the academic staff of the University College, Ibadan (the only university in Nigeria at that time) were invited from time to time to give the committee the benefit of their specialized knowledge. The first

[1] The development plans for the period 1955–60 were extended by the government to cover a further period of two years, and ended in 1962.

[2] Until 1959, when the Southern Cameroons left the Federation of Nigeria.

[3] The Central Bank of Nigeria was established in 1959 (see Chapter 15).

assignment of the committee was the preparation of an economic survey of Nigeria, which was published in 1959.[1]

THE FISCAL SYSTEM

Two major factors brought about changes in the Nigerian fiscal system: first, planning for a more rapid economic development

TABLE 12.1   *Nigerian government revenue, 1946–60 (£000)*

Year ending 31 March	Total revenue	Customs and excise	Direct taxes	Colonial development and welfare grants	Other revenue
1946	13,200	5,664	3,320	349	3,867
1947	14,832	7,095	2,469	791	4,477
1948	18,404	9,129	3,748	791	4,566
1949	23,811	12,623	3,777	1,810	5,601
1950	30,765	17,195	4,830	2,292	5,448
1951	32,794	18,161	5,344	2,271	7,018
1952	50,327	32,106	6,777	2,499	8,945
1953	50,906	33,948	6,810	2,903	7,245
1954	59,256	42,104	5,691	3,027	8,434
1955	62,481	43,960	6,713	1,519	10,289
1956	59,950	44,753	6,757	121	8,319
1957	70,567	50,790	6,557	661	12,559
1958	70,945	51,695	6,666	—	12,584
1959	77,316	55,918	6,678	—	14,720
1960	88,824	63,058	6,291	—	19,475

Sources: *Nigerian Handbook of Commerce and Industry*, and *Annual Abstract of Statistics, 1963.*

increased the demand for funds, which in turn led to the revisions of the fiscal system; and secondly, the constitutional changes which took place led to the re-allocation of revenues among the newly-created regions of Nigeria.

As in previous years, customs and excise continued to form the major source of revenue for the government, its contribution

[1] (Nigerian) National Economic Council, *The Economic Survey of Nigeria, 1959.*

progressively increasing as a result of modifications in the duties. In 1946 it accounted for about 43 per cent of total revenue, and for the years 1950, 1955 and 1960 it increased to 51, 71 and 73 per cent respectively.

TABLE 12.2 *Nigerian government expenditure, 1946–60 (£000)*

Year ending 31 March	Total expenditure	Nigerian government expenditure	Grants and allocations to regions	Development schemes
1946	10,693	10,469	—	224
1947	14,052	13,210	—	842
1948	17,186	15,983	—	1,203
1949	23,898	16,493	6,639	766
1950	28,253	18,533	7,462	2,258
1951	30,388	18,493	9,293	2,602
1952	43,673	29,856	9,968	3,849
1953	44,103	25,917	13,847	4,339
1954	55,003	36,924	13,282	4,797
1955	60,668	31,174	27,416	2,078
1956	55,387	29,185	25,845	357
1957	62,925	25,950	28,386	8,589
1958	65,673	30,542	29,029	6,102
1959	75,414	35,025	31,093	9,296
1960	81,749	40,280	38,469	3,000

Sources: *Nigerian Handbook of Commerce and Industry*, and *Annual Abstract of Statistics, 1963*.

Between 1946 and 1960 import duties were increased, in some cases doubled, on a number of items including alcoholic liquors, bicycles, cotton piece goods, motor vehicles, building materials, petroleum oil and cigarettes. A significant feature of the fiscal policy relating to import duties was the protection of newly established Nigerian industries: a levy was introduced on building materials, particularly cement, and the duties on cigarettes and cotton piece goods increased.[1]

There were considerable increases in export duties on Nigeria's principal export commodities, ranging from 125 per cent increase on palm oil to about 500 per cent on palm kernels. Other

[1] See Chapter 15.

commodities on which duties were raised included cocoa, ground-nuts, hides and skins, and tin. These sharp increases can be attributed to the high prices paid in world markets for Nigerian products immediately after the war, and the government policy of curbing the flow of purchasing power in order to avoid possible inflation and at the same time raise the much-needed revenue for economic development.[1]

In 1950 the government adopted the *ad valorem* system in assessing export duties on cocoa, palm kernel oil, palm kernels and ground-nuts – all these were subject to 6 per cent *ad valorem* duty. The reason for the new system was to avoid the anomaly that might arise with changes in the prices of products, and to avoid unnecessary hardship on the producers. The burden of a specific tax bears more heavily on producers than an *ad valorem* tax, especially when prices are falling. In 1960 export duties on the principal products all carried 10 per cent *ad valorem* duty, with modifications according to the price per ton on any item concerned.

Price-elasticity of supply is extremely difficult to establish in Nigeria because of the presence of a number of uncontrollable variables, e.g. weather, pests and disease. It has been established, however, that the supply of a tree crop, e.g. cocoa, will increase in the long run in response to an increase in price. On the other hand, the supply of a seasonal crop, e.g. groundnuts and cotton, has a more immediate response to a change in price.[2]

Another type of levy which could be regarded as an export duty was the Produce Sales Tax introduced in 1953–4.[3] This tax was on cocoa and palm oil in the Western Region; groundnuts, cotton, benniseed, soya beans, cocoa and palm produce in the Northern Region; and on all agricultural produce in the Eastern Region. It was collected through the buying agents of the marketing boards and the Department of Marketing and Export, and represented a further reduction in the incomes of primary producers.

[1] Carl. K. Eicher and Carl Liedholm (eds), *Growth and Development of the Nigerian Economy*, pp. 119–55.
[2] Ibid., pp. 138–9.
[3] Produce Sales Tax was introduced into Western and Northern Nigeria in 1953. 'The revenue is to meet increasing cost of social services': *Colonial Reports*, Nigeria, 1953, pp. 21–2. It was introduced into Eastern Nigeria in 1954: *Colonial Reports*, Nigeria, 1954, p. 141.

Income tax

In 1946 an income tax ordinance provided for foreigners throughout Nigeria, and Nigerians in the township of Lagos, to pay a graduated income tax.[1] The individual rates imposed in 1943 were increased by 50 per cent in 1946. Nigerians outside the township of Lagos paid the general tax in accordance with various forms of assessment. Tax assessment was particularly difficult among the people because of the diversity of political, social and economic conditions in different areas, and because of the general problem of ascertaining incomes on which correct assessment could be based. There were also administrative and financial difficulties in tax collection.

In Northern Nigeria, there were seven main methods of assessing general tax:[2]

(a) Locally-distributed income tax. This was the most general method, being applied to about 90 per cent of the population. 'The village' was used as the unit of assessment. After careful consideration had been given to the general (agricultural) prosperity and the overall economic conditions of each area, the Head was informed of the total tax assessment of his area. He, in turn, would apportion the tax to his people according to the ability to pay, and with the advice of elders.

(b) Poll tax. Where the differences in the incomes of village inhabitants were not great, a flat rate was payable.

(c) Tax on ascertainable incomes. Civil servants and employees of native authorities and commercial firms who had definitely ascertainable incomes were assessed at the rate of 4d. in the £ up to £72, and 6d. in the £ thereafter.

(d) Wealthy traders' tax. Most traders kept no business accounts, consequently it was difficult to assess their incomes. However, every year rough estimates of their wealth were made by local assessment committees, and on these were based tax assessments.

(e) In mining areas where there was a large and, to some extent, shifting labour force, a tax of 4d. per month was payable by employees on wages of up to 4s. per week; a tax of 6d. per month was payable by tributers and by employees on wages over 4s. but

[1] See Chapter 6.
[2] *Colonial Annual Reports*, Nigeria, 1946, p. 26.

not exceeding 7s. per week. This tax was collected by the mining company's paymaster at the time the labour was paid, and was remitted by him to the District Head.

(*f*) Strangers' tax. The term 'strangers' or 'immigrants' applied to non-Nigerians and to Nigerians who were not of Northern Nigerian origin by birth. The strangers' tax was based on the apparent wealth of the people concerned, and was additional to the amount of the original community assessment. In areas where the poll tax was adopted they paid under that system.

(*g*) Land revenue tax. Based on a detailed assessment of the average productivity per acre in each revenue survey district. This system only applied to five big areas in 1946.

In the old Western Provinces there were no community assessments as in the North, and broadly the system combined a flat rate with an income tax. In 1946 the following types of tax were levied there: flat rate, income tax rate, trade taxes and a tax on unearned incomes. The last two were levied in the Oyo and Ijebu provinces only. The flat rate varied from 7s. to 10s. on incomes below the maximum of between £24 and £30 per annum, and was payable by all male adults, whether employed or unemployed. In the cases of adults who were unemployed or were unable to afford the flat rate, it was the common practice for their relatives to pay for them. In the Abeokuta and Ijebu provinces a flat-rate tax was also levied on all adult females, because many earned an income through retail trading. It was relatively easy for such women traders to pay the tax, but when the adult female did not engage in any trade, her tax was paid by her parents or relatives, or if married, her husband. In any case it was usually an additional burden on the adult males. Income tax was payable by adult males whose incomes exceeded the amount at which flat rates ceased to be payable. The trade taxes in force in the old Oyo and Ijebu provinces were payable in addition to the flat rate by persons engaged in certain trades, e.g. blacksmiths, goldsmiths, cattle-dealers. Also in these two areas a tax was levied on unearned income – 5 per cent and $2\frac{1}{2}$ per cent at Oyo and Ijebu respectively. Unearned income included incomes derived from rents and securities – these were not included in the income under which the individual was assessed to pay tax.

The methods and standards of tax assessment varied in different parts of the country. A common method, however, was the keeping of nominal rolls of all taxpayers by the local authority tax offices: these were revised anually, and formed the basis for computing the amount of flat rate of tax payable by each village or town. It was the task of local assessment committees to assess individuals liable under the income tax rates. Local authorities also enforced the collection of taxes. There were no reliable statistics to show the total number of taxpayers in Nigeria.

Until 1960 the income tax system remained largely on the basis of the 1946 pattern. The only major change took place in 1960 with the introduction by the Western Nigeria government of a flat rate of £1. 17s. 6d. for low incomes, i.e. incomes excluded from the graduated scale of assessment.[1]

For those whose incomes were ascertainable, personal allowances were given before tax assessment. In 1960 such allowances included £200 in respect of a wife living with or maintained by the taxpayer, £40 in respect of each unmarried child (up to a maximum of four), up to £100 in respect of the cost of maintaining a dependant relative, a limited allowance on life assurance premiums and the amount of any income of the taxpayer's wife, up to £200.

Company tax

The company tax was fixed at 5s. in the £ on taxable profit by the income tax ordinance of 1943, but in April 1946 it was increased to 7s. 6d. in the pound. Early in 1948 an arrangement was concluded with the British government for the avoidance of double taxation on businesses. The main result of the arrangement was that the profits of a British trading concern having a permanent establishment in Nigeria would bear the full rate of Nigeria's company tax, and the burden of relieving the resultant double taxation was to be borne by the United Kingdom government. The arrangement was to be backdated to April 1946. Again, in 1949 an agreement was concluded between the United Kingdom and Nigeria in order to avoid double taxation of profits arising from trade effected by United Kingdom firms. Under the agreement, Nigeria levied income tax on profits arising from merchandise exported to Nigeria by United Kingdom firms, leaving the United Kingdom govern-

[1] *Western News* (weekly), 11 May 1960.

ment to tax profits arising from sales of local produce abroad accruing to United Kingdom firms.

In 1950 the company tax on taxable profit was raised to a flat rate of 9s. in the £. In the same year, some changes in business taxation were introduced, including the extension of exemption from

TABLE 12.3   *Company tax by taxable profit,*
             1955–60 (£000)

Year of assessment ending 31 March	Number of companies	Taxable profit	Tax payable*
1955–6	(1) 201	5,138	2,312
	(2) 40	7,017	3,158
1956–7	(1) 218	4,845	2,159
	(2) 40	6,756	3,040
1957–8	(1) 214	4,766	2,042
	(2) 43	6,877	3,113
1958–9	(1) 232	4,882	1,895
	(2) 33	3,505	1,403
1959–60	(1) 310	4,357	1,704
	(2) 47	3,850	1,537

* Tax payable is inclusive of tax reliefs given to pioneer industries and small companies.

Notes:
1. Assessed in Nigeria.
2. Assessed in UK assessments made through office in London, but in no way connected with UK taxation.

Sources: *Digest of Statistics*, vols, 7 and 8 (1958 and 1959), and *Annual Abstract of Statistics, 1963.*

Nigerian income tax to non-resident airlines operating in Nigeria (non-resident shipping lines were already exempt). In 1952 the Nigerian government introduced an ordinance which granted a period of relief from income tax to public companies established as pioneer projects. A new system of granting relief from taxation in respect of capital expenditure was also introduced.[1] Company tax stood at 8s. in the £ in 1960.

[1] See Chapter 15.

Another source of revenue was the Colonial Development and Welfare Grant. The British government provided grants for financing specific plans for social and economic developments including research and surveys, agriculture, communications, education, community development and broadcasting, health and housing. 'Research and surveys' included projects on medical research, and geodetic, topographical and geological surveys. In agriculture, the emphasis was on giving peasant farmers advice and practical help

TABLE 12.4 *Allocation of funds under the
             Colonial Development and
             Welfare Acts, 1945–55 (£000)*

Allocation to colonial territories

Nigeria (general)	23,300
Federal government	3,750
Northern Region	4,750
Eastern Region	2,750
Western Region	500
Southern Cameroons	1,330
Total (Nigeria)	36,380

Source: *The United Kingdom Colonial Development
        and Welfare Acts*, CO1, REP 3400, 1956, appendix II.

though such schemes as soil conservation and the bringing into production of new land by bush clearing, drainage and irrigation, and the provision of water supplies. In 1956 Nigeria received the sum of £2 million for agricultural development. In the same year, £1·5 million was granted for the development of trunk roads in the Federation of Nigeria, and a separate sum of £3·45 million was granted to Northern Nigeria for this purpose. Most of the amount allocated to education was spent on the expansion of primary schooling, although some assistance was given for technical and vocational education. Funds made available for public health were spent on general improvements in the medical services. Total expenditure under the Colonial Development and Welfare Schemes increased from about £2,995,000 in 1948 to £9,408,000 in 1950;[1]

[1] *Report of the Accountant-General, 1950*, Lagos, Government Printer.

and, as shown on table 12.4, to £36,380,000 in 1955. After 1957, however, Nigeria ceased to receive further grants under the Colonial Development and Welfare Acts. The funds which had already been granted before that date were to be spent before 1960; if not, the balance reverted to the British government.

Problems of revenue allocation[1]

The problem of revenue allocation developed from the frequent constitutional changes which took place after 1946. In June 1946 Sir Sydney Phillipson, financial secretary to the Nigerian government, was appointed 'to study comprehensively and make recommendations regarding the problems of administrative and financial procedure to be adopted under the newly-introduced Richard's Constitution'. In his report,[2] he recommended that the revenue of each region should come from two sources: first, from some taxes and fees to be declared regional; and secondly, from a block grant paid to each region by the central government.

In 1950 a Revenue Allocation Commission, under the chairmanship of Professor J. R. Hicks, was appointed to make proposals for the division of revenues under the new constitution; its recommendations[3] were approved by the British government and embodied in the Nigeria (Revenue Allocation) Order in Council made on 4 December 1951.

The new fiscal system which emerged was designed to provide the regions with revenues of their own, with an allocation from the revenues of the Nigerian government to be based on the principles of (*a*) derivation, (*b*) needs and (*c*) national interest. The most important arrangements were:

(i) Certain local revenues should be handed over to complete regional control, with the regions having the power to fix the rates of tax; the import duty on motor spirit should be replaced by regional sales taxes on motor spirit.

[1] For a detailed study of the evolution of federal finance in Nigeria, see Adebayo Adedeji, *Nigerian Federal Finance*.
[2] *Administrative and Financial Procedure under the New Constitution: Financial Relations between the Government of Nigeria and the Native Administration*, Lagos, 1947.
[3] *Report of the Fiscal Commission on Revenue Allocation*, Lagos, Government Printer, 1951.

(ii) Half of the revenue from taxes imposed by the government of Nigeria on tobacco and cigarettes should be allocated to the regions in accordance with their consumption of tobacco products.

(iii) An annual grant, based on the population of each region, should be made from Nigerian government revenues.

(iv) Annual grants should be made to the regions in total reimbursement of the expenditure on native administration police.

(v) A grant of £2 million should be made to the Northern Region, in order to remedy its serious under-equipment in respect of public works and public buildings.

Most of the arrangements contained in the Hicks report were adopted until 1957, when further constitutional changes necessitated a review of the fiscal system,[1] and a Fiscal Commission was appointed, under the chairmanship of Sir Jeremy Raisman.

The commission's report rejected the basic principles of derivation for allocating revenues, yet some of its recommendations could not depart totally from these principles.[2] It recommended that export duties on produce and hide and skins should continue to be returned to the regions of origin of the products. The proceeds of import duties on motor spirit and diesel oil, and of import and excise duties on tobacco and tobacco products, were to continue to be distributed among the regions on the basis of derivation. Fifty per cent of mining fees and mining royalties and rents were to be allocated to the regions of deposit of such minerals. The main departure from the previous system was the recommendation that a 'distributable pool' of funds should be established, into which 30 per cent of all other import revenues and 30 per cent of mining revenues were to be paid. The money in the 'pool' was to be divided among the regions, the North receiving 40 per cent, the West 24 per cent and the East 31 per cent; all the other customs revenues were to be retained by the federal government. It was also recommended that a special grant of £500,000 be made annually to the Northern Region until the new proposals came into operation because, according to the report, this region had been losing money to the others, owing to faulty

[1] *Report by the Nigerian Constitutional Conference held in London in May and July 1957*, Cmd. 207.

[2] *Nigeria: Report of the Fiscal Commission*, Cmd. 481, London, July 1957.

calculations under the derivative principles which operated between 1954 and 1958. The report also recommended that the regions should have control of income tax. These arrangements were in operation until independence in 1960.

TABLE 12.5   *Current revenue from federal sources allocated to the regions, 1953–60 (£000)*

Year ending 31 March	Western Region	Northern Region	Eastern Region	Total
1953	5,043	7,652	4,190	16,885
1954	5,590	4,792	4,398	14,780
1955	11,698	6,907	8,311	26,916
1956	10,570	6,729	6,670	23,969
1957	11,455	7,833	6,904	26,192
1958	12,332	7,850	7,084	27,266
1959	13,499	8,169	7,418	29,086
1960	15,239	11,318	9,373	35,930

Note: For the Northern Region only, customs and excise revenue was included; for the other regions, the total of all federal revenue allocated to each region was included. Special grants from the federal government were also included.

Source: *Annual Abstract of Statistics, 1963.*

National debt

Nigeria needed a great volume of capital investment – more than she could provide herself – for social and economic development projects, which included transport and communications, agricultural development, health and education. Before the second world war the government had been very cautious about incurring public debt for such projects;[1] the most important single item on which public debt was incurred was on the development of the railways. However, after 1946 loans were increasingly sought from both foreign and internal sources to supplement the regular annual revenues. One significant change in the structure of Nigeria's public debt was the

[1] A governor of Southern Nigeria, Sir W. Egerton, once said: 'One of the things I am proudest of in West Africa is that I found Nigeria with hardly any debt, and I left it with a debt of five millions (pounds sterling).' *West Africa,* 31 May 1919, p. 398.

growing proportion of local or internal debt. The first Nigerian local loan of £300,000 was made in 1946. The issue met with an immediate response and was oversubscribed by £549,250. The total public debt of the regional and federal governments soon increased as more development projects were undertaken. Table 12.6 shows federal government borrowing. It must be added that the bulk of the public debt of regional governments were made up of internal loans from the marketing boards.

TABLE 12.6   *Federal government borrowing, 1946–60 (£000)*

Financial year	Amount at beginning of the financial year		
	Total	External	Internal
1946–7	24,859	24,859	—
1949–50	22,075	21,775	300
1950–1	17,598	14,148	3,450
1951–2	17,601	14,163	3,438
1954–5	24,249	20,963	3,286
1955–6	19,982	16,750	3,232
1956–7	21,926	16,750	5,176
1957–8	31,169	16,750	14,419
1958–9	30,743	16,750	13,993
1959–60	34,051	20,501	13,550

Source: *Annual Abstract of Statistics, 1963.*

All Nigeria's external loans were floated on the London money market; the bulk of internal loans, however, were held by individual Nigerians, co-operative marketing and thrift societies, local authorities, commercial banks, insurance companies and commercial firms. The total annual charge on the federal government revenue in respect of interest repayments and sinking fund charges amounted to about £2·5 million in 1960, representing just under 3 per cent of total federal revenue for that year.

DEVELOPMENT INSTITUTIONS

The development plans placed much emphasis on regional autonomy, particularly between 1950 and 1960, and each region jealously guarded its own rights and obligations arising from the constitutions. There were as many development plans as there were regional governments, and it was impossible to avoid wasteful duplications and overlapping of social and economic development projects. No economic targets were – or could be – fixed for the country as a whole, and although the National Economic Council was established late in 1955 to permit the various governments to discuss policies and common economic problems, the development programmes were already formulated by that time.[1] However, apart from the various existing government departments,[2] a number of statutory institutions were established in order to help the speeding-up and co-ordination of a number of projects.

The Federal Loans Board, which was the successor of the former Colony Development Board, was established in 1956 with the object of helping to finance projects designed to further industrial development in the country.[3] The maximum loan which the board could make was £50,000.[4] The federal government provided £300,000 to be used by the loans board during the period of its economic programme, 1955–60. One of the main purposes of the board was to provide medium-term loan capital to those indigenous entrepreneurs who appeared able to employ it profitably. The board was to cater for the entrepreneur whose capital fell short of his ability, and who needed more money for the full development of his latent talent: for example, the trader who wanted to build an office, or the industrial entrepreneur who wished to establish a rubber plantation. Obviously, this involved a certain amount of risk, as it was possible to assess wrongly the credit-worthiness of entrepreneurs or the profitability of proposed projects. In addition, there were very few saleable securities in the country. However, the board was able to approve some loans after proper scrutiny: during the financial

[1] *National Development Plan 1962–8*, Lagos, Federal Ministry of Economic Development, pp. 6–7.

[2] A number of government departments handled some development projects which fell within their functions: for example, the Public Works Department was mainly responsible for the construction of roads and bridges.

[3] For a detailed study, see S. P. Schatz, *Development Bank Lending in Nigeria: The Federal Loans Board*.

[4] The approval of the Federal Minister of Commerce and Industry was required for loans in excess of £5,000, and the approval of the Federal Council of Ministers for loans in excess of £30,000.

year 1957–8, fourteen applications for loans were approved for a total sum of £38,840; and during the following financial year eighteen loans totalling £195,285 were granted.[1] The amount of each loan varied from £140 for a local textile factory to £50,000 for providing launches to operate river transport. Other enterprises which obtained loans included sawmill, furniture, bakery, electrical and upholstery concerns.

The Western Region Development Corporation was the successor to the original Western Regional Production Development Board, and it was responsible for undertaking projects for the development of agriculture and industry in Western Nigeria.[2] The board's funds consisted initially of grants made to it by the former Cocoa and Oil Palm Products marketing boards. After 1955, the corporation was financed by the Western Nigeria government. Under its development programme of 1955–60, the Western Nigeria government set aside a capital provision of £4·5 million for the corporation. The main emphasis of the original board was on agricultural development, but the activities of the new corporation were much wider in scope. Efforts were made to develop partnership schemes on agricultural projects with co-operative societies and local government authorities. Besides its agricultural activities – which included plantations for rubber, oil palm, cocoa, citrus and pineapples – the corporation established canning and rubber-processing factories in Ibadan and Ikpoba respectively. The corporation's non-agricultural activities included a first-class catering rest-house in Ibadan. The corporation also participated both financially and administratively in the direction of a variety of industries, including the manufacture of cement, plastics, metal window frames, asbestos, cement products, aluminium products, pre-stressed concrete, textiles and bedding.

 The Western Region Finance Corporation was established in 1955, and took over the functions of the former Western Region Development (Loans) Board.[3] This corporation granted loans for industrial as well as agricultural and commercial projects; it was also

[1] *Annual Report of the Federal Loans Board, 1958 and 1959*, Lagos, Government Printer.

[2] The corporation derived its powers from the Western Region Law, no. 9 of 1955.

[3] The corporation was established under the Western Region Law, no. 9 of 1955.

empowered to grant loans to non-Nigerians who were in partnership with Western Region enterprises. The corporation intensified its loan activities to farmers, as it was realized that short-term agricultural loans were becoming popular, and established 209 local loans boards. These local boards were corporate entities, administering agricultural and fishing loans under the guidance of the corporation. Corn mill loans were granted to quite a number of people as this was purely a small-scale industry, usually located near marketplaces where the demand for processed grain was likely to justify the establishment of a mill. Loans were also granted for projects including rubber plantations, poultry farming, textile factories, sawmills, sea fishing and transport; and some local authorities even borrowed from the corporation to finance road tarring, market development and improvements to motor parks. By 1960 it had granted loans totalling £1·4 million for industrial purposes. In suitable cases, it made direct equity investments in businesses for which indigenous capital was not readily available, and by 1960 it had invested a total of £1·5 million in this way.

The Eastern Region Development Corporation was established in 1954, and began to function in 1955.[1] It replaced the former Regional Development (Loans) Board and Regional Production Development Board, and latterly the Eastern Region Finance Corporation, which was established in 1954. It was charged with the principal duties of improving the quantity and quality of oil palm produce, on which the economy of the Eastern Region was very largely dependent. The corporation operated a number of agricultural and industrial schemes including pioneer oil mills, oil palm plantations, cashew plantations, a cocoa plantation and a cattle ranch. By 1960 it had issued more than £1·5 million in loans, for the establishment of projects including poultry farms, rubber-processing plants, bakeries, corn mills, lime works and mechanical laundries. A loan of £530,000 was also granted to the Onitsha Urban District Council for the construction of the Onitsha market. Other important ventures for the corporation were the investment of £500,000 in the Nigerian Cement Company Ltd at Nkalagu, and the investment of £490,000 in Oban (Nigeria) Rubber Estates Ltd in Calabar.

The Northern Region Development Corporation was estab-

[1] The corporation was established under the provisions of the Eastern Region Law, no. 12 of 1954, as amended by Eastern Region Law, no. 24 of 1956.

lished in 1955, but did not begin to function till January 1956.[1] Most of its funds were devoted to financing agricultural land settlement, agricultural production development, communications, irrigation and water supplies, and tsetse fly control. The corporation also granted loans to native or local authorities for providing markets, motor parks, abattoirs and printing presses. During the financial year 1959–60, £802,558 was granted in loans. During the same year 1,840 businessmen secured loans for various forms of private enterprise, which ranged over a wide field including a number of village and cottage industries. The popular items for which loans were sought included sewing machines, block-making machines, sugar crushers, corn mills, rice mills, mechanical workshops and garages, and light sawmills.[2]

There were a few other institutions which were directly concerned with economic development in Nigeria. On 2 October 1959 it was announced that, on the invitation of the federal government, the Commonwealth Development Finance Company Ltd,[3] in consultation with leading British and Nigerian business interests, was to organize an investment company for the Federation – the Investment Company of Nigeria Limited.[4] The company was to encourage, and in certain instances to sponsor, the development of local industrial, commercial or agricultural enterprise, and to exploit the country's natural resources by providing financial assistance, attracting expatriate investment capital to private enterprise ventures, seeking technical and managerial expertise, attracting Nigerian investment, and encouraging the growth of a stocks and shares market.

The Colonial Development Corporation also played an important

---

[1] The corporation was established by the Northern Region Law, no. 14 of 1955.

[2] *Northern Region Development Corporation. Annual Report, 1959–60*, Kaduna, Government Printer, pp. 31–2.

[3] The Commonwealth Development Finance Company Ltd was incorporated in March 1953 to 'provide or procure financial facilities of all kinds for the development of the natural and other resources of any part of the Commonwealth'.

[4] The company was incorporated on 17 October 1959. Of the authorized capital of £5 million, one million £1 shares were issued by 1960 and these were fully subscribed by Nigerian, British, French, Swiss, Dutch, American and Canadian firms, companies and corporations.

TABLE 12.7   *Statement of capital expenditure by the*
United Africa group, 1946–60 (£000)

Financial year	Commercial	Industrial	Transport	Total
1946–7	371	403	14	788
1947–8	555	510	72	1,137
1948–9	647	616	142	1,405
1949–50	606	347	442	1,395
1950–1	531	319	854	1,704
1951–2	549	728	529	1,806
1952–3	587	701	516	1,804
1953–4	823	492	166	1,481
1954–5	787	293	310	1,390
1955–6	1,186	346	296	1,828
1956–7	1,624	724*	209	2,557
1957–8	1,351	740*	635	2,726
1958–9	935	897*	263	2,095
1959–60	1,074	1,073*†	40	2,187

* Including agriculture.

† This figure includes the United Africa group's share of capital expenditure by industrial enterprises in which the group is a minority shareholder. It will be noted that the group's capital expenditure in industrial enterprises in 1959–60 accounted for 45 per cent of its total expenditure.

Notes:

1. 'Commercial' includes warehouses, shops, housing, etc.
2. 'Industrial' includes forest activities, factories, plantations (including appropriate housing).
3. 'Transport' includes river craft, plant, wharves, bulk oil installations, etc.
4. Discrepancies between totals and the sums of constituent items are due to rounding off.

Source: *UAC Statistical and Economic Review*, 1953–61.

role in the economic development of Nigeria,[1] investing in a number of projects including the light engineering industry, sawmills and housing development; and by the end of 1956 its current projects in Nigeria amounted to £2,799,000. It encouraged participation in its

[1] The Colonial Development Corporation was created by the Overseas Resources Development Act (UK) of 1948. Its duties were defined as the formulation and carrying out of projects for developing colonial resources.

schemes and the eventual assumption of full responsibility for them by the governments, their agencies or commercial firms.[1]

Some of the major trading companies contributed substantially to the economic development of Nigeria. After 1946, these companies increased their capital expenditure to cover many production fields, including commerce, industry and transport. One of the major companies which made such a contribution was the United Africa Company (UAC) Ltd.

Between 1955 and 1960, the UAC Ltd spent about £6 million on commercial projects in Nigeria, and for the same period it spent about £4·4 million on industrial and agricultural projects and about £1·4 million on transport.

An appraisal of development planning

Between 1946 and 1960, the patterns of social and economic systems changed so fast that it is difficult to assess correctly the achievements or lack of progress which could be associated with any given period of development planning. In general terms, however, it is possible to assess the results of the fifteen years of economic planning by examining the changes which took place in the volume of the national income of the country, and the capital formation among the various sectors of the population.

Total production over the decade 1950–60 grew by approximately 4 per cent per year in real terms. In 1950–1 the national income of Nigeria was estimated at £593·4 million,[2] and a survey of 1956–7 based on current prices put it at £812·3 million. On the face of it, there was an increase of £218·9 million over a period of six years. However, it is now known that the true increase was disguised: different methods of calculating the consumption of certain locally-produced foodstuffs had been adopted, with the result that the 1956–7 survey included values in respect of yams, cassava and guinea corn, which, after allowing for price changes, were 26 per cent lower than those included for 1950–1.[3] Perhaps a clearer illustration of the economic growth of Nigeria is shown by the changes in the gross domestic product of Nigeria (see table 12.8). The gross domestic product of Nigeria at 1957 prices was £688·7 million in 1950.

[1] *UAC Statistical* and *Economic Review*, September 1957.
[2] A. R. Prest and I. G. Stewart, *The National Income of Nigeria 1950–1.*
[3] NNEC, *Economic Survey of Nigeria, 1959*, p. 15.

TABLE 12.8 *Gross domestic product at 1957 prices for fiscal years 1950–60 (£ million)*

Activity	1950	1951	1952	1953	1954	1955	1956	1957	1958	1959	1960
Agriculture (including land development)	385·8	423·2	438·7	454·2	479·5	492·1	468·0	479·6	542·2	526·2	549·4
Livestock	60·1	57·7	52·5	53·5	55·7	56·5	57·6	57·7	52·3	58·7	61·0
Fishing	9·7	9·8	9·9	10·0	10·3	10·3	12·6	13·3	15·0	15·0	15·0
Forest products	9·4	12·0	10·1	11·9	12·3	13·4	13·6	14·6	10·4	13·1	14·6
Mining (including oil exploration)	7·6	7·6	7·9	7·9	8·1	9·0	9·6	9·4	7·0	6·6	8·4
Manufacturing and public utilities	3·9	4·0	5·8	6·3	7·9	8·7	12·0	13·1	25·4	30·6	36·1
Communications	2·7	2·7	3·0	2·9	2·6	2·4	2·6	3·1	2·9	3·1	3·2
Building and civil engineering	20·3	25·4	19·4	25·9	37·8	38·3	36·5	43·0	22·9	32·1	33·3
Ownership of buildings	8·9	9·1	9·2	9·4	9·4	9·7	9·8	10·3	7·9	8·6	9·3
Transport	28·6	34·0	35·3	45·4	50·9	60·2	65·1	74·6	29·1	32·3	37·3
Crafts	15·8	15·9	16·0	16·1	16·2	16·4	16·5	16·7	20·4	20·4	20·4
Missions	6·9	7·0	7·6	7·8	8·7	11·4	12·7	15·9	18·1	21·6	23·3
Government	15·0	16·4	19·9	16·5	17·6	23·4	28·7	30·5	29·1	36·3	35·0
Marketing boards	41·0	10·5	28·0	28·8	42·7	25·0	44·9	11·7	0·7	11·6	5·8
Banking, insurance and the professions	1·5	1·2	1·3	1·7	1·7	2·1	2·2	2·5	3·1	3·7	3·7
Domestic services	4·4	4·4	4·4	4·7	4·8	5·0	5·7	5·5	3·7	3·9	4·0
Miscellaneous services	0·9	1·0	1·1	1·1	1·2	1·5	1·9	2·0	1·8	2·1	3·7
Distribution, residual error, etc.	66·2	99·5	123·4	107·5	104·7	109·8	73·7	106·5	108·0	112·6	117·8
Gross domestic product at factor cost	688·7	741·4	793·5	811·6	872·1	895·2	873·7	910·0	900·0	938·5	981·3

Source: *Annual Abstract of Statistics, 1966.*

It increased to £895·2 million in 1955, and to £981·3 million in 1960.

The interdependence of the different sectors of the economy indicated some increases in the wealth of the country. In 1950 the total gross capital formation in Nigeria was estimated at £36·6 million, of which 45·1 per cent came from the public sector and 54·9 per cent from the private sector. In 1955–6 it increased to £78·3 million, of which the public sector accounted for £45·1, i.e. 57·6 per cent, and the private sector £33·2 million, i.e. 42·4 per cent. Finally, in 1959–60 the total gross capital formation reached the highest value so far of £133·4 million.[1] Of this value the public sector accounted for £88·9 million, i.e. 66·6 per cent, and the private sector 33·4 per cent.

Virtually all sectors of the economy developed rapidly. The quantity of agricultural production grew by 30 per cent – which was more than enough to offset the rise of between 2 and 2½ per cent per annum in the population. The manufacturing industries – though still relatively small – increased about fivefold, and construction works were more than trebled. The supply of electricity and water also increased fourfold. The economic growth of the country was not evenly spaced, as it varied according to the prosperity in agricultural production, which accounted for over 60 per cent of the national income. Increases in the prices of the main agricultural export products, particularly up to 1955, brought prosperity to the entire economy.[2]

There was a significant expansion in the private sector. For example, the gross investment by major companies, which in 1954 was estimated at £11·7 million, rose to £20·5 million in 1959–60. The investments of other enterprises as well as personal investments were estimated to have reached about £52 million in 1960, compared with £31 million in 1954. This expansion was undoubtedly due to the efforts of the governments in providing the economy with the much-needed infrastructure. The production of locally-consumed items also increased; although the rise was less than that for export production, it was nevertheless of the order of 50 per cent over the ten years 1950–60.

[1] *Annual Abstract of Statistics, 1963*, Lagos, Federal Office of Statistics.
[2] *National Development Plan, 1962–8*, pp. 6–13.

13   Transport and communications

The major development of the inland waterways after 1946 concerned the improvement of the Niger–Benue system. The government instituted large-scale studies into the nature and behaviour of these two main river systems, and from 1953 to 1959 teams of hydrological experts carried out detailed investigations of the routes with sea access.[1] Efforts were also made to improve the other important rivers and the numerous creeks by dredging them. The most important project considered in connexion with navigation on the inland waterways was the construction of a multi-purpose dam on the Niger at Kainji.[2] It was thought that by constructing a system of locks on it navigation would be considerably improved.

The volume of foreign trade traffic for Nigeria's transport system increased after the second world war, but river transport enjoyed the least prosperity. Between 1946 and 1957, road transport and rail tonnage increased by about 17·5 per cent and 6·4 per cent per annum respectively, while river transport increased by only 4·1 per cent per annum. Apart from competition from both the railways and roads, one other important constraint upon increased river transport was the limited capacity of the rivers themselves, due to physical defects and lack of artificial improvements. An important disability of the river routes was their seasonality. Only the lower Niger below Onitsha was navigable all the year round. Inevitably, this increased operational costs and led to high freight and passenger fares. Produce had to be stored for long periods while awaiting

---

[1] *Statement of Policy for the Niger and Benue Rivers*, Sessional Paper no. 3 of 1959.
[2] The Kainji Dam Project, one of the major projects conceived under the 1962–8 National Development Plan, is outside the scope of this book.

shipment – a great disadvantage because of the deterioration in quality of produce and high costs of holding stock. The poor conditions of the river ports also contributed to delay and inefficiency in river transport. In fact, most of the improvements to river ports that were made were carried out by private companies, of which the UAC and John Holt were the largest.[1] There were few buoys, and facilities were not available for night navigation.

However, the vast riverain area of the lower Niger was still served practically exclusively by river, and transport by the Benue was of primary importance to the commercial life of the region between Yola and Maiduguri. The government continued to provide a number of marine services. Public transport and ferry services maintained by the Marine Department and later by the Department of Inland Waterways[2] included a passenger ferry between Lagos and Apapa; vehicle ferries across the Niger and the Ethiope at Onitsha and Sapele respectively; inland water services through the lagoons and the delta between Lagos, Warri and Burutu, between Port Harcourt, Degema, Nembe, Brass and Akassa, and between Port Harcourt and Bonny; and coal and coastwise services between Lagos and Port Harcourt.

The services between Lagos and Port Harcourt were provided weekly by government vessels. Fortnightly services were also maintained along the coast between Lagos, Port Harcourt, Calabar and Victoria. Ferries transported passengers as well as motor vehicles. During the financial year 1957–8, 294,543 passengers and 48,363 vehicles were transported on the Sapele–Benin route; and 99,094 passengers and 41,383 vehicles were transported on the Onitsha–Asaba route.[3] Of the 4,200 miles of navigable waterways under the control of the Inland Waterways Department in 1958, only a total of 1,059 miles were inspected and improved for navigation, at a total cost of £8,981. The increasing cost of maintaining the waterways was said to be due to high costs of labour and equipment.[4]

[1] Sessional Paper no. 3 of 1959, p. 7.
[2] The Department of Inland Waterways was established in 1956. *Statement of the Policy proposed by the Government of the Federation for the Establishment of an Inland Waterways Department*, Sessional Paper no. 7 of 1956.
[3] *Annual Report of the Federal Department of Inland Waterways, 1957–8*, Lagos, Government Printer, 1959, p. 20.
[4] Ibid., p. 2.

In addition to government marine services, a very extensive internal traffic, mainly in foodstuffs, was provided by Nigerians who operated with canoes and a few engine-boats. A few expatriate firms also provided river fleets exclusively concerned with foreign trade: these included the Niger River Transport (a branch of the UAC), which in 1960 operated with 24 tugs and 96 barges of a total of 22,220 tons, representing two-thirds of the total river fleet capacity; Holts Transport Ltd (a subsidiary of John Holt & Co. Ltd) which operated with 18 tugs and 59 barges of a total tonnage of 6,650; and a relatively new company, the Niger Benue Transport, with 7 tugs and 25 barges of a total of 4,800 tons.

The Niger River Transport carried goods to the tonnage of 150,000 in 1946–7, 159,000 in 1950–1 and 187,000 in 1959–60 (see table 13.1). The Mobil Oil Nigeria Limited (an oil company operating in the delta) also owned and operated a tank barge-train

TABLE 13.1 *Niger River Transport fleet, 1945–60*

Financial year	Goods		Passengers	
	Tonnage carried ('ooo)	Ton mile ('ooo)	Number of passengers	Revenue* (£,ooo)
1945–6	119	52,257	23	233
1946–7	150	59,218	7	274
1947–8	155	64,028	9	328
1948–9	158	55,385	8	301
1949–50	145	55,882	5	310
1950–1	159	69,048	4	495
1951–2	161	68,212	6	538
1952–3	169	74,625	5	663
1953–4	175	79,028	4	692
1954–5	181	79,470	4	780
1955–6	186	76,043	3	805
1956–7	192	77,053	3	793
1957–8	169	66,684	2	583
1958–9	184	76,429	1	620
1959–60	187	82,220	1	638

* Ninety-five per cent or more of the revenue is obtained from goods traffic.
Source: *UAC Statistical and Economic Review*, 1948–60.

carrying bulk petroleum products from Sapele to up-river installations as far as Garua. The Monrovia Navigation Co. Limited also
operated petroleum tankers for Mobil Oil Nigeria Limited, as far
as Onitsha and beyond to Lokoja and Makurdi at times of high
water. Table 13.2 shows the traffic of the Niger River Transport by
major river port of origin and destination for 1959–60.

TABLE 13.2   *Traffic of the Niger River Transport by major port of*
origin and destination, 1959–60

Port	Downstream		Upstream	
	Tons	*Per cent*	*Tons*	*Per cent*
Baro	42,029	37·3	24,787	37·0
Garua	12,601	11·1	12,217	18·2
Idah	11,922	10·6	1,115	1·7
Onitsha	9,814	8·7	21,345	31·9
Lokoja	9,573	8·5	1,719	2·6
Numan	5,701	5·1	664	1·0
Makurdi	4,352	3·9	0	—
Assay Patani	4,078	3·6	491	0·7
Dalmaro	3,335	3·0	325	0·5
Ibi	2,425	2·2	0	—
Gana Gana/Okpari	2,252	2·0	278	0·4
Yola	1	—	2,093	3·1
Lau	1	—	416	0·6
Other	4,562	4·0	1,560	2·3
Total	112,646	100·0	67,010	100·0

Source: Babafemi Ogundana, *The Changing Role of River Transport in Nigeria*,
University of Ife, unpublished Staff Seminar Paper, 1969–70.

Ports

The increase in the volume of trade meant that the Nigerian ports
had to handle more traffic, particularly cargo. It also meant that
harbour facilities had to be improved in order to cope with this
increased traffic. The ports in order of importance were Lagos, Port
Harcourt, Sapele, Burutu, Warri, Calabar and Degema. The Lagos
port had two sets of quays – those at Apapa on the mainland, and the
customs quay on Lagos island. Apapa was served by rail and was

used for up-country cargoes, while the customs quay, which was road-served only, was used for Lagos cargo. Both the Apapa and the customs quay areas were extended by the reclamation of land from the lagoon. The modern quay at Apapa, with improved harbour facilities, was opened by Queen Elizabeth II on her visit to Nigeria in 1956. The Port Harcourt port was approached by the Bonny river and lies 41 miles from the sea. The approach to its entrance was over the Bonny bar, which vessels could cross only at high water. The importance of this port increased after the establishment of the cement industry and the exploration for petroleum oil in the area it served. The Warri port was some 25 miles above Forcados on the Warri river. The channels of this river were also shallow and demanded great care when used by vessels. The Calabar port was some 40 miles distant from the Fairway buoy, and 5 miles above the main entrance to the Cross river. The approach, as in others, was difficult and dangerous, but ships of 20 feet draught could enter at high tide. The port of Degema was situated on the Sombreiro river, but could only be reached via the Bonny river.

The most significant features of these ports were the narrow passages leading to them, the shallow rivers on which vessels had to sail and the problem of dredging in order to keep them open as much as possible. The Nigerian Ports Authority succeeded the Marine Department in 1954, and became responsible for the provision, improvement and maintenance of harbour facilities and services in all ports. Its duties included dredging, hydrographic surveying, buoyage, pilotage, maintenance of lighthouses, towage and salvage. New buoyage systems were introduced by the ports authority, and special patrols using up-to-date equipment for recording and broadcasting river depths and buoyage details were operated on the Niger and Benue. The ports authority also provided river maps compiled from hydrographic surveys and aerial photography, together with a network of river gauges for the benefit of shipping.

RAILWAYS

The most urgent problem which faced the railway in 1946 was that of making necessary repairs on the coaches and engines, which had been overworked during the war period. In 1947, 14 main line locomotives, ordered by the government from Canada in 1943, were delivered to help replace engines beyond economic use and repair.[1] Even then, the railway's power position was very much under strength. In 1948 another 20 main line railway engines were

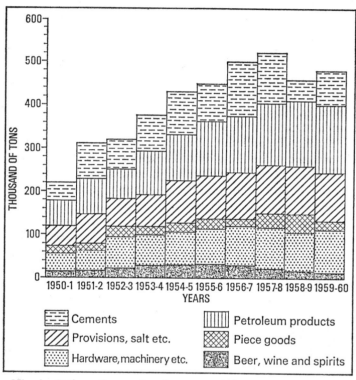

9 Nigerian Railway Corporation: imports carried, 1950–60

bought from the United Kingdom as a partial solution to the problems of providing adequate railway services.

Following the recommendation of the International Bank Mission to Nigeria in 1953, the Nigerian railway came under a corporation in April 1955.[2] The railway corporation made a number of improve-

[1] *Colonial Annual Reports*, Nigeria, 1947, p. 77.
[2] The administration of the Nigerian railway until 1955 was carried on by a General Manager with the highest authority vested in the Director of Railways and Works, subject to the Governor-General's control.

ments to the system. One of the most significant developments was the introduction of diesel locomotives in 1955. These could handle bigger and heavier loads, and could be used more continuously with less maintenance and servicing work. The fact that they did not have

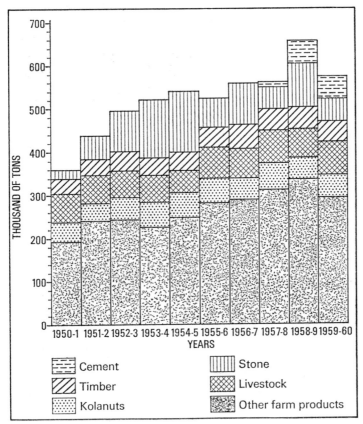

10 Nigerian Railway Corporation: internal traffic, 1950–60

to pick up water also saved time, consequently avoiding the disruptions to running schedules which occurred with steam engines, especially during the dry seasons when there were water shortages in many parts of the country.

Another important development was the extension of the railway system in the north-east of Nigeria. By 1949 approval had already

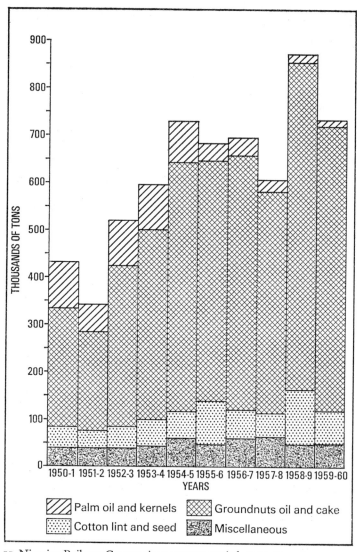

900 —
800 —
700 —
600 —
500 —
400 —
300 —
200 —
100 —
0 —

THOUSANDS OF TONS

1950-1 1951-2 1952-3 1953-4 1954-5 1955-6 1956-7 1957-8 1958-9 1959-60
YEARS

Palm oil and kernels   Groundnuts oil and cake
Cotton lint and seed   Miscellaneous

11 Nigerian Railway Corporation: exports carried, 1950–60

been given by the government to carry out a survey of Bornu province with the object of extending the railway from Nguru to Maiduguri.[1] This was one of the projected extensions contemplated over forty years previously by Lord Lugard, who believed that it would open up the vast plains of Bornu, the soil of which he regarded as very suitable for cotton cultivation. Lugard also considered that such an extension would enable Nigeria to secure the trade of the whole Chad Basin as far north as the Sudan. It was later proved that the Bornu area could grow other crops of equal importance to cotton, such as grain, groundnuts and rice; it also supported vast flocks of sheep, goats and herds of cattle. Three possible extensions had been seriously contemplated: from Lafia, some 60 miles north of Markurdi, a distance of over 400 miles; from Rahama, a distance of some 300 miles; and from Nguru, a distance of some 200 miles through Gasau and Damaturu.

The Mission of the International Bank, which visited Nigeria in 1953, recommended that in order to meet an anticipated expansion of agricultural production in the north-east of Nigeria, either an extension of the railway or a heavy traffic highway should be constructed. The report went on:

> The choice between road and rail transport for this new area must be based on the total cost to the community, and on the possibility of making the users of the facility share that cost. Construction of the railway will require more capital than building a road but on the other hand maintenance costs of a railway are lower and they may be recouped once traffic reaches a certain level.[2]

It concluded that the railway alternative was likely to prove more advantageous to the country. In addition to the railway extension to Maiduguri, the mission also recommended a 40-mile extension of the line from Nguru to Gasau. In order to finance the Bornu railway extension and other development projects on the railway, the Nigerian government borrowed £10 million from the International Bank in 1958.

The 400-mile extension project began in August 1958 from Kuru, south of Jos, across Bauchi and Bornu provinces to Maiduguri in the

[1] *Colonial Annual Reports*, Nigeria, 1949, p. 84.
[2] IBRD, *Economic Development of Nigeria*, p. 309.

north-east corner of Nigeria, and was expected to attract considerable quantities of transit traffic to and from the neighbouring territories, which had no outlet to the sea. While preparations were being made to extend the railway in the north-east, the Bauchi Light Railway, a 2 feet 6 inches gauge line between Jos and Zaria, was closed in 1957 owing to uneconomic returns; this was the first time that any part of the railway had to be closed down.

TABLE 13.3   *Nigerian Railway Corporation: passenger and goods traffic and receipts, 1946–60*

Year	*Traffic*		*Receipts*		
	Number of passengers carried ('000)	*Goods tonnage hauled* ('000)	*Passenger train* (£000)	*Freight train* (£000)	*Total** (£000)
1946	4,262	1,425	748	2,816	3,623
1947	6,256	1,743	1,015	3,517	4,631
1948	6,583	1,604	995	3,612	4,740
1949	6,197	1,841	1,080	4,489	5,716
1950	5,552	1,773	1,015	4,911	6,098
1951	5,585	1,725	1,116	5,027	6,341
1952	5,546	1,752	1,319	6,185	7,758
1953	5,516	2,086	1,470	8,552	10,451
1954	5,454	2,298	1,515	9,740	11,596
1955	5,451	2,602	1,500	11,371	13,251
1956	6,310	2,653	1,696	11,407	13,299
1957	7,271	2,808	1,865	11,942	14,172
1958	7,863	2,739	1,944	11,466	13,664
1959	7,015	3,097	1,884	13,554	15,661
1960	7,881	2,803	1,843	11,545	13,666

* Including sundries.
Source: *Annual Abstract of Statistics, 1963.*

The railway corporation spent about £12 million over the period 1956–60 on general improvements, notably on rolling stock and locomotives, stations, track and signalling improvements, and the establishment of a central technical training school at Zaria for intensifying training in many aspects of railway operation.

While the route mileage remained much the same between 1938 and 1958, and the number of passengers carried varied very little (averaging between 5·5 and 7·5 million a year), the great increase in agricultural export production led to a corresponding increase in rail-freight transport (see figures 9–11). The amount of tonnage

TABLE 13.4 *Number employed by the Nigerian Railway Corporation,* *1947–60*

Period as at 31 March	Civil engineer- ing	Mechani- cal en- gineering	Operating and com- mercial	Adminis- tration	Capital works	Total: all depart- ments
1947	8,355	8,277	3,689	876	2,624	23,821
1948	8,281	8,958	3,938	893	2,548	24,654
1949	8,332	10,057	3,876	948	2,796	26,009
1950	9,080	9,026	4,404	1,000	2,901	27,211
1951	8,225	8,745	5,186	1,220	2,536	25,912
1952	10,983	4,962	9,582	1,521	2,741	29,789
1953	11,778	5,088	10,324	1,532	2,295	31,017
1954	9,581	5,347	9,901	1,717	2,993	29,539
1955	12,886	5,525	9,977	1,745	3,648	33,781
1956	12,186	5,578	9,810	1,689	4,423	33,686
1957	10,023	6,046	10,268	1,848	4,601	32,786
1958	10,413	6,476	10,217	2,254	4,676	34,036
1959	10,177	6,754	10,955	2,305	2,597	32,788
1960	9,752	6,668	10,743	2,413	1,709	31,285

Source: *Annual Abstract of Statistics, 1963.*

hauled between 1955 and 1960 averaged between 2·6 and 2·8 million a year, compared with a tonnage of only 1·4 million in 1946. Traffic receipts also rose from £3·6 million in 1946 to a record of £15·7 million in 1959. The record year for passenger traffic was 1960, when 7,881,000 passengers were carried (see table 13.3). For goods traffic, 1959 proved to be the most successful year, with 3,097,000 tons hauled. By the year ending 31 March 1960, the Nigerian Railway Corporation had 271 steam engine locomotives (215 for use on the main line and 56 for shunting), 39 diesel locomotives, 547 coaching vehicles, 5,489 goods vehicles, 42 goods lorries and 21 goods trailers.[1]

The number of staff employed in various departments increased over the years (see table 13.4 above). Apart from the growing number of university-trained Nigerians, the corporation was able to employ more technical staff through its training schemes, which provided training for craft apprentices, clerks, mechanical engineering assistants and traffic staff-in-training. Of the annual total number of staff, roughly 95 per cent were employed in open line posts, while the remainder were engaged on capital works.

ROADS

After the second world war, a considerable programme of road construction was undertaken under the Colonial Development and Welfare Scheme, and also under the Nigerian government's economic development schemes. The first road financed by the Colonial Development and Welfare Fund was that from Lagos to Ikorodu, joining the road to Shagamu, Ijebu-Ode and Ibadan, and this began in 1945. The following roads were also constructed: Mokwa–Kotangora, Yola–Wukari, Ijebu-Ode–Benin and the Calabar–Mamfe road. By early 1949 a road was completed from Enugu to Mamfe in the Cameroons. The Mokwa–Kotangora road provided a new north–south route which avoided the Kaduna river ferry at Bida; and it was later linked with the main trunk road at Kano. The government's post-war road construction programme was based on an estimated requirement of 40,000 miles of good roads throughout the country.

Before 1952, trunk roads 'A' and 'B' were the responsibility of the public works departments based in Lagos, but from this year regional public works departments were established and assumed responsibility for trunk roads 'B'.[2] The pattern of the road system which developed was that trunk roads 'A', which were constructed and maintained by the federal government, were in the form of a rigid framework on which the rest of the road system was built. The basic components of the trunk 'A' system were two roads running from

[1] *Nigerian Railway Corporation. Report and Accounts for the year ended 31 March 1960.*
[2] This followed the introduction of a new constitution in 1951.

the ports of Lagos and Port Harcourt to the northern boundary, and four east–west roads – two south of the Niger–Benue system, and two north of it. This system linked the federal and the regional capitals with other large towns and ports, and also provided communication between Nigeria and the neighbouring countries. The trunk 'B' system connected provincial and divisional headquarters and other large towns with the trunk 'A' system. Trunk 'B' roads were controlled by the regional governments, and maintained by local authorities with the assistance of grants from the regional governments: these varied between 25 and 100 per cent of the cost of maintenance and construction. Most of the other roads which did not come under either system carried local traffic and acted as feeders to the trunk roads. These were also constructed and maintained by the local authorities, but without grants from the regional governments.

Table 13.5 shows that in 1946 the total road mileage was 25,433, and this increased to 28,042 in 1950; by 1960 the total road mileage was 41,065, of which 5,434 miles were tarred and 35,631 miles were of gravel or earth. In 1960 the road mileage increased to approximately 6,000 miles of trunk road 'A' and about the same mileage of trunk road 'B', with approximately 160,000 miles of local roads. Many of the local roads, particularly in the Eastern Region, were constructed and maintained by voluntary community labour. During the period of its economic development programme 1955–60, the federal government spent about £14 million on new roads, bituminous surfacing, the strengthening of bridges, equipment, etc. The Northern Region government, with the assistance of the Colonial Development and Welfare Fund, spent about £10 million on road development. In Western Nigeria, about £4 million was spent on the tarring of all trunk roads 'B', general improvements of the existing roads and on the construction of new roads where these were an economic necessity. In the Eastern Region about £3 million was spent on roads and bridges.

Nigerian roads varied in standard, and their quality and durability depended partly upon the volume of traffic they carried and partly upon the weather conditions.[1] Most were about 10 feet wide with two verges of 5 feet; these dimensions were considered sufficient for average traffic, but on the busiest roads more widening was under-

[1] A study of road conditions in Nigeria is found in *Colonial Road Problems. Impressions from Visits to Nigeria*, Col. Research Publication no. 8, 1950.

taken, especially after 1955. The reliability of Nigerian roads varied; even some of the trunk roads, which were the best, were impassable at times in the wet season. A deterrent to road-building and repair was the difficulty of moving road-building and earth-moving equipment to where it was needed. Soil erosion also provided

TABLE 13.5   *Length of roads, 1945–60*

Date 31 March	Roads maintained by			Road surfaces		Total
	Local authorities	Govern-ment outside townships	Govern-ment in townships	Tarred	Gravel or earth	
1945	18,419	6,225	276	533	24,387	24,920
1946	18,956	6,246	231	705	24,728	25,433
1947	17,939	6,468	252	760	23,899	24,659*
1948	19,004	6,646	292	802	25,143	25,945
1949	19,025	7,016	303	937	25,407	26,344
1950	20,686	7,066	290	1,024	27,018	28,042
1951	19,774	7,673	312	1,114	26,645	27,759*
1952	20,424	7,382	316	1,256	26,866	28,122
1953	21,274	7,211	322	1,631	27,176	28,807
1954	24,451	7,159	374	2,022	29,962	31,984
1955	23,959	11,376	361	2,442	33,254	35,696
1956	23,860	11,036	367	2,688	32,575	35,263
1957	26,819	8,737	438	3,389	32,605	35,994
1958	25,300	11,022	398	3,905	32,815	36,720
1959	30,225	10,154	454	4,752	36,081	40,833
1960	29,825	10,772	468	5,434	35,631	41,065

* The apparent reduction in total mileage is due to deletion of certain old dry season tracks which were no longer required.

Sources: *Digest of Statistics*, vol. 8 (October 1959), and *Annual Abstract of Statistics, 1963*.

difficulties in many areas. The development of roads necessitated the building and establishment of many bridges and reliable ferries over the numerous rivers and creeks. Many of the Nigerian bridges were single-track, designed to carry a gross load of about 8 tons; but between 1953 and 1960 many on the major roads were strengthened and, where necessary, widened as they were replaced or repaired.

Most of the earlier timber bridges disappeared and were replaced by modern concrete bridges with increased capacity.

In order to cater for the increasing traffic, attention was given to the bearing capacity of the roads. Laboratories were set up in Lagos, Ibadan and in a few centres in Northern Nigeria, in order to exercise control over the materials and methods of construction. For every major road contract, a laboratory on the site was equipped so that tests and control could be carried out continuously. By this means, maximum use was made of the available local materials, and more conventional and expensive methods of construction were avoided. Occasionally cement or stone-based or other expensive methods of construction were employed in order to meet certain requirements. Between 1953 and 1960, the establishment of large firms of civil engineers, both indigenous and expatriate, possessing modern equipment and specialist skill, enabled the government to sub-contract the actual road-building.

The motor transport system continued to compete effectively with the railways, encouraged by the expansion of the economy, particularly the increasing volume of exports and imports, and the construction of better roads. Between 1946 and 1954, there was motor-transport 'mania' in the southern half of the country; because of the great boom in the export trade, which began after the second world war and lasted until 1954, an increasing number of people bought lorries and operated transport services. Table 13.6 shows that in 1946, 1,413 commercial vehicles were registered, and by 1950 the number had risen to 2,898. The upward trend continued, and in 1956 and 1960, 7,184 and 7,879 were registered respectively. The result was that the number of commercial vehicles soon surpassed the volume of the export products to be transported. There was a general deterioration in the standard of the service provided by most transporters, and a number of them incurred great losses and went out of business. An increasing number of taxi-cabs were operated in a few major cities. Neither the road transport system nor the taxi-cab services were organized on a local or national scale; consequently the economic waste of cut-throat competition could not be eliminated.

In addition to the purely commercial road transport system, the Nigerian Railway Corporation operated a motor feeder service, mainly in the groundnut and cotton-growing areas of Sokoto. It

also operated a passenger service between Gasau, Sokoto and
Birnin Kebbi, and by 1960 it employed a fleet of 62 lorries and 20
trailers.[1]

The road transport system provided employment for a number of
Nigerians, as it was the usual practice for a licensed driver to engage

TABLE 13.6   *Registration of road vehicles, 1937–60*

Period	Commercial vehicles	Private cars, including taxis	Motor-cycles	Tractors and trailers	Total
1937	1,819	822	140	—	2,781
1938	550	754	161	—	1,465
1939	559	572	154	—	1,285
1946	1,413	702	352	—	2,467
1947	2,761	1,881	797	—	5,439
1948	1,993	2,199	655	267	5,114
1949	2,356	2,112	667	174	5,309
1950	2,898	2,465	574	303	6,240
1951	2,901	3,457	551	289	7,198
1952	3,788	3,784	538	248	8,358
1953	4,159	3,783	645	275	8,862
1954	4,332	4,026	1,180	357	9,895
1955	5,830	5,398	2,318	401	13,947
1956	7,184	6,185	2,344	474	16,187
1957	5,551	5,830	2,279	449	14,109
1958	7,220	7,459	2,561	367	17,607
1959	6,682	9,257	4,838	796	21,573
1960	7,879	11,615	7,026	487	27,007

Sources: *Digest of Statistics*, vol. 8 (October 1959), and *Annual Abstract of Statistics, 1963*.

some apprentices, who accompanied him on his journeys and who
learnt to drive by watching him, occasionally being allowed to
drive themselves. This went on for a period of between six and
twelve months before the apprentice, on attaining some driving
competence, was sponsored by the master-driver to take an official

[1] *Nigerian Railway Corporation. Report and Accounts for the year ended 31 March 1960.*

driving test. To every commercial vehicle, there were at least four apprentices.

The most important industry which grew out of the road transport system was that of motor repairing. Originally, the few Nigerians who began to provide this service obtained their training and experience while in the service of either the government (e.g. Public Works Department) or a commercial firm (e.g. UAC Motors). They, in turn, trained a number of apprentices to handle simple mechanical faults in vehicles. There are no statistics to show the total number of people employed in the road transport system. However, if one assumes that to every commercial vehicle there were 4 people employed, including the driver, and that there were at least 2 mechanics, then it can be estimated that in 1960 about 47,000 people were employed.

AIR TRANSPORT

After the war the Royal Air Force started an internal air service for Nigeria, but this was abandoned in June 1946 because of inadequate meteorological facilities.[1] However, it was reopened in December 1946, when some improvements had been made: a twice-weekly service, using Dakota aircraft chartered from the British Overseas Airways Corporation came into operation between Lagos–Port Harcourt–Enugu–Jos–Kano, carrying passengers and mail.

The development of commercial air transportation in Nigeria dates from May 1946 when, by an Order in Council, the West Africa Air Transport Authority was constituted for the control and development of commercial civil aviation in British West Africa. The same Order in Council authorized the formation of the West African Airways Corporation to operate services between and within the West African colonies (Ghana, Nigeria, Sierra Leone and Gambia). The corporation bought some aircraft from the United Kingdom and began operating in 1947. By the end of the year it had initiated the connexion by air of the main population centres in the country. There were services between Lagos, Benin, Port Harcourt, Calabar, Enugu and Tiko, operated by Dove aircraft. Meanwhile, the internal Nigerian air service continued to operate on charter by BOAC, alongside the WAAC service; but it was discontinued early

[1] *Annual Colonial Reports*, Nigeria, 1946, p. 78.

in 1948 when the latter took over its routes. The WAAC first operated with small aircraft which proved uneconomical, but in April 1945 larger aircraft were introduced in order to reduce operating and maintenance costs and thereby increase revenue. The newly-manufactured 45-seater Bristol aircraft were introduced, but

TABLE 13.7 *Aircraft arriving from countries outside Nigeria, 1946–60*

Period	Lagos	Kano	Other airports*	Total
1946	596	356	23	975
1947	822	986	3	1,811
1948	712	1,142	9	1,863
1949	677	1,294	5	1,976
1950	744	1,561	2	2,307
1951	810	1,843	288	2,881
1952	963	1,838	71	2,872
1953	1,027	1,851	57	2,935
1954	1,068	2,029	24	3,121
1955	1,260	1,947	42	3,249
1956	1,388	2,534	111	4,033
1957	1,489	2,772	85	4,346
1958	1,456	2,442	77	3,975
1959†	1,428	2,276	48	3,752
1960†	1,500	2,016	72	3,588

* Includes Maiduguri throughout, and Calabar in 1951, 1952 and from fourth quarter 1957.
† Estimates from monthly averages.
Note: Increasing use of Kano Airport can be noticed.
Sources: *Digest of Statistics*, vol. 8 (October 1955), and *Annual Abstract of Statistics, 1963.*

these were grounded in 1955, following an accident near Calabar involving a Bristol 170-type aircraft. When services were resumed they were operated by modified Bristol 170s, de Haviland Dove and Heron aircraft, and a chartered Douglas DC3.

The government of Northern Nigeria started communications flights in 1955, using two Auster aircraft and a Piper Apache small twin-engined aircraft, for operating on the small landing strips in the region. Civil aviation in Nigeria was entirely in the hands of the federal government. Until October 1958 the Department of Civil Aviation was responsible for the management of airfields and ground installations, and for the enforcement of aeronautical regulations. It

TABLE 13.8   *West African Airways Corporation: passenger, freight and mail traffic, 1948–60*

| Year ending 31 March | Passenger traffic | | | Freight | | | |
| | Number carried | Passenger miles ('000) | Passen-ger ton miles ('000) | Mail | | Commercial* | |
				Tons	Ton miles ('000)	Tons	Ton miles ('000)
1948	1,804	376	57	20	8	7	2
1949	13,813	3,948	415	156	54	81	31
1950	15,149	5,220	492	146	50	130	40
1951	32,089	11,387	932	255	79	397	94
1952	42,769	13,453	989	264	82	623	146
1953	57,189	15,973	1,203	352	103	720	193
1954	69,261	18,315	1,651	421	134	903	323
1955	59,982	16,083	1,531	384	118	760	245
1956	52,327	14,449	1,314	433	128	612	228
1957	66,534	19,043	1,790	482	152	770	255
1958	73,473	21,797	2,010	553	178	835	201
1959	68,257	20,270	1,976	597	176	930	324
1960†	59,880	18,372	1,752	468	144	696	240

* Commercial freight includes passengers' excess luggage.
† Estimate from monthly averages.

Notes:
1. The Nigerian Airways, which replaced the former WAAC as from 1 October 1958, operates international services, Lagos–Accra–Dakar, in addition to internal services in Nigeria. Figures in this table up to 30 September 1958 include internal services in Ghana. Internal services in Nigeria accounted for approximately 59 per cent of the total in 1955 and 1956, 60 per cent in 1957, 61 per cent in 1958 and 72 per cent in 1959. All figures exclude Lagos–London flights run in conjunction with BOAC in the recent years.
2. 1 ton=1,000 kilogrammes=2,204 pounds.

Sources: *Digest of Statistics*, vol. 8 (October 1959), and *Annual Abstract of Statistics, 1963*.

was also responsible for air telecommunications in conjunction with the Post and Telegraphs Department, and for construction and maintenance of airfields and buildings, in conjunction with the Public Works Department. These functions were taken over by the Nigerian Airways, inaugurated in October 1958.

The Nigerian Airways was controlled by the federal government, which had 51 per cent of its share capital, and BOAC and the Elder Dempster Lines, which held jointly the remaining 49 per cent of its shares. This arrangement continued at the end of 1960.

Kano was one of the two major airports in Nigeria. It had customs, health and immigration facilities and was used by many of the international air carriers, including BOAC, KLM, Air France, Sabena and Air Liban. It is well placed for providing services as a transit airport because it is situated on the fringes of the Sahara, which makes it a most convenient intermediate stop on several air routes. Lagos Airport – the other major airport – was mainly a terminal which served the southern area of Nigeria, and provided services for direct links with Northern and Eastern Nigeria. This airport also had customs, health and immigration facilities. Tables 13.7 and 13.8 show the number of aircraft arriving in Nigeria, and the passenger and freight traffic respectively.

In 1951 the government created training facilities at Ikeja Airport in order to provide the two main airports with trained personnel. There was also an air traffic control school at Ikeja. The Nigerian Airways, under its training scheme, sponsored a number of young Nigerians to the United Kingdom and to the Sudan to undergo training in many aspects of commercial aviation.

OCEAN SHIPPING

The foreign shipping firms continued to handle and to dominate the export and import trades of Nigeria after 1945. Nine of the shipping lines operating in Nigeria belonged to the West African Lines Conference, which operated a common shipping policy. The increasing volume of foreign trade was reflected in the number of vessels which entered Nigerian ports (see table 13.9).

In 1959 the Nigerian government established the Nigerian National Line. The company was incorporated in Nigeria with an authorized capital of £2 million, and the principal shareholders were

TABLE 13.9 *Shipping movements at Nigerian ports, 1946–60*

| | Vessels registered in | | | | | | | | | |
| | United Kingdom | | France | | Norway | | Other countries | | Total | |
Period	Number	NRT* ('000 tons)	Number	NRT ('000 tons)	Number	NRT ('000 tons)	Number	NRT ('000 tons)	Number	NRT ('000 tons)
1946	475	1,323	23	26	22	72	147	401	667	1,822
1954	682	1,641	81	187	163	388	492	767	1,418	2,983
1955	660	1,622	247	291	143	370	539	889	1,589	3,172
1956	609	1,565	197	298	162	429	586	992	1,554	3,284
1957	794	1,754	159	365	142	368	664	1,169	1,759	3,656
1958	948	2,367	172	485	193	525	799	1,409	2,112	4,786
1959	907	2,395	200	635	231	630	893	1,655	2,231	5,315
1960	858	2,698	200	696	205	598	970	1,966	2,233	5,958

* Net registered tonnage.
Source: *Annual Abstract of Statistics, 1963.*

the federal government with a controlling share of 51 per cent, and Messrs Elder Dempster Lines Ltd and Palm Line Ltd, who between them held the remaining 49 per cent. The government appointed its technical partners as operational agents in order to ensure that the line was competently run, while Nigerians were given the opportunity to learn the skills and acquire the necessary technical knowledge of merchant shipping. The first ship of the Nigerian National Line was MV *Oduduwa*, and by the end of 1960 the line had four ships in service.

POST AND TELEGRAPHS

The postal services advanced dramatically after the second world war, as a result of increasing government expenditure. In 1946 there were 125 post offices and 331 postal agencies in the country. The number of post offices rose to 134 in 1950, and to 176 in 1960; while the number of postal agencies increased to 420 in 1950 and to 1,000 in 1960. Between 1953 and 1960 a number of modern post offices were built to replace the old buildings, while a very useful and economic innovation was the sub post office, run on the lines of an agency but offering a full range of services. The reorganization which the postal services underwent also involved the introduction of new and quicker methods of handling mail, and the intensification of staff training through in-service training schemes. The benefits of the reorganization were particularly noticeable in the internal mail services, where they resulted in an acceleration of mails by as much as forty-eight hours in some parts of Nigeria.[1] New facilities were introduced, for example, stamped envelopes and books of stamps. Mail for destination within Nigeria was charged at surface rates but was carried by the quickest method, air or surface, at the discretion of the postal authorities. Table 13.10 shows the number of postal articles handled between 1945 and 1960.

The modern telegraphic system developed rapidly soon after 1946. In that year there were 116 telegraph transmitting offices, the main ones being at Lagos, Enugu and Kaduna. They were interconnected, so that a breakdown on one line could not interrupt traffic, and landlines were also supplemented by wireless channels.

---

[1] Improved postal services were still to be extended to cover the greater part of the country.

There were 59 telephone exchanges; however, more were introduced between 1946 and 1950, and telegraph services were also extended to cover more areas.

It was generally more convenient to telephone than to telegraph, but an important development between 1950 and 1960 was the introduction of two types of special service, the 'private wire' and

TABLE 13.10   *Number of postal articles handled and annual revenue from postal services, 1945–60*

Year ending 31 March	(a) Estimated number of articles posted in Nigeria	Estimated number despatched abroad included in (a)	Estimated number received from abroad	Total estimated number of postal articles handled	Number of tele-grams handled	Total revenue from postal services (£)
1945	18,822	2,522	3,892	22,714	1,520	151,972
1950	43,362	6,236	10,250	53,612	1,962	310,124
1951	53,001	5,893	10,828	63,829	2,101	349,111
1952	62,342	7,870	11,356	73,698	2,265	441,490
1953	65,637	8,557	11,670	77,307	2,234	487,854
1954	65,692	11,973	11,981	77,673	2,192	590,821
1955	66,365	11,066	12,333	78,698	2,234	663,052
1956	70,947	12,382	12,997	83,944	2,582	765,148
1957	78,386	14,560	13,449	91,835	2,637	977,904
1958	87,426	15,276	13,745	101,171	2,609	1,168,597
1959	76,154	19,345	17,015	93,169	2,135	1,279,970
1960	79,617	10,458	20,521	100,138	2,036	1,413,845

Source: *Annual Abstract of Statistics, 1963.*

the 'telex', in different parts of the country. By means of the private wire, a business subscriber was directly and permanently connected by teleprinter with, for example, his branch office in another town. An international telex service was introduced in co-operation with Messrs Cable & Wireless Ltd, whereby any telex subscriber could obtain connexion to any other telex subscriber in most parts of the world through the Lagos telex switchboard.[1] In 1950 virtually all

[1] By 1960 only Lagos had a telex service: *Annual Report of the Post and Tele-graphs Division for the year 1959–60*, Lagos, Federal Ministry of Information, 1963, p. 15.

transmissions were by morse key, and telegrams were handwritten. However, by 1960 nearly all the major circuits used teleprinters, which automatically printed the telegram at the distant point, and the passage of traffic was further accelerated by the introduction of torn tape relay equipment at Lagos and at the regional capitals.

Early in 1950 the first carrier telephone trunk circuit was put into service between Lagos and Oshogbo, and this was followed almost immediately by extensions to Kaduna and Enugu thus making it possible for people in Lagos and the regional capitals to talk to each other by telephone. In November 1950 the first automatic exchange was opened at Port Harcourt, and in October 1953 the second automatic exchange was opened in the Lagos area.

In 1951 the government decided to provide transmission paths for major trunks by a network of very high frequency radio stations connecting the important centres of the country. These were to replace the overhead lines, which usually followed the railway and were subject to a high rate of fault incidence. The first V.H.F. multi-channel link was opened in 1953 between Lagos and Ibadan, with 12 telephone channels. So rapid was the development of trunk services in modern telecommunication systems, that the demand between Lagos and Ibadan necessitated the installation of ultra high frequency (microwave) equipment, which could provide up to 240 channels on one path. Three such paths were brought into service on 1 January 1960, providing facilities for telephone subscribers in Lagos and Ibadan to dial each other direct.

The introduction of VHF (and later, UHF) circuits did not render superfluous the overhead lines, the capacity of which, on the contrary, increased by the installation of more carrier channels, which gave communication between intermediate centres and which also supplemented the VHF network. Additional overhead lines were constructed using, in many cases, poles made from local timber.

Between 1950 and 1960, the number of exchanges increased from 72 to 130, and the number of telephones from 9,000 to about 39,000. The number of effective trunk calls increased from 701,000 in 1950 to 2,883 000 in 1960. These expansions led to a considerable increase in the number of staff, resulting in greatly improved facilities for training. In 1950 only 3 instructors were regularly employed by the Post and Telegraph Department, and the capacity for resident training at its school at Oshodi was as low as 70 students per annum. By 1960, 50 instructors were permanently employed at the training school (with a further 14 on in-service training), and the capacity of the school (including the three new regional schools) had increased to approximately 500 students per annum.[1]

TABLE 13.11   *Post Office Savings Bank deposits and withdrawals, 1947–60*

Year ending 31 March	Number of accounts* ('000)	Deposits (£000)	Withdrawals (£000)
1947	137	1,594	1,487
1948	148	1,199	890
1949	159	1,216	918
1950	170	1,306	1,086
1951	180	1,450	1,122
1952	188	1,483	1,141
1953	198	1,579	1,280
1954	209	1,467	1,527
1955	225	1,700	1,392
1956	239	1,724	1,643
1957	252	1,595	1,850
1958	259	1,260	1,838
1959	268	1,048	1,487
1960	279	1,212	1,278

* At the end of the year.
Source: *Annual Abstract of Statistics, 1963.*

More people were patronizing the Post Office Savings Bank: table 13.11 shows that the total number of accounts increased from about 137,000 in 1947 to 209,000 and 279,000 in 1954 and 1960 respectively. The total amount deposited fluctuated during this period, but the highest total of about £1,746,000 in 1954 coincided with the last year of the export boom. From 1957 to 1960, total annual withdrawals exceeded annual deposits. This phenomenon coincided with the period when export prices fell. The overall performance of the Post Office Savings Bank was encouraging when one considers

[1] *Annual Report of the Post and Telegraphs Division for the year 1959–60*, p. 18.

TABLE 13.12   *Nigerian Post Office:*
total revenue and
expenditure, 1948–60

Year ending 31 March	Revenue (£000)	Expenditure (£000)
1948	418	639
1949	494	840
1950	550	1,008
1953	864	1,280
1954	993	1,669
1955	1,115	1,795
1956	1,408	2,191
1957	2,024	3,007
1958	2,250	3,642
1959	3,081	4,222
1960	3,532	4,613

Source: *Annual Reports of Post and Telegraphs Department.*

that it faced great competition from the increasing number of commercial banks.[1]

The development of transport enabled the post office to expand its services to many areas. It made use of the road transport system, and employed the railways and the airways for its postal services. However, it can be seen on table 13.12 that the financial position of the Nigerian Post Office was an unhappy one. Although the total annual revenue increased steadily, it was offset by increased capital expenditure, due to the great expansion in postal and telegraphic services of this period. The federal government subsidized the annual losses from its revenue.

[1] See Chapter 16.

14 Agricultural production and the marketing boards

Agricultural production in Nigeria could be divided into two – export crops and locally-consumed produce. However, there was some overlap in that some products, such as palm oil, groundnuts and cotton, were consumed locally as well as being important export crops. The rapidly-increasing population of the country meant that more foodstuffs would have to be produced. Export earnings had to be increased so that more revenues could be obtained, in order to bring to fruition the various programmes of social, economic and industrial development. The main problem of Nigerian agriculture was that of expansion, which depended largely on the degree to which the country could succeed in overcoming and minimizing the effect of such limiting factors as soil deterioration, inadequacy of water supplies in certain areas, low-yielding plant varieties, prevalence of livestock and plant disease, and primitive cultivation methods. The various governments formulated their ideas about agricultural expansion under the development plans, which have already been mentioned.

Most of the major agricultural developments were concentrated on export production. However, the production of locally-consumed foodstuffs continued to expand; indeed, the production of local foodstuffs greatly exceeded in value the production of crops for export. In 1952–3, it was estimated that the value of foodstuffs produced in Nigeria for local consumption was £300 million.[1] In the 1956–7 National Income Survey, the total sum included for locally-consumed foodstuffs was £342·6 million, while the total

[1] IBRD, *Economic Development of Nigeria*, p. 397.

value for export crops was only £84.4 million.[1] It is also known that between 1950 and 1957 (the period for which reliable statistics are available) the production of local produce increased by about 50 per cent (see table 14.1).

TABLE 14.1   *Crops grown primarily for domestic use, 1950 and 1957* (million tons)*

		1950 production	1957 production
Root crops	yam	6·63	6·69
	cassava	3·61	4·66
	cocoyams	0·60	0·67
Cereals	guinea corn	1·38	2·14
	millet	0·92	1·79
	maize	0·47	0·66
	rice	0·19	0·26
Kolanuts		0·08	0·11
Beans		0·07	0·25
Other food crops†		0·76	5·00

* No later estimates available.
† Potatoes, sweet potatoes, pepper, melons, vegetables and acha.
Source: P. N. C. Okigbo, *Nigerian National Accounts, 1950–7.*

There was no problem of food production in Nigeria. There was abundant cultivable land available; and with the greatly improved communications of recent years, areas with surplus foodstuffs could supply those less fortunate. Many farmers learnt from experience that unless their land was cared for, their crops would decrease in quantity and quality. The various government agricultural departments continued to demonstrate the value of the care of land, and the use of fertilizers. There are no statistics on direct farm investments – the peasant farmers never kept records. The bulk of the farmers did not adopt the use of fertilizers, partly because they did not appreciate the improvement they could make to farm production, and partly because they could not afford to buy them. However, they paid

[1] The value included export duties, Produce Sales Taxes and the margin between producer prices for marketing board crops and world parity, but excluded transport and distribution costs: NNEC, *Economic Survey of Nigeria, 1959*, p. 22n.

more attention to weeding, prompt planting and harvesting, and took greater care in processing farm produce. A number of Nigerian farmers were able to improve their methods of production by joining co-operative group-farming and marketing societies, where such improved methods were encouraged.[1]

It was in the production of export crops that the governments' agricultural departments and a few development institutions concentrated their efforts. Statistics on major agricultural export products (1946–60) are shown under foreign trade in Chapter 17.

OIL PALM PRODUCTS[2]

Palm oil, one of Nigeria's principal sources of export earnings, remained in the hands of individual farmers or families; plantations or estates accounted for only about 6–7 per cent of Nigeria's output. The problem the palm oil industry faced was that of expanding the volume of export production and at the same time improving the quality of oil. The development of pioneer oil mills[3] and hand-presses stepped up considerably the quality and quantity of oil extracted from fruit.[4] By 1960 more than 125 pioneer oil mills were operating in Nigeria (four-fifths of which were in Eastern Nigeria), and well over 5,000 hand-presses were in use. The introduction of pioneer oil mills met with vigorous opposition. In many areas palm oil production was largely a female industry, and the women producers received a proportion of the oil and kernels as compensation for their labour. Under mechanical process this source of income was lost. In addition to this problem, many pioneer oil mills were badly sited and had to work under capacity, and consequently at a great loss: for instance, in Western Nigeria the Western Region Production Development Board had to close all its mills for a period.

A number of measures were taken to stimulate the production of

[1] The co-operative movement is discussed in Chapter 18.

[2] An almost up-to-date analysis of the economics of oil palm products is found in Helleiner, op. cit., pp. 91–107.

[3] The first pioneer oil mill was erected at Amuro near Okigwi in Owerri province, and was formally opened on 11 October 1946: *Colonial Annual Reports*, Nigeria, 1946, p. 46.

[4] Pioneer oil mills can extract up to 85 per cent of the oil contained in the pericarp, hand-presses 60–65 per cent and traditional methods only 45–60 per cent: NNEC, *Economic Survey of Nigeria*, p. 28.

palm oil and palm kernels. The West African Institute for Oil Palm Research at Benin continued to supply for sale seedlings of high-yielding strains, and it also provided instructions on the best spacing of palm trees. The use of oil hand-presses was encouraged, and research was conducted into the adoption of an inexpensive power-driven mechanical nut-cracker which could replace the unpopular hand-operated mechanical nut-cracker. Attempts were also made to popularize the harvesting of fruit from trees less than twenty-five feet high by means of Malayan harvesting knives, so as to reduce the need for climbing very high palm trees.

COCOA

Nigeria remained one of the world's major cocoa producers. Cocoa was grown by peasant farmers, and about 95 per cent was produced in Western Nigeria.[1] However, the industry faced many problems immediately after the war: the inadequate marketing facilities experienced during the war continued for a few years; but, more important, there had been a general neglect of cocoa farms as a result of unprofitable farming caused by wild fluctuations in the world cocoa prices, and this had encouraged the spread of pests and diseases which attacked the already old cocoa trees. The three main infections of cocoa in Nigeria were black pods, capsids and swollen shoot, and their combined threat to the industry forced the government to conduct a survey in Western Nigeria. From the commencement of the survey in 1944 to December 1947, a total of 264,705 farms, comprising 461,807 acres of cocoa, were surveyed.[2] The government decided to cut down the affected trees, and although this met with very strong opposition from the farmers, who did not quite understand the problem and regarded the policy as one that could impoverish them, by December 1947 a total of 217,040 affected trees had been cut – equivalent to 540 acres of cocoa. After much agitation by the farmers, the government compensated those whose trees were cut by paying the rehabilitation grant of 2s. 6d. per tree. The fund for the compensation was provided by the Cocoa Marketing Board; and by 1948 a total sum of £54,482 had already been paid out.

[1] K. D. S. Baldwin, *The Marketing of Cocoa in Western Nigeria.*
[2] *Colonial Annual Reports*, Nigeria, 1947, p. 39.

A number of the farmers affected were encouraged to grow citrus, while some whose farms were not badly affected could replant. The cutting-out of diseased trees was made compulsory in 1950; although some opposition was encountered, it was reduced to almost negligible proportions, and real progress was made in arresting the pace of the spread of disease by this means. During the year 1955–6, 27 new centres of infection by swollen shoot disease were recorded in Western Nigeria, bringing the number of centres under treatment to 113. Timely treatment in some centres, particularly the outlying ones at Ife and Ilesha, prevented the disease from spreading into the dense cocoa areas beyond.

Work on black pod control also progressed considerably. In 1956 a total of 12,000 farmers were trained in black pod spraying methods, compared with 11,000 farmers in 1955. This made a grand total of nearly 25,000 farmers trained in the period between 1954, when the scheme started, and the end of 1956. Many of the farmers who received training also helped to train their neighbours. Within a short period the spraying apparatus – pumps and chemicals – was being sold commonly in local markets. Capsids control also passed from the investigational to the field stage. Some enterprising farmers purchased 'Motoblow' (knapsack motor-operated pumps), and sprayed their farms with Gamalin 20. These farmers operated under the strict supervision of the field staff of the Agricultural Department.

COTTON

In the post-war years, increased planting played the greatest part in increasing cotton production (see table 14.2), but the development of higher-yielding strains also played a major role. The seed for well over 90 per cent of the crop was provided from ginneries, thus making possible the rapid dissemination of scientifically-bred seed, which is not found in the case of any other crop. The introduction of the present variety (Samaru 26C), which was developed in the 1940s,[1] increased the yield by over 20 per cent; and by 1959 a new and better variety (Samaru 26J) had been introduced, leading to a further increase in yield of 15 per cent. In 1960 about a dozen ginneries were operating in the cotton-growing areas, all of which were

[1] At the experimental station at Samaru, Northern Nigeria.

established by the British Cotton Growing Association. The association also acted as the ginning agent of the marketing boards.

GROUNDNUTS

Very little effort was made to improve the cultivation methods and yield of groundnuts. However, in 1951 the Northern Region Development Corporation succeeded in introducing a new variety named 'K 50' which performed better than other varieties.[1] It out-yielded others and responded well to fertilizers.

One of the main difficulties with which the groundnuts export industry had to contend was that the nuts were grown in areas up to 1,000 miles away from the main ports to which they had to be transported by road, rail or river. The transporting agencies could not always cope with the vast quantity of nuts produced, particularly in the immediate post-war years, and consequently there were storage problems. Most of the groundnuts awaiting transportation were stored in the open air in a number of huge pyramids covered with tarpaulins, and some were in warehouses. There was inevitably a degree of deterioration when they were left for too long. However, the Stored Products Research Unit succeeded in controlling groundnut pests during storage by spraying.

RUBBER

Although rubber trees had been grown in Nigeria for over half a century, primitive methods still obtained, resulting in the production of poor-quality rubber. However, in the early 1950s – starting from the period of the Korean war – there was greater demand for rubber. But slaughter-tapping of trees threatened to destroy the industry. Again, the increase in the price of crepe (a lower-quality rubber) as compared with sheet rubber tempted tappers to abandon processing and devote their attention to tapping and selling the coagulated latex to the newly-established crepe factories, with a further increase in the rate at which rubber trees were being destroyed.[2] By 1957, some 250,000 acres were under cultivation in the Western and Eastern

---

[1] *Northern Region Development Corporation. Second Annual Report, 1957*, p. 18.
[2] E. I. Oliver, *Overseas Economic Surveys, Nigeria*, London, HMSO, 1957, pp. 118–19; and NNEC, *Economic Survey of Nigeria, 1959*, pp. 34–5.

Regions of Nigeria, but most of these were in the hands of small-holders and included many trees which were diseased or had been mutilated, some beyond recovery, by inexpert tapping. In 1957 the government of Western Nigeria initiated a Rubber Improvement Campaign; in addition, it established more rubber plantations. Large-scale rubber plantations were also undertaken by the United Africa Company of Nigeria, and by Dunlop (Nigeria) Plantations Ltd, in the Calabar province.

TABLE 14.2   *Exports of cotton and rubber, 1946–60*

Year	Cotton (raw) Volume (tons)	Value (£000)	Rubber Volume (tons)	Value (£000)
1946	6,612	536	11,448	1,404
1947	5,248	520	7,445	677
1948	4,635	476	8,019	719
1949	9,984	1,448	6,858	591
1950	12,623	2,975	13,652	2,834
1951	15,374	4,950	20,856	7,483
1952	19,296	6,734	18,331	4,139
1953	17,707	5,518	21,260	3,287
1954	25,959	7,350	20,900	2,907
1955	33,174	9,380	30,380	5,577
1956	27,852	7,113	38,149	6,409
1957	25,196	6,337	39,992	7,022
1958	33,705	7,845	41,206	7,627
1959	36,884	7,301	53,374	11,608
1960	26,974	6,207	52,229	14,239

Source: *Annual Abstract of Statistics, 1963.*

AGRICULTURAL RESEARCH

There were a number of agricultural schools, research institutions and government experimental farms and stations where agricultural research was undertaken. The most important of these were the West African Institute for Oil Palm Research at Benin, the Cocoa Research Institute Substation and the West African Maize Rust Research Unit at Ibadan, the Central Research Organization at

Ibadan, Samaru near Zaria, the Northern Regional Stock Farm at Shika, Zaria, and the Research Station at Samaru. The federal government established a Council of National Resources of Nigeria for co-ordinating research programmes in these fields.[1] The Federal Department of Commerce and Industries also carried out research at its Institute of Applied Technical Research. A few of these projects considered the problem of food storage, since large volumes of local seasonal food crops continued to waste every year.

THE MARKETING BOARDS

The marketing of export products was reviewed immediately after the war, and in 1946 a white paper stated that 'the experience of the war years has shown that Government can achieve a stabilization of seasonal prices to the West African producers....'[2] It was decided to set up statutory marketing organizations for the major export products which were formerly handled by the WAPCB.[3] The Nigerian Cocoa Marketing Board was established by ordinance in 1947, following in 1949 by the Cotton, Groundnut and Oil Palm Produce marketing boards.

A secondary, but important purpose of the boards was to provide funds for the economic development of the areas of production and for scientific research in agriculture.

The bulk-purchase policy which was introduced during the war ceased to apply to cocoa and cotton. 'One reason ... was that the Ministry of Food would have to incur great risks in carrying large stocks bought at spot prices after the restoration of the terminal market, itself regarded as a desirable objective.'[4] The boards wanted an agreement for a longer period for bulk-purchase, and they also wanted the British government to pay prices nearer to open-market prices. Soon after their establishment, the Nigerian Oil Palm Produce and Groundnut marketing boards concluded a three-year agreement (1949–52) with the Ministry of Food (United Kingdom) concerning the latter taking over the whole exportable surplus of palm oil, palm kernels, groundnuts and benniseed. 'A floor price was

[1] Oliver, op. cit., p. 129.
[2] *Statement on Future Marketing of West African Cocoa*, Cmd. 6950, 1946.
[3] See Chapter 11.
[4] C. Leubuscher, *Bulk-Buying from the Colonies*, p. 27.

laid down, while the actual price to be paid each year was to be agreed upon in the preceding October, that is to say, several months before harvesting.'[1] The Ministry of Food was able to pay lower prices because it offered an assured market for the entire available output. The agreement was revised in 1951 because the prices fixed continued to be out of tune with market prices, and eventually in 1954 the Ministry of Food and the marketing boards agreed to terminate all bulk-buying agreements. The marketing boards, as successors to the WAPCB, inherited a large sum of money through the price equalization scheme – £8,320,096 for the period 1939–40 to 1946–7. They continued to accumulate funds in good years, and in performing their functions allocated this money as follows: 70 per cent to be devoted to price stabilization, $7\frac{1}{2}$ per cent to be spent on scientific research and $22\frac{1}{2}$ per cent on the development of the producing areas.

The seasonal prices for the export crops were fixed by the boards after careful consideration of world market conditions and internal marketing costs. Transport costs were allowed according to the kind of transport, the distance to the port or the central marketing station and the ease or frequency of the transport. For example, the ground-nuts board had a policy called the 'price support subsidies', under which it paid subsidies at certain remote buying stations in the Kano area where the cost of evacuation to railhead exceeded £8 per ton (£8 being the standard cost allowed).[2] The collection of the export crops was done by licensed buying agents.

The marketing boards had a selling organization in the United Kingdom – the Nigerian Produce Marketing Company – which sold in the 'open market', i.e. the world market, on behalf of the boards. An additional function performed by the company was the reservation of shipping space, which was done on the basis of forward estimates of availability of produce for shipment supplied by the executive organization, the Marketing Department in Nigeria.

In the 1954–5 season, the marketing system was reorganized to suit constitutional changes, and the previous boards were replaced by four regional marketing boards and a central one. The regional boards handled the marketing of all the 'scheduled' crops (cocoa,

[1] Ibid., p. 14.
[2] *Third Annual Report of the Nigerian Government Marketing Board, 1951–2*, p. 9.

palm products, groundnuts, cotton, benniseed, soya beans, grapefruit and lemons) within their territories. The Central Marketing
Board was a federal body, and its main function was to serve as a
common shipping and selling organization for the regional boards.
Further constitutional changes led to the abolition of the Central
Marketing Board on 1 October 1958, when its function was taken
over by the Nigerian Produce Marketing Company Limited.[1]
Although the form of the marketing board organization underwent
radical changes to conform with constitutional developments in the
country, the overall policy and the practical arrangements for the
purchasing, marketing and overseas sale of Nigerian produce remained virtually the same from the start of the system at the end of
the second world war.

Marketing board operations[2]

Two major aspects of the marketing boards' operations should be
mentioned: first, their price policy. The boards were placed in a
monopsonistic position, as they had absolute control of purchases of
the major export products.

The marketing boards fixed the buying prices at the beginning of
each crop season. However, cocoa and palm kernels have certain
common characteristics: it takes a long time, at least five years,
before they can bear fruit; they bear fruit even if they are not cared
for, in which case it will be of poor quality; and, most important of
all, there was no significant local demand for these crops. Many
farmers, therefore, regarded them as cash-crops, that is, crops grown
with the sole purpose of making money. In such cases, the marketing
boards faced supply curves which were almost perfectly inelastic in

[1] The company was registered in Nigeria and its share capital was entirely
provided by the marketing board it served.
[2] A number of books and journal articles have been written on marketing
board operations. Journal articles on this topic include: P. B. Bauer and F. W.
Paish, 'The Reduction of Fluctuations in the Income of Primary Producers',
and 'The Reduction of Fluctuations in the Income of Primary Producers:
Further Considered'; comments thereon by P. Hill, P. Ady, M. Friedman
and B. Niculescu; P. B. Bauer and B. S. Yamey, 'The Economics of Marketing Reform'; and R. O. Ekundare, 'The Price Equalization Fund in Nigeria'.
Two of the major books on this subject are P. T. Bauer, *West African Trade*,
and G. K. Helleiner, *Peasant Agriculture, Government and Economic Growth in
Nigeria*.

the short run, and consequently they were able to manipulate the prices. In the case of groundnuts, the position was significantly different. Groundnuts take a shorter period, between six to nine months, to bear fruit, and there was a fairly high local demand for the crop. The marketing boards were faced with an elastic supply curve for groundnuts. The price they offered had to be high enough to encourage the cultivation of the crop and to ensure adequate volume of export.

The former exporting firms which became agents to the marketing boards also faced a different kind of competition. The marketing boards paid commission to the agents, who had no influence whatsoever on the buying prices. Since they had to deliver their purchases to the board at the same price, price-cutting was completely eliminated. There was no abnormal profit to be gained by these agents, consequently the trade offered no special attraction to newcomers. The boards only appointed new agents after considering various factors, including the capital resources and the managerial efficiency of intending agents; therefore, freedom of entry as a buyer was almost absent, but not impossible.

Most of the agents employed middlemen to purchase the export crops direct from the primary producers. There was, therefore, a different pattern of competition among the middlemen. But it was difficult to get the true nature of competition in this situation, because there were many middlemen scattered all over wide areas, and the competitive position of each was determined by his area of operation. In some remote parts of the country where there were few transport facilities, often only one or two operated, and the middleman here could pay a much lower price than the one fixed by the marketing board. His freedom over the fixing of the local purchase price depended on the relative elasticity of supply for the product concerned. In some areas where there were several middlemen, each was prepared to bid higher in order to under-buy the others. Price war was often resorted to, but its extent depended on the margin of profit that could be realized over the transaction, bearing in mind that it would be unprofitable to bid above the official price already fixed by the marketing boards. Some middlemen also advanced credits to the producers in order to secure their patronage; those who did provided a special service which made the producers prefer them to other buyers. Often such middlemen fixed lower prices without any fear of retaliation from other middle-men.

Closely connected with the position of the marketing boards and the power to fix prices was the policy of adopting different grades for the same product and paying different prices for each grade. In the case of cocoa, two grades were established, Grade I and Grade II, and the local purchase price of Grade II was lower than Grade I. A similar policy existed for the purchase of palm oil. The grading system was adopted in order to improve the quality of the export products. It was attacked on the grounds that the price incentives offered for the various grades were almost wholly unrelated to ultimate demand, and that the grade differentials found little or no reflection in world markets.[1] However, the policy gave the farmers who were prepared to take a little extra care in preparing their export crop the opportunity of increasing their incomes.[2]

Perhaps the most criticized aspect of the marketing board system was the policy of price equalization.[3] In order to stabilize the price of agricultural export produce, and thus lessen the impact of year-to-year price changes on the Nigerian producer – the main reason for the creation of the marketing boards – producers' prices were set and maintained for an entire crop season. Local prices were fixed very much below world market prices. The boards had to accumulate large reserves to enable them to do this. The WAPCB, the predecessor of the marketing board, had already made a profit of about £9 million in respect of Nigerian cocoa by 1947. Within a short period, particularly between 1947 and 1954, the boards' reserves were built up considerably. This was made possible by the sterling devaluation in England, the raw materials boom caused by the Korean war, and the continuing higher-than-normal world price level thereafter. The boards' surpluses continued to grow after 1955, but at a lower rate. The accumulation of these surpluses brought a number of criticisms. It was considered unfair to withhold a substantial portion of what ought to be the farmers' incomes, either as a measure to combat inflation or as a means of preserving high foreign

[1] Bauer and Paish, op. cit.

[2] 'The boards have successfully used their price-setting powers to bring about great improvements in the quality of export produce': IBRD, *Economic Development of Nigeria*, p. 50.

[3] Helleiner, op. cit., chapters 6 and 7, and Bauer, op. cit., chapters 20-4.

exchange balances.[1] It must be pointed out that before 1954 the high surpluses accumulated by the boards were unpremeditated.[2] However, the report of the International Bank Mission to Nigeria[3] influenced the attitude of the government. This strongly approved of the boards' policy but recommended that

> henceforth the boards' functions be limited to setting quality standards, fixing producers' prices and purchasing and marketing crops. The financing of economic development and agricultural research is a responsibility of government and the boards should not attempt to undertake it. . . . The [. . .] use of the price-fixing function for other purposes, such as the promotion of development or to counteract inflationary or deflationary trends cuts across the responsibility of government.

Despite the repeated arguments against the boards' attempt to usurp the functions of the government, the regional governments virtually accepted the boards as institutions with a definite fiscal role to perform. The boards provided the capital which financed the establishment of the regional production development boards, later known as Development Corporations. By 1954 a cumulative grant of about £24 million had been made to the production boards.[4] The funds made available to the production boards were used for various purposes ranging from the development of agriculture and industry to direct investment in private companies and the granting of loans to companies. The marketing boards also made direct grants and loans to the governments for financing development projects. For example, the Western Nigeria Marketing Board made an outright grant of £10 million and a loan of the same amount to the regional government for the region's development plan of 1955–60.[5]

The price equalization fund policy of the boards was condemned by some economists because it represented a high degree of forced savings or tax on a particular sector of the economy. It is true that forced savings imply a reduction in the money income and in the

[1] Bauer and Paish, op. cit.

[2] Helleiner, op. cit., p. 167.

[3] IBRD, *Economic Development of Nigeria*, p. 51.

[4] Helleiner, op. cit., pp. 172–3.

[5] *Western Region Marketing Board. Sixth Annual Report*, Western Nigeria Legislature, Sessional Paper no. 3 of 1962.

economic welfare of the people concerned. In some cases, as was the case in Nigeria, the policy was unavoidable and should have been implemented so that the disutility of economic welfare created by the policy equalled the utility of economic welfare brought about by the way the forced savings were spent.[1] Forced savings as implemented by the boards had some merits. It was agreed that the amounts involved were too high. However, most Nigerian farmers did not consider agriculture as a business which demanded constant real investments. The level of savings among the farmers was very low, and the little saving that was done through the indigenous savings institution, the Esusu, was collected and spent unproductively on social ceremonies. Only a small amount was devoted by each farmer to buying farm tools, and with no definite object of expanding the farm business. It must be added that various development projects were undertaken by the boards which brought permanent improvements to agriculture on the one hand, and which improved the general standard of living in the country as a whole. The developments undertaken by the government and the various corporations financed by the boards included communications, land settlement, water supply and irrigation. Perhaps one aspect of the boards' policy which could be validly criticized was the lack of co-ordination between the boards and the government in encouraging young people to take up farming as a business. This could have been done by helping schools, particularly at the primary and secondary school levels, to establish small farm estates where the children could be trained in agricultural practice along with other subjects. With the adoption of free primary education, especially in Western Nigeria, there could have been a new generation of better-educated farmers. To encourage young people to adopt farming as a business, the boards could have been less conservative about their price-fixing policies in order to convince them that farming could pay as much as, if not more than, a white-collar job. It would also have been much easier and less wasteful to establish farm settlements with trained young people, rather than those established with men who had never received sufficient training in agriculture. Such young farmers would be able to save and invest more than the uneducated farmers, and a number of government functions which the boards took upon themselves to perform would not have been necessary.

[1] Ekundare, 'The Price Equalization Fund in Nigeria', p. 11.

The disposal of the boards' surpluses, particularly since 1954, has made a number of economists regard the boards' policy as a kind of fiscal policy leading to a very heavy tax on export producers. The farmers were able to bear the burden because of the relative in-elasticity of the supplies of some of the export crops: for example, cocoa, palm oil and palm kernels. Export crops were grown with locally-consumed products; consequently export earnings were often looked upon as merely providing extra cash that the farmer might need. There was sufficient evidence, however, that an increase in prices did encourage greater production.[1] The marketing boards' operations succeeded in reducing the intra-seasonal fluctuations in producer prices, but achieved little success in the much more difficult task of stabilizing producers' incomes.[2]

[1] Helleiner, op. cit., chapter 3.
[2] Helleiner, op. cit., chapter 7.

15 Industrial development

The arguments for and against industrialization, particularly after the second world war, provided the background for the government policy on industrialization. A number of people, notably the extreme nationalists, held the view that industrial development had some political significance. They believed that the creation of industries and hence less dependence on overseas manufactures was vital to political independence. Another group of people regarded industrial development as a cure for poverty.[1] The arguments put forward by both groups failed to bring about a basis for formulating any industrial policy. It is true, of course, that a country should try to diversify her economy, but when political independence is taken to mean self-sufficiency at all costs as implied by the former group, then the argument about industrialization is completely lost. The frequent references to the primary producing countries as poor and underdeveloped influenced the latter group to assume that industrialization is a cure, while failing to realize that agriculture is not necessarily associated with poverty. This becomes obvious when one considers Australia, New Zealand, Denmark, or Iowa and Nebraska in the United States of America. That industrialization is not necessarily associated with prosperity becomes obvious when one considers Italy or Spain.[2]

Also between 1945 and 1950, a crucial period in the constitutional struggle for political independence, a great number of Nigerian politicians and their supporters were opposed to financing any economic or social development projects with foreign loans. Some were

[1] 'The belief that industrialization is an easy, quick road to prosperity is, in some measure, the result of failing to keep up with History': F. J. Pedler, *Economic Geography of West Africa*, p. 93.

[2] Jacob Viner, *International Trade and Economic Development*, pp. 44–5.

even opposed to the presence of foreign investors in Nigeria. It was thought that reliance on foreign capital and foreign investors was incompatible with political independence. When the British government introduced responsible government in 1951, indigenous politicians began to take an active part in the administration of the government. They came to realize that both foreign and local funds were urgently needed to finance economic growth.

In formulating a policy for industrial expansion, the government had to take into account certain factors militating against any rapid progress in this field. There was a lack of indigenous capital as a result of low incomes; and also a reluctance by most people to forsake trade and agriculture for industry, where the rewards are smaller and less certain. Most Nigerians lacked any knowledge of managerial and technical skills required for industrial development.

BUSINESS INCENTIVES

In order to tackle the lack of indigenous capital, the government established development boards in each region and in Lagos to make loans and grants for industrial development. Production development boards were also set up in each region to stimulate and assist industrial projects.[1]

The need to encourage foreign investors in Nigeria was clearly shown in 1952, when the government passed the Aid to Pioneer Industries Ordinance. Any undertaking which was a public limited company registered in Nigeria, and which satisfied the provisions of the ordinance – basically, that the industry was favourable to Nigeria and thus in its interest to assist – might be declared a pioneer industry and granted a Pioneer Industries Certificate. The industry so declared was then relieved from the payment of company tax during the first two years of its operation, or for a further one or three years where fixed capital expenditure had not been less than £15,000 or £100,000 respectively. Also in 1952 the Income Tax (Amendment) Ordinance was passed, allowing both public and private companies to write off from profits, for the purpose of computing taxable income, a large amount of their capital investment in fixed assets during the early years of trading. This enabled them to amortize their capital quickly and to build up liquid reserves at an early date, thereby making

[1] Some details of the functions of these boards are discussed in Chapter 12.

further investment easier. The Aid to Pioneer Industries Ordinance was superseded by the Industrial Development (Income Tax Relief) Ordinance of 1958. The ordinance of 1958 was broadly on the lines of the two earlier ordinances, but it extended the period over which tax holidays could be taken, and also liberalized the procedure for granting pioneer certificates.[1]

After the constitutional changes in 1954, each regional government became responsible for industrial development within its own territory,[2] but as a means of fostering co-operation to ensure that regional development would take place within the framework of a national economic policy, the National Economic Council was set up in 1955. Again, in April 1956, the government established the Institute of Applied Industrial Research within the Federal Department of Commerce and Industries.[3] The functions of the institute were:

(*a*) to carry out basic research into the raw materials available in Nigeria for use in industry, and the processes which can be used most effectively to convert them; (*b*) to carry out pilot-scale trials of processes found in the laboratory to be technically feasible; and (*c*) to calculate by means of larger-scale tests or otherwise the probable viability of such processes if established on a commercial scale.[4]

Its services were to be made available to regional Departments of Commerce and Industries, development agencies, firms or private individuals requiring them.

Some major research projects handled by the institute were the mechanized processing of gari, fish drying, pulp and paper investigations, and solar water heating.

The governments of Nigeria issued a joint policy statement in 1956 under the title 'Opportunities for Overseas Investments in the Federation of Nigeria'.[5] This outlined an agreed national policy

---

[1] While only four pioneer certificates had been issued between 1952 and the end of 1957, seven certificates were issued during 1958.

[2] Industrial development and scientific and industrial research were included as items in the concurrent legislative list.

[3] This followed the recommendation of the International Bank Mission: *Economic Development of Nigeria*, p. 29.

[4] *Nigerian Handbook of Commerce and Industry*, 1960, p. 29.

[5] For the full text, see Oliver, op. cit., appendix II, pp. 181–3. Also NNEC, *Economic Survey of Nigeria, 1959*, appendix VIII b.

applying to industries set up in any part of the country, and indicated some of the types of industrial enterprise in which overseas investment would be welcomed, detailing a number of safeguards and inducements applying to such industries. In 1957 yet another inducement for industrial growth was introduced by the Industrial Development (Import Duties Relief) Ordinance. The ordinance authorized the repayment of part or all of any duty paid on imported raw, semi-processed or processed materials used in the manufacture or processing of goods, or in the provision of services. The federal government carried the whole cost of these concessions.

The Customs Duties (Dumped and Subsidized Goods) Ordinance was passed in 1958, permitting, when necessary, the imposition of a special duty on any goods which were being dumped in Nigeria, or were subsidized by any government or authority outside Nigeria. In exercising this power, the government had to satisfy itself that material injury to a potential or established industry in Nigeria would be threatened or caused by the entry of such goods, and that the imposition of a special duty would not conflict with Nigeria's obligations under the General Agreement on Tariffs and Trade (GATT). Also in 1958, the government brought into force the Customs (Drawback) Regulation, under which importers could claim repayment of import duty in full on goods exported in the same state as that in which they were imported; on materials imported for use in the manufacture of goods and then exported; and on paper imported for use in the manufacture of educational goods where such goods were supplied to recognized educational establishments.

The prospect of industrial investment was further increased in 1959 by the establishment of the Investment Company of Nigeria Ltd. The company was formed by the Commonwealth Development Finance Company Limited on the invitation of the federal government, and in consultation with leading Nigerian and British business interests; and it was to assist enterprises in Nigeria engaged in industrial production, commerce, agriculture and the exploitation of natural resources, by providing finance for their development, modernization or expansion. In addition, the company was to attract supplementary foreign investment capital to private enterprise; seek technical and managerial experts; attract indigenous investment; and actively encourage the growth of a local stocks and shares market. The company had an authorized capital of £5 million, of which one million £1 shares were issued and fully subscribed by Nigerian, British, French, Swiss, Dutch, American and Canadian firms, companies and corporations. The Commonwealth Development Finance Company Limited and the Development Corporation also subscribed.

A number of other companies which directly assisted industrial production in Nigeria included the Northern Nigeria Investments Limited (established in September 1959); and the Industrial and Agricultural Company Limited, established jointly by the Colonial Development Corporation and the Eastern Nigeria government in October 1959.[1]

Other factors which tended to favour industrial growth in Nigeria included the adequate sources of power and the provision of land for industrial estates. Coal production in Nigeria increased from 582,000 tons in 1957 to its highest peak of 925,000 tons in 1958. The Nigerian coal industry was, however, handicapped by the geographical location of the mines (at Udi, Eastern Nigeria), which involved heavy transport costs on any coal used on the western side of the country. Nevertheless, coal provided the main source of power, before the expansion of the electricity and the oil industries. Total electricity generated in Nigeria increased from 6·1 m. kWh in 1950 to 448·3 m. kWh in 1960. Between 1954 and 1960 the proportion of total electricity supply which went to industrial and commercial consumers averaged about 50 per cent annually. Although the production of petroleum oil had not increased greatly by 1960,[2] there was sufficient indication that oil would be a major source of power in the near future.

In order to solve the problem of the land tenure system, which made it difficult to obtain lands with clear titles, the governments of

---

[1] A number of government publications on industrial developments were made available to prospective industrialists, e.g. *Setting up an Industrial Enterprise in Nigeria*, Lagos, Federal Department of Commerce and Industries, 1955, and *The Role of the Federal Government in Promoting Industrial Development in Nigeria*, Sessional Paper no. 3 of 1958. For a most recent survey of incentives for industrial development, see S. A. Aluko, *Fiscal Incentives for Industrial Development in Nigeria*, 1967 (a study conducted for the Research Division of the United Nations Department of Economic and Social Affairs).

[2] In 1960, 6·4 million barrels of petroleum oil were produced in Nigeria.

Nigeria developed a number of industrial estates which could be rented by industrialists. The federal government developed an industrial estate at Apapa in Lagos, and the Western Nigeria government developed a 700-acre industrial estate at Ikeja near Lagos. The government of Eastern Nigeria also acquired lands and developed industrial estates at Enugu and Port Harcourt. In Northern Nigeria, where all land was under the government, approved industrialists could obtain it more easily: the government here provided an added incentive by developing industrial estates at a number of important cities, including Kano, Kaduna and Zaria. Most areas which could attract industrialists were provided with reasonable supplies of water. The government also increased capital expenditure on transport and communication: this rose from £4·7 million (18·1 per cent of total government expenditure) in the financial year 1950–1, to £32·5 million (24·3 per cent of total government expenditure) in the financial year 1959–60. Special priority was given to the construction of feeder roads to industrial estates. Another important social overhead was education, on which the government invested more funds: total expenditure on education (capital and recurrent) increased from £3·4 million in 1950–1 to £21·9 million in 1959–60. These represented 13·3 and 16·4 per cent respectively of total annual expenditure.

Probably the most important attraction to foreign industrialists and investors was the guarantee given by the federal government that profits and dividends arising from sterling and non-sterling capital investments in approved projects could be freely transferred to the country of origin, and that such capital could be repatriated at will.

INDUSTRIAL ESTABLISHMENTS[1]

The selected industries mentioned below include those which were undertaken solely by the various governments of the Federation, and those which were created by private enterprise, sometimes with government participation.

[1] The progress of industrial establishments in Nigeria can be traced in the *Annual Reports of the Federal Department of Commerce and Industries, 1946–60*.

Canning

Among the local industries which the government undertook to develop was the food-canning industry. Food canning was first undertaken by the Department of Commerce and Industries in 1949, when a small experimental cannery using hand-canning machinery

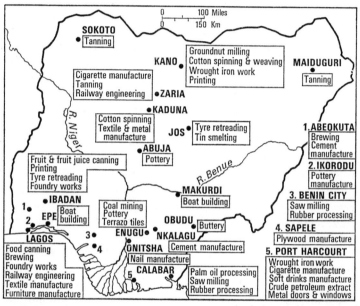

12 Manufacturing industries

was set up in Lagos to investigate the possibility of preserving classified butter, fat, fish, and seasonal surpluses of Nigerian fruits and meat. In 1951 another experimental plant was set up at Ibadan by the same department, but was subsequently taken over by the Western Region Development Corporation.[1] The experiment proved that local pineapple and citrus crops could be successfully canned. In 1952 output at the Ibadan factory included 392,000 cans of grapefruit segments, 58,000 cans of grapefruit juice, 5,000 cans of pineapple crush and slices and 2,000 cans of Nigerian foodstuff. It was hoped

[1] *Annual Report of the Department of Commerce and Industries for the year 1951–2*, Lagos, Government Printer, 1954, pp. 28–9.

that a proportion of the output could be exported, 'but a number of unforeseeable factors, not least the restriction of imports by the United Kingdom and the low price offered by the Ministry of Food (UK) as the sole importer, made this difficult'.[1] In 1954 the Lafia Canning Factory was established at Ibadan, and another factory was started at Kano by the Northern Region Development Corporation. A large proportion of the total output of these factories was consumed in Nigeria. There were some exports to neighbouring countries, but these were small in quantity and in value.

Boat building

In 1950 small experimental boatyards were set up by the Nigerian government at Opobo and Makurdi,[2] with the object of developing the design and construction of shallow-draught vessels suitable for use on the inland waterways – which provided a widespread and economical transport system in some parts of the country, particularly in the South. Initially, the work of the yards was handicapped by the lack of skilled workmen, but the difficulty was overcome by employing qualified British boat-builders to train Nigerian craftsmen. Following the experimental stages, larger boatyards were developed at Opobo, Makurdi and Epe. In 1956 the launchings from these yards included powered vessels for ferrying up to 80 passengers; self-propelled barges with a load capacity of 15 tons; a trawling vessel 39 feet long by 10 feet 6 inches beam; and a 32-foot four-berth fast cruiser powered by two 100 h.p. marine petrol engines, giving a speed of 20 knots.[3] The expansion of the boat-building industry was handicapped by the scarcity of waterside installations and repair and maintenance facilities.

A number of other industrial projects would not have been possible without the aid of foreign enterprises. There were many instances when the government participated jointly with foreign concerns, and a few are mentioned below.

[1] Ibid., p. 30.
[2] *Annual Report of the Department of Commerce and Industries for the year 1951–2*, Lagos, Government Printer, 1954, pp. 27–8.
[3] *Annual Report of the Department of Commerce and Industries for the year 1956–7*, Lagos, Government Printer, 1958, pp. 20–1.

Textiles

Textile production had long been an indigenous craft, predominantly a village industry employing primitive and uneconomic methods. Cotton was grown in nearly all parts of the country. Spinning was carried out mainly by women, while both men and women participated in weaving, the men producing the narrow strips and the women a broader cloth. Like all such primitive industries, the Nigerian textile industry suffered at first from a shortage of home-spun yarn, owing to the insufficiency of spinning caused by the crude techniques adopted. It had long been realized that the country had sufficient raw cotton for considerable expansion in the industry. Small looms were used for the production of the local cloths until 1945, when a textile development programme was incorporated in the Ten-Year Development and Welfare Plan for the country.[1] The framework of the scheme was the establishment of eight territorial centres, each in the charge of a European textile or weaving supervisor. Textile training centres were set up to train operators in the use of looms at Kano, Sokoto, Ilorin, Ado-Ekiti, Oyo, Auchi and Aba, where broad looms, spinning wheels and other preparatory equipment were introduced.[2] The flying shuttle was first introduced at Ado-Ekiti in 1947.

In 1949, the growing interest in textile production found expression in the decision by two indigenous companies to erect textile mills, one near Lagos and the other at Kano.[3] These mills were of small units, planned to allow rapid expansion on the weaving side. Up to 60 looms in each mill were to operate in the initial stage, and the mills were expected to produce between them more than 1·5 million yards of baft, shirting and drills per year when operating on a full scale. The mill at Kano was managed by the Kano Citizen Trading Company, and it was partly financed by a loan from the Northern Region Development Board. The company drew on technical advice and assistance provided by the Department of

[1] Sessional Paper no. 24 of 1945, and *Colonial Annual Reports*, Nigeria, 1946, p. 45.
[2] *Annual Report of the Department of Commerce and Industries for the year 1948*, Lagos, Government Printer, 1950, pp. 4–5.
[3] *Annual Report of the Department of Commerce and Industries for the year 1948–9*, Lagos, Government Printer, 1951, pp. 14–16.

Commerce and Industries. It purchased reconditioned British looms and equipment during a period when the Lancashire (UK) industry was re-equipping with modern machinery.

Production at Kano soon increased under the supervision of two European experts, and, by the beginning of 1957, the factory with its 54 looms was producing about 6,000 yards per week. In its early days it also engaged in the experimental weaving of spun rayon, but this was abandoned, as it was considered that production would not prove competitive enough with imported rayon products.

The factory at Lagos was a private enterprise. It operated with only 30 looms, and was technically assisted by the Federal Department of Commerce and Industries.[1] It utilized yarn produced from Northern Nigerian cotton on 1,600 ring spindles, and it produced mainly dyed drills at the rate of some 4,000 yards a week.

It was soon realized, by both the government and private investors, that if the textile industry was to expand, it was necessary to secure the participation of a reputable overseas textile manufacturing company in order to obtain adequate capital and managerial and technical skills, which the country could not provide from her own resources, and without which the industry could not hope to succeed. In 1952 a British textile firm proposed a financial partnership with Nigerian development authorities to establish a mill of 15,000 spindles and 300 to 350 looms in any suitable location, but the negotiations broke down. However, in March 1955, the Northern Region government made a fresh approach, this time to an old-established Lancashire company, David Whitehead & Sons (Holdings) Ltd. This company, having already set up a cotton textile mill in Southern Rhodesia, had acquired experience of manufacturing under African conditions. In September 1955 a Nigerian public company was formed under the name of Kaduna Textiles Ltd, and granted the benefits of pioneer status under the Aid to Pioneer Industries Ordinance. The total share and loan capital of the company was fixed at £1 million, and the three ordinary shareholders were the Northern Region Marketing Board, the Northern Region Development Corporation and David Whitehead & Sons (Nigeria) Ltd. The last-named company was appointed as the managing agent. Kaduna was chosen for the site of the mill, because

[1] *Annual Report of the Department of Commerce and Industries for the year 1955–6*, Lagos, Government Printer, 1958, pp. 24–5.

it was the only place at which land for the factory, water and electricity supplies and labour were all available. Most of the machinery, weighing nearly 10,000 tons in all, was imported from the United Kingdom, but some specialized equipment was obtained from the United States and Switzerland. The mill went into production in September 1957. It was equipped with 288 automatic looms and was fed with yarn from some 14,000 spindles, all the machines employed being driven by individual electric motors. The cloth produced was believed to be of better quality than imported baft of the same construction, because local cotton was superior to that used by the oriental manufacturers who had been the main suppliers hitherto. When production first began, the factory started to work up to a full single shift with operatives still under training. In December 1957 two-shift working began, and this was followed by three-shift working early in 1958.

By 1960 the volume of cotton piece goods produced in Nigeria remained small and the country continued to rely on imported cotton piece goods, which increased from 149 million square yards, valued at £14·1 million in 1950, to 211 million square yards, valued at £22·3 million in 1960.

Cement

The local manufacture of cement was considered in 1950 after it was discovered that there were large limestone deposits of suitable quality in Nigeria; the only raw material that had to be imported now was gypsum. Four years later, negotiations were completed between the federal government and two United Kingdom firms – cement manufacturers and consulting engineers respectively – for the establishment of a cement factory at Nkalagu.[1] The location of the factory was determined by the extensive limestone deposits in the area, and the proximity of the Enugu coalfields from which the factory could draw its fuel. A considerable amount of auxiliary work was needed, including the construction of an approach road and a 9-mile railway link at Ogbabo with the main railway network for evacuation of the product. The factory was owned and operated as a public company with a capital of £2·25 million subscribed mainly by the federal government, the Eastern Region government, the

[1] *First Annual Report of the Eastern Region Development Corporation, 1955–6,* p. 14.

Eastern Region Development Corporation, the Tunnel Portland Cement Co. Ltd, F. L. Smith & Co. Ltd and the Colonial Development Corporation. The Nigerian public was invited to subscribe £175,000 of the ordinary capital of £1·5 million. The offer was made in 1959 and the response was considerable. It was of great significance that the response came chiefly from small investors – about 84 per cent of the applications were for fifty £1 shares or less, and 51 per cent for the minimum of ten shares.

The cement factory was formally opened in December 1957, but had commenced experimental production three months earlier. Its capacity of 100,000 tons of cement per annum was roughly one-third of Nigeria's cement import in 1957. In 1960 the factory employed about 300 people.

At first, it appeared that the increasing volume of locally-produced cement would reduce the annual volume being imported; however, the increasing demand for cement nullified its impact. In 1958 the volume of imported cement was 477,119 tons, which was about 33,000 tons below that of 1957; but it rose again to 516,190 and 626,488 tons in 1959 and 1960 respectively.

The Nkalagu cement factory was soon followed by another factory in Western Nigeria. Investigations in 1955 and 1956 sponsored by the Associated Portland Cement Manufacturers Limited, with the agreement of the Western Region Development Corporation, revealed that there were limestone deposits in the area from Ilaro to the border of Dahomey; as a result it was decided, in June 1957, that a cement factory should be built. In February 1959 the West African Portland Cement Company Limited was incorporated in Nigeria as a public company to own and operate the cement works.[1] The equity capital of the company was subscribed by the Associated Portland Cement Manufacturers Limited (51 per cent), the Western Nigeria Development Corporation (39 per cent) and the United Africa Company Limited (10 per cent). The rated output was 200,000 tons per annum, which was double the output at Nkalagu. The factory was conveniently sited at Ewekoro at a point where the main trunk road and the railway converge to within 300 yards of each other. Construction started in mid-1958 and production began towards the latter part of 1960. At that time it was

[1] *Annual Report of the Western Region Production Development Board, 1957–8,* pp. 35–6.

the largest single manufacturing undertaking to have been established at one time in the country.

Cigarettes

In 1949 the British American Tobacco Company (later called the Nigerian Tobacco Company) expanded its factory at Ibadan, and it was equipped with new machinery. This was operated by an African staff of over 670, with only the minimum of expert supervision. The output from the factory was at the rate of 200 million cigarettes a month, comprising brands made from the mixtures of imported and Nigerian tobaccos, and cheaper varieties made wholly of locally-grown tobacco. In order to supplement production at Ibadan, two factories were established by the same company, at Port Harcourt and Zaria in 1956 and 1958 respectively. Table 15.1 below shows the

TABLE 15.1   *The growth of domestic*
cigarette production, 1946–60
(million cigarettes)

Year	Domestic production*	Imports
1946	559	282
1947	697	430
1948	729	363
1949	739	454
1950	910	494
1951	1,397	247
1952	1,932	75
1953	2,126	92
1954	2,250	64
1955	2,506	79
1956	2,650	44
1957	2,188	64
1958	2,953	78
1959	2,749	61
1960	2,871	104

* Excludes homemade and smuggled cigarettes.
Sources: (Trade Reports, *UN Statistical Yearbook*, Federal Office
of Statistics); Peter Kilby, *Industrialisation in an Open Economy:
Nigeria 1945–1966*, p. 82.

increasing domestic production of cigarettes and the corresponding decrease in the volume of imported cigarettes.

Soap

In addition to the soap factory established by the West African Soap Company Limited, the Alagbon Industries Limited (a company controlled by Paterson, Zochonis and Company Limited) built a soap factory at Aba in 1957. In 1960 the factory was producing about 5,000 tons of plain and carbolic soaps per annum.

Beer

Beer was a popular beverage in Nigeria, especially after the second world war. The consistent rise in its consumption increased the

TABLE 15.2　*The growth of domestic beer production, 1955–60 ('ooo galls)*

Year	Output of Star Beer	Imports*
1955	1,762	5,675
1956	2,233	6,560
1957	2,407	6,160
1958	3,060	6,271
1959	4,455	6,832
1960	4,459	7,192

* Ale, beer, stout and porter.
Sources: Kilby, op. cit., p. 98, and *Annual Abstract of Statistics, 1963.*

volume of imported beer so much that it was considered more economical to produce it in the country. This led to the establishment of the Nigerian Brewery Company in 1949. The company's product, 'Star Beer', was manufactured from imported hops and malt and, in 1954, was awarded first prize in the Brewers' Exhibition at Olympia, London. A branch of the company was opened at Aba in 1957. Table 15.2 above shows the growth of domestic beer production and imports of ale, beer, stout and porter. Imports of beer increased despite increased production of locally-brewed beer, which enjoyed great popularity in the country.[1]

Margarine

The margarine factory of Van Der Berghs (Nigeria) Limited, the first of its kind in Nigeria, began production in 1954. The industry was suited to Nigeria since it was able to take advantage of the abundant supplies of palm oil and palm kernels which were produced locally. The production capacity of the factory was 1,500 tons per annum, but this was greatly in excess of Nigerian consumption.

Plastics

The production of plastic products started in Nigeria in 1957, at a factory in Ibadan established jointly by the Western Region Development Corporation, the UAC Limited and a UK concern.[2] Initially the factory produced plastic tubes, pipes and conduits, but production was extended to cover a wide range of articles such as combs, beakers and cups, lampshades, casings for telephones, and raincoats.

Oil

The exploration for oil was resumed after the second world war by the Shell-BP Petroleum Development Company of Nigeria.[3] The project met with many disappointments in the early stages, and it was not until November 1953 that oil was struck for the first time. From 1951 to 1959 a total of 70 exploration wells were completed, and only 36 of these were producible. The first of the producible wells was discovered in January 1956 at Oloibiri in the heart of the Niger Delta, and this was followed ten months later by another at Afam in the Aba division. Subsequent wells discovered included Bomu and Ebubu in Ogoni division and Ughelli in the Delta province. Two pipelines were laid in 1957, one a 65-mile, 10-inch

[1] *Annual Report of the Department of Commerce and Industries, 1958–9*, Lagos, Government Printer, p. 13.

[2] *Annual Report of the Western Region Production Development Board, 1957–8*, pp. 29–30.

[3] Direct information about the early years of oil exploration is given in *The Oil Search*, Shell-BP Petroleum Development Company of Nigeria Limited, 1957.

line from Oloibiri to Port Harcourt, and the other a 30-mile, 6-inch line from Afam to Port Harcourt.

Other companies besides Shell-BP participated in Nigerian oil projects. In November 1955 Mobil Exploration Nigeria Incorporated carried out a preliminary geological survey of Sokoto province in the Northern Region; it also explored the Western Region and around Lagos. Other interested companies included the Tennessee

TABLE 15.3   *Production of principal economic minerals, 1947–60*

Year	Coal ('000 tons)	Tin ore (tons)	Columbite (tons)	Gold* (troy oz)
1947	582	12,597	1,282	2,503
1948	605	12,740	1,096	3,294
1949	551	12,171	888	2,858
1950	583	11,391	864	2,543
1951	551	11,778	1,078	1,779
1952	581	11,470	1,293	1,349
1953	700	11,349	1,959	861
1954	636	10,933	2,914	912
1955	749	11,245	3,146	881
1956	787	12,507	2,604	549
1957	815	13,151	1,923	486
1958	925	8,412	806	788
1959	742	7,481	1,588	1,060
1960	562	10,374	2,047	974

* As bullion.
Source: *Annual Abstract of Statistics, 1963.*

Nigeria Incorporated, a subsidiary of Tennessee Gas (USA), and The Gulf, Eastern and the Standard Oil (New Jersey, USA).

The exploration costs incurred by those companies were high, due to the peculiar conditions under which searches had to be conducted. Besides the cost of recruiting experts which the country lacked, and the training of local personnel, the inadequacy of many essential services led to heavy capital outlay in building roads and bridges in difficult and almost inaccessible areas, and in maintaining an independent telecommunications system for regular and frequent contacts with the scattered outposts. Large fleets of cars, lorries and river craft, helicopters and even aircraft all featured in the exploration projects. In the search for oil in the swamp of the Niger Delta, giant drilling barges, houseboats, trailer tractors and amphibious crawler tractors were employed. Up to the end of 1959, Shell-BP had spent £60 million on oil exploration in Nigeria.

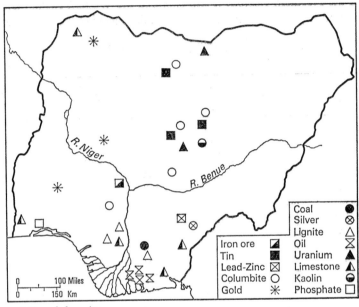

13 Mineral deposits

Other mineral industries

It was not until 1959 that the production of coal began to fall, following the introduction of diesel railway engines on the Nigerian railway from 1955 onwards. Production of tin and columbite, as shown on table 15.3, fluctuated during this period; and there was a decline in the production of gold.

INDUSTRIAL PRODUCTION AND THE NIGERIAN ECONOMY

The gradual growth of industrial establishments meant that the contribution of industrial production to the Nigerian economy slowly increased: on table 12.8 the contributions of two items – mining and oil exploration, and manufacturing and public utilities –

can be used as indicators of industrial growth. In 1950 mining and oil exploration contributed £7·6 million, while manufacturing and public utilities contributed £3·9 million to a total GDP of £688·7 million. These increased to £8·1 million and £7·9 million respectively out of a total GDP of £872·1 million in 1954. The contribution of mining and oil exploration increased to £8·4 million in 1960, while the contribution of manufacturing and public utilities increased to £36·1 million out of a total GDP of £981·3 million.

Increased government expenditure on improving facilities capable of helping industrial establishments, such as better communications, electricity and water, certainly contributed to the rapid growth of industries. Again, the fiscal incentives which have already been mentioned also encouraged foreign capital and investors to come to Nigeria.

The biggest single change in the history of the economy was the rapid increase in the volume of manufacturing production. Table 15.4 shows that the value of total production increased by 398 per

TABLE 15.4 *Gross product of manufacturing in constant 1957 prices* 1950–60 (£000)*

	1950	1954	1957	1960	Percentage increase 1950–60
Bakeries	19·0	66·0	210·0	316·0	1,550
Oil milling	363·6	356·9	2161·6	2610·0	618
Margarine	2·5	12·0	18·2	18·2	630
Beer and soft drinks	275·9	741·1	1683·7	2800·0	911
Tobacco	1395·8	2226·4	2100·6	2190·0	57
Textiles	4·5	50·0	377·0	613·0	1,350
Rubber processing	19·5	137·8	594·8	1368·0	7,080
Tanning	5·9	16·7	39·2	40·5	586
Sawmilling	498·7	1304·4	1531·4	1800·0	261
Cement	—	—	372·4	1160·0	—
Total manufacturing production	3129·3	6474·0	10924·7	15650·0	398

* P. N. C. Okigbo, *Nigerian National Accounts, 1950–7*, and *Estimates of Economic Planning Unit*, Federal Ministry of Economic Development.
Source: *National Development Plan, 1962–8.*

cent between 1950 and 1960. Rubber processing had the biggest increase of 7,080 per cent, while bakeries came next with 1,550 per cent, followed by textiles with 1,350 per cent. The production of beer and soft drinks also went up by over 900 per cent. A significant feature is that the increase in bakeries was achieved almost exclusively by private indigenous enterprise: nearly all the major towns had at least one bakery owned and managed by Nigerians.

The great increase in manufacturing production raised the problem of the supply of labour – skilled and semi-skilled. There are no comprehensive industrial surveys giving the statistics of those employed in manufacturing industries. However, the growth in the number of educated Nigerians in various fields and at various levels afforded industries with a pool of technically trained people, and a large group of other Nigerians who could be trained on the job to operate simple machines, and who could take part in the management of industries.

16   Money, currency and banking

Despite the efforts of the government to popularize the adoption of coins and currency notes issued by the West African Currency Board, one of the old commodity-currencies – the manilla – continued to circulate in the thickly-populated palm oil belt of South-Eastern Nigeria, even though it had ceased to be legal tender in 1911.

No strong measure was adopted against its use until 1948, when the government decided to redeem the manilla.[1] The finance committee of the Legislative Council of Nigeria had already voted the necessary funds for the operation, and the withdrawal operation took place between 1 October 1948 and 31 March 1949. The rates adopted by the government for the redemption were 80 Okpoho (King) manillas to £1, 240 Okombo (Queen) manillas to £1 and 480 Abi or Abbie (Prince) manillas to £1. Holders of manillas could redeem them by presentation at the banks or at the offices of large trading firms, and also at certain government offices. In order to speed up the process, they were accepted as payment of official taxes and dues at the native administration treasuries and courts. The operation met with outstanding success. It was estimated that about 32·5 million manillas were withdrawn, at a net cost of about £284,000, after taking into account the sum of £152,000 obtained from their sale for use as scrap metal.[2] The manilla thus ceased to be a currency, but it was permitted by law for any one person to hold not more than 200 for ceremonial and ritual purposes. The cowrie was

---

[1] *Colonial Annual Reports*, Nigeria, 1948, p. 32; and *UAC Statistical and Economic Review*, no. 3, March 1949.

[2] *Colonial Annual Reports*, Nigeria, 1949, p. 37.

still popular with the 'native' doctors, Shago worshippers and some other pagans who used it for their rituals. The removal of the cowrie and the manilla ended a local trading custom and history which were established many centuries ago.

The West African Currency Board continued to regulate the supply of coins and currency in Nigeria until 1 July 1959, when the newly-established Central Bank of Nigeria became the sole authority for the issue of currency in Nigeria. New Nigerian currency notes of £5, £1, 10s. and 5s. and certain new coins were also issued as from that date. The Nigerian pound was at par with sterling.

It was the practice of the board to make annual distributions from its surplus to the governments of each of the four countries in which it operated. On 30 June 1960 the cumulative sums that had been distributed in this way were as follows:[1]

	£
Nigeria	14,612,709
Ghana	8,344,618
Sierra Leone	2,733,060
The Gambia	569,613
Total	£26,260,000

Over the years, the board also accumulated a large surplus, partly out of retained income and partly out of capital appreciation, as a reserve against contingencies over and above its liabilities. It must be added that it did not make any fiduciary issue of currency even though there was no clause in the regulations to prevent this. The establishment of national currencies in Ghana and Nigeria meant that there was a considerable reduction in the board's liabilities, with the result that its surplus was well in excess of immediate needs. It decided, therefore, to distribute a part of this surplus to Ghana and Nigeria on the basis of the currency withdrawals from the two countries; and in September 1960 Ghana and Nigeria received £3,505,080 and £5,959,336 respectively.

The essence of the currency board system was the convertibility of West African coins and notes on demand into sterling balances in London.[2] The arrangement created the situation whereby the

[1] *UAC Statistical and Economic Review*, no. 26, October 1961, p. 39.
[2] Newlyn and Rowan, op. cit., p. 47.

currency in circulation, whether in the hands of the public or at the commercial banks, fluctuated automatically with the board's receipts or payments in sterling. It had no direct control over the exchange rates of its currency, since the exchange rate of West African currency was directly linked with the exchange rates of sterling: for this reason the board has been described as a passive money changer.[1] As West African currency was a token of indebted-

TABLE 16.1 *Estimated currency in circulation, 1946–60 (£000)*

Year ending 31 March	Notes	Coin	Total	Cash held by banks	Net circulation
1946	3,214	14,926	18,140	1,483	16,657
1947	4,696	18,733	23,429	2,060	21,369
1948	5,336	19,246	24,602	2,364	22,238
1949	8,241	23,531	31,772	3,222	28,550
1950	8,935	22,642	31,577	2,865	28,712
1951	13,958	25,282	39,240	2,661	36,579
1952	19,122	31,164	50,286	5,849	44,437
1953	20,812	30,553	51,365	4,818	46,547
1954	25,693	33,791	59,484	7,713	51,753
1955	25,778	27,938	53,716	6,838	46,878
1956	30,465	27,796	58,261	7,132	51,129
1957	37,318	24,122	61,440	7,634	53,806
1958	33,447	24,391	57,838	7,260	50,578
1959	36,906	21,526	58,432	4,898	53,534
1960*	46,603	20,549	67,152	7,210	59,942

* March quarter includes £45·09 million in Nigerian notes and £7·27 million in Nigerian shillings.
Source: *Annual Abstract of Statistics, 1963.*

ness on the board's part to anybody who deposited sterling with it, the currency in circulation expanded when there was an excess of export earnings over the value of imports, and vice versa. The fact that Nigeria enjoyed a boom in export trade between 1946 and 1954 led to a considerable increase in the amount of money in circulation, as shown on table 16.1. The board was not a banking institution and its functions had little in common with those performed by a central

[1] Perham (ed.), *Mining, Commerce and Finance in Nigeria*, p. 186.

bank. It had no direct relations with the commercial banks, and consequently could not control their activities.

COMMERCIAL BANKING

The first indigenous bank to establish after the war was the Agbon-magbe Bank Ltd, a private company incorporated in Nigeria in 1945, whose name, meaning 'sea never dries', was adopted to gain the confidence of the people and to attract customers. The next bank to establish was the African Continental Bank Ltd, founded by Dr Nnamdi Azikiwe, who became governor-general of Nigeria in 1960.[1]

The others operating in 1960 were: the Merchant Bank Ltd, established in 1952 as a private company incorporated in Nigeria; the Muslim Bank (West Africa) Ltd, established in 1957 as a private company incorporated in Nigeria; the Bank of Lagos Ltd, incorporated in Nigeria in 1958 as a public company; the Bank of the North Ltd, a public company incorporated in Nigeria in 1959; and the National Bank of Nigeria Ltd, which was established in 1933.[2]

Until 1947, when the British and French Bank Ltd opened in Lagos, the BBWA (later known as the Bank of West Africa) and Barclays Bank were the only two expatriate banks operating in Nigeria. The other foreign commercial banks which later began operating in Nigeria were: the Banque de L'Afrique Occidentale, a public company incorporated in France in 1901; and the Berini Bank Limited, a private company incorporated in Nigeria in 1959.

The history of commercial banking in Nigeria is incomplete without mentioning the 'bank mania' of the early fifties. Although there was a recognized need to establish more financial institutions to cope with the expanding economy, the immediate cause was the inflationary pressure in Nigeria during the years 1947–52, brought about by a sharp and sudden rise in the value of Nigerian exports. Some of the people who shared in the trade prosperity established 'mushroom banks', such as the Nigerian Farmers' and Commercial Bank Ltd, the Nigerian Trust Bank Ltd, the Standard Bank Ltd, the Afroseas Credit Bank Ltd, the City Bank Ltd, the Pan-Nigerian

---

[1] The bank was first registered as Tinubu Properties Ltd, but changed its name to the African Continental Bank in 1948.

[2] For the early history of the National Bank of Nigeria Ltd, see Chapter 10.

Bank Ltd, the Provincial Bank of Nigeria Ltd, the Mainland Bank Ltd, the Union Bank of British Africa Ltd, and Group Credit and Agricultural Bank Ltd.

The most popular of these was the Nigerian Farmers' and Commercial Bank Ltd, popularly known as the Farmers' Bank. The history of the Farmers' Bank is typical of the rest. The bank was incorporated in Lagos as a private company in 1947. It started very well, and within a comparatively short period it won the confidence of the public. However, it embarked on an over-ambitious expansion scheme: at the time of its liquidation in 1952 it had thirty-four branch offices in Nigeria, while the BBWA, which had operated for fifty-eight years, had eighteen branches. Again, in common with the other indigenous banks it granted excessive loans to customers: for example, in the financial year ending 31 March 1951 it tied up 40·8 per cent of its assets in loans and advances to customers;[1] this compared with 14·1 per cent and 27·7 per cent by the BBWA[2] and Barclays Bank[3] respectively. It thus reduced its liquidity below the safety margin.

The Farmers' Bank went into compulsory liquidation on 12 December 1952. Small savers suffered very badly, and many businesses, organizations and some Christian missions lost the bulk of their savings. Contributing factors to the disaster were a loss of confidence in the bank, after it had been refused a banking licence that year;[4] bad management; stealing; and a bad accounting system. The crisis was precipitated by the failure of some other 'mushroom banks', which justified the fear of many people about the unsound nature of the indigenous commercial banks. However, some survived the storm,[5] and confidence has since been restored in them.

[1] Nigerian Farmers' and Commercial Bank Ltd, balance sheet at 31 March 1951: *Daily Times*, 1 October 1951.

[2] BBWA Ltd, balance sheet at 31 March 1951: *Daily Times*, 20 July 1951.

[3] Barclays Bank (DCO), statements of accounts at 31 March 1951: *Daily Times*, 14 July 1951.

[4] The Association of African Bankers presented a petition against the Banking Ordinance of 1952: *Daily Times*, 10 March 1952.

[5] The indigenous commercial banks that survived were the National Bank of Nigeria Ltd, the African Continental Bank and the Agbonmagbe Bank.

Branch banking

The nature of the country's economy, which depended mainly on the export earnings on cocoa, oil palm products, cotton and ground-nuts, afforded the banks the opportunity of using surplus cash as loans and advances to farmers and the produce buyers in many parts of the country. The establishment of bank branches was further encouraged, at least after 1950, by the increasing number of foreign and indigenous enterprises. The greatest number of bank branch offices were in Lagos and the Western Region, thus giving these areas the lowest population per bank office.

TABLE 16.2   *Banks and bank branches, September 1960*

| Bank | Branches | | | | |
	Lagos	Western Region	Eastern Region	Northern Region	Total
Bank of West Africa	6	20	10	20	56
Barclays Bank	9	12	14	27	62
National Bank of Nigeria	2	22	1	3	28
African Continental Bank	3	3	7	7	20
British & French Bank	5	1	1	2	9
Agbonmagbe Bank	2	7	—	1	10
Merchant Bank	1	1	—	—	2
Muslim Bank	1	—	—	—	1
Bank of Lagos	1	—	—	—	1
Bank of the North	—	—	—	3	3
Banque de L'Afrique Occidentale	1	—	—	1	2
Berini Bank Ltd	1	—	—	—	1
Total	32	66	33	64	195
Population (million)*	0·4	7	8	20	35
Population per office (million)*		0·012	0·106	0·242	0·311	0·173

* Approximated population estimates (mid-year 1960): *Annual Abstract of Statistics, 1963.*
Source: *Nigerian Handbook of Commerce and Industry, 1960.*

Banking practices

The relationship between the expatriate banks and the Nigerian public was relatively poor. The expatriate banks had little or no knowledge of most of the Nigerian small businesses, consequently advances and loans were seldom granted to them. A survey of the assets and liabilities of these banks revealed certain peculiarities in their operations. The deposits of the banks were made principally by the government, and quasi-government bodies such as the local authorities; and by expatriate businesses and private individuals. The share of Nigerian deposit was very low, because many people preferred demand deposit, which the expatriate banks did not encourage. For liquidity reasons, commercial banks could only grant short-term loans, but there were other reasons for the low levels of advances made by the foreign-owned banks to Nigerians. First, indigenous enterprises did not always satisfy the requirements of the banks; as a borrower, an enterprise should have a good and reliable reputation and thus commercial reliability, but most of the indigenous firms lacked this. Secondly, many indigenous entrepreneurs kept their business accounts by memory, as organized accounting was almost non-existent; consequently credit-worthiness could not be assessed. Thirdly, most of the borrowers had no acceptable securities; and lastly, there were no means by which a close relationship could be maintained between the bankers and the indigenous enterprises, as most of the senior officials of these banks were themselves expatriates. For these reasons, the bulk of the Nigerian public was never satisfied with the services provided by the expatriate banks. There was the general feeling that they discriminated against Nigerians. However, the available facts indicate that the indigenous banks did not depart from the basic principles which ensured adequate bank liquidity; they adopted the English banking tradition, which had been criticized and described as conservative. For example, the National Bank of Nigeria Limited, one of the leading indigenous banks, once advertised as follows:

The National Bank of Nigeria Limited
TRADITION
No organized structure can excel the British conservative system of banking which has become a recognized and respected British

TABLE 16.3a *Assets of principal banks, 1946–60 (£000)*

Date 31 December	Cash	Balance due by other banks — Nigeria	Balance due by other banks — Abroad	Loans and advances	Investments — Nigeria*	Investments — Other†	Other assets	Total
1946	1,272	546	11,142	956	—	47	406	14,369
1947	1,497	393	10,953	1,693	10	32	505	15,083
1948	1,496	415	10,672	3,538	10	40	502	16,673
1949	2,132	144	7,653	3,683	10	31	540	14,193
1950	2,038	140	10,391	4,348	16	30	790	17,753
1951	3,355	596	13,502	5,519	49	31	3,056	26,108
1952	3,856	683	15,961	9,150	322	30	6,037	36,039
1953	5,384	1,165	16,070	10,207	276	30	5,728	38,860
1954	5,310	1,408	24,832	11,895	160	42	8,477	52,124
1955	7,449	1,608	20,467	19,075	380	30	8,734	57,743
1956	6,818	1,821	21,771	25,511	380	56	11,303	67,652
1957	7,023	2,111	16,902	34,462	399	30	11,986	72,913
1958	6,653	3,514	15,888	38,298	261	337	14,751	79,702
1959	8,451	6,101	23,668	40,887	701	616	20,105	100,529
1960	7,967	4,648	21,254	57,000	2,676	179	24,194	117,918

* Including holdings of federal government treasury bills.
† Including holdings of United Kingdom treasury bills.
Source: *Annual Abstract of Statistics, 1963.*

TABLE 16.3b *Liabilities of principal banks, 1946–60 (£000)*

Date 31 December	Deposits — Demand	Deposits — Time	Deposits — Savings banks	Deposits — Total	Balance due to other banks — Nigeria	Balance due to other banks — Abroad	Other liabilities	Total
1946	9,401	2,144	1,116	12,661	1,481	43	184	14,369
1947	10,389	2,108	1,200	13,697	1,109	100	177	15,083
1948	11,435	1,812	1,250	14,497	1,708	194	274	16,673
1949	10,267	1,799	1,397	13,463	123	146	461	14,193
1950	13,190	1,762	1,450	16,402	220	736	395	17,753
1951	18,430	2,362	1,630	22,422	349	979	2,358	26,108
1952	22,230	3,325	2,289	27,844	636	2,441	5,118	36,039
1953	24,468	3,854	2,916	31,238	1,400	1,760	4,462	38,860
1954	32,870	4,289	3,445	40,604	1,918	2,842	6,760	52,124
1955	31,639	4,726	5,864	42,229	1,817	5,271	8,426	57,743
1956	35,352	4,131	6,325	45,808	3,394	7,243	11,007	67,452
1957	37,326	5,648	8,917	51,891	2,357	8,164	10,501	72,913
1958	40,266	6,645	11,145	58,056	3,892	5,600	12,154	79,702
1959	40,168	10,846	14,280	65,294	3,657	12,689	18,889	100,529
1960	41,117	8,954	18,441	68,512	2,499	18,368	28,539	117,918

Source: *Annual Abstract of Statistics, 1963.*

tradition. A system on which is built the strength, solidity and reliability of British financial institutions and which has withstood the vicissitudes of war, tumults, commotions and crises all through the ages.

We follow strictly this British conservative system of banking.

PATRONIZE THE NATIONAL BANK

because it is being built on a solid foundation of tradition and conservatism.[1]

The main difference between the operations of the expatriate banks and the indigenous banks was that the former had fewer contacts with Nigerian businesses. It must be added, however, that the indigenous banks offered more encouragement to small savers; the minimum amount of deposit acceptable to the expatriate banks was higher than that of the indigenous banks, and consequently many people failed to qualify as depositors in the former.

Table 16.3 shows the assets of the principal commercial banks in Nigeria. It can be seen that the total amount of loans and advances increased over the years. In 1946 loans and advances accounted for 6·6 per cent of total banks' assets, but this increased to 26·3 and 48·3 per cent in 1950 and 1960 respectively. In 1946 the commercial banks had no investment in Nigeria, although it must be added that there were no Nigerian securities in which banks could invest. By 1950 a small investment had been made, but it was still less than 0·1 per cent of total assets. However, between June 1959 and December 1960 the Nigerian Central Bank, on behalf of the federal government, issued some treasury bills, and these enabled the banks to increase their investments in Nigeria to 2·3 per cent of their total assets. Table 16.4 shows the main economic activities for which loans and advances were granted. In 1952 loans and advances for the development of agricultural export crops accounted for 34·4 per cent of total loans and advances, but by 1960 it had fallen to 20·5 per cent. In contrast, the percentage of loans for the development of wholesale and retail commerce increased from 34·6 in 1952 to 37·3 in 1960.

The control of commercial banks

Over half a century after the first bank started operating in Nigeria the government began to attempt to control the banking business.

[1] *Daily Times*, 2 April 1952.

TABLE 16.4 *Customers' liabilities to banks for loans and advances, 1952–60 (£000)*

Loans and advances for the development of

Date 31 December	Cocoa	Ground-nuts	Palm produce	Other export crops	Textiles, leather and clothing	Soaps and oils	Buildings in course of erection	Wholesale and retail commerce	Others	Total
1952	1,076	1,424	85	572	39	105	470	3,381	2,030	9,182
1953	823	1,055	163	483	100	268	521	4,140	2,654	10,207
1954	1,630	2,370	347	403	130	17	940	4,088	2,137	12,062
1955	2,038	4,073	411	901	192	237	1,050	7,812	2,734	19,448
1956	2,558	3,565	659	844	272	314	1,021	8,860	7,418	25,511
1957	1,567	8,745	1,032	923	292	588	1,800	11,277	8,416	34,640
1958	3,213	6,094	937	1,367	446	743	2,470	13,399	9,629	38,298
1959	2,581	3,376	824	1,623	486	666	3,068	13,554	14,040	40,218
1960	3,125	5,210	759	2,512	594	675	3,596	21,054	19,013	56,538

Source: *Annual Abstract of Statistics, 1963.*

The rapid growth of indigenous banks immediately after the war called for strict control in order to protect the public; in 1948 the first step was taken when the government invited Mr G. D. Paton, an official of the Bank of England, to make recommendations on the form and extent of control which should be introduced. He included in his report[1] a draft banking ordinance which, he claimed, was designed to protect depositors. This laid down that banking business should be conducted only by a company, and that no banking company should be registered unless it possessed a subscribed capital of at least £25,000, of which £12,500 should be paid up. Because of the difficulty of raising capital in Nigeria, banks were to be given 'three years of grace' in which to meet the latter condition. The report also recommended the supervision of the banks by an officer nominated by the Governor, who should satisfy himself that all were maintaining a sufficient degree of liquidity.

The first banking ordinance, based on Paton's recommendations, was not introduced until 1952, when the government was forced into it following the liquidation of a number of indigenous commercial banks. It was amended in 1958 following a report by Mr J. B. Loynes, an adviser to the Bank of England, who had been invited to look into the possibility of establishing a central bank for Nigeria.[2] In addition to prescribing procedures and standards for the conduct of banking business, and defining permissible capital and reserve structures, the 1958 ordinance provided for the maintenance by banks of a minimum holding of liquid assets as prescribed by the central bank. In November 1959 the liquidity ratio was fixed at 25 per cent of gross demand and time liabilities; and the proportion could be varied as conditions warranted. The law also provided for the regular examination of all licensed commercial banks by the Banking Examiner, who was appointed by the Federal Minister of Finance, and whose task was not only to ensure that banks fulfilled the requirements of the banking ordinance but also to advise and assist them wherever possible, especially the small indigenous banks. By 1960 the indigenous banks had come to realize that the banking legislation was meant to secure a sound banking system, and not

[1] *Report on Banking in Nigeria*, Lagos, 1948.
[2] *Report by Mr J. B. Loynes on the Establishment of a Nigerian Central Bank, the Introduction of a Nigerian Currency and other Associated Matters*, Lagos, Government Printer, 1957.

designed to cripple them. It was, therefore, accepted as an essential factor in the banking policy of any progressive money economy.

THE CENTRAL BANK

The proposal to create a central bank for Nigeria was first made in the House of Representatives in Lagos on 21 March 1952, but it was not debated until it came up again on 9 April.[1] The Financial Secretary to the Nigerian government amended the motion thus: 'that as a practical means of marshalling the financial resources of this country for the purpose of aiding commercial development in all its phases, the Government should examine the possibility of establishing a Central Bank, and report to the House as soon as possible'. This was accepted, and the government invited Mr J. L. Fisher, an adviser to the Bank of England, to examine 'the desirability and practicability of establishing a Central Bank of Nigeria for promoting the economic development of the country'. Mr Fisher, reporting in 1953,[2] thought that the financial environment hardly existed for a central bank to function in Nigeria other than semi-automatically as a bank of issue; that it was highly doubtful if a central bank could be adequately staffed; and that a central bank would be too expensive for the country at that time. He therefore recommended that the Currency Board system should be continued, instead of establishing a central bank. However, the International Bank Mission, which visited the country later in 1953, supported the creation of a 'State Bank of Nigeria' in view of the constitutional progress towards self-government, and its report revived interest in the scheme.

In 1957 the federal government invited Mr J. B. Loynes to advise on a wide range of banking problems in connexion with the establishment of a central bank, in the light of the recommendations made by the International Bank Mission.[3] On the whole his report favoured this proposal, and the Central Bank of Nigeria Ordinance was passed in 1958.[4] It contained the following main provisions, which closely followed Mr Loynes's recommendations:

[1] *Debate in the House of Representatives*, March–April 1952.
[2] *Report on the Desirability and Practicability of Establishing a Central Bank in Nigeria for Promoting the Economic Development of the Country*, Lagos, 1953.
[3] IBRD, *Economic Development of Nigeria*, pp. 56–9.
[4] The Central Bank of Nigeria Ordinance, no. 24 of 1958.

The principal objects of the Bank shall be to issue legal tender currency in Nigeria, to maintain external reserves in order to safeguard the international value of that currency, to promote monetary stability and a sound financial structure in Nigeria and to act as banker and financial adviser to the Federal Government.[1]

TABLE 16.5 *Detailed statement of the Central Bank of Nigeria, 1959 and 1960*

Assets and liabilities	31 December 1959 (£)	31 December 1960 (£)
Assets:		
Convertible currencies, foreign government securities and balance with foreign banks	52,811,195	76,465,457
West African Currency Board notes and coins	4,651,483	1,095,618
Gold	—	—
Total external reserve	57,462,678	77,561,075
Federal government securities	—	1,575,010
Re-discounts and advances	—	1,785,773
Other securities	36,943	56,992
Other assets	453,775	1,465,896
Total assets	57,953,396	82,444,746
Liabilities:		
Capital subscribed and paid up	300,000	1,250,000
General reserve	—	200,872
Nigerian currency in circulation	54,440,376	77,076,571
Deposits:		
Federal and regional government	1,991,779	1,083,054
Bankers	1,010,915	1,448,346
Other	68,266	248,036
(Total deposits	3,070,960	2,779,436)
Other liabilities	142,060	1,137,867
Total liabilities	£57,953,396	£82,444,746

Source: *Annual Abstract of Statistics, 1963.*

[1] Ibid., section 4.

The authorised capital of the Bank shall be one million five hundred thousand Nigerian pounds of which seven hundred and fifty thousand pounds shall be subscribed and paid at par by the Federal Government on the establishment of the Bank.[1]

The unit of currency in Nigeria shall be the Nigerian pound which shall be divided into twenty shillings, each shilling being divided into twelve pence. . . .[2]

The parity of the Nigerian pound shall be one Nigerian pound to one pound sterling.[3]

The relationship between the Central Bank and other banks was defined: 'The Bank may act as banker to other banks in Nigeria and abroad',[4] and 'shall wherever necessary seek the co-operation of, and co-operate with, other banks in Nigeria'.[5]

Building operations began in earnest towards the end of 1958, and on 1 July 1959 the Central Bank of Nigeria was formally opened, with Mr F. P. Fenton, an adviser to the Bank of England, as its first governor. It is difficult to give a full appraisal of its operations for the short period of its life covered in this book, but table 16.5 shows its assets and liabilities. The bank issued the new Nigerian currency notes and coins in 1959, and continued to manage the West African Currency Board notes and coins until they were completely withdrawn. The Central Bank also supervised the management of the country's external reserves, and assisted the government in creating a money market by issues of treasury bills. It served as the bankers' bank, and exercised some control over the credit activities of the commercial banks. Above all, the Central Bank was the banker, agent and financial adviser to the Nigerian government.

THE STOCK EXCHANGE AND THE NIGERIAN MONEY MARKET

In most developed countries, such as Britain and the USA, stock exchanges were formed by the drawing-together of people and firms already engaged in the profession of stockbroking. In Nigeria there were no stockbrokers and comparatively little dealing in stocks and shares; yet the desirability of the establishment of a share market was fully recognized in the early fifties, and this became the subject of discussion by a committee set up by the federal government in

[1] Section 6 (1).   [2] Section 16 (1).   [3] Section 17.   [4] Section 38.   [5] Section 39.

1958. This committee favoured the establishment of a stock exchange but did not think it practicable for some time.[1] However, the Nigerian economy grew rapidly, and as a result some commercial interests, both Nigerian and expatriate, with the support and encouragement of the government and the Central Bank, set up the Lagos Stock Exchange in 1960. The Lagos Exchange was incorporated under the Companies Ordinance of Nigeria as a non profit-making company. It had a small share capital, of which each of the members held a part as a condition of membership.

Very little business was handled by the Lagos Stock Exchange in 1960. However, the main object of its establishment was to provide market facilities for stocks and shares of companies operating in Nigeria. Apart from the conventional sources of raising loans – bank-borrowings – companies could raise substantial capital from the public through a stock exchange.

Before 1960, banks and other financial institutions which accumulated funds in Nigeria at certain times of the year – for example, between the main crop seasons – had little or no opportunity for investing such accumulated funds in short-term securities, which would yield interest and be readily convertible into cash. However, a means of employing short-term funds of this nature became available early in 1960, with the first issue of treasury bills by the Central Bank of Nigeria on behalf of the federal government.[2]

[1] *Report of the Committee appointed to advise on Ways and Means of fostering a Share Market in Nigeria*, Lagos, Government Printer, 1959.
[2] See Charles V. Brown, *The Nigerian Banking System*, p. 151.

17 Foreign trade

After the war, the restrictions on the imports from hard currency countries were continued for some time. The Defence (Finance) Regulations for 1939, amended in 1942, were replaced by the Exchange Control Ordinance, no. 35 of 1950, which was also amended in 1952. The ordinance of 1952 established an exchange control mechanism on United Kingdom lines, giving the government control over dealings in gold and foreign currencies, dealings in securities of various kinds, the import and export of currencies and other measures to protect sterling. However, the reduction of balance of payments difficulties in the sterling area, and the improved world supply position, enabled considerable relaxation to be made in import control regulations in respect of many countries except the United States and Japan. In 1952 restrictions on Japanese goods were sharply tightened by Nigeria, as by most members of the sterling area, following an earlier sterling area deficit with Japan. The restrictions on imports from the United States and Canada continued and only a few items, including a small number of cars, were allowed to be imported. In 1954 Japan negotiated an agreement with the United Kingdom which resulted in a substantial relaxation of restrictions by the United Kingdom and her colonies. Following this agreement, the Nigerian allocation of import licences for Japanese goods was greatly increased.

The primary objects of restrictions on imports were to protect the trading position of the United Kingdom in the world market, and to strengthen the international value of sterling. For many years these restrictions did not confer any direct economic benefits on Nigeria. It was not until after 1955, when industrial production began to increase, that some of the restrictions served to protect a few Nigerian goods from foreign competition.

In the fifties the world supply position and the strength of sterling improved, and the restrictions on imports were relaxed as most commodities were allowed to be freely imported from the United States and other countries (except the Eastern European Countries)[1] under open general licences. From 1 February 1960 the government permitted the importation of all goods except coal, secondhand clothing, gold and articles manufactured wholly or mainly of gold. Goods from Japan enjoyed virtually unrestricted entry into Nigeria under the open general licence, with the exception of singlets, the importation of which was subject to control purely for the protection of a local singlet industry. By the end of 1960, therefore, a position of almost complete liberalization of imports into the Nigerian market was reached, and only goods from East European countries remained subject to quantitative restriction.

The government continued to impose import duties on a variety of goods in order to raise revenue.[2] Such duties, however, increased the prices of the imports concerned, and this in turn led to a gradual reduction in the demand for some of them. One significant change in the policy affecting import duties was the levy introduced on building materials – particularly cement, which had formerly been duty free. This was an attempt to protect the newly established cement factories against the competition of foreign cements.[3]

Besides the fact that export duties were maintained on the major export products,[4] there were a number of prohibitions and restrictions covering the exportation of goods, particularly those of Nigerian origin. In fact, *all* goods were prohibited from export unless covered by an export licence, or scheduled as exempt.

The value of total foreign trade increased from £44·4 million (£3·7 per head of the population) in 1946, to £263·6 million (£8·9 per head) and £385·6 million (£11 per head) in 1954 and 1960 respectively. Table 17.1 shows that the country enjoyed a boom in exports until 1954, after which the value of exports fluctuated; while the value of total imports rose consistently. The value of imports increased by £19·8 million (approximately £1 per head of the

[1] The British government did not encourage her colonies to trade freely with the East European countries.
[2] See Chapter 12.
[3] See Chapter 15.
[4] See Chapter 12.

population) in 1946, to £114 million (£3·7 per head) and £215·9 million (£6·2 per head) in 1954 and 1960 respectively. The value of exports also rose from £24·6 million (£1·3 per head) in 1946 to £149·5 million (£4·9 per head) in 1954. Although the value of total exports was £169·7 million in 1960, its average per head of the population was only £4·8.

TABLE 17.1   *Value of external trade and visible balance,*
1946–60 (£000)

Year	Imports	Domestic export	Re-export including parcel post	Visible balance of trade
1946	19,824	23,738	888	+4,802
1948	41,947	61,163	1,308	+20,524
1949	58,231	79,199	1,868	+22,836
1950	61,866	88,433	1,735	+28,302
1951	84,554	116,610	3,454	+35,510
1952	113,268	125,135	4,395	+16,262
1953	108,290	120,889	3,343	+15,942
1954	114,069	146,242	3,290	+35,463
1955	136,117	129,816	2,718	−3,583
1956	152,713	132,261	2,312	−18,140
1957	152,468	124,177	3,357	−24,934
1958	166,274	132,791	2,759	−30,724
1959	178,405	160,597	2,992	−14,816
1960	215,891	165,619	4,095	−46,177

Source: *Annual Abstract of Statistics, 1963.*

THE EXPORT TRADE

The sharp increases in the value of total domestic exports during the period 1946–52 were partly the result of post-war economic reconstruction in Europe, which led to increased demand for Nigeria's major export products, and partly the result of the Korean war, which forced the USA to stockpile some basic raw materials. However, from 1953 to 1957 the value of total domestic exports fluctuated. But between 1958 and 1960 the position of the export trade improved again, with the value of total domestic exports increasing from about £133 million in 1958 to about £166 million in 1960. The principal export items included palm products, cocoa, groundnuts, cotton, timber, tin, columbite and petroleum.

Palm oil was the principal source of Nigeria's export earnings between 1946 and 1958. There was a considerable increase in its export between 1946 and 1950, but between then and 1960 it fluctuated. Throughout this period efforts were made to improve the competitive position of palm oil in the world market.[1] The volume of export of palm kernels increased, averaging about 400,000 tons per annum from 1952 to 1960. Most of Nigeria's palm products (palm oil and palm kernels) went to the United Kingdom, but after 1933 her share of the products declined because of increasing demand from Western Germany, the Netherlands and the United States. The share of the United Kingdom in palm kernel exports fell from 69·7 per cent in 1954, to 56·3 per cent in 1960, while that of the Netherlands increased from 17·1 per cent in 1954, to 23·4 per cent in 1960.

The cocoa industry faced many difficulties during this period. Immediately after the war there were inadequate marketing facilities, and cocoa pests and diseases ruined some of the trees.[2] For example, in 1949 it was estimated that 25 million cocoa trees were either infected or were liable to become infected by the swollen shoot disease – a total area of about 250 square miles. The government conducted an economic survey of the cocoa-producing areas in the western provinces, and spent a considerable amount of money encouraging farmers to destroy infected trees and replace them where possible with new ones, or other crops. Between 1949 and 1953, the volume of export of cocoa increased steadily. The increase continued until 1960, with occasional fluctuations. Nigerian cocoa was exported mainly to the United Kingdom and the United States of America. In 1954 the United Kingdom took 61·6 per cent of Nigerian cocoa; but this proportion fell drastically to 27·2 per cent in 1960. In contrast, the share of the Netherlands rose from 6·1 per cent in 1954 to 19·8 per cent in 1960, while that of the USA fell from 24·9 per cent in 1954 to 22 per cent in 1960.

Before 1958 groundnuts and groundnut oil were Nigeria's third

[1] See Chapter 14. Nigeria's most powerful competitors in the palm oil trade were the Dutch East Indies and the Congo.
[2] See Chapter 14.

TABLE 17.2   Exports of principal products, 1946–60: quantities

Year	Cocoa ('000 tons)	Palm kernels ('000 tons)	Palm oil ('000 tons)	Ground- nut oil ('000 tons)	Ground- nuts ('000 tons)	Benni- seed ('000 tons)	Colum- bite (tons)	Tin ore (tons)	Coal (tons)	Timber sawn ('000 tons)	Timber logs ('000 cu ft)
1946	100	277	101	—	286	7	1,438	13,929	188,382	720	2,262
1947	111	316	126	—	256	4	1,290	14,090	156,636	749	2,723
1948	91	327	139	—	245	8	1,239	12,169	97,306	521	3,212
1949	104	376	170	—	378	19	945	12,676	63,332	593	4,201
1950	100	410	173	4	317	14	916	11,417	2,718	548	9,218
1951	211	347	150	4	141	11	1,092	11,753	98,605	956	16,845
1952	115	374	167	10	260	14	1,228	10,575	1,472	949	7,706
1953	105	403	201	19	327	12	1,855	12,136	5,071	1,138	11,821
1954	98	464	208	31	428	15	2,525	10,308	25,596	1,282	10,254
1955	88	433	182	32	397	13	3,047	11,399	99,976	1,517	14,504
1956	117	451	185	35	448	22	2,405	13,364	98,393	1,744	10,616
1957	135	406	166	39	302	19	1,145	13,577	101,760	1,875	12,970
1958	87	441	171	40	513	12	737	7,627	98,248	2,223	15,335
1959	143	430	184	48	497	18	1,882	7,536	74,561	2,241	19,316
1960	154	418	183	47	332	27	3,332	10,657	26,780	2,098	22,211

Source: Annual Abstract of Statistics, 1963.

TABLE 17.3 Exports of principal products, 1946–60: values (£000)

Year	Cotton	Palm kernels	Palm oil	Groundnut oil†	Ground-nuts	Benniseed	Columbite	Tin ore	Coal	Timber sawn	Timber logs
1946	3,779	4,160	4,160	—	5,675	77	233	2,861	248	155	203
1947	10,650*	9,491	5,038	7	6,397	142	212	4,091	224	246	462
1948	17,879	11,451	9,048	27	9,806	302	231	4,410	168	158	625
1949	17,697	16,913	11,910	37	18,916	969	224	5,514	119	205	846
1950	18,984	16,694	12,072	267	15,237	704	315	6,020	5	224	2,227
1951	31,381	20,059	12,949	443	9,321	652	837	8,974	186	478	5,078
1952	28,666	22,767	17,091	1,568	22,114	1,133	1,307	7,665	3	507	2,153
1953	24,858	22,185	13,020	2,357	24,928	797	3,698	7,076	13	627	3,223
1954	39,261	22,791	13,431	3,757	29,900	975	5,142	5,171	52	728	2,781
1955	26,187	19,196	13,151	3,152	23,134	883	5,142	5,868	261	881	3,728
1956	23,985	20,440	14,866	4,095	27,764	1,392	1,762	7,223	277	987	2,551
1957	26,036	17,959	13,801	4,600	20,139	1,366	761	7,629	472	919	3,326
1958	26,668	20,450	12,663	3,747	26,948	890	475	3,937	466	1,211	4,141
1959	38,289	25,971	13,808	4,626	27,472	1,157	1,125	4,215	353	1,182	4,877
1960	36,772	26,062	13,982	5,320	22,878	1,851	2,121	6,045	127	1,111	5,928

* Value estimated to have been under-declared by approximately £6 million.
† Groundnut cake was also exported, its value ranging from £1,460,000 in 1954 to £1,179,000 in 1958.
Source: *Annual Abstract of Statistics, 1963.*

largest export earner and were grown principally in Northern Nigeria, where more than 2 million acres were given to groundnut production. After 1959, however, groundnuts and groundnut oil increased both in quantity and value, and displaced palm oil as the biggest single export. The main consumers of Nigeria's groundnuts were the United Kingdom, Italy and the Netherlands.

The export of cotton also increased considerably after 1946. During that year 6,612 tons of cotton were exported, and this rose to 15,374 tons and 33,705 tons in 1951 and 1958 respectively, but fell to 26,974 tons in 1960.

Other agricultural exports included timber (sawn timber and timber logs), hides and skins, rubber, benniseed and bananas. The volume of timber exported increased after the war. The Nigerian Timber Association, whose members handled over 90 per cent of timber exports, inaugurated a voluntary inspection scheme whereby exporters could obtain a survey by qualified inspectors at a nominal fee, in order to improve the quality of Nigerian timber. The export of hides and skins also increased, with occasional fluctuations. During this period there was a gradual revival in the export of rubber. In 1950, 13,652 tons were exported; this increased to 41,802 tons in 1958, and to 57,000 tons in 1960.

After the second world war there were fluctuations in the price of tin. In 1957 the International Tin Council decided that the minimum fixed price at which it would buy tin in order to support the price should be increased from £640 to £730 per ton, while the selling price – the price at which the council sells tin in order to keep the price down – should remain at £880 per ton. This selling price had been fixed in 1953 by the International Conference on Tin held in Geneva. The council therefore maintained a price stabilization policy to iron out and prevent wild fluctuations, such as had been experienced in previous years, especially before 1945. Nigeria, as a member of the council, was a party to the control schemes. From 1946 to 1951 the export of tin increased steadily, and then it began to fluctuate until 1958. However, in 1959 and 1960 it rose again, and in 1960 the International Tin Agreements allocated a greater export quota to Nigeria. The bulk of Nigerian tin was exported to the United Kingdom.

The first recorded export of petroleum oil from Nigeria was in 1958, when a total of 245,000 tons were exported. The vigorous pursuit of oil exploration soon increased oil production from an initial 600 barrels a day in 1958 to 16,500 barrels a day in 1960.[1] Nigeria's exports of petroleum products went mainly to the United Kingdom and the Netherlands.

Another mineral export item was columbite, the export of which increased considerably between 1951 and 1955, partly as a result of the United States policy which offered producers a 100 per cent bonus for all purchases.[2] After 1955 the export of columbite fell sharply – from 3,047 tons in 1955 to 737 tons in 1958; however, in the years 1959 and 1960 it rose again to 1,882 and 3,332 tons respectively.

THE IMPORT TRADE

Imports continued to increase both in number and in volume. The most important single item was cotton piece goods: in 1946, 83,152,000 square yards of cotton piece goods valued at £5,921,000 were imported, accounting for 28·6 per cent of the value of total imports. In 1950, 148,882,000 square yards of cotton goods valued at £14,148,000 were imported, this time accounting for about 22·6 per cent of the value of total imports. In 1960 the highest volume of cotton piece goods imported into the country was reached, being 210,549,000 square yards valued at £22,354,000, representing about 10 per cent of the total value of imports.

This shows that there was an average increase in the volume of cotton piece goods imported over the years, but its importance as an item of import decreased.

The importation of building materials, such as cement and corrugated iron sheets, increased considerably, particularly in the fifties, during the years of export boom when an increasing number of private houses were built. In 1950, 18,174 tons of corrugated iron sheets valued at £1,515,000, were imported, and there were annual increases until 1956, when the peak of 49,877 tons valued at £4,480,000 was reached. The increases in the importation of cement were also significant. In 1950, 153,861 tons of cement valued at £1,098,000 were imported. Four years later, the volume and the value of imported cement were more than doubled; and by 1960

[1] See Chapter 15.
[2] This scheme was discontinued in 1956.

TABLE 17.4 Imports of selected consumer goods, 1946–60: quantities

Year	Beer ('000 galls)	Cotton piece goods ('000 sq yds)	Rayon piece goods ('000 sq yds)	Milk ('000 cwt)	Cement (tons)	Corrugated iron sheets (tons)	Cars	Commercial vehicles	Petroleum oil	Bags and sacks
1946	461	82,152	4,022	10	95,988	1,873	674	1,204	27,102	12,786
1950	2,580	148,882	24,552	37	153,861	18,174	2,154	2,973	64,792	8,067
1951	4,289	121,327	40,669	40	261,057	19,010	3,311	2,757	81,632	8,578
1952	3,662	204,965	67,492	37	205,169	25,140	3,457	5,392	81,018	20,348
1953	5,090	171,961	64,826	55	297,436	34,323	3,338	4,460	82,336	18,010
1954	4,767	170,145	83,749	80	368,108	40,482	3,868	3,766	95,067	15,813
1955	5,675	205,407	104,539	73	425,095	44,875	6,680	5,578	110,371	20,363
1956	6,560	149,389	157,642	104	488,572	49,877	7,025	8,082	126,551	21,872
1957	6,160	156,207	149,934	115	510,237	39,163	7,654	4,884	140,429	17,706
1958	6,270	172,496	151,575	126	477,119	29,891	8,228	6,858	152,699	24,231
1959	6,832	143,631	101,418	144	516,190	42,341	9,973	6,148	177,691	17,768
1960	7,192	200,549	100,575	232	626,488	37,989	14,573	6,394	196,278	21,847

Source: Annual Abstract of Statistics, 1963.

TABLE 17.5 Imports of selected consumer goods, 1946–60: values (£000)

Year	Beer	Cotton piece goods	Rayon piece goods	Milk	Cement	Corrugated iron sheets	Cars	Com- mercial vehicles	Petroleum oil	Bags and sacks
1946	165	5,921	751	58	475	71	202	405	785	731
1950	905	14,148	3,759	265	1,098	1,515	940	1,633	3,437	1,006
1951	1,768	14,898	7,677	296	2,562	2,553	1,637	1,757	4,985	1,539
1952	1,747	24,765	10,364	280	2,236	2,951	1,969	4,355	5,484	3,730
1953	2,390	18,066	9,732	442	2,748	3,274	1,831	3,383	4,871	1,806
1954	2,265	16,488	10,423	554	3,065	3,557	2,114	3,027	5,091	1,610
1955	2,729	18,033	9,893	598	3,631	3,709	3,654	4,536	5,829	2,317
1956	3,201	14,406	14,915	903	4,307	4,480	3,720	7,539	6,718	2,304
1957	3,158	14,469	11,446	971	4,638	3,766	4,143	5,163	7,751	1,932
1958	3,319	16,295	10,790	1,078	4,101	2,472	4,446	6,761	8,303	2,192
1959	3,602	14,923	7,911	1,013	4,428	3,433	5,305	5,775	9,637	1,516
1960	3,898	22,354	8,633	1,932	5,373	3,262	8,245	6,309	10,526	2,382

Source: Annual Abstract of Statistics, 1963.

imported cement was 626,488 tons, valued at £5,373,000. Other imported building materials included nails, glass and paints.

The importation of road vehicles increased during this period, but there were fluctuations in the numbers of imported bicycles. Private cars and taxis were imported in great numbers during the fifties: in 1950 they totalled 2,154 valued at £940,000, and in 1955 the figures rose to 6,680 valued at £3,654,000. The rise continued until 1960, when the number of imported cars stood at 14,573 valued at £8,245,000. Better road conditions, and increased commercial activities and wealth were partly responsible for stimulating the demand for road vehicles. It was also government policy to advance money to senior civil servants for the purchase of cars for use during the course of their duties, in order to increase efficiency. Another reason for the increasing number of private cars was the tremendous success of taxi-cabs in big towns, particularly during the export boom of the early fifties. The number of imported commercial vehicles also increased considerably as a result of the increasing volume of export products which had to be transported to exporting centres. In 1947 imported commercial vehicles were 1,684 (valued at £696,000), and five years later 5,392 commercial vehicles (valued at £4,355,000) were imported. The increase continued annually, except in 1953 and 1954, reaching its highest peak of 8,082 (valued at £7,539,000) in 1956. The increasing number of cars and commercial vehicles led to increases in the volume of imported petroleum oils: in 1950, 64,792,000 imperial gallons of petroleum oil valued at £3,447,000 were imported, and this rose to 82,336,000 gallons (valued at £4,871,000) in 1953. The upward trend continued, and in 1956 and 1960 the volume of imported petroleum was 126,551,000 gallons and 196,278,000 gallons respectively. Other items of import included tobacco (unmanufactured), beer, spirits, salt, sugar, fish and cigarettes.

The consumption of beer and spirits also increased during this period, but these items did not assume the position they occupied among imports before 1914. The importation of salt did not increase significantly, only slightly as a result of the growth in population. Salt is one of those commodities for which the demand is fairly inelastic.

It is important to note that Nigeria depended on imported machinery and equipment for her development projects,

TABLE 17.6 Percentages of total exports and total imports of principal countries of origin, 1946–60

Year	United Kingdom		West Germany		USA		Netherlands		Japan	
	Imports	Exports	Imports	Exports	Imports	Exports	Imports	Exports	Imports	Exports
1946	64·6	75·2	5·0	—	9·6	10·6	1·5	2·8	—	—
1950	59·8	79·3	2·3	1·2	3·9	14·6	2·6	1·7	9·4	—
1954	45·3	71·1	9·4	3·1	4·7	10·5	4·1	6·4	8·2	—
1960	42·9	46·9	7·0	7·6	5·3	9·4	5·3	12·8	12·4	1·5

Source: *Annual Abstract of Statistics, 1963.*

consequently the importation of these items increased as the development projects continued to increase and expand.

Table 17.6 shows the percentages of total exports and total imports by principal countries of origin. After 1946 the volume of imports from various countries increased, but the United Kingdom remained the main source. From 1946 to 1953 more than half of the annual total imports came from Britain, but in 1954 and subsequent years her share dropped by nearly 10 per cent, as a result of increasing competition from other countries. The importation of cotton piece goods from the United Kingdom (her main import item) dropped consistently between 1954 and 1957, with a token revival in 1958. For example, in 1953 the value of cotton piece goods imported from Britain was £9,132,000, which accounted for about 15·8 per cent of the value of total imports from Britain. In 1960 this figure dropped to £4,201,000, representing only about 4·6 per cent of the value of total imports from Britain. In the same period, the Indian and the Japanese shares of imported cotton piece goods increased.

Imports from Germany ceased during the war, but immediately after 1945 West Germany forced her way back into Nigerian trade. (Since Eastern Germany was very much under the control of Russia, there was little trade between her and Nigeria.) Her economic recovery was spectacular: for example, in 1946 Nigerian imports from Germany were valued at £1,000; these rose to £4,130,000 in 1948, to £10,651,000 in 1954 and to £15,212,000 in 1960. The Germans' success was achieved mainly by increases in her share of the vehicle and cotton goods trades.

Nigerian trade with Japan increased considerably after the war, and in 1954 she displaced Britain as the main supplier of rayon piece goods. In 1956 and 1958 this item alone represented about 60 per cent and 47·3 per cent respectively of total imports from Japan. By 1960 the import of cotton piece goods from Japan accounted for about 36 per cent of the value of her total imports.

There were some imports from the United States of America, the main items being petroleum oil and tobacco. Nigeria also imported goods from other countries including Canada, South Africa, Belgium, Czechoslovakia, Italy, the Netherlands and Norway.

TRADE BALANCE AND THE TERMS OF TRADE

Table 17.1 on p. 330 shows that from 1946 to 1954 Nigeria's visible balance of trade consistently showed export surpluses which made possible the accumulation of considerable sterling balances. However, 1955 marked a change from the annual favourable trade balances to a succession of annual deficits, which continued until 1960.

TABLE 17.7   *Terms of trade,*
             1948–60

1948 = 100	
1949	102
1950	110
1951	121
1952	119
1953	116
1954	139
1954 = 100	
1955	90
1956	83
1957	82
1958	86
1959	92
1960	88

Note: The index of the terms of trade is calculated by dividing the price index for domestic exports by the price index for imports. It indicates the quantity of imported goods that can be obtained in exchange for a constant quantity of Nigeria's exports.

Source: *Digest of Statistics.*

During the years of favourable trade balances, the country accumulated budget surpluses, and the marketing boards' funds also rose considerably. Less money was spent on imported goods, partly as the result of inadequate supplies of such goods immediately after the war, and partly as the result of the price policy of the marketing boards which reduced the purchasing power of the farmers. From 1954, however, the increasing number of development projects led to greater importation of various items, especially capital goods. The public authorities also financed larger development programmes, partly by utilizing some of the balances built up in earlier years. In addition, private overseas capital investments increased considerably after 1949. Private investment by major expatriate-owned enterprises increased from £2·3 million in 1949 to £10·5 million, £24·3 million and £31·4 million in 1950, 1955 and 1957 respectively.[1]

If one takes the balance of trade with individual countries, Nigeria had mixed fortunes during this period. Her balance of trade with the United Kingdom showed a consistent annual export surplus over imports. The reason for this was that Nigeria bought

TABLE 17.8   *Balance of payments: overall balance on current transactions, 1952–60 (£ million)*

Year	Receipts	Payments	Balance
1952	144·9	132·3	+12·6
1953	138·2	129·7	+8·5
1954	164·4	136·2	+28·2
1955	150·2	159·5	−9·3
1956	152·1	177·1	−25·0
1957	149·3	180·7	−31·4
1960	186·7	260·6	−73·9

Sources: NNEC, *Economic Survey of Nigeria, 1959,* and *Annual Abstract of Statistics, 1963.*

more goods, particularly those which used to come from Britain, from other countries. The trade with Germany gave an opposite trend to that of Britain. After 1945 imports from Germany consistently exceeded Nigeria's exports to her. The lifting of restrictions on imports led to increased importation of goods from countries outside the Commonwealth. Trade with the United States of America increased during this period, and between 1945 and 1956 Nigeria had a favourable trade balance with her. From 1957 to 1960, however, imports from the United States of America increased, consequently there were trade deficits against Nigeria. Nigeria's trade with India and Japan was not favourable, because both countries supplied goods to Nigeria while demanding few of her products.

Both export and import prices rose following the devaluation

[1] Helleiner, op. cit., table IV-C-2.

of sterling in 1949. The Korean war also helped to push up prices. But by 1954 the index of import prices had dropped back to only 14 per cent above the figure for 1948 (the base year). Export prices fell more slowly, and the index was kept up by extremely high cocoa prices which continued until 1955. In 1952 the index of export prices rose by 63 above the figure for 1948, but dropped to 58 in 1954. Table 17.7 shows that the terms of trade were in Nigeria's favour from 1949 to 1954, after which they were unfavourable.

Until 1955 Nigeria had, for a considerable number of years, a surplus on the current account of her balance of payments: in other words, there were consistent surpluses of exports over imports. But after 1955 the importation of capital goods increased considerably, consequently the country had consistent adverse balance of payments, as shown on table 17.8. The deficits on the balance of payments were balanced partly by drawing on Nigeria's accumulated reserves and partly by the increased inflow of private foreign capital.

TRADE COMPETITION

Monopolistic competition continued to exist in both the import and the export trades of Nigeria. The bulk of the trade was handled by a few expatriate companies. However, after the second world war there was an increasing participation of indigenous firms in Nigeria's foreign trade. Professor Bauer, commenting on the aspect of competition in West African trade, claimed that

the profit margins of the European firms and the Levantine and African intermediaries are believed [by native traders] to depend solely or largely on their own decisions which are only remotely connected with such academic matters as supply and demand. Accumulated wealth is thought to have been earned by the impoverishment of customers and competition. . . . This imperfect understanding of the operation of the market price is most evident in the widespread complaint of Africans that whenever they attempt to establish themselves in business, especially in the direct importing of commodities from overseas, the European merchant firms deliberately reduce prices to put them out of business . . . there may have been instances where firms engaged in localized or temporary underselling with the deliberate intention of destroying a competitor. But Africans are apt to regard any fall in prices as evidence of a deliberate attempt to put them out of business.[1]

The implication of Professor Bauer's view is that the native traders were ignorant of the operation of an exchange and market economy.[2]

The view expressed by Bauer does not reflect the whole story of competition in Nigerian trade, especially after the second world war. It was true that traders and firms hardly concerned themselves with the academic analysis of supply and demand. However, every prospective trader or firm thought in terms of prospective profit. This suggests that a trader thought consciously or unconsciously about the problems of supply and demand, and the price of the product concerned. The optimism of a prospective trader about profit depends on the type of competition existing in the market. A prospective perfect competitor will have to produce at a ruling price on which he has no influence, and the profit he hopes to get is a 'normal profit'. Under oligopoly, however, the position is different. Oligopoly, by its nature, gives a few firms a certain margin of profit usually higher than the normal profit which exists under perfect competition. The prospective oligopolist is therefore influenced by the abnormal profit which he knows or believes to exist. But his belief or forecast may be wrong. If we assume that he is right, then he will be tempted to join in the business; but he will have to provide the necessary capital and skill required. If one puts the indigenous traders of Nigeria in the situation explained above, it is possible to understand more clearly the nature of competition between these traders and foreign firms during this period.

The Nigerian traders relied on small individual capital resources. Partnerships and joint-stock companies were not favoured by most people, partly because of the desire to be independent of others, and partly because of the lack of confidence in partners. Thus trading operations were small, and such indigenous traders were more vulnerable to price-cutting and depressions. The hostility of established firms meant that price-cutting and other obstacles were often placed in the way of newcomers. A big firm with great capital resources could withstand the effect of a price war more than the

[1] Bauer, op. cit., pp. 9–10.
[2] Ibid., p. 9.

small firms. The complaint by Nigerians about a few trading firms exploiting the buyers sprang from the realization that imperfect competition existed in the import trade, and that they (Nigerians) had no adequate capital resources which could enable them to enter the trade, and thus make it more competitive. Another important factor which hindered the progress of the indigenous traders was that they found it difficult to make contact with foreign manufacturers. These manufacturers tended to deal with the older, more reputable firms, which were usually foreign; they doubted the commercial trustworthiness of the indigenous traders. This was quite understandable, because foreign manufacturers had more knowledge about foreign firms, especially those having offices in Europe. During this period, barriers to entry were the key elements in monopoly or oligopsony.[1]

Many of the big foreign firms were engaged in both wholesale and retail trades. They were also involved in the marketing of export produce. With the appearance of new and strong indigenous businesses after 1946, many of these firms, including the UAC and John Holt, withdrew from retail trade and from collecting export produce direct from farmers. As a result, most of their trading posts in the interior were closed. There are no statistics to indicate the total number of indigenous businesses established during this period. However, the increasing participation of indigenous businesses in foreign trade is clearly shown by the increase in the number of indigenous licensed buying agents of the marketing boards: for example, indigenous agents in Western Nigeria increased from 13 in 1950 to 37 in 1960. It must be added that the withdrawal of foreign firms from some aspects of foreign trade was due to both political and economic reasons: political in the sense that many indigenous businessmen were influential in Nigerian politics, and that the large foreign firms wanted to avoid being indirectly dragged into local politics – in fact, the politicians expressed the view, through the Nigerian ministers, that they expected expatriate trading firms to leave the retailing business to Nigerians; economic in the sense that

---

[1] 'The economic strength of the existing firms, their contacts and influence with the suppliers and customers, their power to influence prices, and the possibility of special action directed against newcomers may be deterrents to newcomers additional to any other natural or contrived obstacles': ibid., p. 97.

even if the expatriate firms wanted to continue in retail trading, the cost of keeping retailing posts in several isolated parts of the country had risen very sharply, thus making it less profitable.

Another aspect of imperfect competition in the import trade was found in the appointment of certain special agencies to sell some imported goods, including motor cars, lorries, bicycles, tractors, tyres and matches.[1] Prices were dictated by the suppliers; the reputations of these products, and perhaps the special conditions of sale offered, made it possible for such firms to maintain a steady flow of demand. In other words, the firms had loyal customers, consequently they could fix any price, or at least fix a price which would ensure reasonable sales and profit. The favourable terms which the agents got from the suppliers could be regarded as restrictive practices to active competition. Resale price maintenance policy was not common in Nigeria, but it was known to have existed in the selling of cigarettes and sewing-thread.[2]

[1] Ibid., p. 131.   [2] Ibid., pp. 133-4.

Part 5   Life, labour and society

HEALTH AND POPULATION

By modern standards, life in Nigeria, particularly before 1930, was
far from pleasant. Most towns and villages were isolated, with a few
bush paths connecting some of them. The quietness of village life was
often interrupted by the cries and shouting of people mourning the
victims of poverty and disease. There were a few traditional social
clubs, and social events were arranged to coincide with ritual ceremonies or the new year and other celebrations. Apart from these, the
routine of life was fairly rigid. The best part of the day was spent on
the farm by the bulk of the population, with only a few families
engaged in some traditional industries, such as carving, blacksmithing and weaving.

   The mud-houses covered with leaves and straw in which most
people lived were usually too damp during the rainy season, and
were therefore unhealthy for habitation. In fact the mortality rate
was very high in Nigeria. The malnutrition of both expectant
mothers and young children caused high rates of infant mortality.
The health of the population was entrusted to the indigenous
doctors who were skilled in herbs. There were a few families which
specialized in herbs, and their long experience helped a great deal in
diagnosing and treating various diseases. Most of the medicines and
the way they were administered could not be easily explained in
modern scientific terms; but the doctors effected the curing of
various common diseases which prevailed among the people. There
were two factors which diminished their success: first, it was difficult
for the people to appreciate the appropriate time to consult a
doctor, and diseases were not reported or brought for treatment until

the condition of the victim had worsened, thus making it difficult to effect any cure; secondly, even when a sick person was brought for treatment, crude methods of prescribing medicine were adopted, as there was no standard by which the correct dose could be measured. Even with these handicaps, the indigenous doctors were respected for their skill in saving lives, particularly in curing common diseases like fever. But to live to old age was really a case of the 'survival of the fittest'.

The first population census to be held in Nigeria was confined to the area of the Lagos Colony in 1870, and showed a total population of 41,236.[1] Population censuses for Lagos Colony were also held in 1880, 1890 and 1900. Since the inception of population estimates and censuses in Nigeria it has been extremely difficult to arrive at any accurate figures. For example, the population figures for Lagos were given as 60,221 and 85,607 for 1880 and 1891 respectively,[2] but in 1909 and 1911 they were reported as 60,716 and 72,703 respectively.[3] Similarly inaccurate population figures were given for the other areas of Nigeria: in 1904 the population of Northern Nigeria was given as 9,161,700,[4] but in 1908–9 it was given as 7,164,751.[5] However, the first countrywide population estimate was made in 1900, when it was estimated that about 15 million people lived in Nigeria, of which 9 million were in Northern Nigeria. In 1921 the population estimate for Nigeria was 18·9 million. However, in 1931 the first countrywide population census was held, and it showed that 19,555,000 people lived in Nigeria: 11,434,000 in the North, 4,266,000 in the East; 3,729,000 in the West; and 126,000 in Lagos.[6] Another population census was held in 1952–3, and showed a total population of 30,417,000.

These censuses were not accurate for a number of reasons, but they were the only two attempts at population censuses up to 1960.

[1] CO151/8, Lagos, 1870.

[2] CO151/19, Lagos, 1881; CO151/29, Lagos, 1891; and *Colonial Report*, no. 58, Lagos, 1891.

[3] *Colonial Annual Reports*, no. 665, Southern Nigeria, 1909, p. 21; and *Colonial Annual Reports*, no. 735, Southern Nigeria, 1911, p. 23.

[4] *Colonial Annual Reports*, no. 476, Northern Nigeria, 1904, p. 84. Indeed, it was reported that 'Barth in 1954 estimated the population of Northern Nigeria at from 30 to 50 million': ibid.

[5] *Colonial Annual Reports*, no. 633, Northern Nigeria, 1908–9.

[6] *Census of Nigeria, 1931*, London, Crown Agents, 1933.

Some people were superstitious about the counting of human beings, as it was believed that people who allowed themselves to be counted would die young. It was widely believed that the government would use a population census for the purpose of tax assessment. It must be added that most of the official enumerators had no knowledge of statistics, and therefore were unable to appreciate the importance of accurately recorded returns of the population.

TABLE 18.1 *Population and population estimates: selected years, 1900–60 ('000)*

| Year | Nigeria | Regions | | | |
		Lagos (township)	West	East	North
1900 estimates	15,000	n.a.	n.a.	n.a.	n.a.
1921	18,900	100	n.a.	n.a.	n.a.
1931 census	19,555*	126	3,729	4,266	11,434
1952–3	30,417*	272	6,087	7,218	16,840
Mid-year					
1953 estimates	30,803	277	6,144	7,229	17,153
1954	31,381	288	6,258	7,363	17,472
1955	31,971	300	6,374	7,500	17,797
1956	32,572	312	6,492	7,640	18,128
1958	33,808	337	6,736	7,927	18,808
1960	35,091	364	6,989	8,224	19,514

n.a. Not available.
* Excluding Southern Cameroons.
Note: For the regions, the population is estimated from 1953 to increase at the rate of nearly 2 per cent per annum; the Lagos rate is estimated at 4 per cent per annum.
Sources: *Digest of Statistics*, vol. 8 (1959), and *Annual Abstract of Statistics, 1963*.

However, some significant changes were noticed in the population of Nigeria. It was estimated, for example, that it was increasing at the rate of between 1·5 and 2 per cent per annum. An example of the changes can be illustrated by the population census for Lagos. Between 1918 and 1939 the average death rate for Lagos fell from 30 to 20 per 1,000 of the population; and for the same period the birth rate remained fairly constant at 24 per 1,000. In 1918 the infant mortality rate was 285 per 1,000, but it fell to 123 per 1,000 in 1939. Similar improvements were experienced in some other parts of the country, and these continued during and after the second world war.

The increases in the population of Nigeria were due mainly to the gradual reduction in the death rate, brought about by a combination of two factors: increasing medical facilities and an improved standard of living. At first, many people were slow to avail themselves of the services provided by the few hospitals, dispensaries and maternity homes which were established by the governments and the missionaries. As educational facilities increased and were made to cover more areas, more people became enlightened and an increasing number obtained medical treatment. The number of hospitals which were capable of handling important medical cases were too few at first, but the government built more from time to time and supplemented the services of these hospitals by helping the local authorities to build a number of dispensaries. For example, in 1919, there were 23 hospitals in Northern Nigeria,[1] and 11 in the Colony and southern provinces (i.e. Lagos, Western and Eastern Regions). By 1960, however, Lagos had 23 general hospitals (including nursing homes) and 24 maternity centres (including clinics and rural centres). The number of general hospitals and maternity centres in Eastern Nigeria were 58 and 373 respectively; in Western Nigeria, they were 54 and 387 respectively; and in Northern Nigeria, they were 74 and 55 respectively. For the whole country the number of dispensaries increased from 2 in 1900 to 89 in 1930, and to 1,655 in 1960. A number of special hospitals were built to cater for orthopaedic treatment, tuberculosis and other infectious diseases, and mental disease.

With the exception of the principal towns, where waterworks were established to provide pipe-borne water, the bulk of the Nigerian population obtained their water supply from the streams, rivers, springs and wells. In semi-desert areas the government provided wells for public use. Domestic refuse was often dumped into rivers and streams, while some of the refuse dumped on waste lands was carried by rain into them. After 1946, however, more water-

---

[1] Twenty of the hospitals in the North were classified as native hospitals. These figures included the regional government missions and private medical institutions.

works were constructed to provide water for the smaller towns, and in a few cases for some villages. There were no properly organized public sewage systems: the best alternatives provided were wells dug purposely for night soil; otherwise, the bushes provided the 'toilet'. But in the fifties an increasing number of private houses were provided with privately-installed sewage systems. The unhygienic sources of water supplies led to the spread of many water-borne diseases such as cholera, dysentery, typhoid and guineaworm. In

TABLE 18.2 *Central government expenditure on education and medical services, 1922–48*

Year	Education		Medical services*	
	Amount (£000)	Percentage of total expenditure†	Amount (£000)	Percentage of total expenditure†
1922–3	100	1·5	253	3·9
1924–5	116	2·0	254	4·4
1929–30	262	4·1	471	7·3
1930–1	287	4·5	486	7·6
1934–5	225	4·7	385	8·0
1939–40	264	4·2	442	7·0
1944–5	485	5·4	677	7·8
1947–8	1,391	9·5	1,143	7·8

* Including sanitary services.
† Total ordinary expenditure.
Source: *Annual Reports of the Accountant-General of Nigeria.*

addition to these bad conditions, most dwelling houses were badly ventilated and there was overcrowding nearly everywhere. The absence of good drainage systems led to very filthy street conditions. Improvements came very slowly as hygiene was taught at schools, and a great deal of sanitary work and supervision was undertaken by the Medical Department of the government through the government sanitary inspectors.[1] The sanitary inspectors were trained

1 'The sanitary condition leaves much to be desired but steps are being taken by constant instruction, and in the more advanced places by organised inspection, to secure attention to the ordinary sanitary usages, which have been codified and widely circulated in a series of simple "Observations"': *Colonial Annual Reports*, no. 1569, Nigeria, 1931, p. 16.

locally and received instruction from doctors on basic hygiene as best implemented under tropical conditions. For example, the Yaba Higher College, which opened early in 1932, trained a number of medical assistants, dispensers, chemists and druggists. Sanitary inspection training was also provided at Kano in 1931, Ibadan in 1933 and Umudike (Eastern Nigeria) in 1934.[1] A number of missions as well as government hospitals also helped to train nurses, and some local sanitary inspectors who served the local authorities. Pharmacists were later trained at the Nigerian College of Arts and Technology (Ibadan branch), and the University of Ibadan Teaching Hospital trained doctors and nurses.

In addition to locally-trained medical personnel, an increasing number of Nigerians qualified annually from various medical institutions overseas. In 1960 Nigeria had 425 registered physicians and surgeons, of whom 167 were expatriates (67·6 per cent of expatriate doctors were in Northern Nigeria).[2] With the estimated population of Nigeria at 35,091,000 in 1960, there were 82,569 people per medical doctor. Similar shortages were experienced in the supply of other medical and health personnel.

There were some population movements in Nigeria during this period. The few public works which the governments provided attracted a number of people from the rural areas into the urban areas. The construction of roads and railways attracted some labour to the construction centres, which were usually the towns. The erection of public buildings (offices and government quarters) also attracted labour to the towns. The spread of education and missionary work tended to increase the number of people seeking employment in urban areas, for here the schools, churches and government offices which absorbed the bulk of the educated few were to be found. It must be added that movements of the population were more noticeable during the depression years and during the second world war. From the later twenties until 1945, people came to the big cities where there were better prospects of obtaining work. During the second world war, population movements were considerably encouraged by opportunities of employment in the army, and in construction and other public works undertaken in connexion with the war effort.

[1] *Colonial Annual Reports*, no. 1710, Nigeria, 1934, p. 22.
[2] *Annual Abstract of Statistics, 1963*.

There are no reliable figures showing movements of population; the best available show population growth in the main cities and towns of Nigeria (see table 18.3). In the Western Region, large population growths were noticeable in many towns including

TABLE 18.3 *Growth of towns, 1921–52/3 ('000)*

Towns	1921*	1931	1952–3
Abeokuta	29	46	84
Benin	—	—	54
Calabar	—	17	47
Enugu	41	28	63
Ibadan	238	387	459
Ijebu-Ode	22	28	28
Ilesha	—	22	72
Ilorin	39	48	41
Iwo	54	57	100
Jos	—	15	39
Kaduna	—	11	39
Kano	50	97	130
Katsina	17	23	53
Lagos	100	126	267
Maiduguri	—	25	55
Ogbomosho	85	87	140
Onitsha	—	18	77
Oshogbo	51	50	123
Oyo	40	49	72
Port Harcourt	—	15	72
Sokoto	19	20	48
Zaria	23	28	54

* Estimates.
Sources: *Nigerian Censuses 1931 and 1952–3.*

Abeokuta, Ibadan, Ilesha, Oshogbo, Iwo and Oyo, where between the censuses of 1931 and 1952–3 there were population increases of 40 per cent and above. Similar population growth was experienced in Kano, Katsina, Jos, Sokoto and Zaria in Northern Nigeria; and in Port Harcourt, Enugu and Onitsha in Eastern Nigeria. The population of Lagos also increased by more than 100 per cent. The movement to the large commercial and administrative towns continued at a faster rate in the fifties up till 1960, as an increasing number of young educated Nigerians continued to look for jobs in these towns.

The family or clan was the very vital social force, and its members looked after and supported one another in sickness, old age or any other misfortune. It was remarked in one of the colonial reports that 'The people of Nigeria have not advanced to that stage of civilization where it has become necessary for the state to make provision for its destitute members. . . .'[1] Most people regarded it as more humane and socially desirable for each family to care for its destitute members.

EDUCATION

In the field of education, the missionaries had been the first to establish a few schools in the nineteenth century. After an initially unenthusiastic response, parents began to regard the education of a child as an investment which would yield dividends when the child passed out of school and took employment (often as a teacher or a clerk in the civil service or the local authority). The salary of the child on starting work was often regarded as the dividend which should normally go to the parents; hence the reluctance to train girls, who were considered as wasteful investments since they would eventually marry into another family. However, the attitude of parents soon changed, and an increasing number of children, both boys and girls, were released by their parents to attend schools. The opening of schools started much earlier in Southern Nigeria, where the missionaries first established their posts. Attendances at schools were fairly regular where the missionaries were most successful: in Northern Nigeria, where most people were either Moslems or pagans, attendances were irregular. In the Moslem areas children only attended schools in the afternoons, having devoted the mornings to Arabic lessons. In some areas special schools had to be created for the sons and nominees of chiefs.

The number of schools which existed before 1944 was very small, considering the population which they were supposed to serve. For example, in 1913 there were 43 elementary schools and only 1 primary school in the whole of Northern Nigeria, and all were

---

[1] *Colonial Annual Reports*, no. 1569, Nigeria, 1931, p. 42.

supported by the various missionary societies.[1] In contrast there were 14,611 Moslem schools in Northern Nigeria in the same year. In Southern Nigeria in 1913 there were 534 schools, which included elementary, primary and secondary schools.[2] After the first world war the number of schools increased. Apart from the missionary schools, which were the greatest in number, some government schools were established, and some individuals established what were popularly called 'private schools'. The activities of the governments in regard to education soon increased and more funds were made available (see table 18.2 above). High standards of education were encouraged by the establishment of the school inspectorate system, by which schools were visited regularly by education officers. On the basis of the inspections, good schools were assisted financially by the government, while bad ones were advised to improve or close down.

For the few secondary schools in the South, the government introduced the Cambridge University Local Examinations in 1910 for students passing out at the end of a six-year course.[3] The first Cambridge examinations were held in 1910. As more secondary schools were established the examinations became popular and countrywide. However, the last Cambridge Junior Certificate Examination was held in Nigeria in 1949, and the last Senior Certificate Examination was held in 1952. These were replaced in 1953 by the West African School Certificate Examination and the General Certificate of Education Examinations, under the control of the West African Examinations Council.

For many years the government concentrated on ensuring that there were adequately staffed and well-run primary schools to produce a supply of candidates for further education and for administrative jobs. After the first world war the demand for education was so great that the bulk of it could only be met by unassisted schools, opened mainly by missionary bodies and financed entirely by fees and voluntary contributions. In 1937 there were 36 government schools, 58 native administration schools, 339 private schools assisted by the government and 3,086 unassisted schools – all catering for 267,788 pupils. The expansion continued, and it entailed the employment of increasing numbers of untrained teachers, who

[1] *Colonial Annual Reports*, no. 821, Northern Nigeria, 1913, pp. 7–9.
[2] *Colonial Annual Reports*, no. 825, Southern Nigeria, 1913, p. 18.
[3] *Colonial Annual Reports*, no. 695, Southern Nigeria, 1910, p. 23.

by 1960 had come to outnumber the trained and certificated teachers by about six to one.

After the second world war and until 1960 the government, with assistance from the Colonial Development and Welfare Fund, promoted the development of primary education to cover as many children of school age as possible. Many teacher-training schools were established, particularly in Eastern and Western Nigeria. In the development programme for 1955–60 free primary education was introduced in Lagos, Eastern and Western Nigeria. The introduction of free primary education increased the shortage of school accommodation and more particularly the shortage of trained teachers. At the end of 1960 there were 112 primary schools in Lagos catering for 74,468 children; 6,540 primary schools in Western Nigeria, catering for about 1,125,000 children; 6,451 primary schools in Eastern Nigeria, with about 1,431,000 pupils; and 2,600 schools in Northern Nigeria, catering for about 283,000 pupils.

The governments of Nigeria also assisted in developing post-primary education by assisting in the establishment and the running of secondary schools. In 1955 secondary modern schools were introduced in Western Nigeria, to provide a three-year education course for young primary school leavers who were unable to enter the secondary schools and were too young for employment. At the end of 1960 there were 700 secondary schools in Western Nigeria, and these were catering for 109,249 children. Similar increases in the number of secondary schools and pupils took place in Eastern Nigeria. In Northern Nigeria at the end of 1960 there were 41 secondary schools catering for 6,264 pupils.

The development of technical education was slow in Nigeria. Most early educated Nigerians, and for that matter West Africans, were employed as clerks, teachers and pastors. With increasing industrial production it became clearer than ever before that technical education had been neglected and that not enough indigenous technicians were available. Indeed, an appropriate reaction to the 'overproduction' of clerks *vis-à-vis* technicians and tradesmen was by a Governor of the Gold Coast (Ghana), who, commenting on the establishment of trade schools, said '. . . over the door of the school there is going to be inscribed *Abandon ye who enter here all hope of becoming a clerk*'.[1] Nigeria had to employ a large number of foreign

[1] Governor G. Guggisberg commenting in *West Africa*, 27 August 1921, p. 946.

technicians in order to cope with industrial production and in order to execute the major development projects. In 1960 there were only four main technical institutions in the country: the Yaba Technical Institute, Enugu Technical Institute, Kaduna Technical Institute and the College of Technology in Ibadan. In addition to these there were a number of trade centres in many important towns. The technical institutes and the trade centres provided training over a wide field, including civil and electrical engineers, motor mechanics, machinists, fitters, carpenters, bricklayers, sheet-metal workers, electricians, painters, cabinet workers, wood machinists and blacksmiths.

University education developed in Nigeria after the second world war. Hitherto, most Nigerians who were qualified to undertake undergraduate courses attended Fourah Bay College in Sierra Leone.[1] A few other Nigerians, with rich parents, were educated in the United States of America and in the United Kingdom. It was the Fourah Bay College, however, which trained the bulk of the new labour force needed to maintain an efficient civil service and supply teachers for the secondary schools.

Before 1948 Nigeria had only the Yaba Higher College, established in 1932, which provided a few diploma courses for medical and engineering assistants;[2] but in that year, following the report of the Elliot Commission on Higher Education, plans were made to open a university college at Ibadan.[3] The Yaba Higher College was closed down and some of its students continued at the new college in the academic year 1948–9. Until 1960, University College Ibadan prepared students for the degrees awarded by the University of London, under a scheme of special relationship. Departments included agriculture, biology, botany, chemistry, classics, education, English, geography, physics, history, economics, mathematics, mycology, parasitology and medicine. The University College Teaching Hospital (an offshoot of the Ibadan University) was opened in 1956, and provided local training for doctors and nurses.

In 1959 the government set up a Commission on Higher Educa-

[1] Fourah Bay College was established in 1814. In the early years of the college only theologians and teachers were trained, but after its affiliation with Durham University in England in 1876, more courses, particularly Arts, were provided.

[2] *Colonial Annual Reports*, no. 1625, Nigeria, 1932, p. 52.

[3] *Report of the Commission on Higher Education in West Africa*, Cmd. 6655, 1945.

tion under the chairmanship of Sir Eric Ashby. The commission was to recommend various measures for improving higher education in the country up to 1970, and in its report it favoured the establishment of more universities in order to cater for the future manpower needs of the country.[1]

In 1960 the Eastern Nigeria government established the University of Nigeria at Nsukka. At its inception the university had two main faculties, arts and science, and it also provided professional training in accountancy, secretaryship, librarianship and journalism. In 1952 the Nigerian College of Arts, Science and Technology had been opened to meet the need for higher education of a type not normally provided by a university. The college, which had three branches (Ibadan, Enugu and Zaria), confined itself to professional education, and provided training for civil, mechanical, electrical and mining engineering; land surveying; mining surveying; pharmacy; accountancy; secretaryship; fine arts; agriculture and estate management. In addition, the college admitted students reading for the General Certificate of Education at advanced levels, in preparation for university education. The future of these colleges was also considered in the Ashby Report, and it was recommended that they should be developed gradually into regional universities.

LABOUR

Nigeria is primarily an agricultural country and in the early fifties the bulk of her working population was engaged in agricultural production.

Table 18.4 shows that the total working population was 14,498,000, which represented about 47·7 per cent of total population. Of this working population about 78 per cent were engaged in agriculture, forestry, animal husbandry, fishing and hunting. The greater number of the women engaged in agriculture assisted their husbands on the farms, and only a few had separate farms of their own. Apart from providing labour on the farms, the most usual job among women was retail trading. Most of the population, therefore, was self-employed and non-wage earning. As the economy of the country expanded with the increasing development projects

[1] The commission's report, entitled *Investment in Education*, was presented in September 1960.

undertaken by the governments (e.g. railway and road construction), and with the increasing commercial and mining activities of foreign companies, some of the agricultural labour drifted into the big towns. It must be added that a number of people were engaged in indigenous crafts, like weaving and blacksmithing, and supplemented their earnings with agricultural production. The increasing importance of the cash-crops gradually enlarged the number of

TABLE 18.4 *Primary occupations of Nigerians: 1952–3 census*

Region	Males						Females			Total both sexes
	Agriculture, forestry, animal husbandry, fishing, hunting	*Craftsmen, workers engaged in producing articles*	*Traders and employees engaged in commerce*	*All government and local government professional workers*	*Other occupations*	*Sub-total*	*Agriculture and fishing*	*Trading and clerical*	*Sub-total*	
Lagos township	4	11	21	16	32	84	3	33	36	120
Western Region	1,154	119	145	54	125	1,597	1,187	420	1,607	3,204
Northern Region	3,876	291	151	104	245	4,667	2,069	836	2,905	7,572
Eastern Region	1,306	75	148	50	142	1,721	1,737	144	1,881	3,602
Total	6,340	496	465	224	544	8,069	4,996	1,433	6,429	14,498

people who derived their income from agricultural production, either as farmers, or produce buyers, or motor transport magnates who were engaged in the evacuation of produce to the ports of shipment.

The introduction of education also brought new classes of workers. Some of the educated few were engaged as clerks in government and local government offices, while others were engaged by the foreign firms operating in the country. Some people who were trained by the Christian missions became teachers and pastors serving the institutions which trained them. Although a few of the early young workers kept in touch with farming by working part-time on the farms, particularly at weekends, in due course a gradual decline in agricultural labour became noticeable. Between 1945 and 1960 increasing numbers of young men and women were being educated and kept for long periods in schools and colleges; and by the time they finished their courses (which usually took at least eight to ten years), the farm offered no further attraction to them.[1] In Northern Nigeria, seasonal fluctuations of labour were experienced: as the annual rains approached there were general contractions in the supplies of unskilled labour employed by the government and the business companies, because the peasants who provided this labour tended to return to their farms until the approach of the next dry season. On most occasions the offers of wage incentives failed to check the seasonal movements away from the urban centres.

Between 1939 and 1960 there was a steady drift of people from the rural areas to the big towns, and it was greatest in Western Nigeria and the area of Lagos. The drift was first accentuated by heavy demands for labour on military works during the second world war; but the main reason was undoubtedly the attraction of higher wage rates and increasing social amenities in the towns with which, owing to improved transport and communications, the people in rural areas were becoming increasingly familiar. In 1946 the drift was most marked in Lagos where, out of 6,575 able-bodied men registered at the Labour Registration Office, only 46·5 per cent were from Lagos and surrounding towns, the remainder having come from distant parts of the country, attracted by the rumours of well-paid employment available through the Labour Exchange.[2] In 1946 the total number employed in wage-earning occupations was 236,000, and of these the government and native administration employed 135,000, while non-government enterprises employed 101,500 – of which 68,000 were employed by European firms, 16,000 by Christian missions, 15,000 by African firms and 2,000 by Syrian, Lebanese and other enterprises.[3] The number of people employed by African firms can be regarded as a mere estimate, because many indigenous enterprises employed family labour for which no definite wage or salary was paid. As the economy of the country expanded, more employment opportunities were created for the increasing working population. In 1960 the total number of people employed by the government (including federal,

[1] A. C. Callaway, 'Unemployment among African School Leavers'.
[2] *Colonial Annual Reports*, Nigeria, 1946, p. 17.
[3] See *Digest of Statistics*, Lagos, 1962.

regional and local governments) was 184,225, and the number employed by non-government enterprises (including public corporations, commercial firms and missions) was 238,650.

The first Employment Exchange in Nigeria was set up in Lagos in 1944. This was followed by two Employment Registration Centres at Ibadan and Benin in 1946, another at Sapele in 1947, and the system was later extended to cover a number of big towns. It was created in order to centralize the supply and demand of unskilled and semi-skilled labour in urban areas. The standard weekly hours of work varied with different kinds of employment: for example, farmers and traditional craftsmen had no regular hours of work as they spent virtually the whole day on their jobs, except for the regular rest hours; other fixed hours of work ranged from 34 per week for clerical workers to 45 for technical workers. The wage rates in the civil service were fixed by the government, and were usually adopted or slightly modified by quasi-government institutions like the corporations, local authorities and business companies. They were occasionally revised to take into account supply and demand for the various kinds of labour, and the gradual increases in the cost of living which were experienced as money economy developed.

At the start of the twentieth century, unskilled labour earned between 6*d*. and 10*d*. per day; and by the late thirties it earned between 1*s*. and 1*s*. 6*d*. per day. After 1946 wages for unskilled labour gradually increased from between 7*d*. and 2*s*. 6*d*. to between 3*s*. and 6*s*. 2*d*. per day in 1960. In 1946 semi-skilled labour received between 11*d*. and 4*s*. 4½*d*. per day, but in 1960 this increased to between 3*s*. 1*d*. and 8*s*. 6*d*. Also in 1946 wages for artisans varied from 2*s*. 6*d*. to 8*s*. 6*d*. per day, and in 1960 rose to between 8*s*. 8*d*. and 18*s*. 6*d*. In fixing the wage rates the government always made allowance for variations in the cost of living in different towns: for example, labour in Lagos received a higher rate than its counterpart in the provinces.

It is difficult to relate these increases in wages to the cost of living, for there are no reliable statistics of price indices; those that are available relate to about six main cities, and thus do not reflect clearly the average condition in the country. However, if one takes Lagos the minimum wage paid to general unskilled labour increased by 70·7 per cent – from 3*s*. 5*d*. per day to 5*s*. 10*d*. – between 1953 and 1960, while the cost of living index for the same period rose by 32 per cent.[1] Similar patterns between increases in wages and cost of living indices were recorded in Ibadan, Enugu and Kaduna. However, the margins which existed between wage increases and the cost of living indices did not reflect correctly the actual cost of living of an average Nigerian, for the most important item of expenditure, on family commitments under the extended family system, was not included in computing the indices. Most wage-earners spent 25–50 per cent of their annual incomes on such commitments.

Since 1945 a number of commissions have been set up to review the wage structure of government employees, and to advise the government on the problem of wages. These include the Tudor Davies Commission of 1945;[2] the Harragin Commission of 1946;[3] the Miller Committee of 1947;[4] the Gorsuch Commission of 1955;[5] and the Mbanefo and Morgan Commissions of 1959.[6] Before the Harragin Commission of 1946, the initial basic salary of a Nigerian administrative officer was £300 per annum, but by 1960 this had increased to £720 per annum – an increase of nearly 150 per cent. Similar and, at times, greater increases were experienced for other posts in the civil service. Generally, the government of Nigeria was the wage pacemaker. It has been suggested that the wages structure, particularly between 1955 and 1960, was largely influenced by politics, and that there was a tendency to increase wages in order to satisfy political supporters.[7] It was noticeable, however, that whenever the government revised wages upwards, a series of industrial disputes usually followed in private business undertakings.

[1] Helleiner, op. cit., tables I-B-6 and III-B-1.
[2] *Enquiry into the Cost of Living and the Control of the Cost of Living in the Colony and Protectorate of Nigeria.*
[3] *Report of the Commission on the Civil Services of British West Africa*, Col. no. 209, 1947.
[4] The Miller Committee considered the recommendations made by Sir Walter Harragin in respect of salary-earners, and brought unestablished or daily-rated labour into line with these recommendations.
[5] *The Report of the Commission on the Public Services of the Government in the Federation of Nigeria 1954–5*, Lagos, Government Printer, 1955.
[6] *Review of Salaries and Wages. Report by the Commission appointed by the Governments of the Federation, the Northern Region, the Eastern Region and the Southern Cameroons*, Lagos, Government Printer, 1959; *Report on the Commission for the Review of Wages and Salaries in the Public Service of the Western Region 1960*, Sessional Paper no. 5 of 1960.
[7] T. M. Yesufu, 'The Wages Structure and its Determinants in Nigeria'.

Commercial firms were understandably reluctant to follow the pattern of the government wage structure during this period, for, unlike the government, they were constantly faced with the problem of costs of production and the struggle to make profits.

In an effort to review wages and conditions of work, a number of boards were established. In 1943, legislation was passed setting up wage-fixing machinery, and thus the Labour Advisory Boards were created. In 1948 the National Whitley Councils were established, but they were replaced in 1955 by a newly constituted Federal Industrial Whitley Council.

The Department of Labour, which was established in 1944, was supervised by the Commissioner for Labour until the Ministry of Labour was created in 1953. The Commissioner (later the Minister of Labour) was the government's principal adviser on all matters of labour policy. The functions of his department included the enforcement of labour legislation, the constant revision of conditions of employment in all areas and occupations, the guidance of trade unions, the prevention of trade disputes and assistance in the orderly settlements of those which could not be prevented, and the operation of Employment Exchanges.

One aspect of labour in Nigeria was that of emigrant labour. Some people, particularly in Eastern Nigeria, drifted to Gabon (French Equatorial Africa) and Fernando Po (a Spanish territory) to find employment. At first emigrant labour was uncontrolled, but with the increasing reports of ill-treatment of Nigerian workers in these territories, the government decided to act. In 1950 it concluded an agreement with the French Authorities regulating the employment of Nigerian labour.[1] Mr W. I. Brinkworth was appointed as labour officer and British vice-consul at Gabon, in order to protect Nigerian interests. The government concluded a similar agreement with the Spanish Authorities regarding Nigerian labour in Fernando Po. In 1953 the recruitment of Nigerian labour was placed under the supervision of the Anglo-Spanish Employment Agency at Calabar. Prospective recruits received travelling and subsistence allowances from the place of recruitment to the transit camp at Calabar. While awaiting embarkation they received free board and lodging, and were required by law to be examined by a medical officer appointed by the Nigerian government. Contracts of

[1] *Colonial Annual Reports*, Nigeria, 1950, p. 16.

employment were drawn up and attested by an officer of the Nigerian government.

The treaties between the Nigerian government and the governments of the Spanish territories of the Gulf of Guinea, and of French Equatorial Africa, contained similar conditions of service for the Nigerian workers: free medical attention and hospital treatment; free housing; a daily food ration approved by the medical authorities; compensation in respect of injury or death arising out of employment; and the repatriation of the worker and his family at the expense of the employer on completion of a contract or in circumstances beyond the control of the worker. Wages were payable in two parts: there was a monthly wage paid in local currency, and a deferred wage of 14s. for each completed month of service, which was sent to the Nigerian government for payment to the worker on his return to Nigeria. The first contract was to be no longer than two years, and if it was renewed, the employer had to pay for the repatriation and subsequent return of the worker and his family. In the event of a fatal accident arising out of his employment, a sum equal to thirty times the total monthly wage was paid to the relatives of the deceased in accordance with local customs. Most of the workers recruited were unskilled, and many of them have settled permanently in these territories.

Until 1945 the general conditions of labour in Nigeria were governed by the Labour Ordinance of 1929, the Forced Labour Ordinance of 1933 and the Labour (Wage-Fixing and Registration) Ordinance of 1943. An attempt was made to bring together the existing legislation in the Labour Code Ordinance of that year; this was replaced by the Labour Code Ordinance of 1948 and subsequent amending legislation based on the United Kingdom system of labour law.[1] The 1948 ordinance applied to all directly-employed manual and non-manual workers earning not more than £75 per annum, but not to domestic servants.

[1] See 'Labour Code', *Laws of the Federation of Nigeria and Lagos, 1958*, chapter 91.

Trade unions[1]

Before 1930 a number of organizations and societies existed which had similar aims and policies to trade unions, and there are some records of strike action by workers. For example, there was the Lagos Strike of 1897, when government workers went on strike against the government's decision to alter their conditions of work, especially the hours;[2] and in 1929 the coalminers at Udi organized a strike because of alleged illegal deductions from their wages.[3] Both strike actions were successful. Workers felt the need to organize trade unions, for the purpose of demanding higher wages and for improving conditions of work, long before they were given public recognition by the Trade Union Ordinance, no. 44 of 1948.[4] This gave legal recognition to trade unions, allowed them to organize peaceful picketing and protected them against actions for tort. During the war years more were established, the most important being the Railway Workers Union which called a general strike in 1945. In January 1946 there were 121 registered trade unions in Nigeria, but due to amalgamations, cancellations and dissolutions the actual number of unions functioning effectively at the end of the year was 100, with a declared membership of 52,747. In order to cope with this increase and to protect their members, the Trade Union Ordinance was amended in 1947 to empower the Registrar of Trade Unions to take necessary steps to ensure that union accounts were properly kept, and to institute criminal and civil proceedings on behalf of any trade union for the recovery of funds where no proper account was produced. The Criminal Code of Nigeria was also amended in 1947 to guard against possible strike actions which might affect the supply of electricity and water, and other services vital to human life and public health.[5] The legal position of the trade unions remained unchanged in 1960.

The Nigerian trade unions, like those of other countries, were

[1] For a detailed account of the Nigerian trade unions, see T. M. Yesufu, *An Introduction to Industrial Relations in Nigeria.*

[2] For full details, see A. G. Hopkins, 'The Lagos Strike of 1897: An Exploration in Nigerian Labour History'.

[3] *Colonial Annual Reports*, no. 1493, Nigeria, 1929, p. 10.

[4] 'Trade Unions', *Laws of Nigeria, 1948*, chapter 218: no fundamental alterations were made to this law between 1948 and 1960.

[5] *Laws of the Federation of Nigeria and Lagos, 1958*, chapter 42.

active in demanding better pay and improved conditions of service for their members, but they were faced by many problems. First, most of the union leaders had no trade union education, and some had no education at all; secondly, the union subscriptions were usually low, consequently they were not financially strong; and lastly they often suffered from dishonest secretaries and treasurers. In 1946 the government appointed a labour officer charged solely with trade union affairs, and a special office was opened in Lagos in the Department of Labour for the purpose of helping and advising in their proper development. The Labour Department also started educational classes for union leaders on the principles and organization of trade unions. An annual trade union school was started in 1947, and in 1948 92 students from 32 unions attended the course. At the end of 1948 the government decided on a scholarship scheme for trade unionists,[1] the purpose being to facilitate trade union studies in the United Kingdom by awarding six annual scholarships.

But this scheme met with some problems, both financial and practical, and it was eventually abandoned. However, in 1949 the government decided to provide an alternative training course for the trade unionists.[2] A correspondence course of twelve monthly lessons was started by the trade union officer on the same lines as that run by Ruskin College, Oxford, for colonial trade unionists. The number of trade unionists who took the course in 1949 was 154, representing 54 trade unions. Special emphasis was placed on the preparation of union accounts.

In April 1950 union representatives at a conference in Lagos decided to set up a Trade Union Education Committee for Lagos and the colony area. Four classes were started during June 1950, and continued for three months with a weekly average attendance of about 200 students. More classes were held in November 1950. Outside Lagos there were fewer facilities for unionists: only some trade union discussion groups and weekend schools at Ibadan and Benin, and annual lectures at University College, Ibadan, where a tutor on industrial relations, responsible for trade union education,

---

[1] *Annual Report on the Department of Labour and on the Resettlement of Ex-Servicemen, 1948*, Lagos, Government Printer, p. 17.

[2] *Colonial Reports*, Nigeria, 1949, p. 23; *Annual Report on the Department of Labour and on the Resettlement of Ex-Servicemen, 1949–50*, Lagos, Government Printer, 1950, p. 16.

was employed. In 1952 a number of union leaders from Western Nigeria attended courses on labour management arranged by University College, and others attended one in Ghana, organized by the International Conference of Free Trade Unions.

TABLE 18.5   *Trade union membership,*
              1944–60

Year	Total numbers of registered unions	Total membership
1944	91	—
1945	97	—
1946	100	52,747
1947	109	76,362
1948	127	90,864
1949–50*	140	109,998
1950–1	144	144,385
1951–2	124	152,230
1952–3	131	143,282
1953–4	152	153,089
1954–5	177	165,130
1955–6	232	175,987
1956–7	270	198,265
1957–8	298	235,742
1958–9	318	254,097
1959–60	347	259,072

* Financial year ending 31 March.
Source: *Annual Report on the Department of Labour, 1959–60.*

Table 18.5 shows the increases in the number of registered trade unions and their membership. However, development was hindered by the lack of capable and responsible leadership, by rivalry among the leaders, and by the embezzlement of union funds. In 1946 the Trades Union Congress of Nigeria was formed by 59 affiliated unions, with a total membership of 42,300, and during the following year the first regrouping and reorganization took place. The tendency was towards amalgamation, and in this way the Nigerian Motor Transport Drivers Union, the Amalgamated Union of UAC

Workers of Nigeria, the Amalgamated Union of Clerical and Allied Workers, and a tin-mine workers union were formed.[1]

In December 1948 the Secretary-General of the Trades Union Congress of Nigeria, who had recently returned from studying in the United Kingdom with a scholarship awarded by the British Trades Union Congress, put forward some proposals for reorganization. These were accepted, and the British Trades Union Congress donated £110 towards them; but before they could be implemented, the movement suffered a set-back. A split in the Congress developed in 1949, caused by a clash of personalities among the leaders, and a rival body was set up – the Nigerian National Federation of Labour. The two groups were temporarily united in 1950, with the formation of a new body called the Nigerian Labour Congress; but this collapsed in 1952, having failed to attract the support it needed from the local trade unions. During this year more trade unions appointed full-time organizers, but there was no co-ordination between the policies of unions in different parts of the country. In 1953 a new All-Nigeria Trade Union Federation was formed, and in 1954 it had 39 affiliated unions of a total membership of 95,000. Two years later it broke down, like its predecessors, giving birth to two rival central trade union organizations: the National Council of Trade Unions and what was left of the All-Nigeria Trade Union Federation. The Labour Department made fruitless efforts to weld them together into one strong central body, and the confused situation remained unresolved in 1960.

The big trade unions which existed were found in agriculture, teaching, community and business services, and building and construction; but by far the largest and best organized was the Nigerian Union of Teachers. This had many advantages over the rest of the country's unions: all its members were educated and able to appreciate the purpose and functions of a trade union; it had a better financial standing than most, and it also had paid officials, who were able to devote enough time to its organization. Many other unions had a low percentage of educated members; so their leaders were able to run them without adequate explanation of their actions, and the incidence of embezzlement of union funds was very high.

In pursuing their policy of improving the working conditions of

[1] *Annual Report on the Department of Labour and on the Resettlement of Ex-Servicemen, 1948*, Lagos, Government Printer, p. 17.

their members, the unions were often involved in trade disputes. The first one of any significance resulted in the General Strike of 1945. It arose between the Nigerian Railway and the Nigerian Railway Workers Union, when the union asked for substantial wage increases for its members to meet the increasing cost of living, and the Nigerian Railway, as the employer, rejected their claims. The union then sought the support of the other unions in a general strike. As a countrywide movement this was a failure, but a measure of dislocation was caused in Lagos and in a few big towns, and the Nigerian Railway suffered long-range repercussions mainly through the loss of revenue. However, it did mean that more trade unions became strike-conscious. In 1946, 16 labour disputes were reported to the Labour Department, 10 of which led to strikes. The longest strike lasted for more than three weeks, but most of the others lasted for less than four days. The main cause of the disputes was the disagreement on pay awards granted by the government in June 1946. Others included protests against the dismissal of union members, and dissatisfaction with the hours and conditions of work generally. In 1948 the Federation of Government and Municipal Non-Clerical Workers Union demanded a 40-hour week, and, in the face of continued pressure, the government commissioned a report.[1] This recommended a 44-hour week, which was accepted by the union as an interim measure. Around this time, many unions began to show a new outlook in the matter of trade disputes, as many disputes were resolved by negotiations between employers and employees, and only in a comparatively few cases were other methods adopted. In 1948 a total of 20 industrial disputes resulted in strike actions involving about 7,375 workers. The longest lasted 13 days, while others lasted for periods varying from 2 to 7 days. In 1949 there were 70 industrial disputes of which 36 led to strike actions involving some 46,698 workers. The four longest strikes lasted for periods varying from 27 to 30 days, while the others were of a few hours to 18 days duration, the average being 6 days. Approximately 500,000 man-days were lost by these stoppages. One of the strike actions involved the Public Utility Technical and General Workers Union, Kaduna Branch, and the Public Works Department: the union demanded a 100 per cent increase in pay, but the government offered less than 5 per cent, and the ensuing strike was only called off after the government had agreed to review the claims. Another strike was between the Railway Station Staff Union and the Nigerian Railway, and was caused by dissatisfaction with previous arbitration. The union called a countrywide strike among its members, which completely paralysed the railway system between 17 and 20 July 1949, and which was called off on the appointment of a commission of inquiry. The railway unions objected to the appointments of two members of the commission, suggesting substitutes, and when the government refused to yield to this demand the union staged a twenty-four hour strike of railway workers in Lagos. This failed to produce the desired effect, and the union finally refused to give evidence before the commission.

The most important labour dispute in Nigeria involved the Colliery Workers Union at Enugu and the Colliery Department in 1949.[1] The union demanded increases in pay and better conditions of work, and these were rejected by the government. The miners went on strike, and this was followed by a series of demonstrations in the big towns in Eastern Nigeria. At Enugu, during one of the riots which resulted from demonstrations, some twenty-one miners were killed when police opened fire on the demonstrators while trying to restore order. This incident brought a wave of sharp protests from all parts of the country. The government appointed a commission of enquiry, headed by a former Chief Justice of Palestine, William Fitzgerald, to look into the disturbances in the colliery at Enugu. The report, issued on 10 June 1950, proposed the establishment of a Ministry of Labour Conciliation Board and a National Tribunal.[2] The government accepted this in principle, and arrangements were made for a small group of experts in trade union organization and labour relations to investigate the problems involved. Representatives of the trade unions, individual employers and government officials were consulted, and a number of valuable suggestions designed to improve industrial relations were made; but industrial disputes continued.

In 1950 there were 82 disputes and of these 26 resulted in strike action, involving some 26,876 workers. As these statistics show, many were resolved by negotiations and only in a few cases was it

[1] *Annual Report on the Department of Labour and on the Resettlement of Ex-Servicemen, 1949–50*, Lagos, Government Printer, pp. 21–3.
[2] *Report of the Commission of Enquiry into the Disorders in the Eastern Provinces of Nigeria, November 1949*, HMSO, no. 256 of 1950.

necessary for the Commissioner of Labour to appoint conciliators. Two of these disputes are of particular interest in the study of trade union problems. The first was between the Armels Transport Workers Union and the Director of Armels Transport Ltd. The union demanded higher wages and better conditions, and when these were rejected they took strike action. But after eighteen days the workers went back to work on the employer's terms: they failed because of insufficient financial support. Another dispute involved the Amalgamated Union of UAC African Workers and the UAC Ltd. The union renewed a strike notice suspended in May 1949, and demanded arbitration before 2 August 1950. An arbitrator and two assessors, nominated by the union and the company respectively, were appointed, and as a result, four of the union's eleven claims were accepted. A 12·5 per cent cost-of-living allowance was awarded to all junior staff by the company, but disagreement arose as to the effective date of the awards. Another less successful strike followed on 14 December 1950 and lasted for about twelve days.

Labour disputes continued to be frequent, as many leaders felt this was the only effective means of bargaining with employers. In 1952, 59 disputes were dealt with by the Labour Department. Many were resolved by negotiation, but 39 resulted in strike actions involving 11,580 workers, and approximately 63,930 man-days were lost through these stoppages. In 1953, 54 disputes were dealt with by the Labour Department, and 31 of these resulted in strike actions, involving 8,403 workers and the loss of 13,860 man-days. There were the same number of industrial disputes in 1954, but 34 resulted in strike actions. In 1957, 137 trade disputes were notified to the Department of Labour, and more than 50 per cent of these affected the transport and constructional industries and the commercial firms. Stoppages of work occurred in 52 cases involving 22,784 workers and the loss of 48,955 man-days, which was about 14 per cent of the man-days lost in 1956, when the number of industrial disputes and strikes reached their highest. For the year 1959–60, 115 trade disputes came to the Ministry of Labour, 54 of which resulted in stoppages of work involving 23,250 workers and a loss of 70,862 man-days.

The constitution of each trade union provided that friendly benefits, e.g. sickness benefits, be paid to deserving members.

However, between 1950 and 1960 an annual average of about 2 per cent of union funds was spent on friendly benefits.[1] It could be argued that this small proportion of expenditure on such an important item resulted partly from the fact that conditions of service of most trade union members provided for such benefits under the Workmen's Compensation Ordinance, and partly from the benefits which people enjoyed under the extended family system. A number of workers also obtained financial help from friendly and semi-political societies such as tribal unions.

As early as 1946, the Trades Union Congress had set up a working committee which consulted with the Commissioner of Labour on labour problems. In 1949, following investigations made into the trade union movement, three Whitley Councils were set up for government services – one for senior and two for junior civil servants.[2] But after little more than twelve months of existence, they broke down because the staff side was dissatisfied with the rate of progress and the extent of the improvements in conditions which had so far been secured. They were later revived, but broke down once again, and in 1955 a newly constituted Federal Industrial Whitley Council was formed. The machinery for statutory wage-fixing was governed by the Wages Board Ordinance, which came into force in 1957 and set up a Wages Board to regulate remuneration and other conditions of work.[3] The Ministry of Labour concentrated on encouraging voluntary collective bargaining, which was considered the most satisfactory method of fixing wages. Joint industrial councils operated in the electricity, coal and tin-mining industries, the Divisional Wages Committees functioning exclusively in Northern Nigeria. The ordinance also made provision for the establishment of Wages Boards in any industry or occupation where, in the opinion of the Minister of Labour and Welfare, wages were unreasonably low, or no adequate machinery existed for the effective regulation of wages and other conditions of employment.

[1] T. M. Yesufu, *An Introduction to Industrial Relations in Nigeria*, pp. 66–70
[2] *Annual Report of the Department of Labour and on the Resettlement of Ex-Servicemen, 1948*, Lagos, Government Printer, p. 8.
[3] 'Wages Boards', *Laws of the Federation of Nigeria and Lagos, 1958*, chapter 211.

Factories and mining legislation

Before 1946 there was no factory legislation in Nigeria, mainly because there was no substantial industrial development which merited elaborate regulations. However, the welfare of workers in the mines had been a primary concern of the government.

The principle of legal enforcement of a minimum standard of welfare in all industries emerged very slowly. Between 1927 and 1929 the government passed a number of Safe Mining Regulations which laid down safety conditions, and the Minerals Ordinance also provided for compensation to be paid to injured miners.[1] The first attempt by the government to secure an improved standard of life for industrial workers was in 1929, when the 'labour health area' was constituted under the Labour Ordinance of the same year.[2] The ordinance prescribed minimum standards of housing, water supply, sanitation and medical attention and treatment. It was applied to the coal mines at Enugu in 1936, thus making it the first among the mining industries to attempt to provide better environmental conditions for its workers.

After the second world war the conditions in the mines attracted more attention. In 1945 the Safe Mining Regulation under the Minerals Ordinance[3] was amended to provide a variety of measures including the supervision and adequate fencing of dangerous machinery, the storage and use of explosives, and special precautions required for open-cast, alluvial and underground mining. Measures concerning underground mining included fire shafts, windings, haulage and dredging. The ordinance also provided a minimum penalty of £200, or two years imprisonment or both, for the breach of any of the regulations, but this was amended to a fine of £50 or six months imprisonment in 1947.

In 1948 rules were formed to provide for the better working of workmen's compensation measures, by requiring employers and insurers to render six-monthly returns giving details of accidents and workmen injured and the compensation admitted and paid. Despite

[1] Minerals Regulations, nos. 4 and 30 of 1927, no. 29 of 1929; and *Laws of the Federation of Nigeria and Lagos, 1958*, chapter 121.
[2] Labour Ordinance, no. 1 of 1929. See Perham (ed.), *Mining, Commerce and Finance in Nigeria*, p. 9.
[3] *Laws of the Federation of Nigeria and Lagos, 1958*, chapter 121.

these rules, the response of private employers was disappointing, as they failed to furnish full and regular particulars.

The first Factories Ordinance was passed in 1955 and it came into force on 1 September 1956.[1] It was based on the factory legislation in the United Kingdom. A factory was defined as a place employing ten or more manual workers making or processing articles, and included shipyards, dry docks, railway workshops, electricity-generating stations and waterworks. The ordinance laid down the minimum standards for the safety, health and welfare of workers in factories, but did not apply to the mines, which were covered by the Minerals Ordinance. All factories had to be registered with the Chief Inspector of Factories, who was also responsible for ensuring the enforcement of the legislation.

Cases of industrial diseases were rare in Nigeria because industrial development was fairly recent. However, there were a few cases of lead poisoning in the mines, and suspected cases of pneumo-coniosis, which was thought to be due to the inhalation of dust and cotton fibres.

A number of private concerns provided dispensaries, maternity homes and hospitals for the benefit of their workers. These facilities were usually placed at the disposal of the workers' families as well. In a few other cases, employers arranged for doctors to call at regular intervals to attend to workers who might have any complaint regarding their health. The Red Cross Society also provided first-aid classes for factory workers in several centres throughout the country. Modern cloakrooms, washing facilities and sanitary accommodation were provided by the few large firms. The number of canteens and mess-rooms gradually increased, and workers could either buy the food provided there, usually at subsidized prices, or bring their own food and consume it in the mess-rooms.

THE CO-OPERATIVE MOVEMENT

The co-operative movement in Nigeria first appeared in agricultural production. The early co-operative societies, which were in Western Nigeria, took the form of group-farming societies, and concentrated on providing labour on the farms. After 1924, however, some began to organize collective sales of cocoa under the supervision of the

[1] *Laws of the Federation of Nigeria and Lagos, 1958*, chapter 66.

Agricultural Department.[1] Thus a society of middlemen, some of whom owned cocoa farms, developed, and by 1933 the movement in the cocoa-growing area of Western Nigeria was so advanced that the government felt the need to set these societies on a more definitely co-operative basis, and to appoint a registrar of co-operative societies.[2] In February 1936 Captain E. F. G. Haig, an administrative officer, was appointed; and the Co-operative Department thus created became responsible for the co-operative movement affairs.[3] The office and staff quarters were located at Moor Plantation (an agricultural research station) at Ibadan, the area with the largest number of 'indigenous' co-operative societies.[4]

The immediate task of the department was to train the three Nigerian officials who formed the nucleus of an inspectorate, and whose job it was to instil the basic principles of co-operation, to apply them to practical problems involving the existing cocoa-marketing organization, and to teach a sound and simple system of accounting.[5] Farmers who desired to form a society were encouraged to do so, and where a society already existed, it was encouraged to become a government-recognized co-operative organization.

The Nigerian co-operative movement followed three basic principles:

(a) The share capital of the society was provided by its members. The shares could not be sold and they neither appreciated nor depreciated in value; and so a member was in much the same position as a debenture-holder in a joint-stock company.

(b) The society operated on the principle of one man, one vote, regardless of capital holding or the scale of participation in the society's activities. The management of the society was in the hands of a committee appointed by all its members.

[1] The early co-operatives in agricultural production were known as 'agricultural associations': *Annual Report on the Agricultural Department, 1924*, Lagos, Government Printer, p. 10.

[2] *Annual Report on the Agricultural Department, 1934*, Lagos, Government Printer, p. 20.

[3] *Report on the Progress of Co-operation in Nigeria, 1935–7*. Issued as Sessional Paper no. 2 of 1938.

[4] These were the societies (agricultural associations) formed voluntarily without any government assistance.

[5] *Report on the Progress of Co-operation in Nigeria, 1935–7*, op.cit., p. 1.

(c) The society did not make profit, but 'surplus', which was allocated at the end of the financial year to members in proportion to
their purchases as consumers or their sales as producers. The
society was, therefore, excluded from the provisions of the
company tax.

TABLE 18.6   *Number of co-operative societies supervised by the
Co-operative Department: selected years, 1939–60*

Year 31 March	Produce marketing societies	Thrift and loan societies	Thrift and credit societies	Con-sumers' societies	Other societies (*)	Total
1939	113	9	8	—	—	†
1940	140	32	9	—	—	†
1945	187	200	61	—	—	†
1947	242	265	141	4	40	692
1950	310	314	388	38	42	1,092
1955	545	273	913	43	116	1,890
1958	1,243	293	1,093	51	261	2,941
1959	1,493	308	1,183	39	357	3,380
1960	—	—	1,237	34	195	†

* Including secondary organizations.
† Total not reliable because of lack of statistics about other co-operative
societies.
Source: *Annual Abstract of Statistics, 1963.*

Before 1945 development was slow, but thereafter more societies
were formed and they began to play an increasing role in the
country's economy. Table 18.6 shows that the total number of
co-operative societies increased from 692 in 1947 to 1,092 in 1950,
1,890 in 1955 and 3,380 in 1959. In the 1945–6 cocoa season there
were 219 co-operative marketing societies, and this number rose to
310 in 1950, 545 in 1955 and to 1,493 in 1959; they grew rapidly,
particularly in the Western Region, which in 1960 had more than
two-thirds of the marketing societies in the country.

It was in the marketing of cocoa that the societies were most active:
table 18.7 shows the proportion of Nigeria's production of cocoa
which came through them. The increase in primary wealth and
exports, and the subsequent advance in the living standards of the

people, brought about a remarkable increase in the number of co-operatives, particularly in the produce marketing and thrift and credit sectors. The Association of Nigerian Co-operative Exporters, which later became a licensed buying agent of the Western Region Marketing Board, was responsible for selling the products supplied by the produce marketing societies.[1] It also handled the societies' non-marketing board produce, such as rubber, copra, coffee, ginger and castor seed.

TABLE 18.7 *Co-operative marketing societies and Nigerian cocoa production, 1935–60*

Year	(a) Nigeria (tons)	(b) Co-operative marketing societies (tons)	Percentage (b) to (a)
1935–6	79,469	2,161	2·7
1939–40	112,841	5,915	5·2
1945–6	95,189	13,762	14·5
1949–50	100,520	9,697	9·7
1959–60	154,595	29,300*	19·0

* Approximate figure.
Source: *Annual Reports of the Registrar of Co-operative Societies in Nigeria.*

The Co-operative Thrift and Loan Societies, which cater primarily for salary earners, were among the earliest co-operatives to be formed in the country. Originally they existed only in government departments, but the movement later spread to mercantile houses, schools and corporations. They increased in number from 224 in 1946, to 314 in 1950, dropped to 273 in 1955, but increased again to 308 in 1959. Their total savings increased steadily between 1948 and 1959. However, in 1957 total withdrawals exceeded total savings for the first time. This was due to a number of factors:

(a) the increased cost of living, especially in Lagos where most of the societies existed, made it more difficult for salary earners to save;

[1] *Annual Report on the Progress of Co-operation in Nigeria*, Lagos, Government Printer.

(*b*) housing difficulties in Lagos forced up rents, and several months' rent was often demanded in advance;

(*c*) it became common practice for members to use the society as a current account savings bank, thereby making frequent withdrawals for purposes not provided in the bye-laws;

(*d*) the liquidation of a number of societies, and the amalgamation of others, necessitated heavy withdrawals.

Members of the thrift and loan societies were allowed to borrow from the society, or against their savings, for objects of permanent use: for example, for buying land or buildings. They were encouraged to save the minimum of 1*s*. per pound of salary, and to limit savings to what they could afford. The accumulated savings were invested in various accounts; part was kept in the commercial banks and, from 1953, at a co-operative bank;[1] some deposits were made with the Post Office Savings Bank; while some of the societies also invested in government stocks. Co-operative Thrift and Credit Societies for non-salary earners grew considerably after 1946, the number rising from 98 in 1946, to 388 in 1950, 913 in 1955 and 1,237 in 1960. The credit societies had great support among farmers and small traders, particularly at Calabar in Eastern Nigeria. The Co-operative Consumer Societies, on the other hand, were slow to develop for three main reasons: first, they faced competition from the multitude of small traders with low overhead costs; secondly, there were inadequate funds to develop the societies and extend their operations; and thirdly, the societies were often managed by people without any experience. The number of consumers' societies increased from 4 in 1947, to 38 in 1950, 43 in 1955 and to 51 in 1958, but fell to 34 in 1960. Other Nigerian co-operative societies which came into existence after 1945 included craft and artisans societies (covering raffia-work, wood-carving, ironwork, carpentry and fancy-leather work), farming societies, building societies, and co-operative schools and maternity homes.

The co-operative movement was also extended to cover banking. The first co-operative bank was established in Western Nigeria in 1953 with a capital of £1 million granted by the Nigerian Cocoa Marketing Board. It was followed in 1955 by the Eastern Nigeria Co-operative Bank, which started with a capital of £20,000. The

---

[1] Co-operative banking is discussed below.

primary function of the bank was to provide a source of capital for co-operative societies. Membership was open to any registered co-operative society within the area of the bank's operations, provided that the necessary minimum share capital of £1 was paid. There was no maximum limit to the amount of share capital which a society could hold. The funds of the bank were composed of £1 shares from the co-operative societies, deposits from members and from the public, loans sanctioned by the Registrar of Co-operative Societies, grants from any source and undistributed surpluses.

The bank granted loans and advances to co-operative societies, but these were not automatic: they were only granted after careful consideration, and only if adequate material securities were available – the society had to produce the names of persons prepared to guarantee the loans. The bank also served the public through its 'ordinary banking business' as understood in commercial banking.

The day-to-day operation of any co-operative society was governed by a bye-law which was based on the Co-operative Societies Ordinance.[1] Until the early fifties, when training was provided, most of the financial transactions of the societies were handled by the secretaries, who were entrusted with large sums of money. Since most of the society's members were illiterate, secretaries were often dishonest without any fear of detection; cases of embezzlements of societies' funds were common, and unfortunately many of the people involved in such malpractices got away without punishment because their frauds were discovered too late. After 1950, more training courses for the secretaries were organized by the Co-operative Department to improve efficiency, but it was obvious that improvement could only come if better-educated people were encouraged to take up such appointments, and if better wages were offered. In 1953 the government opened a Co-operative Training School at Ibadan for inspectors and auditors.[2]

The co-operative movement in Nigeria played an important role in the social and economic life of the people. Indeed, social conditions in the country were such that without the movement, many of the smaller traders and agriculturists would have found it difficult to

[1] *Laws of the Federation of Nigeria and Lagos, 1958*, chapter 39.
[2] The governments of the other (former) British West African colonies (The Gambia, Sierra Leone and Ghana) sent their officers to be trained at this school.

operate. The movement also improved the savings habit, particularly in rural communities. Generally, businesses among Nigerians tended to operate in small units, but the co-operative movement set the example of partnership and co-operation needed for economic growth to be achieved and sustained.

19 Epilogue: the post-independence years to 1972

PHILOSOPHY ON ECONOMIC GROWTH

In the preceding chapters, we have traced the process of economic revolution in Nigeria. A purely subsistence economy a century ago has been transformed into a fairly sophisticated market economy. It is important, therefore, to examine very briefly the philosophy which motivated economic growth in Nigeria within a comparatively short period, and which has sustained growth to the present day.

Every economic history is premised on a philosophy, explicitly stated or implied; a philosophy which reveals the conception of the economic world in which a people have lived. In substance, the philosophy behind the economic history of Nigeria is based on 'Competitive Capitalism'. This is most practicable in a free-enterprise economy in which certain fundamental principles are observed and accepted: the private ownership of factors of production; the right to organize such factors for productive purposes and for profit motives; and the exercise of these rights within the legal framework of the country.

An individual, therefore, could own factors of production, set himself up in business, join others in partnership, or own shares in a joint-stock venture. He could then sell his produce for profit without any government intervention on observing all the basic laws which made it possible for him and the other citizens to enjoy 'competitive capitalism'.[1]

The British administration in Nigeria between 1860 and 1960 was made relatively easy by the fact that it met with a philosophy of

[1] R. O. Ekundare, 'The Political Economy of Private Investment in Nigeria'.

economic growth on which the modern system was built. The adoption of the indirect-rule policy by the British[1] was made possible by the indigenous economic system which was not completely alien to the British, and which encouraged Britain to adopt the colonial economy as an arm of the British economic system. There was nothing on record to indicate that Nigerians were 'socialists' or 'communists'. The fact that the indigenous social and economic systems of the country were based largely on the extended family system tended to give the impression that Nigerians were 'natural socialists'. This impression, which was often adopted by the protagonists of socialism in Nigeria, had no economic foundation. In a developing country, where the process of division of labour and exchange had not been fully entrenched into the economic system, a reliance on subsistence production, which is the main economic characteristic of the extended family system, was inevitable. Indeed, subsistence production did not preclude exchange. While the main motive for production in this subsistence economy was to satisfy individual wants, surplus production over and above the subsistence level often formed the nucleus of an exchange system – either barter or money exchange. The fact that a wealthy member of a family was obliged to help his less fortunate brethren was not a sufficient reason to brand him as a socialist. The question was, how did he acquire his wealth? Surely not through any socialist system, but by working hard enough to earn a reasonably high income from which he accumulated his wealth. Indeed, he would prefer to help his brethren in such a way as to ensure ultimately that they had individual economic independence. The economics of the slave trade and that of the legitimate trade which followed – and which had its foundation in 'rural' agricultural capitalism – had strengthened the claim of a long-established competitive capitalism in Nigeria.

With the rapid development of a modern exchange economy, the extended family system was gradually losing its firm grip on Nigerian society. It was a slow but inevitable process of change in what was fast becoming a highly materialistic society.[2] Some family obligations, such as the care of the sick, and financial support for education, had become partly the responsibility of the government.

[1] See Perham, *Native Administration in Nigeria*.
[2] R. O. Ekundare, *Introduction to Economics for West African Students*, New York, Nok Publishers Ltd: in preparation.

The philosophy of competitive capitalism gave scope for government enterprise, for private enterprise (corporate and individual), as well as for a combination of both, to participate in shaping the economic history of the country. However, the general responsibility of government for pacemaking and overall direction of economic and social activity was, nevertheless, inevitable and paramount. The colonial administration which ended in 1960 provided the kind of economic leadership compatible with imperialism. At independence, however, three sectors of economic activity clearly emerged: first, the public sector which was dominated by the activities of the government and its agencies; second, the semi-public sector in which the government joined with private enterprise as partner or sponsor; and thirdly, the private sector for private corporate and individual activity.

THE POLITICAL ECONOMY OF SECTORAL PARTICIPATION

As the main policy of the government was to increase the country's rate of economic growth, every sector had to increase its participation in the general level of economic activity. However, political stability was essential to economic progress. It was the main factor which could encourage a government to plan, and which could help it to execute such a plan successfully. It also constituted the essential link among the various sectors of the economy.

Despite a number of political crises since independence, the public sector increased its participation in economic activity. The public sector was a monopoly of the government, federal, state or both, extending over certain basic activities and amenities such as the provision of education and health facilities; transportation infrastructure; power; currency and central banking; technical, scientific and research services; national surveys and planned utilization of natural resources, including minerals of strategic value or of basic importance to the security of the nation; and the manufacture of arms and ammunition.

The semi-public sector was by nature flexible since within it the government sought to encourage private enterprise through sponsorship, or to enter into partnership with private enterprise in areas where the government had primary responsibility, such as the ownership and use of mineral wealth, but in which, for one reason or another, it sought to share its activities with private enterprise. The trend since 1960 has been that of increased participation of the semi-public sector in various economic activities, including shipping and oil exploration.

The third sector, which was the private sector, could be divided into two groups – foreign and indigenous private investors. The relatively low levels of private saving and investment in Nigeria necessarily limited the economic functions of indigenous private enterprise. For this reason, it was argued – and to a large extent accepted – that, in order to achieve faster rates of economic growth, a substantial volume of foreign private investment would be needed to supplement indigenous investment.

Even if the public sector intended to take over the most important aspects of development, there were limits to the government's financial resources, which depended largely on customs duties and which, until the very recent increases in oil revenue, had fluctuated over the years. There was also a limit to government economic activities if the principle of free enterprise was not to be violated.

The various incentives to private investors mentioned in Chapter 15 were continued in the first two years of independence. However, the government continued to face increasing demands from the Nigerian public for the Nigerianization of the private sector. As a result of this pressure, the Immigration Act of 1963 was introduced. Among other things, the act prescribed the number of foreigners *vis-à-vis* Nigerians to be employed by foreign entrepreneurs. Indeed, it sought to control directly the establishment of any foreign business, stipulating that no alien might, either on his own account or in partnership with any person, including a Nigerian citizen, practise a profession without the prior written approval of the Minister, to be obtained before the entrepreneur himself could enter the country.

The Nigerian Civil War also forced the government to take a number of measures which affected private foreign investment. At the outbreak of the civil war the government imposed full economic sanctions against the 'breakaway' Eastern Region. Stricter foreign exchange control was operated and a number of import items were prohibited. Since 1970, however, the wartime control has been relaxed as many of the restrictions have been lifted.

A new government policy on private investment was introduced in 1972 with the introduction of Decree No. 4 – Nigerian Enterprises Promotion Decree, 1972.[1] This established the Nigerian Enterprises Promotion Board, which had the power to advance the promotion of Nigerian enterprises. It also established the Enterprises Promotion Committee in each state of the Federation with certain powers to assist and advise the board on the implementation of the decree, and to ensure that the provisions of the decree were complied with by aliens resident in every state.

Under the decree, the establishment and operation of certain enterprises – including newspaper publishing and printing; rice-milling; singlet manufacture; blending and bottling of alcoholic drinks; all aspects of pool betting business and lotteries; haulage of goods by road; and all assembly of radios, radiograms, record changers, television sets, tape recorders and other electric domestic appliances not combined with manufacture of components – were exclusively reserved for Nigerian citizens, companies and associations. In addition, certain other enterprises could not be operated or carried on by aliens in Nigeria unless they fulfilled certain specified conditions. However, the decree provided that exemptions might be granted in certain circumstances.

Any person who acted as a front for the purpose of defeating the object of the decree was liable to be prosecuted, and any contravention of any of the provisions of the decree was an offence punishable with a fine or imprisonment or both. The board also had power to take over, sell or otherwise dispose of any enterprises where there was a contravention. An aggrieved person might, however, petition the government for a review of his case.

The main objective of the government in its indigenization policy under the decree, which is to be fully operative from 31 March 1974, was to gradually reduce the area of foreign participation in most economic activities. Outside the specified areas of activities, foreign private enterprises could operate with the advantages of a number of incentives which already existed for the encouragement of foreign private investment.

[1] *Federal Republic of Nigeria. Official Gazette,* vol. 59, no. 10 (28 February 1972), Lagos, Federal Ministry of Information.

THE NATIONAL DEVELOPMENT PLANS

The economics of the post-independence era to 1972 has been dominated by two development plans – the National Development Plan 1962–8,[1] and the Second National Development Plan 1970–4.[2] It has always been difficult to assess the achievements and failures of any development plan within the plan-period or shortly afterwards. Economic activities are not rigid. Economic variables, therefore, tend to react independently and sometimes together with repercussions which tend to 'vibrate' beyond the plan-period.

The first National Development Plan 1962–8 aimed at a growth rate of at least 4 per cent compound per annum, as against 3·9 per cent per annum achieved in the preceding ten years. In furtherance of this aim, 15 per cent of the gross domestic product was to be invested while *per capita* consumption was to be raised by about 1 per cent per year. The plan anticipated that, by the end of the third or fourth national plan, the Nigerian economy would have attained self-sustaining growth. It stressed that the domestic savings ratio had to increase from about 9·5 per cent of GDP in 1960–1 to about 15 per cent or higher by 1975 in order to sustain the bulk of domestic investment. The development of transportation infrastructure, general improvement in manpower resources and improved power supplies were among the priorities.

There were two main issues which featured prominently in the plan: first, the participation of the private sector in the development process, and second, the position of the Nigerian economy in the world. The government wanted Nigerian businessmen to control greater portions of the Nigerian economy, not through nationalization but by the accelerated training of businessmen, the provision of advisory and training services, and the improved flow of capital and technical and market information. Because the economy depended largely on the fortunes of its export sector, whose prices and output depended on weather and world markets, it was necessary to diversify the country's exports, and to encourage the establishment of industries which would efficiently produce substitutes for essential

---

[1] *National Development Plan 1962–8*, Lagos, Federal Ministry of Economic Development.

[2] *Second National Development Plan 1970–4*, Lagos, Federal Ministry of Information.

imports as well as those which would serve to augment exports. Increased trade among African countries was accorded the highest priority, and the possibilities of establishing closer economic links with other African countries were constantly examined.

The total planned fixed investment for the first national plan was £1,183 million. About £390 million was to be invested in the private sector at an average of £65 million annually. The plan assumed that £793 million would be invested in projects in the public sector at an average annual investment of £132·3 million. Measured in terms of the allocation of funds, transport, electricity, primary production, trade and industry, and education, in that descending order, dominated investment in the public sector.

Public investment, which in the first year of the plan-period amounted to £64·6 million, declined slightly to £63·4 million in 1963. Thereafter, it rose gradually to approximately £90·0 million in 1966. The expected average annual investment of £112·8 million was really never achieved. In absolute terms, total annual fixed investment for the economy as a whole in the first two years fell short of the expected average level of £197·2 million. In subsequent years, however, the targets were considerably exceeded right up to and including 1965. The growth rate of recorded capital formation not only declined with the 1966 crisis, but was actually negative by 1967, mainly because of the exclusion of the three eastern states. However, actual investment in both public and private sectors combined in 1966 exceeded the estimated annual average of about 37 per cent. Also by then, 85 per cent of the total planned fixed investment for the economy as a whole during the plan-period had been achieved. This was attributed to the better performance of the private sector, where the target of £390 million for the plan-period was already exceeded by about 64 per cent in 1966. The estimated average annual investment of £65 million proved to be an under-estimation of the expected performance of the private sector.

The apparent contrast in the behaviour of the economy between the 'pre-crisis' and the 'crisis' period notwithstanding, the overall performance of the national economy during the plan-period, as reflected in changes in GDP, was one of unsteady expansion. The growth rate was 6·7 per cent in 1963–4, but only 3·8 per cent in 1964–6, when the lowest growth rate was recorded. Thereafter, it rose to 5·7 per cent in 1965–6 and fell again to 4·2 per cent in 1966–7.

More significant, however, was the uneven growth from sector to sector. Agriculture occupied a dominant position in the economy, as it accounted for about 65 per cent of GDP in 1962–3 and 63 per cent in 1966–7. With the faster growth of the non-agricultural sectors, however, the relative position of agriculture was understandably declining. Local industries accepted the challenge of the imposition of import restrictions necessitated by the crisis, using this as a spur for further industrialization. The share of industry in GDP grew from 5·3 per cent in 1963–4 to 7 per cent in 1966–7. The fastest growing sector of the economy was mining. It was also later to be the hardest hit by the war as a result of production stoppage in the oilfields of the eastern states; but in spite of this, the contribution of the sector to GDP rose from 1·9 per cent in 1962–3 to about 3·4 per cent in 1966–7.

The list of major projects successfully completed during the plan-period includes an oil refinery, the Nigerian Security and Minting Plant, a paper mill, a sugar mill, the Niger dam, the Niger bridge, some trunk roads and port extensions. The behaviour of the national economy during this period reflected a good potentiality for expansion greater than the 4 per cent minimum annual growth rate set by the planners.

The Second National Development Plan 1970–4 claimed that national planning should be aimed at the transformation of the whole society. It stated that it '. . . recognises explicitly the possibilities of using planning as a deliberate weapon of social change by correcting defects in existing social relations in various spheres of production, distribution and exchange'.[1] The national objectives of the plan were described as being to establish Nigeria firmly as

(i) a united, strong and self-reliant nation;
(ii) a great and dynamic society;
(iii) a just and egalitarian society;
(iv) a land bright and full of opportunities for all citizens; and
(v) a free and democratic society.[2]

These five basic objectives constituted the foundation for the social changes which the federal government planned to bring about between 1970 and 1974.

[1] Ibid., p. 37.
[2] Ibid., p. 32.

The first major problem which faced Nigeria at the time this plan was formulated was that of national unity.[1] The plan argued that

> ... the war-time experience of Nigeria has demonstrated the necessity for a sustained social will harnessed to a common social goal as a basis for national survival and greatness. Post-war conditions, rather than remove this necessity, indeed underline its undiminished importance. ... For planning purposes, a set of national objectives must deal simultaneously with the community's standard as well as quality of life. ... The first is a quantitative phenomenon and easier to measure. The second is a qualitative notion which is not susceptible to quantitative analysis but which is crucial to the pace of economic development and social change. It is relatively easy to quantify targets such as output, growth rates or changes in *per capita* income. Yet it is becoming increasingly appreciated that the development process is a function of the innate forces of a society.[2]

The main emphasis on social change was a new and important aspect of economic planning in the country. Indeed, it reinforced the basic economic philosophy that economic behaviour is a function of social change.

In each sector, the main purpose of maintaining a steady social equilibrium was carefully emphasized. For the agricultural sector, all the governments of the Federation planned a capital expenditure of £132·7 million which was to be spent on, among other things, a National Agricultural Bank; improvements in land use; irrigation and conservation schemes; agricultural education and research programmes; and improvements in livestock, fisheries and forestry. However, the main obstacle to a much needed agrarian revolution – the land tenure system – still remained. Because of the delicate social nature of this system, the plan remained very vague as to what changes were necessary. It suggested that in the southern states the local communities should consolidate the fragmented holdings and redistribute them into economic units suitable for tree crops and mixed food crops. Any spontaneous move among the people for the

[1] R. O. Ekundare, 'Nigeria's Second National Development Plan As A Weapon of Social Change'.
[2] Ibid., p. 31.

consolidation of land was, however, very unlikely, and it appeared that whatever initiative there was would have to come from the government.

The total planned public investment for the industrial sector was £86·1 million. The plan listed the objectives of the new industrial policy, the first of which, 'to promote even development and fair distribution of industries in all parts of the country', was relevant to the issue of maintaining social equilibrium.[1] This seemed to suggest that economic considerations would be secondary when deciding on where to locate new industries. However, the plan further explained that 'industries sponsored by the Federal and State governments will as a matter of location policy be sited purely on economic considerations. A measure of administrative dissemination will, however, be allowed in favour of less industrially developed towns and districts when considering the marginal levels of selective incentives. Any such subsidies will be specific and explicit.'[2]

The government, through this reservation, gave itself the opportunity to use its discretion as to what it considered to be in the public interest as far as industrial location was concerned. If the siting of an industrial project in a given area was uneconomical but could help to promote political and social unity, the government could disregard those economic considerations which favoured its establishment elsewhere. It might be possible for the government to adhere to this policy in respect of any industrial project which was to be financed entirely from public funds. It would be difficult, however, to expect private enterprise – in particular foreign private capital – to co-operate with the government in establishing industry in an area where optimum production and profit could not be achieved.

The government accepted its responsibility to reduce the educational gap between the different states and between the urban and rural areas, and to increase the supply of high- and intermediate-level personnel. Closely related to the problem of education and the availability of trained manpower was that of full employment. The plan accepted that '. . . full employment of resources, especially of the labour force, is the necessary policy objective for any economy dedicated to rapid growth and social harmony. The existence of excess capacity means resource waste and lost economic opportuni-

[1] Ibid., p. 143.
[2] Ibid., p. 144.

ties which an economy like Nigeria can ill afford.'[1] It was also vague as to what policy of full employment to pursue. While it recognized the essential need for full employment of resources, it went on to say that '. . . it does not mean an obligation on the part of government to find wage employment for everybody, irrespective of his skill, wish or aspiration'. Undoubtedly the main obstacle to any definite policy on full employment was that of mobility, particularly mobility of labour. The greatest obstacle to such mobility in Nigeria was the mistrust which had been created over the years among the various ethnic groups. Indeed, the issue of free mobility of labour constituted the main social barrier to the economic and political stability of the country. Improvements in the manpower potential of the country would have little impact on the economy unless socially, economically and politically every citizen was accepted in any part of the country and among any ethnic group.

The plan did not overlook the international position of Nigeria. From the point of view of outside industrial powers, Nigeria was of interest as a major market: 'Nigeria has the largest concentration of natural and human resources on the continent of Africa. With a probable population of about 64 million in 1970 and an estimated 80 million by the end of the second United Nations Development Decade in 1980, Nigeria is the most attractive single market in Africa.'[2] But perhaps more important, Nigerian industrial experience and development potential could provide the focal point in the active pursuit of West African economic integration, and the plan argued that the economic prosperity and political stability of Nigeria was vital to the future of Africa. It continued: 'In the context of modern power relations in the world and especially of the international threats facing the African peoples, Nigeria cannot be truly strong and united without a prosperous economic base. Material power exerts a disproportionate influence on international morality. Nigeria will, therefore, pursue relentlessly the task of development to make the national economy strong, dynamic, and responsive to the challenge of world competition.'

Nigeria believed in the economic integration of Africa. Her main concern, however, was with closer economic and political relations with her immediate neighbours. She advocated the abolition of

[1] Ibid., p. 34.
[2] Ibid., p. 29.

various restrictions – economic and political – which tended to
hinder proper integration. The aim was to eliminate the situation
which made some countries in the sub-region of West Africa grant
preferences to America and industrial countries in Europe, and
discriminate against fellow West African countries by imposing
artificial barriers to trade. It was believed that if the West African
countries could maintain non-discriminatory duties, intra-West
African trade in manufactures would be greatly expanded, and
would promote a more rapid economic growth in the sub-region of
West Africa.

It could be argued that the Nigerian policy of 'economic liberal-
ism' had its foundation in the gradual industrialization of the country; and on the bright prospect of her economy there was no doubt
that, given an optimum utilization of resources, the economy could
achieve increased production capable of yielding substantial surpluses over and above domestic needs. Nigeria could therefore
provide West Africa with agricultural foodstuffs and, at the initial
stage, with a limited range of industrial goods.

The performance of the Nigerian economy under the Second
National Development Plan was reviewed in June 1972. A government progress report compared the plan forecast with current
estimates of some of the principal economic indicators as shown in
table 19.1.[1] It admitted that more than a year was lost because
funds for projects under the plan were not released until April
1971.[2]

The projected levels of GDP at constant 1962–3 factor cost in the
plan were £1,585·6 million for 1970–1 and £1,685·9 million for
1971–2. The implied rates of growth were 4·7 per cent and 6·3 per
cent respectively. The estimates of the Central Planning Office put
GDP at £1,995·9 million for 1970–1 and £2,234·9 million for
1971–2, which substantially exceeded the plan estimates.

One significant feature of the economic changes was the declining
percentage contribution of agriculture to GDP as shown in table
19.2. The contribution of agriculture fell substantially from 53·8 per
cent in 1966–7 to 41·6 per cent in 1971–2. In contrast, the contribution of mining and quarrying more than doubled from 7·2 per cent

[1] *Second National Development Plan 1970–4. First Progress Report*, Lagos, Central
Planning Office, 1972.
[2] Ibid., p. 7.

TABLE 19.1 *Comparison of plan forecasts with current estimates, 1970–1 and 1971–2*

	1970–1			1971–2		
	Plan figures	Current estimates	Increase decrease (+)/(−)	Plan figures	Current estimates	Increase decrease (+)/(−)
Gross domestic product (£m)^a	1,585·6	1,995·9	+410·3	1,685·9	2,234·9	+549·0
Growth rate (%)	4·7	9·6	+4·9	6·3	12·0	+5·7
Capital formation (£m)^b	355·0	381·3	+26·3	399·0	465·4	+66·4
Investment ratio (%)^c	18·4	14·4	−4·0	18·9	14·7	−4·2
Traditional exports (£m)	201·8	187·0	−14·8	214·2	187·0	−27·2
Oil exports (£m)	260·3	292·6	+32·3	329·5	580·0	+250·5
Total exports (£m)	462·1	479·6	+17·5	543·7	767·0	+223·3
Imports (£m)	330·0	419·9	+89·9	362·9	530·0	+167·1
Current account balance (£m)^d	−34·6	−99·1	−64·5	−20·5	+2·0	+22·5
Gross national savings^d	164·2	222·8	+58·6	193·5	427·4	+233·9
Savings ratio (%)^e	9·2	8·8	−0·4	10·0	14·3	+4·3
Marginal rate of saving (%)	—	—	—	19·0	45·0	+26·0
Government recurrent revenue	318·6	425·3	+106·7	397·2	718·0	+320·8
Government recurrent expenditure	285·9	395·7	+109·8	321·5	425·0	+103·5
Budget surplus	32·7	29·6	−3·1	75·7	293·0	+217·3
Rate of inflation (%)	1·5	6·0	+4·5	1·5	6·5	+5·0

^a At constant 1962–3 factor cost.
^b At current market prices.
^c Ratio of capital formation at current market prices to GDP current market prices.
^d GNP at current market prices minus consumption expenditure.
^e Ratio of gross national saving to GNP at current market prices.
Source: *Second National Development Plan 1970–4. First Progress Report.*

to 18·5 per cent. Manufacturing also increased its share from 7 per cent to 8·5 per cent.

The changing structure of the economy was a reflection of the differential growth rates of the various sectors. Except for agriculture, education, health and other services, in no case did the compound rate of growth fall below 5 per cent. The most rapid growth

TABLE 19.2   *Sectoral contribution to gross domestic product of Nigeria at 1962–3 factor cost*

Sectors	Percentage contribution 1966–7	Percentage contribution 1971–2	Compound rate of growth 1966–71
Agriculture, livestock, etc.	53·8	41·6	1·5
Mining and quarrying	7·2	18·5	28·9
Manufacturing and crafts	7·0	8·5	10·8
Electricity and water	0·6	0·6	5·8
Building and construction	5·0	4·9	6·2
Distribution	12·4	11·5	5·0
Transport and communications	4·0	3·7	5·3
General government	3·2	5·3	18·1
Education	3·4	2·6	0·7
Health	0·8	0·7	3·3
Other services	2·6	2·1	2·1
Total	100·0	100·0	6·7

Source: *Second National Development Plan 1970–4. First Progress Report.*

rates were, however, recorded by mining and quarrying (28·9 per cent), general government (18·1 per cent) and manufacturing (10·8 per cent). These were the results of increased production of oil, rapid expansion of manufacturing activity and increased government involvement in economic activity.

The aggregate growth rate of GDP increased from 3·5 per cent in 1966–7 to 12 per cent in 1971–2. The growth rate of 12 per cent for 1971–2 was significant in that it was almost double the growth rate of 6·3 per cent projected in the plan. Indeed, it illustrated the dynamism of the economy and its rapid recovery from the shocks of the civil war. Undoubtedly, a large part of the rapid growth was due to increased production of oil, which continued to earn more revenue for the country. In fact, the sectoral breakdown of aggregate growth rate for 1971–2 showed that the oil industry accounted for 5·7 per cent, nearly half of the estimated growth rate of 12 per cent of GDP.

ECONOMIC INDICATORS

There were great changes in the Nigerian economy between 1960 and 1972. To start with, the population of the country increased from 55·7 million in 1963 to an estimated figure of about 64 million in 1972. Naturally, increases in population had some economic implications. The potential labour force of the country increased. The population in the age group 15–49 years, from which the bulk of the labour supply came, increased from 14·5 million in 1952–3 to 28·1 million in 1963, an increase of about 94 per cent. The number of people in this group continued to increase, and by 1972 it was estimated to have increased by 120 per cent over the 1952–3 figure. Within this group was contained a large contingent of school-leavers, a great proportion of whom were unemployed until 1967 when the civil war absorbed some of them. In other words, the population contained an increasing proportion of 'non-productive' elements, who were to be fed along with the rest of the population. A rapid expansion of the education system brought more children to school. Many children who in the past provided agricultural labour were no longer available. On leaving school, the children had completely lost touch with farming. In addition, the construction works and the establishment of modern industries attracted a large number of adults to the big cities. There was a marked drift of young people from the rural areas to the urban areas – a new phenomenon which put a great strain on the supply of agricultural foodstuffs.

The value of total foreign trade for Nigeria increased from £385·6 million in 1960 to about £821 million in 1970. In other words, the value of total trade per head of the population increased from about £7·4 in 1960 to £14·8 in 1970.[1] The trend of adverse

[1] R. O. Ekundare, 'Salary and Wages Reviews since 1946'.

balance of trade and adverse balance of international payments which began in 1954 continued until 1966. Thereafter and until 1972 Nigeria had favourable trade balances. The indices of Nigeria's foreign trade showed that by using 1960 as the base year, the value of total domestic export increased by 158·9 per cent in 1965 and by 264·7 per cent in 1970. The value of merchandise imports, also using 1960 as the base year, increased by 127·6 per cent in 1965 and by 175·2 per cent in 1970.

Apart from the major development projects already mentioned, Nigeria had to finance a civil war between 1967 and 1970, and it was estimated that this cost about £300 million.[1] A huge amount was spent on military weapons and equipment, and in maintaining the army, which had increased in number from 6,650 in 1956 to 10,500 in 1966,[2] and to more than 20,000 in 1970.[3] Federal government expenditure on military and defence (including personal emoluments) increased from £2·3 million in the financial year of 1955–6, to £7·7 million in 1966–7, £20·2 million in 1967–8, £49·6 million in 1968–9 and to £124·6 million in 1969–70.[4] Such expenditure did not contribute directly to the material well-being of the population, and the resultant multiplier effect led to an abnormally high general level of prices. In addition, certain vital sectors of the economy declined, especially agriculture, transport and distribution.[5]

Another indicator of growth was provided by the credit system of the commercial banks. Loans and advances granted by the banks, and which went mainly to the private sector, increased from £57 million at the end of 1960 to £135 million in 1965 and to £175·6 million at the end of 1970. An analysis of the structure of the credit system indicates substantial increases in loans and advances for agriculture, manufacturing, mining, real estate and construction. In addition to the enlarged credit system of the commercial banks, the federal government itself resorted to deficit financing. In the financial year 1967–8 the federal government deficit amounted to £71·4

[1] Barclays Bank, *Overseas Review* (March 1970).
[2] N. J. Miners, *The Nigerian Army, 1956–1966*, London, Methuen, 1971, pp. 15, 27.
[3] *West Africa*, 22 October 1971, p. 1235.
[4] *Recurrent Estimates of the Government of the Federal Republic of Nigeria*, 1955–6 and 1966–71.
[5] O. Aboyade and A. Ayida, 'The War Economy in Perspective', *Nigerian Journal of Social Studies*, vol. 13, no. 1 (March 1971), pp. 28, 32.

million, and this increased to £204·4 million in 1969–70. Government borrowing from the Central Bank increased, and in the two-year period from December 1967 to December 1969, Central Bank net credit to the government sector increased by £10 million. Also in the same period, credit from commercial banks to the government sector, in the form of treasury bills and treasury certificates, increased by £154·5 million.

The performance of the economy was not consistent during the period 1960–70. For example, between 1962 and 1965, national production increased at the rate of 5·5 per cent per annum, but declined to an average rate of 0·8 per cent per annum between 1965 and 1970. Increases in the levels of public and private expenditure led to the creation of demand for various goods and services far in excess of available supplies. Undoubtedly, the period of the 'war economy' worsened the situation. The indices of estimated (net) currency in circulation, using 1960 as the base year, increased by 146·0 per cent in 1965, and by 285·5 per cent in 1971. The purchasing power of the public had greatly increased. The pressure of demand on supplies of both local products, including foodstuffs, and imported goods, many of which were either prohibited or restricted, was reflected in increases in the cost of living indices as shown on table A3 of the Statistical Appendix. While these indices do not represent the overall nationwide pattern of consumption, they provide a guide to the general trend of the cost of living in the country.

The expected reaction to the rising cost of living was the demand for more wages. The cost of living argument formed the major basis for three wage reviews during the period 1960–71. As wages were reviewed upwards by each Wages Review Commission, the cost of living index continued to rise. In fact, no sooner had wage increases been granted than fresh agitations for more wages began. By 1972 threats of industrial action by a large section of the workers in support of wage claims constituted a real danger to the stability of the economy.

One recent and important development, which will have far-reaching economic implications, was the introduction of decimal coinage. The new unit of currency, the Naira, is equivalent in value to the old Nigerian 10s. There are 100 Kobo to 1 Naira. On 3 July 1972 the Kobo in units of 5 and 10 were brought into circulation.

Other units of 2·5 and 25 Kobo, along with currency notes of Naira and its units, were introduced on 1 January 1973.

There is a strong belief that the Nigerian economy has passed the stage of economic 'take-off' and reached that of self-sustaining growth. Nigeria was one of the few African countries to realize that the survival of modern competitive capitalism as a philosophy of economic growth depends not so much on attacks on the economic systems of other countries, as on the ability and the willingness of capitalism, guided by a proper national policy, to accept the increasing challenge facing it in a rapidly developing country. A realistic economic policy which pays due regard to the feelings and aspirations of the government and the people of Nigeria will ensure continued economic progress and prosperity, and increasing economic and political influence in the world.

Statistical appendix
Bibliography
Index

Statistical appendix

TABLE A1 *Population of Nigeria by region, sex and age groups, 1952–3 and 1963 ('000)*

Areas and sex		0–14 years 1952–3	0–14 years 1963	15–49 years 1952–3	15–49 years 1963	50 years and over 1952–3	50 years and over 1963	Total population 1952–3	Total population 1963
Nigeria	total	13,458	23,925	14,504	28,127	2,448	3,617	30,410	55,670
	male	6,945	12,326	6,800	13,703	1,126	2,082	14,869	28,112
	female	6,515	11,599	7,704	14,424	1,322	1,535	15,541	27,558
North	total	7,128	13,220	8,116	14,658	1,591	1,931	16,835	29,809
	male	3,714	6,933	3,796	7,021	719	1,132	8,229	15,086
	female	3,414	6,287	4,320	7,637	872	799	8,606	14,723
East	total	3,333	5,677	3,521	6,003	361	713	7,215	12,394
	male	1,687	2,837	1,633	2,874	168	411	3,488	6,121
	female	1,646	2,840	1,888	3,129	193	302	3,727	6,273
West†	total	2,899	3,734	2,712	5,997	484	734	6,085*	10,266
	male	1,493	1,907	1,285	2,952	233	410	3,001*	5,268
	female	1,406	1,827	1,427	3,045	251	324	3,084*	4,998
Mid-West‡	total	—	1,052	—	1,283	—	201	—	2,536
	male	—	532	—	614	—	11	—	1,258
	female	—	520	—	666	—	90	—	1,277
Lagos	total	98	242	155	389	12	33	265*	665
	male	49	118	86	241	6	16	141*	375
	female	49	124	69	147	6	17	124*	288

* Including those of unstated age.
† West included Ikeja division now in Lagos state.
‡ Mid-West was still part of Western Nigeria.
Note: Figures may not add up to totals because of rounding-off errors.
Source: *Annual Abstract of Statistics, 1963 and 1969.*

TABLE A2　*Population of Nigeria by ethnic group*
　　　　　　('ooo)

Ethnic group	1921*	1931	1952–3
Edo	473	508	468
Fulani	1,950	2,027	3,030
Hausa	3,337	3,630	5,544
Ibibio	960	750	757
Ibo	3,930	3,185	5,458
Kanuri	637	931	1,301
Nupe	347	327	358
Tiv	446	577	781
Yoruba	2,509	3,166	5,045
Others	4,038	4,822	7,619
Non-Nigerians	4	5	41
Total	18,631	19,928	30,402

* These figures are estimates.
Source: *Census of Nigeria, 1931 and 1952–3.*

TABLE A3 *Cost of living index: principal towns*

Year	Lagos (1953 = 100)	Ibadan (1953 = 100)	Enugu (1953 = 100)	Kaduna (1957 = 100)
1953	100	100	100	—
1954	105	105	112	—
1955	108	108	105	—
1956	117	114	112	—
1957	119	117	112	100
1958	119	110	115	103
1959	124	112	119	109
1960	132 (1960 = 100)	117	119	108
1961	106	127	122	115
1962	110	137	149	122
1963	110	128	143	119
1964	112	127	147	118
1965	117	131	148	122
1966	127	146	166	131
1967	122	141	*	128
1968	124	136	*	130
1969	136	148	*	147

* Figures for Enugu not available because of the civil war.
Sources: *Digest of Statistics*, and *Annual Abstract of Statistics*.

TABLE A4　*Nigerian central government finance, 1900–60*
$(£ooo)^e$

Year	Gross revenue *a, c, f*	Customs and excise revenue	Gross expenditure *c, f*	Surplus or deficit
1900	639	601	735	—96
1901	675	603	865	—190
1902	868	732	1,099	—231
1903	909	753	1,280	—371
1904	1,047	846	1,391	—344
1905	1,035	802	1,382	—347
1906	1,281	771	1,555	—274
1907	1,673	1,262	1,716	—43
1908	1,636	1,105	1,898	—262
1909	1,645	1,076	2,215	—570
1910	2,278	1,536	2,158	+120
1911	2,571	1,537	2,545	+26
1912	2,754	1,656	2,821	—67
1913^b	3,327	1,773	2,916	+411
1914	2,940	1,506	3,596	—656
1915	2,603	1,383	3,434	—831
1916	2,843	1,149	3,610	—767
1917	3,417	1,196	3,220	+197
1918	3,964	1,382	3,460	+504
1919	4,959	1,876	4,529	+430
1920	6,819	3,094	6,493	+326
1921–2	4,876	1,680	7,172	—2,296
1922–3	5,562^d	2,539^d	6,565^d	—1,003
1923–4	6,261	2,626	5,501	+760
1924–5	6,944	2,935	5,769	+1,175
1925–6	8,269	3,613	6,583	+1,686
1926–7	7,734	2,929	7,585	+149
1927–8	6,305^c	3,541	6,724^c	—419
1928–9	5,895	3,438	6,861	—966
1929–30	6,045	3,360	6,200	—155
1930–1	5,622	2,981	6,330	—708
1931–2	4,858	2,077	6,188	—1,330
1932–3	4,985	2,377	4,984	+1
1933–4	4,887	2,133	5,036	—149
1934–5	4,961	2,069	4,837	+124
1935–6	5,996	2,912	5,757	+239

Year	Gross revenue *a, c, f*	Customs and excise revenue	Gross expenditure *c, f*	Surplus or deficit
1936–7	6,260	3,624	6,061	+199
1937–8	7,342	3,505	7,376	−34
1938–9	5,811	2,472	6,867	−1,056
1939–40	6,113	2,487	6,499	−386
1940–1	7,273	2,433	7,254	+19
1941–2	7,975	3,085	7,027	+948
1942–3	9,034	3,622	8,999	+35
1943–4	10,913	4,897	9,977	+936
1944–5	11,445	5,242	10,133	+1,312
1945–6	13,200	5,664	10,693	+2,507
1946–7	14,832	7,095	14,052	+780
1947–8	18,404	9,129	17,186	+1,218
1948–9	23,811	12,623	23,898	−87
1949–50	30,765	17,195	28,253	+2,512
1950–1	32,794	18,161	30,388	+2,406
1951–2	50,327	32,106	43,673	+6,654
1952–3	50,906	33,948	44,103	+6,803
1953–4	59,256	42,104	55,003	+4,253
1954–5	62,481	43,960	60,668	+1,813
1955–6	59,950	44,753	55,030	+4,920
1956–7	70,591	50,790	67,080	+3,511
1957–8	72,057	51,695	76,701	−4,644
1958–9	78,119	55,918	94,197	−16,078
1959–60	89,825	63,058	114,579	−24,754

a Excluding grants-in-aid, which amounted to £4,872,000 between 1897 and 1919.

b The figures to 1913 are combined totals for the Colony and Protectorate of Southern Nigeria and the Protectorate of Northern Nigeria. There is a slight duplication where duties collected on goods for Northern Nigeria by Southern Nigeria are included in the revenues of both.

c As from 1927 net railway revenue only is included, instead of the gross railway revenues and expenditures as hitherto.

d To 31 December up to 1920. As from 1921, for the twelve months ended 31 March of the second year stated.

e Includes the mandated area of British Cameroons until its separation in 1960.

f From 1956–7 on, revenue includes receipts of the capital fund other than proceeds of loans and transfers from the current budget, and expenditures include those out of the capital fund (and exclude transfers from current to capital budget).

Source: Helleiner, op. cit., pp. 557–8.

TABLE A5   *Nigerian funded public debt*
            outstanding, 1900–60

31 December	1900	973·0
	1906	2,000·0
	1908	4,000·0
	1911	10,000·0
	1918	11,997·0
31 March	1923	13,609·0
	1929	23,559·2
	1931	28,350·6
	1939	24,764·6
	1945	24,764·6
	1949	22,064·6
	1950	14,438·0
	1953	21,238·0
	1955	17,050·0
	1959	17,050·0
	1960	19,405·4

Source: Helleiner, op. cit., p. 563.

TABLE A6   *Regional governments' revenue and expenditure:
total all regions (£000)*

Period: year ending 31 March	Current revenue				Current expenditure[c]	Capital[a]		Expenditure
	Total	Federal sources[a]	Regional	External[b]		Revenue Grants[e]	Loans	
1951	8,455	—	—	—	7,823	—	—	—
1952	9,761	—	—	—	9,433	—	—	—
1953	18,938	16,885	2,053	—	14,034	—	—	—
1954	18,993	14,780	4,213	—	17,319	—	—	—
1955	36,238	26,916	8,106	1,216	26,823	—	—	—
1956	37,137	23,969	9,580	3,588	34,409	—	—	—
1957	42,255	26,192	14,810	1,253	39,641	23,293	13,502	15,602
1958	43,408	27,266	14,203	1,939	39,100	3,264	2,501	10,202
1959	45,899	29,086	15,902	911	38,421	2,417	2,021	12,560
1960	51,164	35,930	15,234	—	49,564	4,174	3,381	20,968

TABLE A6a   *Revenue and expenditure: Northern Nigeria*

Period: year ending 31 March	Current revenue				Current expenditure[c]	Capital[a]		Expenditure
	Total	Federal sources[a]	Regional	External[b]		Revenue Grants[e]	Loans	
1951	3,134	2,495	639	—	2,991	—	—	—
1952	4,354	3,603	751	—	3,576	—	—	—
1953	8,540	7,652	888	—	4,955	—	—	—
1954	6,338	4,792	1,546	—	6,055	—	—	—
1955	13,123	6,907	5,423	793	9,957	—	—	—
1956	13,748	6,729	4,939	2,080	14,949	—	—	—
1957	14,549	7,833	5,774	942	15,747	4,892	2,500	5,724
1958	14,319	7,850	5,201	1,268	13,459	1,914	2,500	6,216
1959	15,034	8,169	6,865	—	12,806	1,541	2,000	6,126
1960	16,608	11,318	5,290	—	14,551	1,714	2,767	5,678

TABLE A6b　*Revenue and expenditure: Eastern Nigeria*

| Period: year ending 31 March | Current revenue | | | | Current expen- diture[c] | Capital[d] | | Expen- diture |
	Total	Federal sources[a]	Regional	Ex- ternal[b]		Revenue Grants[e]	Loans	
1951	2,947	2,713	234	—	2,814	—	—	—
1952	3,008	2,659	349	—	3,158	—	—	—
1953	4,730	4,190	540	—	4,322	—	—	—
1954	5,348	4,398	950	—	4,736	—	—	—
1955	9,397	8,311	793	293	5,577	—	—	—
1956	9,008	6,670	2,338	—	6,653	—	—	—
1957	12,184	6,904	4,969	311	12,607	—	—	—
1958	13,380	7,084	5,625	671	13,536	—	—	—
1959	14,216	7,418	5,887	911	12,076	—	—	—
1960	14,875	9,373	5,502	—	12,861	1,092	589	3,579

TABLE A6c　*Revenue and expenditure: Western Nigeria*

| Period: year ending 31 March | Current revenue | | | | Current expen- diture[c] | Capital[d] | | Expen- diture |
	Total	Federal sources[a]	Regional	Ex- ternal[b]		Revenue Grants[e]	Loans	
1951	2,374	—	—	—	2,038	—	—	—
1952	2,399	—	—	—	2,699	—	—	—
1953	5,668	5,043	625	—	4,757	—	—	—
1954	7,307	5,590	1,717	—	6,528	—	—	—
1955	13,718	11,698	1,890	130	11,289	—	—	—
1956	14,381	10,570	2,303	1,508	12,807	—	—	—
1957	15,522	11,455	4,067	—	11,287	18,401	11,002	9,878
1958	15,709	12,332	3,377	—	12,105	1,350	1	3,986
1959	16,649	13,499	3,150	—	13,539	876	21	6,434
1960	19,681	15,239	4,442	—	22,152	1,368	25	11,711

[a] For Northern Nigeria only, customs and excise (and mining for 1950–2) revenue is included; for all other regions the total of all federal revenue allocated to the region is included. Special grants from the federal government have also been included.

[b] Includes C.D. and W. grants from the United Kingdom government and also I.C.A. grants from the United States of America government.

[c] Includes payments into the Capital Development funds from the current accounts.

[d] Capital revenue and expenditure shown is that pertaining to the special Capital Development accounts set up by Western and Northern Nigeria.

[e] Capital grants received from both external and local sources.

Note: All figures in the table of consolidated revenue and expenditure for all regions include that of the Southern Cameroons from 1955–6, and as from 1 October 1960 Southern Cameroons is excluded.

Source: *Annual Abstract of Statistics, 1963.*

TABLE A7 *Value of exports and imports*
1900–60 (£,000)

	Domestic exports	Re-exports	Imports
1900	1,887	—	1,735
1901	2,020	—	1,812
1902	2,512	—	1,977
1903	2,357	—	2,129
1904	2,781	—	2,423
1905	2,672	—	2,710
1906	2,950	—	2,837
1907	3,612	252	3,839
1908	3,102	234	4,046
1909	3,829	285	4,530
1910	4,964	295	5,122
1911	5,072	282	5,235
1912	5,477	297	5,952
1913	5,779	318	6,332
1914	6,151	270	6,277
1915	4,874	72	4,984
1916	5,884	146	5,174
1917	8,483	120	5,809
1918	9,359	153	7,423
1919	14,501	175	10,799
1920	16,718	236	20,763
1921	8,028	230	10,237
1922	8,793	253	10,304
1923	10,803	82	10,271
1924	14,391	140	10,948
1925	16,906	57	14,783
1926	16,539	142	12,761
1927	15,470	204	14,438
1928	16,927	148	15,765
1929	17,581	176	13,219

	Domestic exports	Re-exports	Imports
1930	14,778	251	12,617
1931	8,553	218	6,511
1932	9,279	198	7,195
1933	8,560	167	7,195
1934	8,734	140	5,364
1935	11,473	142	7,804
1936	14,930	147	10,830
1937	19,242	194	14,625
1938	9,463	239	8,632
1939	10,203	266	6,757
1940	11,232	372	7,479
1941	13,124	658	6,505
1942	13,696	824	10,490
1943	14,320	830	12,418
1944	16,203	986	15,748
1945	17,123	866	13,583
1946	23,738	888	19,824
1947	43,103	1,211	32,636
1948	61,165	1,308	41,947
1949	79,199	1,868	58,231
1950	88,487	1,735	61,866
1951	116,610	3,455	84,554
1952	125,135	4,395	113,268
1953	120,889	3,343	108,290
1954	146,242	3,290	114,069
1955	129,816	2,718	136,117
1956	132,261	2,312	152,770
1957	124,177	3,357	152,468
1958	132,791	2,759	166,274
1959	160,505	2,992	178,405
1960	165,619	4,095	215,891

Sources: *Trade Reports, Annual Abstract of Statistics* and *Blue Books.*

TABLE A8   *Prices and retail price indices: basic producer prices for palm produce (£ per ton)*

		Grades of palm oil			
			Technical		
Period	Palm kernels	Special	I	II	III
1948	21	—	32·25	30·0	28·5
1949	26	—	42·75	37·1	33·0
1950	26	53·0	42·75	37·1	33·0
1951	32	71·0	55·00	43·0	34·0
1952	36	80·0	61·00	47·0	35·0
1953	34	75·5	58·00	45·0	34·5
1954	34	65·0	50·00	38·0	33·0
1955	31	A60·0	43·00	36·0	28·0
		B52·0			
1956 and 1957	31	54·0	43·00	36·0	28·0
1958	31	53·0	43·00	34·0	27·0
North	31	54·0	45·00	38·0	30·0
West	30	54·0	45·00	38·0	30·0
East	29	48·0	40·00	34·0	26·0
1960					
North	31	54·0	45·00	38·0	30·0
West	30	54·0	45·00	38·0	30·0
East	29	48·0	40·00	34·0	26·0

Notes:

1. The basis of these prices is as follows: Palm kernels – 'naked ex scale' at port of shipment. Palm oil – at bulk oil plant.
2. The maximum allowable free fatty acid content for the different grades of palm oil is as follows:

    Special A=4½ % to 1954, 3½ % from 1955; B=4½ %, 3½ % from 1956.
    Grade I   9%
    Grade II   18%
    Grade III 27% to 1952, 30% from 1953.

3. From 1953 in the North, West and East actual payments to producers were reduced through the application of Purchase Sales Tax (North, West) and Produce Purchase Tax (East) by £1 per ton on palm kernels and £4 per ton on palm oil. For 1958 and 1959 the Eastern Region prices are those actually paid to producers, the board paying the Produce Purchase Tax.

Source: *Annual Abstract of Statistics, 1963.*

TABLE A9   *Prices and retail price indices: basic producer prices for cocoa, groundnuts, benniseed and cotton*

Period (group seasons)	Cocoa (main crop)[a] Grade I	Grade II	Groundnuts Kano area Standard grades	Special grades	Rivers area	Benniseed (£ per ton)	Cotton (N.A.I.) (d. per ton)
1947–8	62·5	60·0	16·0	—	15·0	—	—
1948–9	120·0	115·0	19·2	—	18·0	18·0	4·0
1949–50	100·0	95·0	21·2	—	20·0	20·0	4·0
1950–1	120·0	100·0	21·2	—	20·0	19·2	4·0
1951–2	170·0	155·0	36·0	—	36·0	32·0	6·0
1952–3	170·0	155·0	36·0	—	36·0	36·0	6·0
1953–4[b]	170·0	155·0	36·0	—	36·0	36·0	6·0
1954–5	200·0	185·0	36·5	—	36·0	36·0	6·1
1955–6	200·0	185·0	36·4	37·9	37·5	36·0	6·1
1956–7	150·0	135·0	33·4	36·9	36·5	36·0	6·0
1957–8	150·0	135·0	33·4	38·4	38·0	38·0	6·1
1958–9	150·0	135·0	29·9	34·9	39·5	40·0	6·1
1959–60	c		45·2	d	45·2	40·0 North	6·2
				e	46·5	39·5 East	

[a] The maximum allowance of unfermented beans for the different grades of cocoa is as follows: Grade I, 5 per cent; Grade II, 10 per cent. Prices of light crop cocoa were £2–£3 lower in 1947–8 and £5 lower in 1948–9 to 1952–3. Since then they have been the same as for main crop cocoa.

[b] Through the operation of the Sales of Produce (Taxation) Ordinance of 1953, payments to producers, beginning from the 1953–4 buying seasons, were reduced by the application of such taxes as follows: in the Western and Northern Regions as from 1 January 1953, £4 per ton on cocoa, £1 per ton on groundnuts, 10s. per ton on benniseed and 1d. per lb on cotton (discontinued in the West as from 1954–5).

[c] For the Eastern Region, direct payments of Produce Purchase Tax are made by the board at the following rates per ton: £4 on cocoa, and 10s. on benniseed. At present no produce tax is levied on groundnuts. For 1959–60, separate prices for each region were announced as follows:

	East	North	West
Grade I	156	160	160
Grade II	141	145	145

[d] For 1959–60 only one grade, 'Exportable Quality', replaced the former grades for Kano area.

[e] The price for the Eastern Region is £34.

Note: The basis of these prices is as follows:

Cocoa – 'naked ex scale' at port of shipment. Eastern Region cocoa prices for 1958–9 were £171 for Grade I and £156 for Grade II.
Groundnuts – Kano area: 'naked at railhead, Kano'. From 1954 to 1955, differential prices arising from varying freights were introduced, and there are over 250 different buying station prices. Rivers area: 1st Zone or Zone A buying stations up to 1957–8; for 1958–9, price zones do not apply and the Makurdi price is shown.
Benniseed – all buying stations.
Cotton – all buying stations to 1957–8. Differentials introduced with effect from 1958 to 1959, and 1st Zone ginnery price shown.

Source: *Annual Abstract of Statistics, 1963.*

TABLE A10 *External trade: value of exports* through each port (£000)*

Period	Lagos	Sapele	Warri	Burutu	Degema	Port Harcourt	Calabar	Other ports	Parcel post	Total
1950	50,509	4,989	784	1,315	3,470	20,028	5,947	155	111	87,308
1951	69,434	9,853	1,397	1,790	4,682	21,777	7,083	387	139	116,542
1952	70,592	6,839	1,404	2,970	4,728	29,888	8,670	536	154	125,781
1953	64,823	7,680	1,055	3,312	3,230	31,221	6,810	407	126	118,664
1954	87,233	9,852	1,866	3,351	3,338	30,266	8,014	569	134	144,623
1955	76,211	11,042	1,599	2,383	3,293	25,968	6,811	995	190	128,492
1956	74,589	10,828	1,550	2,933	3,583	28,320	7,144	1,233	156	130,336
1957	67,360	12,022	1,835	3,456	2,558	25,766	7,424	1,618	154	122,193
1958	70,241	13,846	1,508	3,258	2,488	28,138	7,376	1,680	92	128,627
1959	87,319	18,450	3,066	3,691	1,941	32,095	7,905	1,755	74	156,296
1960	83,685	22,571	3,052	4,879	1,435	38,027	7,276	2,174	196	163,295

* Includes re-exports.
Source: *Annual Abstract of Statistics, 1963.*

TABLE AII *External trade: value of imports through each port (£000)*

Period	Lagos	Sapele	Warri	Burutu	Degema	Port Harcourt	Calabar	Other ports	Parcel post	Total
1950	45,215	1,012	1,370	1,370	126	8,850	1,499	409	916	60,951
1951	60,273	1,663	2,257	1,462	98	13,388	2,185	706	1,365	83,397
1952	81,028	1,810	2,604	1,626	147	18,707	2,890	1,120	1,381	111,313
1953	75,951	1,984	2,295	1,377	71	19,000	3,228	1,017	1,758	106,681
1954	79,143	1,863	2,384	1,403	115	21,926	2,985	856	1,729	112,404
1955	96,217	2,266	2,751	1,851	160	24,238	2,747	1,588	2,208	134,026
1956	108,691	2,663	2,942	1,803	84	28,020	2,680	1,330	2,491	150,704
1957	101,611	2,680	2,461	1,015	153	34,922	2,439	1,748	2,284	149,313
1958	112,926	2,558	2,247	2,239	84	37,259	2,260	1,655	2,120	163,348
1959	119,902	2,838	2,660	2,315	73	40,465	2,273	3,170	2,206	175,902
1960	150,226	4,008	4,445	2,378	58	46,260	1,882	1,501	2,945	213,703

Source: *Annual Abstract of Statistics, 1963.*

Bibliography

SELECTED BOOKS

*mentioned in the text

ABOYADE, O., *Foundations of an African Economy: a Study of Investment and Growth in Nigeria*, New York, Frederick A. Praeger, 1966.

ADEDEJI, A., *Nigerian Federal Finance*, London, Hutchinson Educational, 1969.

ADY, P. and COURCIER, M., *Systems of National Accounts in Africa*, Paris, OEEC, 1960.

*AJAYI, J. F. A., *Christian Missions in Nigeria, 1841–1891*, London, Longmans, 1965.

*AJAYI, J. F. A. and SMITH, R., *Yoruba Warfare in the Nineteenth Century*, Cambridge, Cambridge University Press, 1964.

*AJISAFE, A. K., *The Laws and Customs of the Yoruba People*, London, Routledge & Sons, 1924.

ALLEN, CAPTAIN WILLIAM, *A Narrative of the Expedition sent by Her Majesty's Government to the River Niger in 1841*, London, Richard Bentley, 1848, 2 vols.

ANANABA, W., *The Trade Union Movement in Nigeria*, London, C. Hurst & Co., 1969.

ANENE, J. C., *Southern Nigeria in Transition 1885–1906*, Cambridge, Cambridge University Press, 1966.

*ARIKPO, OKOI, *The Development of Modern Nigeria*, Harmondsworth, Penguin Books, 1967.

*AYANDELE, E. A., *The Missionary Impact on Modern Nigeria 1842–1914*, London, Longmans, 1966.

—— *Holy Johnson: Pioneer of African Nationalism, 1836–1917*, London, Frank Cass, 1970.

*BALDWIN, K. D. S., *The Marketing of Cocoa in Western Nigeria*, London and Ibadan, Oxford University Press, 1954.

—— *The Niger Agricultural Project. An Experiment in African Development*, Oxford, Basil Blackwell, 1957.

*BANDINEL, JAMES, *Some Account of the Trade in Slaves from Africa*, London, Frank Cass, 1969.

*BAREAU, PAUL, *The Sterling Area*, London, Longmans, 1948.

*BARTH, H., *Travels and Discoveries in North and Central Africa*, London, Longman, 1857, 5 vols.

BASDEN, G. T., *Among the Ibos of Nigeria*, London, Frank Cass, 1966.

BATTEN, T. R., *Problems of African Development*, London, Oxford University Press, 1947.

*BAUER, P. T., *West African Trade. A Study of Competition, Oligopoly and Monopoly in a Changing Economy*, Cambridge, Cambridge University Press, 1954.

BIOBAKU, S. O., *The Egba and their Neighbours 1842–1872*, Oxford, Clarendon Press, 1957.

BLAKE, J. W., *European Beginnings in West Africa, 1454–1578*, London, Longmans, 1937.

*BLITZ, L. FRANKLIN (ed.), *The Politics and Administration of Nigerian Government*, London, Sweet & Maxwell, and Lagos, African Universities Press, 1965.

*BOAHEN, A. ADU, *Britain, the Sahara and the Western Sudan, 1788–1861*, Oxford, Clarendon Press, 1964.

*—— *Topics in West African History*, London, Longmans, 1966.

BOHANNAN, PAUL and BOHANNAN, LAURA, *The Tiv of Central Nigeria*, London, International African Institute, 1953.

BOHANNAN, PAUL and DALTON, GEORGE (eds), *Markets in Africa*, Evanston, Ill., Northwestern University Press, 1965.

*BOURRET, F. M., *The Gold Coast 1919–1946*, London, Oxford University Press, 1949.

*BOVILL, E. W., *The Golden Trade of the Moors*, London, Oxford University Press, 1968.

BOWER, P. A., *The Balance of Payments of Nigeria in 1936*, Oxford, Basil Blackwell, 1949.

BRETTON, HENRY L., *Power and Stability in Nigeria. The Politics of Decolonization*, New York, Frederick A. Praeger, 1962.

*BROWN, C. V., *The Nigerian Banking System*, London, Allen & Unwin, 1966.

BUCHANAN, K. M. and PUGH, J. C., *Land and People in Nigeria*, London, University of London Press, 1955.

*BURNS, SIR ALAN, *History of Nigeria*, 5th ed., London, Allen & Unwin, 1955.

BURTON, R. F., *Wanderings in West Africa*, London, Tinsley Bros, 1863, 2 vols.

*BUXTON, T. F., *The African Slave Trade and its Remedy*, London, John Murray, 1839.

CALVERT, A. F., *Nigeria and its Tin Fields*, London, Edward Stanford, 1910.

CARNEY, DAVID E., *Government and Economy in British West Africa*, New York, Bookman Associates, 1961.

CARSON, PATRICIA, *Materials for West African History in French Archives*, London, Athlone Press, 1968.

CARY, JOYCE, *Britain and West Africa*, London, Longmans, 1946.

CHALMERS, R., *History of Currency in the British Colonies*, London, HMSO, 1893.

CHUBB, L. T., *Ibo Land Tenure*, 2nd ed., Ibadan, Ibadan University Press, 1961.

COMMONWEALTH OFFICE, *Handbook of Railways in Africa*, London, C B 910, vol. I.

COOK, A. A., *British Enterprise in Nigeria*, Philadelphia, Pa., University of Pennsylvania Press, 1943.

*COUPLAND, SIR REGINALD, *The British Anti-Slavery Movement*, London, Butterworth, 1933.

*COX-GEORGE, N. A. W., *Finance and Development in West Africa. The Sierra Leone Experience*, London, Dennis Dobson, 1961.

CROCKER, W. R., *Nigeria: A Critique of British Colonial Administration*, London, Allen & Unwin, 1936.

*CROWDER, MICHAEL, *The Story of Nigeria*, London, Faber & Faber, 1962.

*—— *West Africa under Colonial Rule*, London, Hutchinson, 1968.

CROWDER, MICHAEL and IKIME, OBARO (eds), *West African Chiefs: Their Changing Status under Colonial Rule and Independence*, Ile-Ife, University of Ife Press, 1970.

CRUICKSHANK, BRODIE, *Eighteen Years on the Gold Coast of Africa*, new ed., London, Frank Cass, 1966, 2 vols.

*CURREY, C. H., *The British Commonwealth since 1815*, Sydney, Angus & Robertson, 1952, 2 vols.

*CURTIN, P. D., *The Atlantic Slave Trade: A Census*, Madison, Wis., University of Wisconsin Press, 1969.

*DAVIDSON, BASIL, *A History of West Africa 1000–1800*, London, Longmans, 1965.

*DAVIES, K. G., *The Royal African Company*, London, Longmans, 1957.

*DAVIES, OLIVER, *West Africa before the Europeans*, London, Methuen, 1967.

*DENHAM, D. and CLAPPERTON, H., *Narrative of Travels and Discoveries in Northern and Central Africa in the Years 1822, 1823 and 1824*, London, John Murray, 1826.

*DERRY, T. K. and WILLIAMS, T. I., *A Short History of Technology*, Oxford, Clarendon Press, 1960.

DIEJOMAOH, VICTOR, *Economic Development in Nigeria; its problems, challenges and prospects*, Princeton, N.J., Princeton University Press, 1965.

DIKE, K. O., *Trade and Politics in the Niger Delta, 1830–1885. An introduction to the economic and political history of Nigeria*, Oxford, Clarendon Press, 1956.

DUE, JOHN F., *Taxation and Economic Development in Tropical Africa*, Cambridge, Mass., Massachusetts Institute of Technology Press, 1963.

*EICHER, CARL K. and LIEDHOLM, CARL (eds), *Growth and Development of the Nigerian Economy*, East Lansing, Mich., Michigan State University Press, 1970.

*EKUNDARE, R. OLUFEMI, *Marriage and Divorce under Yoruba Customary Law*, Ile-Ife, University of Ife Press, 1969.

*ELIAS, T. O., *Groundwork of Nigerian Law*, London, Routledge & Kegan Paul, 1954.

ENGLISH, M. C., *An Outline of Nigerian History*, London, Longmans, 1959.

EVANS, IFOR L., *The British in Tropical Africa. An Historical Outline*, Cambridge, Cambridge University Press, 1929.

EZERA, K., *Constitutional Developments in Nigeria*, Cambridge, Cambridge University Press, 1960.

*FAGE, J. D., *An Atlas of African History*, London, Edward Arnold, 1958.

—— *An Introduction to the History of West Africa*, Cambridge, Cambridge University Press, 1955.

FAULKNER, O. T. and MACKIE, J. R., *West African Agriculture*, Cambridge, Cambridge University Press, 1933.

*FORDE, DARYLL and KABERRY, P. M. (eds), *West African Kingdoms in the Nineteenth Century*, London, Oxford University Press, 1967.

FRANKEL, HERBERT S., *Capital Investment in Africa, its Course and Effects*, New York, Oxford University Press, 1938.

GALLETTI, R., BALDWIN, K. D. S. and DINA, I. O., *Nigerian Cocoa Farmers: An Economic Survey of Yoruba Cocoa Farming Families*, London, Oxford University Press, 1956.

*GEARY, SIR WILLIAM, *Nigeria under British Rule*, London, Frank Cass, 1965 (first published by Methuen, 1927).

*GOUROU, PIERRE, *The Tropical World. Its Social and Economic Conditions and its Future Status*, 3rd ed., London, Longmans, 1961.

*GUGGISBERG, G., *The Gold Coast (1920–1926)*, Accra, Government Printer, 1927.

*HAILEY, LORD W. M., *An African Survey. Revised to 1956. A study of problems arising in Africa south of the Sahara*, London, Oxford University Press, 1957.

HAINES, C. G. (ed.), *Africa Today*, Baltimore, Johns Hopkins Press, 1955.

*HALLETT, ROBIN (ed.), *The Niger Journal of Richard and John Lander*, London, Routledge & Kegan Paul, 1965.

*—— (ed.), *Records of the African Association 1788–1831*, London, Thomas Nelson, 1964.

HANCE, WILLIAM A., *African Economic Development*, London, Oxford University Press, 1958.

*HANCOCK, W. K., *A Survey of British Commonwealth Affairs*, vol. II, part 2, London, Oxford University Press, 1942.

*HARGREAVES, J. D., *Prelude to the Partition of West Africa*, London, Macmillan, and New York, St Martin's Press, 1963.

HARRIS, T. H., *Domestic Slavery in Southern Nigeria*, London, 1912.

HARRISON-CHURCH, R. J., *West Africa: a study of the environment and of man's use of it*, London, Longmans, 1957.

HAWKINS, E. K., *Road Transport in Nigeria. A Study of African Enterprise*, London, Oxford University Press, 1958.

*HELLEINER, GERALD K., *Peasant Agriculture, Government and Economic Growth in Nigeria*, Homewood, Ill., Richard D. Irwin, 1966.

HERKOVITS, M. J. and HARWITZ, M., *Economic Transition in Africa*, Evanston, Ill., Northwestern University Press, 1964.

HICKS, URSULA K., *Development From Below: Local Government and Finance in Developing Countries of the Commonwealth*, Oxford, Clarendon Press, 1961.

HILL, POLLY, *The Gold Coast Cocoa-Farmer*, London, Oxford University Press, 1956.

—— *The Migrant Cocoa-Farmers of Southern Ghana. A Study in Rural Capitalism*, Cambridge, Cambridge University Press, 1963.

HILLIARD, F. H., *A Short History of Education in British West Africa*, London, Thomas Nelson, 1957.

*HODDER, B. W. and UKWU, V. I., *Markets in West Africa*, Ibadan, Ibadan University Press, 1969.

HOGG, V. W. and ROELANDTS, C. M., *Nigerian Motor Vehicle Traffic. An Economic Forecast*, London, Oxford University Press, 1962.

*HUISH, ROBERT, *The Travels of Richard and John Lander*, London, J. Saunders, 1836.

HUXLEY, E., *Four Guineas, a journey through West Africa*, London, Chatto & Windus, 1954.

IDOWU, E. B., *Oludumare: God in Yoruba Belief*, London, Longmans, 1962.

IKIME, OBARO, *Niger Delta rivalry: Itsekiri–Urhobo relations and the European Presence 1884–1934*, London, Longmans, 1969.

IRVINE, F. R., *A Textbook of West African Agriculture*, 2nd ed., London, Oxford University Press, 1953.

JACKSON, I. C., *Advance in Africa. A study of community development in Eastern Nigeria*, London, Oxford University Press, 1956.

JOHNSON, BRUCE F., *The Staple Food Economies of West Tropical Africa*, Stanford, Calif., Stanford University Press, 1958.

JOHNSON, SAMUEL, *The History of the Yorubas*, Lagos, CMS Bookshops, 1921.

JONES, G. H., *The Earth Goddess. A Study of Native Farming on the West Coast of Africa*, London, Royal Empire Society (Imperial Studies 12), 1936.

*JONES, G. I., *The Trading States of the Oil Rivers*, London, Oxford University Press, 1963.

KILBY, PETER, *Industrialisation in an Open Economy: Nigeria 1945–1966*, Cambridge, Cambridge University Press, 1969.

KINGSLEY, M. H., *West African Studies*, 3rd ed., London, Frank Cass, 1964.

—— *Travels in West Africa*, 3rd ed. (with a new introduction by J. E. Flint), London, Frank Cass, 1964.

KIRK-GREENE, A. H. M., *Lugard and the Amalgamation of Nigeria*, London, Frank Cass, 1968.

*—— *Crisis and Conflict in Nigeria: A Documentary Source Book 1966–1970*, London, Oxford University Press, 1971, 2 vols.

*KLINGBERG, FRANK, *The Anti-Slavery Movement in England, A Study of English Humanitarianism*, New Haven, 1926.

KNOOR, KLAVS E., *British Colonial Theories, 1570–1850*, Toronto, 1944.

KNOWLES, L. C. A. and KNOWLES, C. M., *The Economic Development of the British Overseas Empire*, London, Routledge & Sons, 1936.

KOPYTOFF, J. K., *A preface to modern Nigeria: the 'Sierra Leonians' in Yoruba, 1830–1890*, Madison, Wis., University of Wisconsin Press, 1965.

LAWRENCE, A. W., *Trade Castles and Forts of West Africa*, London, Jonathan Cape, 1963.

*LEUBUSCHER, CHARLOTTE, *Bulk-Buying from the Colonies*, London, Oxford University Press, 1956.

*LEWIS, W. ARTHUR (ed.), *Tropical Development 1880–1913*, London, Allen & Unwin, 1970.

*LLOYD, C. CHRISTOPHER, *The Navy and the Slave Trade*, London, Longmans, 1949.

LOYNES, J. B., *The West African Currency Board 1912–1962*, London, WACB, 1962.

LUGARD, LADY FLORA, *A Tropical Dependency*, London, James Nisbet, 1905.

*LUGARD, LORD, *The Dual Mandate in British Tropical Africa*, Edinburgh and London, Blackwood & Sons, 1922.

MACDONALD, A. J., *Trade, Politics and Christianity in Africa and the East*, London, Longmans, 1916.

MACFARLANE, DAVID L. and OWOREN, MARTIN A., *Investment in Oil Palm Plantations in Nigeria: A Financial and Economic Appraisal*, Enugu, Economic Development Institute, 1965.

*MACKINTOSH, JOHN P., *Nigerian Government and Politics*, London, Allen & Unwin, 1966.

*MACMILLAN, ALLISTER (ed.), *The Red Book of West Africa*, London, Frank Cass, 1969.

MACMUNN, SIR G. F., *Slavery through the Ages*, London, Nicolson & Watson, 1938.

*MANNIX, DANIEL, with COWLEY, MALCOLM, *Black Cargoes. A History of the Atlantic Slave Trade, 1518–1865*, London, Longmans, 1963.

*MARTIN, ANNE, *The Oil Palm Economy of the Ibibio Farmer*, Ibadan, Ibadan University Press, 1956.

*MARTIN, E. C., *The British West African Settlements 1750–1821*, London, Longmans, 1927.

*MCPHEE, ALLAN, *The Economic Revolution in British West Africa*, London, Routledge & Sons, 1926.

MEEK, C. K., *Land Law and Custom in the Colonies*, London, Oxford University Press, 1946.

*MILNE, A. H., *Sir Alfred Lewis Jones: A Story of Energy and Success*, Liverpool, H. Young & Sons, 1914.

*MOREL, E. D., *Nigeria: its Peoples and its Problems*, 3rd ed., London, Frank Cass, 1968.

*NADEL, S. F., *A Black Byzantium*, London, Oxford University Press, 1942.

NEWBURY, C. W., *British Policy towards West Africa. Select Documents 1786–1874*, Oxford, Clarendon Press, 1965.

*—— *The Western Slave Coast and its Rulers*, Oxford, Clarendon Press, 1961.

*NEWLYN, W. T. and ROWAN, D. C., *Money and Banking in British Colonial Africa*, Oxford, Clarendon Press, 1954.

NEWMARK, DANIEL S., *Foreign Trade and Economic Development in Africa*, Stanford, Calif., Stanford University Press, 1963.

*NICOLSON, I. F., *The Administration of Nigeria 1900–1960*, Oxford, Clarendon Press, 1969.

NIVEN, C. R., *The Land and People of West Africa*, London, A. & C. Black, 1958.

*NIVEN, SIR REX, *The War of Nigerian Unity*, Ibadan, Evans Brothers, 1970.

*OJO, G. J. A., *Yoruba Palaces*, London, University of London Press, 1966.

*OKIGBO, P. N. C., *Nigerian National Accounts, 1950–7*, Enugu, Government Printer, 1962.

—— *Nigerian Public Finance*, Lagos, Longmans of Nigeria, 1966.

*OLIVER, E., *Economic and Commercial Conditions in Nigeria*, London, HMSO, 1957.

OLUWASANMI, H. A., *Agriculture and Nigerian Economic Development*, Ibadan and London, Oxford University Press, 1966.

ONYEMELUKWE, C. C., *Problems of Industrial Planning and Management in Nigeria*, Lagos, Longmans of Nigeria, 1966.

*OREWA, G. O., *Taxation in Western Nigeria*, London, Oxford University Press, 1962.

*ORR, SIR CHARLES, *The Making of Northern Nigeria* (with a new introduction by A. H. M. Kirk-Greene), London, Frank Cass, 1965.

PALMER, SIR HERBERT RICHMOND, *The Carthaginian Voyage to West Africa in 500 BC*, Bathurst, Government Printer, 1931.

*PEDLER, F. J., *Economic Geography of West Africa*, London, Longmans, 1955.

*PERHAM, MARGERY, *Native Administration in Nigeria*, London, Oxford University Press, 1937.

—— *Africans and British Rule*, London, Oxford University Press, 1941.

*—— (ed.), *Mining, Commerce and Finance in Nigeria*, London, Faber & Faber, 1946–8.

*—— (ed.), *The Native Economics of Nigeria*, London, Faber & Faber, 1946–8.

PERSONS, H. A., *Colonial Coinages of British Africa, with the adjacent islands*, London, Spink, 1950.

*PETCH, G. A., *Economic Development and Modern West Africa*, London, University of London Press, 1961.

PIM, SIR A., *The Financial and Economic History of the African Tropical Territories*, Oxford, Clarendon Press, 1940.

—— *Colonial Agricultural Production*, London, Oxford University Press, 1946.

PREST, A. R., *War Economics of Primary Producing Countries*, Cambridge, Cambridge University Press, 1948.

—— *The Investigation of National Income in British Tropical Dependencies*, London, Athlone Press, 1957.

—— *Public Finance in Underdeveloped Countries*, London, Weidenfeld & Nicolson, 1962.

PREST, A. R. and STEWART, I. G., *The National Income of Nigeria 1950–1*, London, HMSO (Colonial Research Studies 11), 1954.

RODNEY, W., *A History of the Upper Guinea Coast 1545–1800*, Oxford, Clarendon Press, 1970.

ROOT, J. W., *The Trade Relations of the British Empire*, Liverpool, 1903.

ROX, RALPH, *The Colonial Policy of British Imperialism*, New York, 1934.

*SCHATZ, SAYRE P., *Development Bank Lending in Nigeria: The Federal Loans Board*, Ibadan and London, Oxford University Press, 1964.

—— *Economics, Politics and Administration in Government Lending: The Regional Loans Boards of Nigeria*, Ibadan, Oxford University Press, 1970.

*SMITH, ADAM, *The Wealth of Nations*, London, J. M. Dent & Sons (Everyman Library edition), 2 vols.

SMITH, T. E. and BLACKER, J. G. C., *Population Characteristics of the Commonwealth Countries of Tropical Africa*, London, Athlone Press (Commonwealth Paper 9), 1963.

STAMP, L. D., *Africa: A Study in Tropical Development*, London, Chapman & Hall, 1953.

STEWART, I. G. and ORD, H. W. (eds), *African Primary Products and International Trade*, Edinburgh, Edinburgh University Press, 1965.

STRICKLAND, CLAUDE, *Co-operation for Africa*, London, Oxford University Press, 1933.

*TALBOT, P. A., *The Peoples of Southern Nigeria*, London, Humphrey Milford, 1926, vol. 1.

*THOMSON, JOSEPH, *Mungo Park and the Niger*, London, G. Philip & Son, 1890.

*VINER, JACOB, *International Trade and Economic Development*, Oxford, Clarendon Press, 1953.

*WALKER, GILBERT, *Traffic and Transport in Nigeria*, London, HMSO (Colonial Research Studies 27), 1959.

WALLIS, C. B., *The Advance of our West African Empire*, London, T. Fisher Unwin, 1903.

*WARD, W. E. F., *Government in West Africa*, London, Allen & Unwin, 1965.

*WELLESLEY, DOROTHY, *Sir George Goldie, Founder of Nigeria*, London, Macmillan, 1934.

*WHITFORD, JOHN, *Trading Life in Western and Central Africa*, London, Frank Cass, 1967.

*WILLIAMS, ERIC E., *Capitalism and Slavery*, Chapel Hill, N.C., University of North Carolina Press, 1945.

*WILSON, CHARLES, *A History of Unilever. A Study in Economic Growth and Social Change*, London, Cassell & Co., 1954, 2 vols.

*WOOLF, L. S., *Empire and Commerce in Africa*, London, Allen & Unwin, 1920.

WRAITH, RONALD E., *Local Government in West Africa*, London, Allen & Unwin, 1964.

*WYNDHAM, H., *The Atlantic and Slavery*, London, Oxford University Press, 1935.

*YESUFU, T. M., *An Introduction to Industrial Relations in Nigeria*, Ibadan, Oxford University Press, 1962.

—— (ed.), *Manpower Problems and Economics Development in Nigeria*, Ibadan, Oxford University Press, 1969.

SELECTED JOURNAL ARTICLES

ABOYADE, O., 'Some Implications of Nigerian Imports Structure', *Nigerian Journal of Economic and Social Studies*, vol. 4, no. 1 (March 1962), pp. 51–61.

ADEJUWON, J. O., 'Crop–Climate Relationships: The Example of Cocoa in Western Nigeria', *Nigerian Geographical Journal*, vol. 5, no. 1 (January 1962), pp. 21–31.

ADERIBIGBE, A. B., 'Trade and British Expansion in the Lagos Area in the Second Half of the Nineteenth Century', *Nigerian Journal of Economic and Social Studies*, vol. 4, no. 2 (July 1962), pp. 188–95.

ADLER, JOHN H., 'The Economic Development of Nigeria: Reply', *Journal of Political Economy*, vol. 64, no. 5 (October 1956), pp. 435–41.

ADY, P., 'Bulk Purchasing and the Colonial Producer', *Bulletin of the Oxford University Institute of Statistics*, vol. 9, no. 10 (October 1947), pp. 321–40.

—— 'Trends in Cocoa Production in British West Africa', *Bulletin of the Oxford University Institute of Statistics*, vol. 11, no. 12 (December 1949), pp. 389–404.

—— 'Fluctuations in Incomes of Primary Producers, A Comment', *Economic Journal*, vol. 3, no. 251 (September 1953), pp. 594–606.

AJAYI, F. J. A., 'The British Occupation of Lagos, 1851–61', *Nigerian Magazine*, vol. 69 (August 1961), pp. 96–105.

ALUKO, S. A., 'Agriculture and Economic Development in Nigeria', *Nigerian Journal of Economic and Social Studies*, vol. 1, no. 1 (May 1959), pp. 27–40.

—— 'Financing Economic Development in Nigeria', *Nigerian Journal of Economic and Social Studies*, vol. 3, no. 1 (November 1961), pp. 39–67.

—— 'How many Nigerians? An Analysis of Nigeria's Census Problems, 1901–63', *Journal of Modern African Studies*, vol. 3 (1965), pp. 371–92.

ANJORIN, A. O., 'The Background to the Amalgamation of Nigeria in 1914', *ODU: Journal of African Studies, University of Ife*, vol. 3, no. 2 (January 1967), pp. 72–86.

AYANDELE, E. A., 'Observation and Some Social and Economic Aspects of Slavery in Pre-Colonial Northern Nigeria', *Nigerian Journal of Economic and Social Studies*, vol. 9, no. 3 (November 1967), pp. 329–38.

BASCOM, W. R., 'The Esusu: A Credit Institution of the Yoruba', *Journal of the Royal Anthropological Institute*, vol. 82, part 1 (1952), pp. 63–9.

—— 'Urbanization Among the Yorubas', *American Journal of Sociology*, vol. 60, no. 5 (March 1955), pp. 446–54.

BAUER, P. B., 'The Economic Development of Nigeria', *Journal of Political Economy*, vol. 63, no. 5 (October 1955), pp. 398–411.

BAUER, P. B. and PAISH, F. W., 'The Reduction of Fluctuations in the Income of Primary Producers', *Economic Journal*, vol. 62, no. 248 (December 1952), pp. 750–80.

—— 'The Reduction of Fluctuations in the Income of Primary Producers: Further Considered', *Economic Journal*, vol. 64, no. 256 (December 1954), pp. 704–29.

BAUER, P. B. and YAMEY, B. S., 'The Economics of Marketing Reform', *Journal of Political Economy*, vol. 62, no. 3 (June 1954), pp. 210–35.

—— 'A Case Study of Response to Price in an Under-Developed Country', *Economic Journal*, vol. 69, no. 276 (December 1959), pp. 800–5.

BERRY, S. S., 'Christianity and the Rise of Cocoa-Growing in Ibadan and Ondo', *Journal of the Historical Society of Nigeria*, vol. 4, no. 3 (December 1968), pp. 439–51.

BOHANNAN, PAUL, 'The Impact of Money on an African Subsistence Economy', *Journal of Economic History*, vol. 19, no. 4 (December 1959), pp. 491–503.

BROWN, C. V., 'The Supply of Bank Money in Nigeria', *The Banker's Magazine* (November and December 1960).

CALLAWAY, A. C., 'Unemployment among African School Leavers', *Journal of Modern African Studies*, vol. 1, no. 3 (September 1963), pp. 351–71.

—— 'Nigeria's Indigenous Education: The Apprentice System', *ODU: Journal of African Studies, University of Ife*, vol. 1, no. 1 (July 1964), pp. 62–79.

CHARLE, EDWIN G., JR, 'An Appraisal of British Imperial Policy with Respect to the Extraction of Mineral Resources in Nigeria', *Journal of Economics and Social Studies*, vol. 6, no. 1 (March 1964), pp. 37–42.

CLIFFORD, SIR HUGH, 'United Nigeria', *Journal of the Royal African Society*,[1] vol. 21 (1921–2), pp. 1–14.

COPPOCK, J. T., 'Agricultural Geography in Nigeria', *Nigerian Geographical Journal*, vol. 7, no. 2 (December 1964), pp. 67–90.

COWAN, ALEX A., 'Early Trading Conditions in the Bight of Biafra', *Journal of the Royal African Society*, vol. 35 (1935–6), pp. 53–4.

COX-GEORGE, N. A. W., 'Fiscal Experiments in Eastern Nigeria', *Public Finance*, vol. 12, no. 2 (1957), pp. 173–80.

CRABTREE, W. A., 'Great Britain in West Africa', *Journal of the Royal African Society*, vol. 19 (1919–20), pp. 196–205.

DAAKU, K. YEBOA, 'Pre-European Currencies of West Africa and Western Sudan', *Bulletin of the Historical Society of Ghana*, no. 2 (1961), p. 13.

DENNETT, R. E., 'Agricultural Progress in Nigeria', *Journal of the Royal African Society*, vol. 18 (1918–19), pp. 266–89.

DENTON, SIR GEORGE, 'Twenty-three years in Lagos and the Gambia', *Journal of the Royal African Society*, vol. 11 (1911–12), p. 130.

[1] Later published as *African Affairs*.

DOSSER, DOUGLAS, 'The Formation of Development Plans in British Colonies', *Economic Journal*, vol. 69, no. 274 (June 1959), pp. 255–66.

DUGGAN, E. DE C., 'The Cotton Growing Industry of Nigeria', *Journal of the Royal African Society*, vol. 21 (1921–2), pp. 199–207.

—— 'The Cotton Prospects of Northern Nigeria', *Journal of the Royal African Society*, vol. 26 (1926–7), pp. 10–20.

ECONOMIST INTELLIGENCE UNIT, 'The Natural Rubber Production in Nigeria', *Rubber Trends*, no. 7 (September 1960), pp. 23–8.

EDOKPAYI, S. I., 'The Niger and the Benue in Nigeria's Economy: Past, Present and Future', *Nigerian Journal of Economic and Social Studies*, vol. 3, no. 1 (November 1961), pp. 68–77.

EKUNDARE, R. O., 'The Price Equalization Fund in Nigeria', *Nigerian Journal of Economic and Social Studies*, vol. 2, no. 1 (June 1960), pp. 6–11.

—— 'The Evolution of Nigeria's Income Tax Systems from the Colonial Period to 1945', *Quarterly Journal of Administration, University of Ife*, vol. 4, no. 3 (April 1970), pp. 255–67.

—— 'Nigeria's Second National Development Plan As A Weapon of Social Change', *African Affairs*, vol. 70, no. 279 (April 1971).

—— 'Salary and Wages Reviews since 1946', *Quarterly Journal of Administration, University of Ife*, vol. 6, no. 2 (January 1972), pp. 157–70.

—— 'The Political Economy of Private Investment in Nigeria', *Journal of Modern African Studies*, vol. 10, no. 1 (May 1972), pp. 37–56.

FAGE, J. D., 'Slavery and the Slave Trade in the Context of West African History', *Journal of African History*, vol. 10, no. 3 (1969), pp. 393–404.

FELL, SIR MILTON, 'The Tin Mining Industry in Nigeria', *Journal of the Royal African Society*, vol. 38 (1938–9), pp. 246–58.

FRIEDMAN, MILTON, 'The Reduction of Fluctuations in the Incomes of Primary Producers', *Economic Journal*, vol. 64, no. 256 (December 1954), pp. 698–703.

GREAVES, IDA, 'Sterling Balances of Colonial Territories', *Economic Journal*, vol. 61, no. 242 (June 1951), pp. 433–9.

—— 'Sterling Balances and the Colonial Currency System: A Comment', *Economic Journal*, vol. 63, no. 252 (December 1953), pp. 921–3.

—— 'The Character of British Colonial Trade', *Journal of Political Economy*, vol. 62, no. 1 (February 1954), pp. 1–11.

GROVE, A. T., 'Soil Erosion and Population Problems in South-East Nigeria', *Geographical Journal*, vol. 117, part III (September 1951), pp. 291–306.

HAIG, E. F. G., 'Co-operatives in Nigeria', *Journal of the Royal African Society*, vol. 49 (1949–50), pp. 41–50.

HANSON, A. H., 'Public Enterprise in Nigeria: I, Federal Public Utilities', *Public Administration*, vol. 36 (Winter 1958), pp. 366–84.

—— 'Public Enterprise in Nigeria: II, Development Corporations', *Public Administration*, vol. 37 (Winter 1959), pp. 21–40.

HARRIS, JOHN R., 'Nigerian Enterprise in the Printing Industry', *Nigerian Journal of Economic and Social Studies*, vol. 10, no. 2 (July 1968), pp. 215–27.

HAWKINS, E. K., 'A Note on the Terms of Trade of Nigeria', *Review of Economic Studies*, vol. 22 (1), no. 57 (1954–5), pp. 47–56.

—— 'The Growth of a Money Economy in Nigeria and Ghana', *Oxford Economic Papers*, vol. 10, no. 3 (October 1958), pp. 339–54.

—— 'Marketing Boards and Economic Development in Nigeria and Ghana', *Review of Economic Studies*, vol. 26 (1), no. 69 (October 1958), pp. 51–2.

—— 'Capital Formation in Nigeria and Ghana, 1946–1955', *Bulletin of the Oxford University Institute of Statistics*, vol. 21, no. 1 (February 1959), pp. 39–46.

HAZLEWOOD, A., 'Sterling Balances and the Colonial Currency System (A Note)', *Economic Journal*, vol. 62, no. 248 (December 1952), pp. 942–5.

—— 'A Reply', *Economic Journal*, vol. 64, no. 255 (September 1954), pp. 616–17.

—— 'Trade Balances and Statutory Marketing in Primary Export Economics', *Economic Journal*, vol. 67, no. 265 (March 1957), pp. 74–82.

HELLEINER, GERALD K., 'The Eastern Nigeria Development Corporation: A Study in Sources and Uses of Public Development Funds, 1949–1962', *Nigerian Journal of Economic and Social Studies*, vol. 6, no. 1 (March 1964), pp. 98–123.

—— 'The Northern Region Development Corporation: a Wide-Ranging Development Institution, 1949–1962', *Nigerian Journal of Economic and Social Studies*, vol. 6, no. 2 (July 1964), pp. 239–57.

—— 'The Fiscal Role of the Marketing Boards in Nigerian Economic Development, 1947–61', *Economic Journal*, vol. 74, no. 295 (September 1964), pp. 582–610.

—— 'Marketing Boards and Domestic Stabilization in Nigeria', *Review of Economics and Statistics*, vol. 48, no. 1 (February 1966).

HICKS, U. K., 'The New Tax System in Eastern Nigeria', *Journal of African Administration*, vol. 8, no. 4 (October 1956), pp. 202–5.

HILL, P., 'Fluctuations in Incomes of Primary Producers', *Economic Journal*, vol. 63, no. 250 (June 1953), pp. 468–741.

HIMBURY, W. H., 'Empire Cotton', *Journal of the Royal African Society*, vol. 17 (1917–18), pp. 262–75.

HODDER, B. W., 'Rural Periodic Day Markets in Part of Yorubaland, Western Nigeria', *Transactions and Papers of the British Institute of Geographers*, publication no. 29 (1961), pp. 149–59.

HOPKINS, A. G., 'The Lagos Strike of 1897: An Exploration in Nigerian Labour History', *Past and Present*, no. 35 (December 1966), pp. 133–55.

—— 'The Currency Revolution in South-West Nigeria in the Late Nineteenth Century', *Journal of the Historical Society of Nigeria*, vol. 3, no. 3 (December 1966), pp. 471–83.

—— 'Economic Imperialism in West Africa: Lagos, 1880–1892', *Economic History Review*, vol. 21, no. 3 (December 1968), pp. 580–606.

—— 'The Creation of a Colonial Monetary System: The Origins of the West African Currency Board', *African Historical Studies*, vol. 3, no. 1 (1970), pp. 101–32.

HOWES, F. N., 'The Early Introduction of Cocoa to West Africa', *Journal of the Royal African Society*, vol. 45 (1945–6), pp. 152–3.

JOHNSON, MARION, 'The Cowrie Currencies of West Africa', *Journal of African History*, vol. 11, nos. 1 and 3 (1970), pp. 17–49 and 331–53 respectively.

JOHNSRUB, ROBERT O., 'A Decade of Nigerian Cotton, 1949–1958', *Nigerian Geographical Journal*, vol. 3, no. 2 (November 1960), pp. 1–14.

JONES, G. I., 'The Beef Cattle Trade in Nigeria', *Africa*, vol. 16, no. 1 (January 1946), pp. 29–30.

KILBY, PETER, 'Organisation and Productivity in Backward Economies', *Quarterly Journal of Economics*, vol. 76, no. 2 (May 1962), pp. 303–10.

—— 'Technical Education in Nigeria', *Bulletin of the Oxford University Institute of Economics and Statistics*, vol. 26, no. 2 (1964), pp. 181–94.

KIRK-GREENE, A. H. M., 'The Major Currencies in Nigerian History', *Journal of the Historical Society of Nigeria*, vol. 2, no. 1 (December 1960), pp. 132–50.

LAMB, P. H., 'Agricultural Development in Nigeria', *Journal of the Royal African Society*, vol. 30 (1930–1), pp. 119–27.

LEUBUSCHER, CHARLOTTE, 'Marketing Schemes for Native-grown Produce in African Territories', *Africa*, vol. 12, no. 2 (1939), pp. 163–87.

LLOYD, P. C., 'The Integration of the new Economic Classes with Local Government in Western Nigeria', *Journal of the Royal African Society*, vol. 52 (1951–2), pp. 327–34.

MABOGUNJE, AKIN L., 'The Economic Implications of the Pattern of Urbanization in Nigeria', *Nigerian Journal of Economic and Social Studies*, vol. 7, no. 1 (March 1965), pp. 9–30.

MABOGUNJE, AKIN L. and GLEAVE, MICHAEL B., 'Changing Agricultural Landscape in Southern Nigeria: The Example of Egba Division, 1850–1950', *Nigerian Geographical Journal*, vol. 7, no. 1 (June 1964), pp. 1–15.

MANNING, PATRICK, 'Some Export Statistics for Nigeria 1880–1905', *Nigerian Journal of Economic and Social Studies*, vol. 9, no. 2 (July 1967).

MYINT, H. L. A., 'The "Classical Theory" of International Trade and Underdeveloped Countries', *Economic Journal*, vol. 68, no. 270 (June 1958), pp. 317–37.

NICULESCU, B., 'The Reduction of Fluctuations in the Incomes of Primary Producers', *Economic Journal*, vol. 64, no. 256 (December 1954), pp. 730–43.

NWOGU, E. D., 'Oil in Nigeria', *Nigerian Geographical Journal*, vol. 3, no. 2 (November 1960), pp. 15–25.

OGUNSHEYE, AYO, 'Marketing Boards and the Stabilization of Producer Prices and Incomes in Nigeria', *Nigerian Journal of Economic and Social Studies*, vol. 7, no. 2 (July 1965), pp. 131–9.

OLAKANPO, O., 'Distributive Trade – A Critique of Government Policy', *Nigerian Journal of Economic and Social Studies*, vol. 5, no. 2 (July 1963), pp. 237–46.

OLUWASANMI, H. A. and ALAO, J. A., 'The Role of Credit in the

Transformation of Traditional Agriculture: The Western Nigerian Experience', *Nigerian Journal of Economic and Social Studies*, vol. 7, no. 1 (March 1965), pp. 31–50.

ONI, S. A., 'Production Response in Nigerian Agriculture: A Study of Palm Produce, 1949–1966', *Nigerian Journal of Economic and Social Studies*, vol. 11, no. 1 (March 1969), pp. 81–92.

ONITIRI, H. M. A., 'Import Duties and the Nigerian Balance of External Payments', *Nigerian Journal of Economic and Social Studies*, vol. 2, no. 1 (June 1960), pp. 26–40.

—— 'Recent Trends in Nigerian Balance of Payments', *Nigerian Journal of Economic and Social Studies*, vol. 7, no. 2 (July 1965), pp. 145–57.

ORME-SMITH, R., 'Maiduguri Market – Northern Nigeria', *Journal of the Royal African Society*, vol. 37 (1937–8), pp. 318–25.

OSOBA, S. O., 'The Phenomenon of Labour Migration in the Era of British Colonial Rule: A Neglected Aspect of Nigeria's Social History', *Journal of the Historical Society of Nigeria*, vol. 4, no. 4 (June 1969), pp. 515–38.

RATTRAY, R. S., 'The Drum Language of West Africa', *Journal of the Royal African Society*, vol. 22 (1922–3), pp. 226–36.

ROBINSON, STANLEY, 'Resources of West Africa', *Journal of the Royal African Society*, vol. 18 (1918–19), pp. 190–7.

ROOT, J. W., 'British Trade with West Africa', *Journal of the Royal African Society*, vol. 1 (1901–2), pp. 40–63.

ROWAN, D. C. 'The Native Banking Boom in Nigeria', *The Banker*, vol. 97, no. 309 (October 1951), pp. 244–9.

SCHATZ, SAYRE P., 'Under-utilized Resources, Directed Demand, and Deficit Financing, Illustrated by Reference to Nigeria', *Quarterly Journal of Economics*, vol. 73, no. 4 (November 1959), pp. 633–44.

—— 'Obstacles to Nigerian Private Investment', *Nigerian Journal of Economic and Social Studies*, vol. 4, no. 1 (March 1962), pp. 66–73.

SCHATZ, SAYRE P. and EDOKPAYI, S. I., 'Economic Attitudes of Nigerian Businessmen', *Nigerian Journal of Economic and Social Studies*, vol. 4, no. 3 (November 1962), pp. 247–56.

SHELFORD, CAPTAIN F., 'Transport in Africa by Road, Rail, Air and Water', *Journal of the Royal African Society*, vol. 19 (1919–20), pp. 165–75.

SONUBI, O., 'A Note on Nigeria's Youth Employment Problems',

Nigerian Journal of Economic and Social Studies, vol. 4, no. 3 (November 1962), pp. 228–32.

STAMP, L. DUDLEY, 'Land Utilization and Soil Erosion in Nigeria', *Geographical Review*, vol. 28 (1938), pp. 32–45.

STEWART, IAN G., 'Nigeria's Economic Prospects', *Three Banks Reviews*, no. 49 (March 1961), pp. 3–15.

UGOH, S. U., 'The Nigerian Cement Company', *Nigerian Journal of Economic and Social Studies*, vol. 6, no. 1 (March 1964), pp. 72–91.

UZOAGA, W. OKEFIE, 'Bank Money in Nigeria, 1950–62', *Nigerian Journal of Economic and Social Studies*, vol. 6, no. 1 (March 1964), pp. 92–7.

VIELROSE, EGON, 'Import and Export Substitution in Nigeria', *Nigerian Journal of Economic and Social Studies*, vol. 10, no. 2 (July 1968), pp. 183–90.

WEBSTER, J. B., 'The Bible and the Plough', *Journal of the Historical Society of Nigeria*, vol. 2, no. 4 (December 1963), pp. 418–34.

WELLS, J. C., 'Government Investment in Nigerian Agriculture: Some Unsettled Issues', *Nigerian Journal of Economic and Social Studies*, vol. 8, no. 1 (March 1966), pp. 37–48.

WILLIAMS, D. M., 'West African Marketing Boards', *Journal of Royal African Society*, vol. 52 (1951–2), pp. 45–54.

WILLIAMS, J. B., 'The Development of British Trade with West Africa, 1750–1850', *Political Science Quarterly*, vol. 1 (1935), pp. 194–213.

WILLIAMS, R. W., 'Trade Unions in Africa', *Journal of the Royal African Society*, vol. 54 (1954–5), pp. 267–79.

WILLIAMS, SIMON, 'Start-up of a Textile Industry, Cost and Benefits to the Economy of an Under-developed Country', *Nigerian Journal of Economic and Social Studies*, vol. 4, no. 3 (November 1962), pp. 247–56.

WRIGLEY, CHRISTOPHER, 'Historicism in Africa: Slavery and State Formation', *African Affairs*, vol. 70, no. 279 (April 1971), pp. 113–24.

YESUFU, T. M., 'Nigerian Manpower Problems (A Preliminary Assessment)', *Nigerian Journal of Economic and Social Studies*, vol. 4, no. 3 (November 1962), pp. 207–27.

—— 'The Wages Structure and its Determinants in Nigeria', *Management*, vol. 2, no. 5 (January–February 1967), pp. 201–6.

SELECTED OFFICIAL PUBLICATIONS

Imperial (UK) Command Papers

Report of the Committee of Inquiry into the Liquor Trade of Southern Nigeria, 1909, Cmd. 4906.

Report of Departmental Committee appointed to inquire into matters affecting the Currency of the British West African Colonies and Protectorates. Reports and Minutes of Evidence, Cmd. 6426 and 6427, 1912.

Report of Committee on Edible and Oil-producing Nuts and Seeds, 1916, Cmd. 8247.

Amalgamation of Northern and Southern Nigeria, and Administration, 1912–1919, Cmd. 468, 1919.

West Africa: Minutes of Evidence taken before the Committee on Trade and Taxation for British West Africa, 1922, Cmd. 1600.

Private Enterprise in British Tropical Africa, 1924, Cmd. 2016.

Education Policy in British Tropical Africa. Memorandum by Advisory Committee on Native Education in the British Tropical African Dependencies, 1925, Cmd. 2374.

Report by the Hon. W. G. A. Ormsby-Gore, M.P. (Parliamentary Under-Secretary of State for the Colonies) on his visit to West Africa during the year 1926, Cmd. 2744.

Colonial Development Act, 1929. Memorandum explaining Financial Resolutions, 1929, Cmd. 3357.

Despatch from the Secretary of State to the Officer Administering the Government of Nigeria regarding the Report of the Commission of Inquiry into the Disturbances at Aba and other places in South-Eastern Nigeria in November and December 1929, Cmd. 3781, 1931.

Papers relating to the International Tin Control Scheme, Cmd. 4825, 1935.

Remission of Payments to Exchequer under the Royal Niger Company Act, 1899. Memorandum on the Financial Resolution, Cmd. 5488, 1937.

Report of Commission on the Marketing of West African Cocoa, Cmd. 5845, 1938.

Papers relating to the International Tin Control Scheme, Main Control Scheme, Buffer Stock Scheme, Research Scheme, Cmd. 5879, 1938.

Importation of Spirituous Beverages into certain Territories under British Administration in Africa, and Import Duties levied thereon. Report for 1938, Cmd. 6082, 1939.

Colonial Development and Welfare Act, 1940. Statement of Policy, Cmd. 6175, 1940.

Labour Conditions in West Africa. Report by Major G. St J. Orde Browne, Cmd. 6277, 1941.

Report on Cocoa Control in West Africa, 1939–43, and Statement on Future Policy, Cmd. 6554, 1944.

Report of the Commission on Higher Education in West Africa, Cmd. 6655, 1945.

Proposals for the Revision of the Constitution of Nigeria, Cmd. 6599, 1945.

Statement on the future Marketing of West African Cocoa, Cmd. 6950, 1946.

Nigeria: Report of the Fiscal Commission, Cmd. 481, 1951.

Report by the Conference on the Nigerian Constitution held in London in July and August 1953, Cmd. 8934.

Report of the resumed Nigerian Constitutional Conference held in London in September and October 1954, Cmd. 569.

Report by the Conference on the Nigerian Constitution held in London in May and June 1957, Cmd. 207.

Colonial Office Publications

West Africa, Palm Oil and Palm Kernels. Report of a Committee appointed by the Secretary of State for the Colonies, September 1923, to consider the best means of securing improved and increased production, Col. no. 10, 1925.

An Economic Survey of the Colonial Empire, 1932, Col. no. 95.

Census of Nigeria, 1931. Vols I—VI, London, Crown Agents, 1933.

An Economic Survey of the Colonial Empire, 1937, Col. no. 179.

The Useful Plants of West Tropical Africa (J. M. Dalziel), London, Crown Agents, 1937.

An Enquiry into the Cost of Living and the Control of the Cost of Living in the Colony and Protectorate of Nigeria (W. Tudor Davies).

Report of the Commission on the Civil Services of British West Africa (Sir Walter Harragin), Col. no. 209, 1947.

Report of the Mission appointed to enquire into the Production and Transport of Vegetable Oils and Oilseeds produced in the West African Colonies, Col. no. 211, 1947.

Report of the West African Oilseeds Mission, Col. no. 224, 1948.

Colonial Road Problems. Impressions from Visits to Nigeria (H. W. W. Pollitt), Colonial Research Publications, no. 1 of 1948.

Report of a Survey of Problems in the Mechanization of Native Agriculture in Tropical African Colonies, 1949, Colonial Advisory Council Publications, no. 1 of 1950.

Report of the Commission of Enquiry into the Disorders in the Eastern Provinces of Nigeria, November 1949, HMSO, no. 256 of 1950.

British African Land Utilization Conference. Jos, Nigeria, 1951. Final Report, 1951, HMSO.

An Economic Survey of the Colonial Territories, 1951. Vol. III, The West African Territories – The Gambia, The Gold Coast, Nigeria and Sierra Leone, and St Helena, Col. nos. 281–3, 1953.

The National Income of Nigeria 1950–1 (A. R. Prest and I. G. Stewart), Colonial Research Studies, no. 11 of 1953.

Nigerian Government Papers

Report on the Groundnut Trade in Kano Province (H. H. Middleton), Sessional Paper no. 41 of 1924.

Report on Livestock Problems in Nigeria (J. P. du Toit), Sessional Paper no. 5 of 1927.

Report on the Oil Palm Industry in British West Africa (F. M. Dyke), Lagos, Government Printer, 1927.

Report of Committee upon the System of Produce Inspection in Nigeria, 1931, Sessional Paper no. 1 of 1932.

Report of Committee on Road v. Railway Competition, Sessional Paper no. 21 of 1933.

Report of the Committee appointed by His Excellency the Governor to enquire into the Question of Unemployment, Sessional Paper no. 46 of 1935.

Interim Report of the Road–Rail Competition Committee, 1936, Sessional Paper no. 16 of 1937.

Report of a Committee appointed in Nigeria to examine recommendations made by the Commission on the Marketing of West African Cocoa, Sessional Paper no. 20 of 1939.

The Implementation of Sessional Paper no. 14 of 1945. Political and Constitutional Future of Nigeria, 1945.

Preliminary Statement on Development Planning in Nigeria, Sessional Paper no. 16 of 1945.

A Ten-Year Plan of Development and Welfare in Nigeria, Sessional Paper no. 24 of 1945.

Administrative and Financial Procedure under the New Constitution: Financial Relations between the Government of Nigeria and the Native Administration, Lagos, 1947.

Report on Banking in Nigeria, Lagos, 1948.

Laws of Nigeria, 1948.

Report of the Fiscal Commission on Revenue Allocation, Lagos, 1951.

Debate of the House of Representatives, March–April 1952.

Report on the Desirability and Practicability of Establishing a Central Bank in Nigeria for Promoting the Economic Development of the Country, Lagos, 1953.

Setting up an Industrial Enterprise in Nigeria, Lagos, Federal Department of Commerce and Industries, 1955.

Report of the Commission on the Public Services of the Government in the Federation of Nigeria, 1954–5 (The Gorsuch Report), Lagos, 1955.

Report by Mr J. B. Loynes on the Establishment of a Nigerian Central Bank, the Introduction of a Nigerian Currency and other Associated Matters, Lagos, 1957.

Laws of the Federation of Nigeria and Lagos, 1958.

Report by the Ad Hoc meeting on the Nigerian Constitutional Conference held in Lagos in February 1958, Lagos, 1958.

The Role of the Federal Government in Promoting Industrial Development in Nigeria, Sessional Paper no. 3 of 1958.

Report of the Ad Hoc Committee of the Conference on the Nigerian Constitution, Lagos, April 1959.

An Economic Survey of Nigeria, 1959.

Report of the Committee appointed to advise on Ways and Means of fostering a Share Market in Nigeria, Lagos, 1959.

Review of Salaries and Wages. Report by the Commission appointed by the Governments of the Federation, the Northern Region, the Eastern Region and the Southern Cameroons (The Mbanefo Commission), Lagos, 1959.

Investment in Education (The Ashby Commission Report), 1960.

Report on the Commission for the Review of Wages and Salaries in the Public Service of the Western Region, 1960 (The Morgan Commission), Sessional Paper no. 5 of 1960.

Handbook of Commerce and Industry in Nigeria, Lagos, 1960.

National Development Plan 1962–8, Lagos, 1962.

Annual Reports

Blue Books: Lagos, Niger Coast Protectorate, Southern Nigeria, Northern Nigeria, and Nigeria.

Accountant-General's Report
Accounts and Finances (published before 1936 as Treasurer's Report)
Agriculture
Colliery (published with Railway Report before 1938)
Commerce and Industry
Co-operation, Progress of
Development Corporations
Digest of Statistics
Education
Government Railway and Colliery (divided since 1938)
Labour (from 1940)
Loans Board
Marine
Marketing Boards
Medical Services
Mines
Ports (Ports Authority)
Posts and Telegraphs, and Post Office Savings Bank (divided since 1936–7)
Public Works
Trade Summary

Note: The United Africa Company's *Statistical and Economic Review* series contains a number of articles on various aspects of economic development in Nigeria.

Index

Aba, 155, 193, 302
Abakaliki, 184
Abeokuta, town and province, 111, 170, 173, 237, 355; communications, 73, 74, 148, 154, 170, 198
Aboynia river, 129
Action Group, political party, 227
Adamawa province, 198
administration, cost of colonial, 68–9, 116
Ado-Ekiti, 302
Adukpani, 142
Adulteration of Produce Ordinances, 89, 160, 161–2
Afam, 308
Africa: Berlin Conference partition, 63; economic links within, 389
African Association Ltd, 26, 87, 217, 220
African Banking Corporation, 86–7
African Continental Bank, 316, 317n, 318
African and Eastern Trade Corporation, 220
African Merchants of Bristol, 91
African Shipping Company, 27, 75
Afroseas Credit Bank Ltd, 316
Agba, 142
Agbonmagbe Bank, 316, 317n, 318
Agbor, 142
Agege, 142, 173
Agricultural Department, 166, 171
Agricultural Research Station, Vom, 159, 174
Agricultural School, Ibadan, 159

Agricultural Station, Samaru, 160
agriculture, 10, 120, 156–7, 159, 164, 201, 248, 279, 280–1, 292; cash-crops encouraged, 197–201; and Development Plans, 20, 390, 391, 394; economic importance, 15–16, 18, 251; employment in, 360, 397; finance of, 116–17, 164, 247–8, 321; machinery used in, 163, 164, 165, 166, 171; productivity, 201, 252; research institutions, 125, 159–60, 283, 285–6
Aid to Pioneer Industries Ordinance 1952, 295, 303
Air, 21
Air Services Development Committee, 149
air transport, 17, 149–50, 269–72; airmail services, 150
Akassa, 254
Akure, 145
Alagbon Industries Ltd, 307
Algiers, and caravan trade, 23
All-Nigeria Trade Union Federation, 370
Amalgamated Union of Clerical and Allied Workers, 370
Amalgamated Union of UAC African Workers, 369–70; strike, 373
Ameka, 184
Amuro, 281n
Anambra river, 4, 129
Anglo-African Bank, 192
Anglo-African Company, 91
Anglo-French Convention 1899, 104

458   *An economic history of Nigeria*